Robert B. Coote is Professor of [Old] Testament at San Francisco Theological Seminary, San Anselmo, California.

David Robert Ord is pastor of Trinity Presbyterian Church, Jonesville, Louisiana.

The Bible's First History

The Bible's First History

ROBERT B. COOTE
and
DAVID ROBERT ORD

FORTRESS PRESS   PHILADELPHIA

BS
1225.2
.C66
1989

Library of Congress Cataloging-in-Publication Data

Coote, Robert B., 1944–
　The Bible's first history.

　　1. J document (Biblical criticism)　I. Ord, David
Robert.　II. Title.
BS1225.2.C66　1988　　　222'.106　　　88–45234
ISBN 0–8006–0878–X

3468F88　Printed in the United States of America　1–878

—Well, God's a good man.

Dogberry (*Much Ado About Nothing*, act 3, sc.5)

Contents

Preface

This is a book about an ancient writer and his ancient work of political imagination. It forms the earliest part of the first four books of the Bible. Because the work usually refers to God as Yahweh (which is spelled with a J in Europe, where the work first came to notice, and is frequently printed as Jehovah in English Bibles), historians call both the writer and his work J. The writer has also been called the Yahwist, especially more recently. We prefer to retain the classic designation. Although the vast majority of people have never heard of J, its stories will be familiar to many because they are among the most popular to be found in Genesis and Exodus. Indeed, these stories are so embedded in our culture in trivialized, bowdlerized, and dogmatized versions that many of us have been familiar with them since childhood. But as originally told, these stories were not children's stories, and the purpose of this book is to present the whole of J as it was in the beginning, as a work treating matters of justice and prosperity which concern us as intensely as they concerned its original hearers.

This book is the product of collaboration between a historian and a minister. Although the analysis it is based on is specialized, the results are of importance to everyone with an interest in the Bible. The communication of these results requires special skill as well. We hope that by joining the skills of a historian with those of a minister, we may make the results of our study as widely accessible as possible.

Because J was written three thousand years ago, and in a culture quite different from our own, some of its assumptions will no longer be shared by many people in today's world. In particular, J makes God male. For many people, God as male remains essential to their understanding of God. For others of us, including the two authors, the maleness of God as portrayed in the Bible is no longer adequate or acceptable as a way of talking to or about God. Nevertheless, in discussing J we follow his practice of referring to God as male because, as will become evident, God's male sex plays an integral role in J's history.

It is our hope that those interested in the Bible will find J's whole story as it was first heard more engrossing and illuminating than the pieces with which they may already be familiar. We are about to encounter a story that may not have been heard as J intended it for almost three thousand years. It has lost nothing of its greatness for its age.

We would like to express our thanks to Polly Coote, Mary McCormick Maaga, Derek Taylor, and our book editor, John A. Hollar, who read this book in typescript and made many valuable suggestions, and to Kristin Saldine, who helped prepare the genealogical chart.

1 _____

What Is the Bible's First History?

_____

In an era when printing presses and photocopying machines turn out billions of pages of print each year, literature is commonplace and serves an endless variety of purposes. In our society almost everyone reads. But in the ancient world, literacy was extremely limited and the production of texts was a restricted craft. To know why a certain few people undertook the laborious and exclusive task of writing texts and to identify who these people were can be a great help in understanding the meaning of a text.

Writing as we know it goes back about five thousand years. Until recently in human history, however, few people practiced the art in any particular society. At first, in order to write a person had to know upward of several hundred signs. It would have been possible to write quite clearly with only a hundred signs, but scribes tended to belong to an exclusive social group who magnified the difficulty of their skill in order to reinforce their exclusivity. Even after the invention of the alphabet about thirty-seven hundred years ago, which made available a writing system requiring the knowledge of a mere twenty-five or so simple signs, knowledge of writing did not spread much beyond the scribal class. The limitation on literacy had less to do with the complexity of the system than with the usefulness of the skill. Only a few people within the society had good reason to make extensive use of the skill.

The population of Palestine was essentially divided into a ruling class and a lower class. Rulers themselves tended not to be literate, but they employed a literate and partially literate class—scribes and priests—to keep records for them. Not surprisingly, writing was first developed for the purposes of taxation. When the local lord sent men into a nearby village to see whether the peasants had paid their taxes, he was entirely dependent on the scribes. In addition to record keeping, writing was useful to the ruling class for marking ownership. Needless to say, the scribe or recorder in the royal court exercised a great deal of power in ancient society. The scribes were the language specialists of their day.

Another important function of ancient scribes was that of composing literary documents that reflected how the rulers understood themselves and their role in society. Rulers, who could retain and influence scribes, had the privilege of having their self-image mirrored back to them in the powerful, sophisticated, and even sublime medium of the written word. But writing of this kind had far more than a private value. Such documents also set forth a social image for public consumption, even when the public was limited to the royal court and its visitors. This image became, or reinforced, the prevailing way in which people generally understood themselves and their place in society. It defined what political, social, and religious issues were to be considered important—what, in the interest of the rulers, people were supposed to believe and become concerned about, and what by implication they were supposed to ignore or be indifferent toward. It also set the criteria by which the rule of a few over the masses was justified and applied those criteria for the benefit of the rulers.[1] By projecting a sense of social place onto the people of a society, the literary image produced by writers in ancient courts assisted in the necessary maintenance of law and order.

The literature of the courts and chapels of ancient rulers—the places where nearly all ancient literature was produced—thereby functioned in much the same way as newspapers do in our society. In the United States, the bulk of the copy is devoted to disasters, local politics, and the advertise-

1. On the scribe's role in the ancient court, see Gideon Sjoberg, *The Preindustrial City: Past and Present* (New York: Free Press, Macmillan Co., 1960), 224–31 ("Legitimization of the Elite's Rule"); William W. Hallo, "New Viewpoints on Cuneiform Literature," *Israel Exploration Journal* 12 (1962): 13–26; A. Leo Oppenheim, "A Note on the Scribes in Mesopotamia," in *Essays in Honor of Benno Landsberger,* Assyriological Studies, 16 (Chicago: University of Chicago Press, 1968), 253–56; R. J. Williams, " 'A People Come Out of Egypt,' " *Supplements to Vetus Testamentum* 28 (1975): 231–52; Frank Moore Cross, "Newly Found Inscriptions in Old Canaanite and Early Phoenician Scripts," *Bulletin of the American Schools of Oriental Research* 238 (1980): 13–15; Nadav Na῾aman, "A Royal Scribe and His Scribal Products in the Alalakh IV Court," *Orientalia Analecta* 19 (1980): 107–16; Jack M. Sasson, "Literary Criticism, Folklore Scholarship, and Ugaritic Literature," in *Ugarit in Retrospect,* ed. G. D. Young (Winona Lake, Ind.: Eisenbrauns, 1981), 96–98; and idem, "On Idrimi and Sharruwa, the Scribe," in *Studies on the Civilization of Nuzi and the Hurrians in Honor of Ernest R. Lacheman,* ed. M. A. Morrison and D. I. Owen (Winona Lake, Ind.: Eisenbrauns, 1981), 309–24; M. Haran, "On the Diffusion of Literacy and Schools in Ancient Israel," in J. A. Emerton, ed., *Congress Volume Jerusalem 1986* (Vetus Testamentum, Supplement 40), Leiden: E. J. Brill, 1988; E. Lipinski, "Royal and State Scribes in Ancient Jerusalem," idem. The useful reviews by Alan R. Millard, "An Assessment of the Evidence for Writing in Ancient Israel, in *Biblical Archaeology Today, Proceedings of the International Congress on Biblical Archaeology, Jerusalem, April 1984* (Jerusalem: Israel Exploration Society, 1985), 301–12, and "The Question of Israelite Literacy," *Bible Review* 3 (1987): 22–31, raise again the possibility that writing was widespread in biblical Palestine. This notion, agreed to by many, ignores the macrosocial factor in the incidence of writing. A similar review of the occurrence of writing in any better-known society would fail to explain the social and political parameters of its use.

ment of products. In the Soviet Union, attention focuses instead on the social contribution of labor, developments in local industries and worker organizations, and administrative changes. In both cases, there is coverage of cultural and foreign affairs, but from quite different perspectives. Newspapers in other countries vary in similar ways. The particular emphasis of newspapers in each country reflects the society's self-understanding and values and reinforces the way in which the society is supposed to work. The differences in what is regarded as news do not reflect so much different realities as different understandings of what is important, understandings linked to the nature and agenda of each society.

The lower class[2] formed the bulk of the population and consisted mainly of the people of the villages. These were peasants. They performed virtually all the productive work of the society. It was their hands that grew the food, made the clothing, built the dwellings and the monuments, and produced or gathered the trade commodities of the society. For none of these activities was writing essential. The peasantry were nearly all illiterate. Where writing was used in the village, it was usually under the supervision of an elite craftsman or supervisor. With few exceptions, villagers' experiences and how they understood themselves and their place in society were not recorded in writing. Where this was done, it was by incorporation into court documents whose primary concern was with the court rather than the village. To the extent that village life was influenced by written texts, this influence derived from the political and economic decisions of the urban elite. Through this means the elite tended to conceive of the peasants' identity for them.[3]

One of the ways that court scribes created a social image was to incorporate traditions into written texts. Historians distinguish between two kinds of tradition, including religious tradition, in ancient societies. These are sometimes called the great tradition and the little tradition.[4] The great tradition belonged in the urban context. It came out of the interests of the major religious institutions of a society and their officialdom. It tended to be comprehensive and systematic, so that all aspects of society and belief were brought into relation with one another in an attempt to put everything in its proper conceptual place. Major components of the traditional histories and mythologies of the society were integrated into a single grand

2. A distinction merely between upper and lower classes is of course an oversimplification. For many issues, however, such as literacy, it conveys the right impression.

3. Conor Cruise O'Brien, "Press Freedom and the Need to Please," *Times Literary Supplement* (London), 21 Feb., 1986: 179–80; and Shanto Iyengar and Donald R. Kinder, *News That Matters: Television and American Opinion* (Chicago: University of Chicago Press, 1987).

4. Eric R. Wolf, *Peasants* (Englewood Cliffs, N.J.: Prentice-Hall, 1966), 100–106.

statement. The guardians of the great tradition were full-time officers wholly dedicated to its formulation, revision, and preservation.

It has long been noticed that the masses of recent agrarian societies, no doubt like the masses of ancient societies, relate only distantly to this kind of tradition. Village life was instead characterized by local, even parochial concerns, related especially to the direct production of food and the other necessities of the village, concerns that were of little interest to the elite guardians of the great tradition. The little tradition concerned local spirits and local cults and shrines. It consisted of superstitions, many of which would seem trivial to the guardians of the great tradition. Peasant religious life often centered around what we would call magic, the attempt to manipulate the forces of nature to favor fertility and production. The parochial and seemingly unsophisticated character of peasant tradition was a direct result of the peasants' dependence on the day-to-day precariousness and unpredictability of sun, rain, health, and safety and on their lesser control over basic economic factors.[5]

Before the time of Saul and David, the people who came under their rule lived in villages in the highlands of Palestine. The political form under which they were organized is not known to historians. There was probably no state over them—no fixed taxing power with a standing army and bureaucracy. Nor were there many large cities. The villages were situated in the mountains of Palestine rather than in its plains and valleys. Hence the villages were separated from each other in pockets of distinct local climates and local traditions. The traditions of these mountain villages were little traditions, not a great tradition. The prerequisites for a great tradition—an official state religion, an established priesthood, a well-supported scribal class—did not exist in early Israel. It is possible that the idea that there was a single, unified society called early Israel is mistaken. Such an idea might itself be the product of a later great tradition.

Eventually early Israel evolved into a state. The first state under Saul was weak. David replaced Saul and created a strong state. Under his rule the prerequisites for a great tradition were set in place. He created an official state religion out of certain elements of the most important shrines of early Israel. He established a dual urban priesthood representing on the one hand the rise to power of his own household and on the other the interests of an important shrine of tribal Israel in a new urban context. He supported a scribal class in his capital who helped him administer his new empire and

---

5. For a nuanced consideration of this distinction, see Gary A. Herion, "The Role of Historical Narrative in Biblical Thought: The Tendencies Underlying Old Testament Historiography," *Journal for the Study of the Old Testament* 21 (1981): 25–57.

produced a body of literature that legitimated his rise to power over Saul's kingdom.

The bulk of our Old Testament literature belongs to a great tradition. It originated not among the common folk—the illiterate masses of the countryside—but in the nation's urban courts sometime after Israel became a state. The views and traditions represented in Old Testament literature are not so much those of the people of Israel as of their rulers, who may or may not have enjoyed the support of the populace.

Although Genesis, Exodus, Leviticus, Numbers, and Deuteronomy appear to have been composed prior to the founding of the Israelite state and the Davidic royal court, the internal evidence of the books reveals that in their earliest form the traditions were not arranged as the five books with which we are familiar and that they underwent a progressive composition that took place over a span of centuries. By studying the Pentateuch carefully, one can discern that what appears as a single narrative is a composite intertwining of several narratives of different kinds. No one really knows exactly how many kinds of narrative there are in the Pentateuch or exactly how the different kinds originated and were combined into the present composite, although it is generally agreed that there exist four particularly distinctive kinds, known as strands or, less accurately, sources. Because we do not know the names of those who composed the four literary strands that form the basis of the first five books of the Bible, they are commonly referred to by the letters J, E, D, and P.

From the internal evidence of these literary works it is possible to suggest who wrote them and why. In each case it is evident that these works did not arise in a vacuum, simply because someone thought it would be nice to compose a major new literary work; rather, they were composed at periods of transition in Israel's history, in response to a crisis precipitated by societal and religious changes. Each of them is a fresh articulation of the world view of a particular group of Israelites to meet the needs of their changed circumstances.

Our concern here is with J. When and why was it written? J could not have been composed earlier than the united monarchy of David and Solomon, because it is by nature a product of an urban great tradition. J's optimism and sweep reflect the expanding horizons of the united monarchy and its empire and the untrammeled expectations of a newly emergent and rapidly upwardly mobile elite.

If J could not have been composed earlier than David, it could not have been composed later than Solomon, because its conception of a uniting Israel indicates no awareness either of the division of the kingdoms of Judah and Israel that took place following the death of Solomon or of significant events in their subsequent history.[6] J also shows interest in the same set of nations as those held in vassalage in the united monarchy's empire.[7] Further, J shows no awareness that northern Israel ceased to exist as a state in the eighth century.[8] Indeed, J pays no significant attention to either Assyria or Babylon other than in a couple of literary symbolic references and gives no hint of addressing such devastating events as the destruction of the temple or the deportation of the Jerusalemite governing class to Babylon. Stylistic and thematic similarities between J and the earliest constituent documents of 1 and 2 Samuel, which are widely regarded as going back in origin to the united monarchy, also suggest that J was written in the same period. And, as we shall see in due course, all indications are that the rise of nationalism that occurred with David and Solomon would have included the writing of a nationalist history, J or something very much like it.[9]

The immediate occasion for the composition of J was the necessity of validating the establishment of the Davidic royal house, which replaced a much less centralized political arrangement in the highlands of Palestine.

6. The sons of Jacob group themselves in a way that indicates neither regional animosities nor separate northern and southern state territories. The singling out of Judah and the failure to link Simeon with Judah also reflect the Davidic house's rule of the united monarchy rather than a southern Judah's relation to an independent northern state. Further, J's treatment of Bethel, which became the national shrine of northern Israel after the division of the kingdoms, is extremely positive. If the story of the golden calf is an anti-Bethel polemic, and if it belongs in any sense to J, then it is probably a post-Solomonic supplement. A few might want to argue that this positive treatment of Bethel reflects a ninth-century Judahite capture of Bethel. Why, then, is there not even one allusion to the division of the kingdom, and why does J have a similarly positive interest in the northern sites of Shechem and Penuel? Moreover, if, as seems probable, J made direct references to literary cuneiform texts, why would it not have referred to an existing Hebrew history as well? Incorporating cuneiform literary traditions into an Israelite nationalist history itself makes little sense in any period other than the united monarchy, before the scribal office in Jerusalem became fully Hebraized.

7. By itself this agreement would count for little, were it not that J combines relationships with Aram to the north and with Edom to the south in the single story of Jacob. These relationships would have been of a distinctly different character and interest to Judah following the death of Solomon and the secession of the north. It might even be said that relationships with Aram were significant to Judah in detail, as opposed to an undifferentiated event like Aram's joining the siege of Jerusalem in the reign of Ahaz, only during the united monarchy.

8. J's valuation of northern sanctuary towns is so different from the Deuteronomistic insistence on Zion's exclusive legitimacy that it would be difficult to argue that J was written in seventh-century Jerusalem, quite apart from other objections that could be raised. In addition, the possibility remains that a Deuteronomist revised J and positioned it in its present location ahead of the Deuteronomistic History.

9. Each reason given can by itself generate considerable debate, but no other dating has produced as extensive and comprehensive a group of reasons. Cf. Hans Walter Wolff, "The Kerygma of the Yahwist," in *The Vitality of Old Testament Traditions*, W. Brueggemann and H. W. Wolff, 2d ed. (Atlanta: John Knox Press, 1982), 43–45; and Werner H. Schmidt, "A Theologian of the Solomonic Era? A Plea for the Yahwist," in *Studies in the Period of David and Solomon and Other Essays*, ed. T. Ishida (Winona Lake, Ind.: Eisenbrauns, 1982), 55–73.

In other words, J was a "social product." The imposition of the Davidic state involved massive changes, not only in terms of a new political system but also economically, socially, and religiously. Such changes were no small matter, and it was to address and justify these changes, even when indirectly, that the J document was commissioned.

In the course of the history of monarchic Israel, of its court scribes and official priesthoods, this document was imitated, lengthened, and supplemented in a complex process of periodic recomposition.[10] This whole process reflects the same great–tradition interest that J itself reflects. It took place within urban contexts at the behest of rulers and for purposes that often had little to do with most of the concerns of Palestinian villagers. Although David founded the state, it was his son Solomon who followed the custom of other Mediterranean states and established a Phoenician-style temple as the dynastic chapel. Throughout the Old Testament there is constant tension between the localized religion of the country people, who built shrines wherever they pleased, and the state religion that was promoted in the royal chapel. It was here that the nation's traditions were molded in the period of the monarchy, until the Davidic state came to an end in 587 B.C.E. The end result of this process we now know as the Pentateuch and the Former Prophets in the Hebrew Bible, or the books of Genesis through 2 Kings (excepting Ruth, which comes much later in the Hebrew Bible).

10. J made sense in new ways to later interpreters. The exilic priesthood deemed it suitably applicable to their own perception of Israel and its destiny to use it as the basis of their updating and recording of their own traditions. It seems to have been an influence, like everything else in Israelite tradition, on the author of Second Isaiah. But it would not have been composed afresh in any period following the death of Solomon.

2

Four Different Stories

For some readers of this book, the evidence for strands has been disregarded, downplayed, or even ridiculed by scholars, teachers, ministers, priests, and rabbis they rightly respect. In our view, one reason for this tendency to dismiss strand analysis has been the failure of the scholarly community to explain clearly what each strand is really like, what it is about, and why the evidence for it should be taken seriously.

It is possible, though not easy, to separate the bulk of J, E, D, and P out from the Pentateuch. Of the four strands, J contributes the greatest quantity of the Pentateuch's story, including a majority of the more familiar episodes, much as Mark's Gospel serves as the basis of Matthew's, which is a composite of Mark and other traditions. J is the warp through which the other strands cross as woof to produce the present fabric from Genesis to Numbers.[1] E and P are only partial as stories. They came into being as supplementary revisions of J. Neither was ever a complete work in its own right. D is a complete story, although the part contained in the Pentateuch, mostly in the Book of Deuteronomy, is only the beginning of its story, which continues all the way through the Books of Kings.

Many have never heard about these strands—which is a little like not having heard about the atomic elements that make up the world of objects we take so much for granted. Others do not take seriously what they have heard or are understandably put off because they have not had the opportunity to consider the strands fully enough to see the real value, or to think through the full implications, of this kind of interpretation. Nor is it easy for them to take the strands seriously, because they are forced to read a text, not to speak of a translation, in which the strands are woven together and

---

1. For a treatment of revision and conflation in early biblical texts, see E. Tov, "The Composition of 1 Samuel 16—18 in the Light of the Septuagint Version," in *Empirical Models for Biblical Criticism*, ed J. Tigay (Philadelphia: University of Pennsylvania Press, 1985), 97–130.

their distinctive qualities more or less blurred, much as nature forces us to see paper clips and zebras, not atoms. Although the strands are all found together in the Pentateuch as part of what seems at first to be the same story, J, E, D, and P in fact tell vastly different stories. Most readers of the Bible never learn just how different from one another they are.[2] This book presents one of the strands in a new way. When readers have seen the whole story of one of these strands presented in its totality, many will recognize for the first time the value of such literary analysis.

It is our intention to present J as nearly as possible as it was originally intended to be read or heard. This will be done by bracketing whatever isn't J—in other words, by leaving aside E, D, and P—and then integrating J as though it were all the story we had and the other strands had never been layered over it. We shall isolate the warp and then read. For when this "warp" is isolated from the Pentateuch, it is found to represent a complete fabric in its own right.

While there is broad agreement on the authorship of many passages, historians continue to differ on other passages. With few exceptions, our approach is to give weight in our interpretation to those passages which are most generally agreed to be from J. What this amounts to in practice is determining which passages most clearly represent the characteristics of J in the view of the majority of historians. Since it is not a matter of strict definition with uniform certainty, but of more or less relation to a well agreed but rather small set of passages that determine the definition of J, we have not provided the standard listing of passages from J. In those places where we go against the weight of historical opinion, we make sure readers are aware of the peculiarity of our view.

Various oral and written sources contribute to the story of J. We will pay some attention to them as we go along. Our focus, however, will be on the story of J as an integrated whole. To understand J, we must examine it as a whole, keeping in mind all the other parts as we read any one part.

One way to integrate a complex whole is to find its determinative part. The one story in J that has the most bearing on all others is the story of the revolt and escape of a band of disenfranchised, oppressed laborers from Egypt. If J represents the cardiovascular system of the Pentateuch, then this episode, often referred to as the exodus, represents its heart. It is this which gives vitality and meaning to the rest of J and to which we must repeatedly return if we are to keep the whole of J in perspective. Every story in J,

---

2. Those interested in reading further in this subject may consult Norman C. Habel, *Literary Criticism of the Old Testament* (Philadelphia: Fortress Press, 1971); Lloyd R. Bailey, *The Pentateuch* (Nashville: Abingdon Press, 1981); and Richard E. Friedman, *Who Wrote the Bible?* (New York: Summit Books, 1987).

insofar as it is a part of a larger whole, must be understood as it relates directly to this pivotal event.

Recall, for instance, the episode in which Moses killed the Egyptian taskmaster who was beating a Hebrew slave (Exod. 2:11–12). If we bracket P and E, we can see clearly that this killing is the first thing that J relates about Moses. J says nothing about Hebrew midwives, maidens coming with pharaoh's daughter to the river to wash, or a foundling in the bulrushes. These are from E. In J, before we find out anything else about Moses, we learn that this man killed a slave driver who was beating a slave.

This was a determinative deed. In J, unlike P and E, it is the reason Yahweh selected Moses rather than someone else to lead the slave rebellion, and it foreshadows and helps to define the meaning of Yahweh's killing the firstborn son of the king of Egypt and eventually the king of Egypt himself. These killings—distressing to us though they seem—lie at the center of gravity of what it is J most wants to say.

They are in turn the reason J's story gets fully under way at the point where Cain, the firstborn son of Adam and Eve, killed Abel. As soon as we realize that the purpose of the story of Adam and Eve, as far as J is concerned, is to explain how the firstborn came into being and how he could conceive of killing Abel, and thus why Moses eventually had to kill the Egyptian and Yahweh had to kill pharaoh's firstborn and eventually pharaoh himself, we are in a position to relate the story of Adam and Eve to the workers' revolt and hence the beginning of J to the heart and whole of J.

When put in so many words, this procedure seems obvious. Yet it has never been done with J in its entirety. Nor is it easy to do. If, for instance, someone were to cut out of an English translation the parts of the strand, isolating them from the composite context, and to sew them together again in sequence, then this text, based as it is on the translation of the composite, would already have obscured many of J's essential characteristics.[3]

We can see this by returning to the incident in which Moses killed the Egyptian taskmaster. It begins, "In those days." Which days? In the present composite text, Moses relinquished the privileges of his elite Egyptian upbringing and owned his Hebrew kinship through the decisive act of killing. This meaning conveyed by the composite text could conceivably belong to early Hebrew tradition, but it is not J's meaning. We have already indicated that J says nothing of Moses' upbringing. It makes a huge difference that J says nothing of this. J has it that before anything else is known about Moses, it is known that this man killed a taskmaster who was beating a laborer. This is no insignificant matter, and indeed is what J

---

3. For examples of this latter procedure, see Smend, *Biblische Zeugnisse: Literatur des alten Israel* (Frankfurt: Fischer, 1967), 27–87; and Peter J. Ellis, *The Yahwist: The Bible's First Theologian* (Collegeville, Minn.: Liturgical Press, 1968), 225–95.

means when he speaks of "in those days." In J this phrase refers exclusively to the time when pharaoh forced Palestinian herders to build grain-storage facilities in his cities. But even if we realize that the intervening story from Exod. 1:15—2:10 comes from E and 2:11—12 from J, and even if we are reading a more literal translation in which the words "in those days" appear, it still requires a strenuous effort of the imagination to avoid understanding "those days" in the light of the composite text and hence as referring to the time of Moses' growing up in pharaoh's court.

The act of killing by itself defines Moses as the person who acts justly in the view of the writer. And not *a* person but *the* person. This meaning is stressed to the degree that others are excluded. The episode then joins the two that follow—Moses' judging for the Palestinian herder in the right and intervening to rescue the Midianite women at the watering hole—and together they indicate why Yahweh chose this person Moses and not some other to lead the workers' revolt against pharaoh. The point in J is not ethnic identity, that Moses is one with the Hebrews (which may be E's point, or is P's for the exilic period). J takes that for granted. J's point is that, unlike all the rest of his kin, gang work or its supervision has not voided Moses' sense of justice or made him impotent to act on it. Moses is one with the oppressed and will correctly identify and struggle against the oppressor.

Nonliteral translations, more so than literal translations, unavoidably leave the reader less able to discern this distinctive J meaning. The RSV, for instance, translates "one day" rather than "in those days." The reader thus has no chance whatever of making the connection just described. This translation continues, ". . . when Moses had grown up." The Hebrew for "had grown up" is exactly the same as for "grew" in the E story in Exod. 2:10, so it is nearly impossible when reading or translating the composite text to avoid the impression that these two identical words right next to each other refer to the same growth of Moses. But the Hebrew word, which might literally be rendered "he was or became large," can also mean "he became important" or "he rose in status" or the like. As is verifiable from J's other uses of the word, this seems to be its meaning here. Even though Moses was rising in status among the Palestinian laborers (there were different ranks of foremen), his upward mobility failed to erode his sense of justice. A free translation of Exod. 2:11 as J intended it would begin, "In the days of Hebrew oppression, as Moses gradually succeeded in making the system of oppression work to his personal advantage . . . ."

Does J make a similar point elsewhere that might confirm this under-standing? Indeed, in Exodus 5 he expands on how hard it is for the upwardly mobile to identify with the oppressed—harder probably than for all but the most elite. Once the E story of finding the baby Moses is added, however, and "he grew" in Exod. 2:10 nudges the original J meaning of the same Hebrew word in 2:11 out of consideration, the translator is nearly compelled, for the sake of the assumed homogeneity of the composite text (as indeed intended by E), to translate 2:11 so as to preclude its direct and exclusive connection with 1:8–12 and obscure its distinctive J meanings.

This, then, is the concern of the way we present J in this book. To get at what J wanted to say as distinct from E, D, and P, it is necessary to take careful note of the Hebrew text and translate it from scratch.[4]

4. The translation of J appearing in sections beginning with chapter 7 in this volume is not always literal or strict. In places, it represents more paraphrase than translation, in order to keep it readable within the flow of the discussion.

3

A Royal History

Once *Tom Sawyer* and *Huckleberry Finn* were banished from the children's room of the Brooklyn Public Library. Some of Mark Twain's supporters insisted that he protest. "I wrote *Tom Sawyer* and *Huck Finn*," he replied, "for adults exclusively and it always distresses me when I find boys and girls have been allowed access to them. The mind that becomes soiled in youth can never again be washed clean; to this day I cherish an unappeasable bitterness against the unfaithful guardians of my young life, who not only permitted but compelled me to read an unexpurgated Bible through before I was fifteen years old. None can do that and ever draw a clean, sweet breath again this side of the grave."

Most of the good stories in Genesis, Exodus, and Numbers are about explicit sex, bloody violence, and systemic injustice. If they are not children's stories, just what kind of writing are they? They could perhaps best be described as history. But having said this, we must qualify it. We are taught that there are basically two types of writing—fact and fiction. In bookstores, you find the fiction in one section and everything else, including history, grouped under nonfiction in another section. This may be practical from the point of view of organizing the shelves of bookstores or the pages of the *New York Times Book Review*, but it is a limited and potentially misleading distinction.

History is commonly thought of as a factual record of the events that took place in a particular period of the past. Fact in the ultimate sense of what happened is something we cannot know; and even if we could know all the facts, they would have no meaning. Facts by themselves are meaningless. Only when they are selected and arranged in an order that makes sense of them do they become significant.

Suppose you were to record every single event that happened within just one month to you, your family, and your community. You would have far

more information than would fit into ten thousand volumes. But although
you might have an accurate record of everything that took place in this
thirty-day period, you would not have a history. Not only would the sheer
size of the work make it impossible for anyone to digest but an outsider
reading it would find no arrangement of the events into meaningful categories that would tell the story of your life, your family, and your community.

A history requires the selection of material and the grouping of that
material so that it tells a story. Someone has to decide that some events are
more significant than others and then has to arrange them into categories.
The historical task is not to describe what happened but to select the
hundred out of a hundred billion events that happened and to group and
organize them so that they convey meaning. Since only a small percentage
of the events that took place will be included in the history, the selection
will inevitably be highly subjective, reflecting the concerns of the one
making the selection. Another person, with a different perspective, might
select an entirely different set of events or describe the same events with an
entirely different set of categories. A history spanning a one-month period
in a township in the South during the era of slavery told from the vantage
of a white plantation owner would be different from a history of the same
community told by a black mother, because the interests and concerns of
each are at opposite poles.

It is an axiom of history that the categories by which history is written
are the categories of the historian's here-and-now analysis. The historian is
interested in those events in the past which have relevance for his or her
world in the present. There isn't a history that doesn't reflect the historian's
world. A reading of the history of so recent an event as World War II as told
by the Germans, the Japanese, the Russians, the French, the British, and
the Americans shows how differently people can interpret the same events.
What people "see" is governed by their perspective. There is then a very
real sense in which history is fictional, though not in the sense that fiction
is opposed to fact.

J's history is no different. The material he selected for inclusion in his
history was selected because it had bearing upon the period in which he
was living. He was not so much interested in collecting and relating
random traditions about Israel's past as in arranging events into a fictional
scheme that had meaning for the present. This raises the question of
whether the story is about what it appears to be about on the surface, or
whether it is about something else, or both. To illustrate the importance of
this decision from a modern work, George Orwell's *Animal Farm*, which
ostensibly is a story about animals that take over a farm from humans and
attempt to establish equality among all the inhabitants of the farm, is

generally considered to be a satire about communism in the 1930s. Although *Animal Farm* is fantasy, it addresses a real-life phenomenon in a way that helps one see it as it might not otherwise be seen.

In the case of J, there is no story except what it points to, but what it points to is not different from the context of assumptions and preunderstandings within which it was composed. There isn't such a thing as just the simple story: the story has to be interpreted. No text has any meaning whatever except through interpretation. The question is, in relation to what, or in terms of what, is it to be interpreted? Is it going to be our context alone, or can we strive to include a specific historical context as well?

J presents himself as telling the early history of Israel, which in his conception spans roughly five hundred years. How many things happen in five hundred years? Think back to 1492. How did J decide what to include in his history? Certainly he did not have thousands of volumes at his disposal, bursting with the details of the past five hundred years preceding his lifetime. To compose his history he therefore had to look at his world, the traditions of his people (already similarly selected), the sense of national identity he desired to be embodied in those people, and the objectives he wished to achieve by writing this history. Then he constructed the history by treating present realities in terms of the past. And in the world of J the principal reality was the royal household by which he was employed.

In preindustrial societies the government was not so much an official government as proprietary, or literally owned by its head. Rule was as much possession as office. As Louis XIV stated, "L'état c'est moi"—"I am the state." The state was embodied in the head of the ruling family. And because the political economy, beginning with the bulk of the arable land of the kingdom, was owned by the ruling family, they had the opportunity and the prerogative to tell the history of their people and the history of the world in any way that suited their purpose. Indeed, we have abundant evidence that histories composed by dynastic scribes tended to reflect the world view of the particular family. This is especially true for rulers like David who were new to the throne and did not have the automatic legitimacy that the son or daughter of the previous ruler would.

In J's history, Israel is represented in Abram, Isaac, Jacob, and the twelve brothers, who were essentially sheepherders. When Jacob and his extended family went to Egypt, Joseph told pharaoh, "My brothers and my father's household, who were in the land of Canaan, have come to me; and the men are shepherds, for they have been keepers of cattle; and they have brought their flocks, and their herds, and all that they have" (Gen. 46:31–32). Such peoples are known to anthropologists as pastoral nomads, and their experiences as related by J can be understood in terms of the typical experiences of bedouin of the Philistine plain, the Negev, and the Sinai from as long ago as the Early Bronze Age. Egyptian records show that it was common practice for such pastoral nomads to cross the Negev into Egyptian territory to graze their flocks. Here they were sometimes commandeered by the pharaoh to work without pay for the Egyptian state. This tax in labor is known as corvée.[1]

But even though J portrays their immediate forebears as such, the vast majority of Israelite Palestinians of his time were not in fact pastoral nomads. At least 80 percent of those who would class themselves as Israelites during the time of the united monarchy were and had been all along peasants. Why, then, does J represent them as pastoral nomads, who were at most only 10 percent of Israel's subjects? The answer is that although J's history purports, through the use of named ancestors of the nation of Israel, or eponyms,[2] to speak for the people as a whole, in reality it is a highly "factionalized" history told from the perspective of the ruling household. So although the peasants formed the bulk of the population, their lives were all but ignored by the story. That this is not unique to ancient literature may be seen in the following excerpt from a *New York Times* essay entitled "Workers in Fiction: Locked Out"[3]:

Many politicians will appear at Labor Day gatherings tomorrow mouthing platitudes about industrial workers being the backbone of the United States, but few of these speakers will believe what they say. For many Americans in this age of high technology, industrial workers are at best an anachronism, at worst an embarrassment.

Steelworkers, truck drivers and men and women on assembly lines have not entirely vanished from the pages of American fiction, but they are no longer the heroes they occasionally were at earlier times in our literature. Since World War II, few novels about the working class have been set in the present; instead, the authors have nostalgically looked to bygone eras of labor militancy. . . .

It is tempting to suggest that the current literary uninterest in workers is a reflection of the present atmosphere of political conservatism and that the mood is likely to pass if the pendulum swings back toward liberalism. There is, though, little in American literature's past treatment of workers to support such a view. Throughout most of this nation's history the industrial working class has been largely ignored in our fiction. . . .

Here lies an indication of the reasons behind Americans' general uninterest in

1. R. North, *"mas,"* *Theologisches Wörterbuch zum Alten Testament,* ed. G. J. Botterweck et al. (Stuttgart: W. Kohlhammer, 1984), vol. 4, cols. 1006–10.

2. The technical term for an ancestor who purports to stand for the whole of a later group is "eponym," of which the adjective is "eponymous."

3. Robert S. McElvaine, 1 Sept., 1985, *New York Times Book Review* section. We quote at length because the point, then and now, is so significant. See Sacvan Bercovitch and Myra Jehlen, eds., *Ideology and Classic American Literature* (Cambridge: Cambridge University Press, 1986).

industrial workers: those workers have never fit the self-image that Americans like to maintain. . . .

Americans cherish the myth of success as much as they do the agrarian myth. It's permissible to be a laborer early in life, as long as you rise to better things later; but he who remains an industrial worker is seen by most Americans as unsuccessful.

While most scholars concur that J must have originated during the united monarchy, they have had difficulty locating the document convincingly in a specific historical context so that it might be interpreted in the light of that context. This is because the question of why J portrays Israel in terms of bedouin when in reality they were principally peasants is never asked. When this question is addressed, it becomes possible to interpret J for the first time in a specific historical context.

4

Who Were Israel?

To a person accustomed to reading the Old Testament story of the founding of Israel in terms of the descent of the patriarchs and their families into Egypt and their subsequent exodus as a great nation, it comes as a surprise to learn that the name Israel appears only once in the wealth of non-Israelite literature from before the ninth century B.C.E. and that even then it is only a passing reference in a victory hymn of Pharaoh Merneptah, who ruled Egypt toward the end of the thirteenth century B.C.E.[1] Neither the presence of Moses and the descendants of Abram, Isaac, and Jacob in Egypt, the exodus of several million people, the destruction of the pharaoh and all of the nation's firstborn sons, and the establishment of the Davidic kingdom, nor the splendor of Solomon's empire receives a single mention in the literature of Egypt or of any of Israel's neighbors, of which we have no small amount.

The first definite information about Israel based on contemporary documents preserved in the Old Testament comes from the time of David and Solomon. The historical picture of what the highlands of Palestine, where Israel came into being, looked like for the two hundred years before David is extremely hazy. The documents in the Old Testament that appear to tell about the emergence of Israel come from much later, during the monarchy, and their themes and details say much more about the time and circumstances of their writing and the issues of importance to their writers than about the emergence of Israel. How, then, is anything to be said about the actual history of the emergence of Israel?

Within the last century, historians have proposed three different models of the emergence of Israel in an attempt to make sense of the extremely sparse information available from the biblical and other texts as well as

---

1. Donald B. Redford, "The Ashkelon Relief at Karnak and the Israel Stela," *Israel Exploration Journal* 36 (1986): 188–200.

from archaeology.[2] Our concern is not to discuss the pros and cons of these models in detail but to indicate how they treat J's history of Israel's beginnings. The reason for mentioning them at all is to show how little biblical texts such as J have to do with the emergence of Israel. To appreciate what J is about, it is necessary to realize that J is not about the actual emergence of Israel.

The conquest model. This model posits that a unified Israel approached the land of Palestine from Egypt and conquered it in a single campaign. This is the way many people have thought Joshua 1–12 describes the emergence of Israel. When we examine Joshua and Judges closely, however, not only do we find that Judges places some of the traditions about the taking of the land after Joshua's death, whereas in Joshua there is a unified conquest of the land under Joshua himself, but also the traditions in Judges 1 picture the tribes taking possession of their territories in separate attacks, whereas the Book of Joshua rules out such separate military actions and asserts that all the tribes moved as one to possess the land. Furthermore, within Joshua not much of the land is actually captured. Most of the attention is focused on a ritual-like crossing of the Jordan, probably based on later liturgical practice, the taking of Jericho and Ai, and two limited sweeps through the Judahite foothills and the eastern Galilee.

It is now clear that Jericho was uninhabited at the time of the emergence of Israel and had been for several hundred years. And there is not a trace of the destruction described in the Book of Joshua. Similarly, Ai was destroyed around 2500 B.C.E. and continued to be unoccupied until the twelfth century B.C.E., when it was reoccupied by new highland inhabitants, usually identified with early Israel, until about 1050 B.C.E. In general, many of the cities described in Joshua as being destroyed were not destroyed, and many cities that are known, from archaeological investigation, to have been destroyed are not named.

Clearly the writers of Joshua were not entirely familiar with the period they were writing about. The few general characterizations of conquest in the Book of Joshua, as well as the linkage of certain cities into the two sweeps mentioned, come from the hand of the Deuteronomistic historian

---

2. These models are conveniently described by Norman K. Gottwald, *The Tribes of Yahweh: A Sociology of the Religion of Liberated Israel, 1250–1050 B.C.* (Maryknoll, N.Y.: Orbis Books, 1979), 191–227; and by Marvin L. Chaney, "Ancient Palestinian Peasant Movements and the Formation of Premonarchic Israel," in *Palestine in Transition: The Emergence of Ancient Israel,* ed. D. N. Freedman and D. F. Graf (Sheffield, Eng.: Almond Press, 1983), 39–90. All three models have serious liabilities, and historians are currently rethinking the problem in terms of the growing body of archaeological and comparative historical data. See Volkmar Fritz, "Conquest or Settlement? The Early Iron Age in Palestine," *Biblical Archaeologist* 50 (1987): 84–100; and Robert B. Coote and Keith W. Whitelam, *The Emergence of Early Israel in Historical Perspective* (Sheffield, Eng.: Almond Press, 1987, with bibliography).

in the seventh century B.C.E., six hundred years after the supposed event. Recently it has become clear that the figure of Joshua is modeled on Josiah, the king who had the Deuteronomistic History written. Probably the Deuteronomistic picture of conquest is a picture not of the emergence of Israel but of Josiah's own campaigns to recover erstwhile Israelite lands to his north and west.[3]

The infiltration model. This model suggests that nomads out of the steppe and desert gradually settled in the Palestinian highland by a process of peaceful immigration. How these nomads came to be in the steppe and desert is left unexplained: they simply infiltrate the supposedly vacant highland from their former steppe and desert abodes. Since this model was first suggested, anthropologists have shown that pastoral nomads did not emerge from the desert but were based in the more fertile areas and journeyed into the steppe and desert to graze their flocks during the period of the year when these regions could support livestock. The direction of movement was toward the desert rather than out of it.

This model sees J's history coming about through a "brick and mortar" process, with the various small seminomadic tribes that infiltrated and settled in Palestine developing localized oral traditions that in due course coalesced and were embellished into the written traditions which have been preserved. There is a religious basis to these traditions, as is evident from the stories about tribal ancestors hovering around Beersheba, Hebron, and Bethel—all were centers of worship. In this view, J would be one version of this early written tradition and E another. Although the model recognizes the diversity of early Israelite population, its great weakness is that it was developed prior to the time when archaeology could offer a significant contribution to our understanding of Palestinian society in this period.

The revolt and frontier settlement model. This model—of which already several versions have been proposed—attempts to account for the rise of Israel in terms of a struggle for liberation from class oppression. In this model there was no conquest of Palestine from without. Instead, it is suggested the evidence points to an organized peasant revolt. According to this model, Egyptian domination of Palestine, which was maintained by Canaanite city-state rulers who exercised local control on behalf of the pharaoh, was at a low ebb at the time Israel is envisioned as coming into existence. Evidence for this is gleaned from the correspondence of the city-

3. Marvin L. Chaney, "The Book of Joshua," in *The Books of the Bible,* ed. B. W. Anderson (New York: Charles Scribner's Sons, vol. 1, 1989).

state rulers with the Egyptian imperial power, which has been made available to us by the discovery of the fourteenth-century El-Amarna diplomatic archives. It was during this period of supposed Egyptian decline that there arrived in the Palestinian highlands a contingent of peoples who had escaped from Egypt, very likely the Levites. With them they brought the religion of Yahwistic monotheism, which rejected the gods of the Canaanite rulers. They are seen as the core group who provided the ideological focus for peasant revolt. We might liken them to the Pilgrim Fathers, who brought with them a religious ideology that was to play a significant role in the shaping of America. Even though the bulk of the people in North America do not trace their roots back to those who arrived aboard the *Mayflower,* the story of these people has nevertheless become the founding myth of the United States. With the help of this exodus group and their faith, the Palestinian peasants rebelled against their overlords and established a tribal society in the highlands. But within two hundred years the experiment in egalitarianism failed because the arrival of the Sea Peoples, known in biblical literature as the Philistines, on the coast of Palestine posed a mounting military threat that caused Israel to seek a leader who could organize them to withstand the enemy. Thus the Philistines were the catalyst that precipitated the formation of the Israelite state.

The revolt model is the one most recently formulated. It takes account of evidence that indicates that the people identified with early Israel were indeed indigenous to Palestine. The complete shift in understanding required by this new evidence is gradually making its way through scholarly, and even some lay, circles. Although it involves a sophisticated and valuable social analysis, the revolt model falters in its analysis of the politics and economics typical of Palestinian history. For instance, it does not take seriously enough the fact that the bedouin peoples of Palestine typically play a distinct sociopolitical role from the peasantry, while it makes too much of the permanent effect of peasant unrest when it is difficult to point in the historical record to any other "successful" peasant revolt in Palestine or the Near East. Although it correctly takes account of the importance of the village population of Palestine as a distinct social entity, and of the endemic social unrest that characterized their existence, it does not give a convincing explanation as to why such unrest should lead to a regional revolt at the time the model suggests it did.[4] Furthermore, if Israel emerged

---

4. See Gerhard Lenski, review of *The Tribes of Yahweh,* by Norman K. Gottwald, *Religious Studies Review* 6: (1980): 275–78, and the response by Gottwald, "Two Models for the Origins of Ancient Israel: Social Revolution or Frontier Development," in *The Quest for the Kingdom of God: Studies in Honor of George E. Mendenhall,* ed. H. B. Huffmon et al. (Winona Lake, Ind.: Eisenbrauns, 1983), 5–24.

as the result of such a revolt, then it is difficult to understand the marked lack of fortifications around most of the highland settlements.

All three models attempt to fit the historical evidence into what is generally accepted as the biblical picture without first conducting a serious study of J. In effect, they function as an apologetic for a popular understanding of Scripture, attempting to show that it bears witness to actual events in the emergence of Israel. But if what can be known of Palestinian history during this period is taken seriously, a different picture emerges. When what is known to have occurred provides the framework that allows the Bible to be understood, rather than the other way around, the biblical literature makes eminent sense and can be seen to relate well with the known historical data. Instead of constantly having to provide an apology for the Bible, we are set free to utilize it as a faith document that preserves the life, shape, and identity of the interpretive communities of faith.

Historically, what can we say about the emergence of Israel with some degree of certainty? It is commonly agreed that there was a sudden expansion of village settlement in the Palestinian highlands during the early Iron Age, or Iron I, the period from 1200 to 1000 B.C.E. Indeed, this is one of the few statements about the emergence of Israel that we may take with certainty. But when it is viewed against the backdrop of regular and recurrent trends in the history of Palestine, it opens up a window through which we may begin to catch a glimpse of how Israel came into being.

How are we to account for the rapid spread of highland villages and towns? One of the more likely possible scenarios runs like this: The city-state economy of Palestine prior to the emergence of Israel was structured for the benefit of an urban elite and sustained by military subsidy and trade. Concurrent with the fall of the Mycenaean and Hittite empires, and the eventual weakening of Egypt, there was a serious decline in international trade. Many groups in Palestine who operated as political substitutes for the Egyptians, with Egyptian support, found their backing and support drying up with the drop in trade on which Egyptian control was ultimately based. Groups such as dominant bedouin tribes,[5] bandits, and youth gangs played regularly as hirelings in the political and military games of the ruling elite and shared in the economic support of elite politics that moved from village to city and between cities. Such groups often controlled extensive domains in the more marginal areas of Palestine, in the highlands and deserts. These domains had not necessarily been settled and farmed, since the groups that controlled them had other sources of support and food. As their urban support fell off because of the decline of trade, however, they had an incentive to arrange for the settlement of their

5. One very large tribe or tribal grouping was called the Israelites.

domains where possible, in order to supply the foodstuffs previously available to them as mercenaries and bandits. In some cases they themselves settled and farmed more extensively than usual, while in other cases they made it possible, by providing "protection," for expanding peasant families and villages to move from elsewhere into these more marginal domains. With the decrease in city-state powers in the region, these new village settlements enjoyed some freedom from urban domination, if not from every form of exploitation, for a few generations. The occupation of the highlands was therefore an attempt to find an alternative means of subsistence.

Since the development of the highland was not the work of an organized group of people such as a league of tribes banded together around a single religiopolitical ideology, though the tribal designation Israel was apparently the prevailing one, how did these competitive and sometimes hostile settlements become a state? This occurred with the gradual reestablishment of international trade. The people who had withdrawn to the highland were a mix of social classes and soon found themselves swept up in the process of socioeconomic stratification which is common to emerging agrarian societies. With the restoration of interregional trade, surpluses were sold, with those located nearest to the trade routes gaining an economic advantage over those farther away. At the same time, it was becoming less and less profitable to expand agriculture by opening up new highland territory, since this required an increasing amount of long-term investment in terracing. This precipitated a switch to practices of agricultural intensification. Tree crops, requiring many years to become lucrative, called for residential stability if their development was to be worthwhile. It was clearly in the interests of those with the greatest investment to protect their investment through a gradual movement toward centralized rule. This process may be seen in the clan heads, local chieftains, tribal sheikhs, and lowland mercenaries described in sections of the Deuteronomistic History going back to the time of Saul and David. Some of these were wealthy; others started out relatively disadvantaged and had to build up support over time. In due course one such person, David, became king.[6] It is the story of how this came about to which we now turn. The important point to note is that J does not describe the processes that were in operation in Palestine during the two centuries or so prior to David. It is not a history of early Israel as a historian today would understand that history.[7]

6. P. Kyle McCarter, Jr., "The Historical David," *Interpretation* 40 (1986): 117–29.

7. Robert B. Coote and Keith W. Whitelam, "The Emergence of Israel: Social Transformation and State Formation Following the Decline in Late Bronze Age Trade," *Semeia* 37 (1986): 107–47.

5

A Window Opens

The chief large-scale political-economic forms of Late Bronze Mediterranean civilization were the Mycenaean empire, the Hittite empire, the Assyrian empire, and the Egyptian empire, which one might loosely describe as the four quarters of west, north, east, and south. The Egyptian empire in Asia was a prime feature of the New Kingdom period—essentially the Eighteenth, Nineteenth, and Twentieth Dynasties, spanning from about 1550 to 1150 B.C.E., and roughly coterminous with the Late Bronze Age. From the sixteenth century B.C.E. to the end of the tenth century the Egyptians had the capacity to exercise sovereignty in Palestine. The rise of the Davidic state represented a brief departure from Egyptian rule, but even this development took shape against the background of a persistent Egyptian threat.

At one time it was thought that the Amarna letters from the early- to mid-fourteenth century, dispatches from Palestinian warlords to their Egyptian sovereign, indicated severe social disruption and the decline of Egyptian influence in Palestine. The "cultic revolution" of Akhenaton, which involved the creation of the cult of Aton at Amarna, was also taken to indicate a political disintegration from which the New Kingdom never recovered. It was therefore assumed that Egyptian power in Palestine peaked with the Eighteenth Dynasty and receded during the first half of the fourteenth century. Accordingly, it was conjectured that this imperial power vacuum was what made it possible for an independent Palestinian society, Israel, to emerge.

More recent historical study shows that Egyptian New Kingdom power, an important aspect of which was the ability to maintain sovereignty over Palestine, continued at least through the period of Ramses II, down to around 1240 B.C.E. The latest view is that this power extended all the way through Ramses III, deep into the twelfth century.[1] Egyptian influence was therefore quite strong, particularly along the coast, well into the period when the villages of the people whom we come to know as Israel in the time of David had already sprouted in the highland, often quite close to Egyptian-controlled cities. The emergence of these highland settlements resulted not from a waning of Egyptian power, which did not come until later, but from economic factors that had to do with survival.

Around 1275 B.C.E., Ramses II and the Hittite Hattusilis III had formed a treaty whereby the Egyptian sphere of influence bordered the Hittite sphere of influence in Palestine. The result was a degree of political-economic coherence in the world that allowed the flow and exchange of goods and military services. This was an era of a high level of communication, transportation, and prosperity at the urban level. The cities of Ugarit and Byblos, for instance, thrived. The benefits enjoyed by the urban populations drew people into the cities, so that even though the number of settlements remained static, the size of urban centers increased,[2] facilitating the influence that Ramses II and Ramses III had on Palestine in this period, since city populations were more readily governed.

With the end of the Late Bronze Age, this coherence of the Middle Eastern and Mediterranean world went into serious decline.[3] One of our prime sources of information is monumental inscriptions on the temples of Ramses II and Ramses III. At the death of Ramses III (about 1150 B.C.E.) there was a drastic ebb of Egyptian influence in Palestine, so much so that the Egyptians didn't have the resources to build monuments and carve grand inscriptions as had their predecessors. The Wen-amun papyrus from about 1050 B.C.E. describes how the pharaoh sent his envoy to Byblos on the Phoenician coast to acquire wood, which Egypt had to import from Cyrenaica on the west and from the Levantine coast on the east. Upon arrival in Byblos he was spurned and treated in a degrading manner that demonstrated the temporary loss of Egyptian power along the coast of the eastern Mediterranean. The inscription indicates that the coasts had become dangerous for trade as Sea People pirates took advantage of the breakdown of communication between the major powers.

1. James M. Weinstein, "The Egyptian Empire in Palestine: A Reassessment," *Bulletin of the American Schools of Oriental Research* 241 (1981): 1–28; Itamar Singer, "Merneptah's Campaign to Canaan and the Egyptian Occupation of the Southern Coastal Plain of Palestine in the Ramesside Period," *Bulletin of the American Schools of Oriental Research* 269 (1988): 1–10.

2. Rivka Gonen, "Urban Canaan in the Late Bronze Period," *Bulletin of the American Schools of Oriental Research* 253 (1984): 61–73.

3. The exact causes of this decline are not yet known. Only a tiny fraction of the Middle East and the Mediterranean world has been excavated—perhaps as low as 1 or 2 percent of what is available for excavation.

By the tenth century the danger from pirates had diminished and trade routes were once again developing. The Phoenicians, notably Hiram at Tyre on the coast, took over the role of the Mycenaeans, establishing a commodity trade that extended out into the Mediterranean.

The rise of the house of David was contemporaneous with this gradual reintegration of the eastern Mediterranean, so that David and Solomon were able to take advantage of the reemerging trade network. Although the full-blown coherence of Mediterranean–Middle Eastern trade did not return until the ninth century, Israelite cities in the interior and Tyre on the coast became major centers of trade. There was also an overland north-south trade in horses and chariots, run by Solomon. Horses were expensive in the Middle East so as to be high-value, high-grade military equipment.

This period of Israelite independence, which lasted only sixty years or so, was a window of opportunity that went quite against the pattern of domination of Palestine by outside powers. Political autonomy of this kind in Palestine was an anomaly. Self-directed regimes which were not in any way beholden to the empires, and which could set their own price, simply did not flourish often in Palestine, even during the period of the Israelite monarchies. For this brief period, the economic influence of David and Solomon extended into the Negev, into the Transjordan, and up into the Aramean region, enabling them to exercise a wide sovereignty.[4]

In the tenth century—the time of David and Solomon—Egypt was once more a threat, particularly under Shishak in the latter part of the century. The brief revival of Egyptian power toward the end of the Twenty-first Dynasty[5] sparked a Judahite-Philistine alliance under David, with Egypt as the common enemy.

One indication of Egyptian influence in Palestine was the role of the Egyptian monarchy in the secession of Israel from the Davidic state at the death of Solomon (1 Kings 12). Far from being merely a peasant rebellion, the split in the kingdom was an instance of imperial manipulation. Political figures from the Israelite empire, from Edom and Aram, were resident as refugees in the court of pharaoh (1 Kings 11). Jeroboam was essentially an Egyptian puppet, sent up from the Egyptian court to lead the rebellion

4. For a recent summary statement of the classical view that J was composed during the time of the "united monarchy" under David and Solomon, see Werner H. Schmidt, "A Theologian of the Solomonic Era? A Plea for the Yahwist," in *Studies in the Period of David and Solomon and Other Essays,* ed. T. Ishida (Winona Lake, Ind.: Eisenbrauns, 1982), 55–73. Although some scholars support alternatives, this is still the common view. Almost all regard J as Solomonic. Our discussion will focus on why it is probably Davidic instead. See B. Mazar, "The Historical Background of the Book of Genesis," *Journal of Near Eastern Studies* 28 (1969): 73–83.

5. David O'Connor, "New Kingdom and Third Intermediate Period, 1552–664 B.C." in B. G. Trigger et al., *Ancient Egypt: A Social History* (Cambridge: Cambridge University Press, 1983), 229–35.

against the house of David. This may explain why, in the fifth year of Rehoboam, Shishak invaded the Davidic state and took tribute but apparently did not reduce the northern kingdom.

Who were the Philistines? We met them earlier as part of the various Sea Peoples. They were a migrating and mercenary population. As they migrated they plundered. They were able to exercise a power that local rulers were not able to maintain, because the period of their migration coincided with the decline in Middle Eastern trade at the end of the Late Bronze Age and the beginning of the Iron Age. Circumstances afforded an opportunity for such migrants to ensconce themselves as a new elite, at first alien, in the Palestinian plain during the twelfth, eleventh, and beginning of the tenth centuries. In a short time they became integrated into Palestinian society and adopted the Palestinian pantheon and the Palestinian language.

Just as those who became identified as Israelites with the emergence of the Davidic state did not have ethnic coherence prior to the formation of the state, so too the lowland population had no single ethnic identity. When one excavates a Philistine site—mostly lowland cities, such as Ashdod, Ashkelon, and other coastal sites—identifiable Philistine artifacts amount to only a tiny proportion of the finds. Only at Ashdod has this been as high as 50 percent, with the majority of sites yielding a mere 5 to 25 percent. In other words, what the Philistine presence represented was not a new ethnic identity but a replacement ruling class of lowland Palestine. Population change was not significant: what was significant was the newcomers' politics. Several texts from the period show that the Sea Peoples functioned not only as opponents of Egypt but also as mercenaries within the Egyptian forces. They were an elite power with which Egypt had to come to grips, either as ally or as opponent. At first they only represented Egyptian suzerainty, and it is significant that, upon the diplomatic marriage of Solomon to an Egyptian princess, the city of Gezer on the traditional Philistine border changed hands.

The conflict between Saul and the Philistines was not a question of Israel versus the Philistines, as if two national entities were vying for power—the picture portrayed in most literature. Rather, the battle was between a highland elite, for whom Saul had emerged as leader, and a lowland elite. Earlier the lowland elite had ruled with the backing of Egypt, and now they were supported by other Palestinians, including the highlander David.

Our treatment of the J strand assumes that the narratives of the rise of David in 1 Samuel, which tell how he usurped the throne from Saul, are among the earliest prose historical documents in the Bible. We have abundant evidence that those who usurped another family's royal prerogatives—the main prerogative being sovereignty over the arable land—wrote narratives justifying their usurpation. This is precisely what we have in the story of the rise of David: 1 Sam. 16:14—2 Sam. 5:12 is an apology for the house of David. That this text belongs to the genre of apology tells us it came from the time itself and addressed contemporary pressing political issues rather than being a history composed at a later date.

David became Saul's particular enemy when he became the vassal of a Philistine lord. Indeed, he had to defend himself mightily in his more direct apologetic literature for having any connection with the Philistines in the first place. Sections of 1 Samuel attempt to answer the charge that he took the lowland side against the highland people who were to emerge as the nation of Israel when he came to power. They explain away his alignment with the lowland elite by blaming Saul for alienating him and by asserting that he only feigned raiding the highland peoples (1 Samuel 27). The Davidic court documents, however, reveal that even after he gained control of the throne, David's own personal army comprised Philistine and Cretan mercenaries (the Kerethites and Pelethites) under the command of Benaiah.[6]

Although the Philistine elite play a major role in the apology of David, they figure little in J. Why isn't the enemy in J the Philistines? In 2 Samuel 8, David defeats the Ammonites, the Moabites, the Arameans, and the Philistines: why isn't J all about this? Not only does J not make the Philistines the enemy, he is very careful to have Abram and Isaac make friends with the Philistines, and Jacob makes friends with the Edomites, against the prime enemy, which in J is Egypt.

J is an anti-Egyptian document that represents the circumstances of David's reign, not Solomon's. It was the Egyptians, not the Philistines, who posed the greatest threat to the house of David. In the time of Solomon there was no need to portray Egypt as the enemy, because Solomon had already come to terms with the Egyptian threat and arranged a diplomatic

---

6. Cf. 2 Sam. 20:23. The documents contained in whole or in part in the Bible that come directly from the court of David or Solomon are all known to have a significant propagandistic element, so it comes as no surprise that J does also. See P. Kyle McCarter, Jr., "The Apology of David," *Journal of Biblical Literature* 99 (1980): 489–504; idem, " 'Plots, True or False': The Succession Narrative as Court Apologetic," *Interpretation* 35 (1981): 355–67; Keith W. Whitelam, "The Defence of David," *Journal for the Study of the Old Testament* 29 (1984): 61–87; and Walter Brueggemann, *David's Truth in Israel's Imagination and Memory* (Philadelphia: Fortress Press, 1985). Brueggemann's book follows on an early set of superb studies related to J: "David and His Theologian," *Catholic Biblical Quarterly* 30 (1968): 156–81; "Israel's Moment of Freedom," *The Bible Today* (April 1969): 2917–25; "The Trusted Creature," *Catholic Biblical Quarterly* 31 (1969): 484–98; "The Triumphalist Tendency in Exegetical History," *Journal of the American Academy of Religion* 38 (1970): 367–80; "Of the Same Flesh and Bone (Gn 2:23a)," *Catholic Biblical Quarterly* 32 (1970): 532–42; "Kingship and Chaos," *Catholic Biblical Quarterly* 33 (1971): 317–32; "Weariness, Exile and Chaos," *Catholic Biblical Quarterly* 34 (1972): 19–38; "From Dust to Kingship," *Zeitschrift für die alttestamentliche Wissenschaft* 84 (1972): 1–18; "On Trust and Freedom," *Interpretation* 26 (1972): 3–19; "Life and Death in Tenth Century Israel," *Journal of the American Academy of Religion* 40 (1972): 96–109; and "On Coping with Curse: A Study of 2 Sam 16:5–14," *Catholic Biblical Quarterly* 36 (1974): 175–92.

marriage alliance with pharaoh. This is what made it possible for him to establish strong land-based trade relations between Egypt and the Hittite realm to the north, with himself as the middleman. While David's economy was essentially built on peripheral produce that was going out through the Phoenician ports, Solomon's economy was Middle Eastern, stretching from Asia Minor to Egypt and the Arabian coast. Instead of representing Egypt as the enemy, he needed to find a way of reading J that would allow the court to view Egypt as friendly at this point. The document could either be read pseudo-historically as referring to what Israel had been in origin but was no longer or it could have been hidden or discarded. Apparently Solomon's court chose the former strategy.

J is an upbeat, optimistic document that assumes basic acquiescence to its projection of an ethnic identity. This is more likely to be true under David, given what we know of the large numbers of people who did not acquiesce to Solomon's rule and joined in the secession to create the separate state of northern Israel under Jeroboam. Whatever the basis of the twelve-tribe schema represented in J,[7] David allowed, or was forced to allow, tribal identities and territories to persist, while Solomon attempted to override them through an administrative redivision of the nation. The emphasis in J on tribal identities in the history of Israel and his sons reflects David's policy, not Solomon's. J's critique of urban culture on behalf of the posited nation under David is expressive of, among other things, the preservation of some degree of premonarchic tribal identity. Solomonic politics generated a range of tensions and hostilities within society, none of which are addressed by J. Rather, J reflects the sociopolitical issues that we know were uppermost in the Davidic period. To treat J's optimism as a courtly, secular optimism due to the wealth and success of the Solomonic royal household, as many scholars do, ignores the ideological purpose of J, which was to project an identity for the mix of peoples who became the state of Israel under Davidic rule and to give the cult of Yahweh under David a sacral basis in history. J is a history of the world written by David's scribes with the kingdom of David as its center and culmination. It is a history in which the experiences, perceptions, and purposes of the ruling house of David in the time of David are set forth.[8]

J became the basic document in the court of the house of David in subsequent centuries because it came into existence early in the history of

7. See Norman K. Gottwald, *The Tribes of Yahweh: A Sociology of the Religion of Liberated Israel, 1250–1050 B.C.* (Maryknoll, N.Y.: Orbis Books, 1979), 358–75.

8. It is tantalizing to speculate whether J was the scribe Shausa mentioned in the lists of David's court officers, 2 Sam. 8:17 and 20:25, or one of his apprentices. On this form of his name, see P. Kyle McCarter, Jr., *II Samuel,* Anchor Bible (Garden City, N.Y.: Doubleday & Co., 1984), 253–56, 433. Zadok, from the house of Jehoiada in southern Judah, is another possible candidate.

30

the house of David and because it represented Israelite identity at a time of political autonomy. Although such autonomy was not usual in Palestine, nevertheless its representation in J gained great popularity with reigning descendants of David in retrospect.[9]

9. A few historians have analyzed J in terms of David. Volkmar Fritz in *Israel in der Wüste* (Marburg, 1970), 121, cites H. Schulze, "Die Grossreichsidee Davids wie sie sich im Werke des Jahwisten spiegelt" (diss., Mainz, 1952).

6

Real People by Another Name

The reason usually given for why Egypt, rather than the Philistines, is the foil[1] of J's story is that Israel had its origin in an escape from Egypt. The usual interpretation of the story of that escape is that it is a narrative connected with the cult of premonarchic Israel, a narrative that reflects historically the origins of Israel. Even in the peasant revolt model, these "exodus" people are treated as the core of the Israelite peasantry. In view of what we have already seen about the actual emergence of Israel, we need to look more closely at this notion.

The exodus story in J is essentially a bedouin story, describing the release from corvée labor of a group of Negev and Judahite highland bedouin who found themselves jeopardized as they rose in power within the Egyptian kingdom. The question is, why should J have selected these traditions to function as the founding myth of the nation of Israel? Why single out the events that happened to a handful of bedouin to represent the vast majority of Israelites who were peasants, not pastoral nomads?

Except in periods and areas of extremely high political-economic integration, in which a centralized regime exercised effective control over a large definable territory, the ones who controlled the marginal regions in Palestine were those whose subsistence and whose sociopolitical organization allowed them to exist in areas where villages were not so prevalent and where the pathways of communication and transportation passed through more desolate regions such as mountains and arid land. These marginal areas included the Negev, which bordered on the Philistine plains, and mountainous passes up and down the Transjordan. Empires and those who wished to rule from cities had to come to grips with this military force (and therefore political power) which we call the bedouin.

---

1. Something that by contrast sets off another thing to advantage. In this case, Egypt sets off David's state. Egypt is portrayed as bad so that the Davidic state can appear good.

The bedouin were able to take advantage of the sparse vegetation of the ecologically more marginal areas.[2] Consequently, they formed a buffer between the major political entities. Bedouin bands did not diminish during the period of the demise of the New Kingdom at the end of the tenth century B.C.E.; on the contrary, as happened periodically in Palestine during periods of major political activity and extension of settlement, their influence probably increased. Recent study of an extension of pastoralist settlements in the western Negev dates them in the eleventh century.[3] Israel emerged in regions where bedouin and bandit groups exercised political control. We know that the bedouin were influential during the time of the rise of the Israelite monarchy because the Midianites and the Amalekites, who were bedouin of the Negev and similar regions, are referred to by J and the traditional materials in Judges. Indeed, the Amalekites played a significant role in the rise of David, according to documents directly from David's court.

David used diplomatic maneuvers, marriage, and military strength to surround the heartlands, gaining political influence in border lands and in marginal dry lands: the Judah–Negev boundary, the Judahite desert on the east, and the Philistine plain–Negev boundary to the southwest. The arena of his operation, where he hid in caves and oases, is well described in 1 Samuel. When he came to power he was able relatively easily, with forces developed in these areas, to conquer and dominate similar areas in the Transjordan along the desert boundary of the dominions of Edom, Moab, the Ammonites, and the Arameans. At first his military strength was not that of the Philistine mercenary force he hired once on the throne, nor a chariot force such as could be used to control the plains. Rather, his strength came from a tactical strike force suited to marginal, buffer zones.

According to 1 Samuel, not only did David defeat the Amalekites, who controlled this area, but the prime point of apology vis-à-vis Saul in the narrative is that Saul did not destroy the Amalekites, which is what led to his downfall.[4] After the throne was turned over to David, the Amalekites reemerged to give David his excuse for not being present at the death of Saul and Jonathan. David was not responsible for the death of the king and the rightful heir to the throne, because he was away chasing the Amalekites! In the apology, it was one who might be dubbed the "last of

2. A. G. Baron, "Adaptive Strategies in the Archaeology of the Negev," *Bulletin of the American Schools of Oriental Research* 242 (1981): 51–81.

3. Israel Finkelstein, "The Iron Ages Sites in the Negev Highlands—Military Fortresses or Nomads Settling Down?" *Biblical Archaeology Review* 12/4 (1986): 46–53; Ernst Axel Knauf, *Zeitschrift des Deutschen Palästina-Vereins* 102 (1986): 175.

4. 1 Sam. 28:17–18. This passage comes from a "prophetic" reworking of David's apology but indicates the traditional importance of David's treatment of the Amalekites. See P. Kyle McCarter, Jr., *I Samuel*, Anchor Bible (Garden City, N.Y.: Doubleday & Co., 1980), 18–23, 422–23.

the Amalekites" who reported the demise of Saul and Jonathan; and David had this one slaughtered for bringing him this bad news, as he wept crocodile tears over the death of his opponents Saul and Jonathan.

Saul had captured (RSV: "taken"; 1 Sam. 14:47) the royal dominion, taking to himself the prerogative of taxing the arable land. David was pitted against him, claiming that this prerogative had been turned over to him by God. Saul could use the agricultural heartland of the highland to create an army by rewarding allegiance with economic power in the form of "vineyards, olive orchards and fields" (1 Sam. 22:7). Since David did not control the heartland, he could not raise a military force as Saul could. Therefore his strategy was to control the margins, placing himself in the same political niche as the bedouin, who were organized in paramilitary bands, and becoming, like them, an outlaw from the state. If David was to rule, he must supplant these with supporters. The defeat of the Amalekites is a paradigm of that replacement. Presumably there were lots of Amalekite-like groups, but the Bible mentions only one in order to use it against Saul. It is the people whom David used to replace them that J is particularly interested in. These are the ancestors of Israel, according to J.

J is not about the settlers in the highland, the more than four-fifths of David's Israelite subjects who were peasants. It is about the people along the border of Palestine and Egypt whose fate was bound up with the Egyptian threat.[5] If these Negev bedouin had names, their names would be of the same type as Abram, Isaac, and Jacob.[6] They occupied the same

5. It was not Solomon who represented Israel as nomads, because he didn't have to come to terms with nomads and use nomadic regions the way David did. Most historians believe that archaeology shows the Negev was garrisoned and fortressed under Solomon, perhaps by bedouin. Early in his career, Solomon was in control of the area and didn't have to deal with the distinctive sociopolitical forces of the Negev. The apologetic history of David's rise addresses issues of internal highland politics; J's scope extends to the peripheries of the kingdom and far beyond.

6. See V. Worschech, *Abraham: Eine sozialgeschichtliche Studie* (Frankfurt and Bern, 1983); J. J. Scullion, "Some Reflections on the Present State of the Patriarchal Studies: The Present State of the Question," *Abr-Nahrain* 21 (1982/83): 50–65; and Thomas L. Thompson, *The Historicity of the Patriarchal Narratives* (Berlin: Walter de Gruyter, 1974). William G. Dever and W. M. Clark, "The Patriarchal Traditions," in *Israelite and Judaean History,* ed. J. H. Hayes and J. M. Miller (London: SCM Press; Philadelphia: Westminster Press, 1977), 70–148, give an excellent review of the anthropological data and interpretation available as of ten years ago. They apply this material, however, as do most, to the ancestors in some supposed earlier period, following the indication of J. The use of information about bedouin is different in this book. Here the question is not, "Who were the patriarchs?" but rather, "How do the bedouin traditions as selected and composed by J reflect the pastoral nomadic politics and economics in David's day, particularly in southwestern Palestine?" But see two studies that have cast some doubt on the assumption in this question: John Van Seters, *Abraham in History and Tradition* (New Haven, Conn.: Yale University Press, 1975), 1–38 ("The Nomadism of the Patriarchs"), part of Van Seters's attempt to demonstrate that J was written only after the monarchic period; and Norman K. Gottwald, *The Tribes of Yahweh: A Sociology of the Religion of Liberated Israel, 1250–1050 B.C.* (Maryknoll, N.Y.: Orbis Books, 1979), 448–59. For a preliminary treatment of early Iron Age Palestinian bedouin as understood here, see Niels Peter Lemche, *Early Israel* (Leiden: E. J. Brill, 1985), 82–163; and Robert B. Coote and Keith W.

region and did the same things as did the "ancestors" in J's history. If one compares the material in the second half of 1 Samuel with J's stories of Abram, Isaac, and Jacob, it becomes apparent that the arena of David's rise to power was identical to the arena of the stories of Israel's ancestral families. Although J presents them as eponyms stretching back many generations before the Davidic state was born, in reality they were the sheikhs of David's time. Names of the *type* Abram, Isaac, and Jacob were as commonplace among such groups as Tom, Dick, and Harry.[7] Their names suggest that they were fictionalized individuals, because the names are so fully integrated into the narrative points that J wants to make; but even though the names are fictionalized, the social configuration to which they refer was real. Abram, Isaac, and Jacob were real people by another name, much like the characters in James Herriot's novels and television series *All Creatures Great and Small.* Abram, Isaac, Jacob and his heirs inhabited David's Israel.[8]

Abram is portrayed as ruling at Hebron, a sheepherder, who was extremely wealthy by bedouin norms. David was dealing not only with militarized bands but with wealthy sheikhs who were sheepherders. Bedouin were employed in Egypt as state sheepherders. David was a village outlaw from a relatively well-to-do family. The process by which he ended up with control of the arable in Palestine was one of encirclement through the creation of military and economic alliances with the likes of Abram. He came to power controlling the produce of marginal boundaries and ruled in Hebron for seven years. He might just as well have been a bedouin sheikh. He displaced those bedouin who did not align themselves with him, represented by the Amalekites, by forming an alliance with those who wanted to be on his side.

Like most bedouin in the whole area of Syria and Palestine, the bedouin of the Negev tended to maintain a form of political independence from the state, when they did not themselves provide the head of state. One of J's aims was to make such bedouin allies of David feel that they were a part of

Whitelam, *The Emergence of Early Israel in Historical Perspective* (Sheffield, Eng.: Almond Press, 1987), 94–111.

7. The name Jacob occurs often in Palestine and Egypt at the end of the Middle Bronze Age, referring to at least two generations of Palestinian lords, who ruled in Egypt as well as coastal Palestine. It does not occur in the archaeological record in the Late Bronze or the Early Iron age. See Aharon Kempinski, "Jacob in History," *Biblical Archaeology Review* 14/1 (January/February 1988): 42–47.

8. The recognition of a connection between Abram and David is a commonplace in biblical studies. See Ronald Clements, *Abraham and David: Genesis 15 and Its Meaning for Israelite Tradition* (London: SCM Press, 1967). For a critique of this point of view, see N. E. Wagner,"Abraham and David?" in *Studies on the Ancient Palestinian World,* ed. J. W. Wevers and D. B. Redford (Toronto: University of Toronto Press, 1972), 117–40. Most historians have not felt it necessary to distinguish David from Solomon when discussing the "Davidic" setting of J.

David's political economy and to reinforce the bedouin's feeling of independence from the Egyptian state. J was not simply public literature meant to be broadcast far and wide throughout David's realm. Instead, it was intended mainly for private consumption in the court of David. It is easy to imagine David entertaining influential sheikhs such as Abram and Isaac in his court and having the history of his nation read aloud to them.[9] They would have been interested to hear that the people whom David ruled descended from their kind of people and that, like David, they too enjoyed the privileges of the court at the head of the people.[10] Such an idea, coupled with economic favors, no doubt greatly enhanced the sheikhs' support of David's court and its policies.[11]

9. An interesting partial parallel occurs in the sources for nineteenth-century Palestine. In 1852–55 Turkey was at war with Russia and had to transfer troops from Palestine to the Russian front. This allowed rebels to crop up in Palestine. A wealthy landowner named Abderrahman took over Hebron with a force numbering up to eight hundred men. A key to his temporary success was his alliance with the Taamri bedouin of the Judean wilderness. The British consul at the time described a secret meeting he attended in a village north of Hebron between Abderrahman's brother and the head sheikh of the Taamri. See Arnold Blumberg, *A View from Jerusalem, 1849–1858* (East Brunswick, N.J.: Fairleigh Dickinson University Press, 1980), 128; and idem, *Zion Before Zionism, 1838–1880* (Syracuse, N.Y.: Syracuse University Press, 1985), 69, 80–83.

10. See the remarks of George E. Mendenhall, "The Nature and Purpose of the Abraham Narratives," in *Ancient Israelite Religion: Essays in Honor of Frank Moore Cross*, ed. P. D. Miller et al. (Philadelphia: Fortress Press, 1987), 337–40.

11. A thorough study of state use of bedouin alliances in Palestine is required. It is a frequent feature of the history of the area. For preliminary indications, see M. B. Rowton, "Autonomy and Nomadism in Western Asia," *Orientalia* 42 (1973): 247–58; Victor Harold Matthews, *Pastoral Nomadism in the Mari Kingdom (ca. 1830–1760 B.C.)* (Cambridge: American Schools of Oriental Research, 1978), 95–103, 131–78; Ernst Axel Knauf, *Ismael: Untersuchungen zur Geschichte Palästinas und Nordarabiens im 1. Jahrtausend v. Christi* (Wiesbaden: Harrassowitz, 1985); Israel Eph'al, *The Ancient Arabs: Nomads on the Borders of the Fertile Crescent, 9th–5th Centuries B.C.* (Jerusalem: Magnes Press, 1982); David F. Graf, "The Saracens and the Defense of the Arabian Frontier," *Bulletin of the American Schools of Oriental Research* 229 (1978): 1–26; Philip Mayerson, "The Saracens and the *Limes*," *Bulletin of the American Schools of Oriental Research* 262 (1986); 35–47; S. Thomas Parker, *Romans and Saracens: A History of the Arabian Frontier* (Winona Lake, Ind.: Eisenbrauns, 1986); Berthold Rubin, *Das Zeitalter Justinians* (Berlin: Walter de Gruyter, 1960), 268–79; Fred McGraw Donner, *The Early Islamic Conquests* (Princeton: Princeton University Press, 1981), chap. 1 ("State and Society in Pre-Islamic Arabia"), 11–49; M. Sharon, "The Political Role of the Bedouins in Palestine in the Sixteenth and Seventeenth Centuries," in *Studies on Palestine During the Ottoman Period*, ed. M. Ma'oz (Jerusalem: Magnes Press, 1975), 11–48; Abdul-Rahim Abu-Husayn, *Provincial Leaderships in Syria 1575–1650* (Syracuse, N.Y.: Syracuse University Press, 1986), 153–98 (chap. 4: "Three Dynasties of Bedouin Chiefs of the Biqa', Transjordan and Palestine: the Furaykhs, the Qansuhs and the Turabays"); Amnon Cohen, *Palestine in the 18th Century: Patterns of Government and Administration* (Jerusalem: Magnes Press, 1973), 90–110; Walter P. Zenner, "Aqiili Agha: The Strongman in the Ethnic Relations of the Ottoman Galilee," *Comparative Studies in Society and History* 14 (1972): 169–88; Afaf Lutfi al-Sayyid Marsot, *Egypt in the Reign of Muhammad Ali* (Cambridge: Cambridge University Press, 1984), 122–25; and Robert Springborg, *Family, Power, and Politics in Egypt* (Philadelphia: University of Pennsylvania Press, 1982), 3–27. For a theoretical discussion of this relationship, see Daniel G. Bates, "The Role of the State in Peasant-Nomad Mutualism," *Anthropological Quarterly* 44 (1971): 109–31. More recent work by Knauf at Heidelberg promises to further our understanding in the area significantly.

David had been the ruler of Ziklag in Gerar, which was a Philistine town: the Philistines had turned it over to him. When J talks about the Philistine area of Gerar in the stories of Abram and Isaac, he is talking about the region of Ziklag.[12] The area where David established his military base as a Philistine vassal is the very area in which Isaac created the conditions of peace with Abimeleck (Genesis 26). The picture of the ancestors in Genesis making peace with the Philistines reflects the situation in the reign of David, not the premonarchic period. David integrated this area politically—reducing hostility and coordinating the barrier against Egyptian influence—with the support of his bedouin allies centered in Hebron and Beersheba.[13]

The Davidic state was centered in the highlands of central Palestine; it was an all-highland state by sometime after the Davidic capital came to be in Jerusalem. We know little about the premonarchic highland social and political forms that were transformed into the Davidic state. The Israel to which Pharaoh Merneptah referred may have been a bedouin tribe once serving as an Egyptian-allied force in the buffer zone with the Hittite lands, and conceivably one of those strong tribes which sponsored the settlement of the highlands. Certainly it is not a reference to the whole of later Israelite society from far north to far south. It would be as erroneous to read into this early use of the name the political and social forms associated with the Davidic state as it would be to read what we know today as the United States into a seventeenth-century reference to America. When did the peoples who became Israel achieve a sense of ethnic coherence, so that we might think of them loosely as having a national identity? It is possible that this sense of ethnic coherence is a creation of Davidic ideology and that J is the first major statement of it. With the emergence of the Davidic state, an unusually large number of people in Palestine were supposed to identify themselves with a political-economic form of which they were to see themselves as beneficiaries.[14] In J, the Davidic state centered in Jerusalem

12. See Eliezer D. Oren, "Ziklag: A Biblical City on the Edge of the Negev," *Biblical Archaeologist* 45 (1982): 155–66; Joe D. Seger, "The Location of Biblical Ziklag," *Biblical Archaeologist* 47 (1984): 47–53; and J. D. Ray, "Two Etymologies: Ziklag and Phicol," *Vetus Testamentum* 36 (1986): 355–61.

13. For an alternative understanding of the "pastoral motifs" in J, see Herbert N. Schneidau, *Sacred Discontent: The Bible and Western Tradition* (Berkeley and Los Angeles: University of California Press, 1976), 104–73 ("The Hebrews Against the High Cultures: Pastoral Motifs").

14. Nationalism as we know it today developed only with industrial societies. It is essential not to posit a uniform ethnic or social identity for ancient "Israel" at any stage. "The social organization of agrarian society . . . generates political units which are either smaller or much larger than cultural boundaries would indicate." See Ernest Gellner, *Nations and Nationalism* (Ithaca, N.Y.: Cornell University Press, 1983), esp. chap 2 ("Culture in Agrarian Society"), 8–18; the quote is from p. 39. In this book, we use terms such as "nationalism" and "national identity" to refer to *an inherently limited notion of political consensus held mainly in the royal court*

represents its tenure of state territory in terms of a bedouin grant. Since the bedouin grantee was a powerful sheikh, he was able, as David his heir presumed to be able, to traverse Palestine. In the third generation after great Abram, the territory was blanketed by the claims of his twelve powerful great-grandsons. This tribal concept of extensive tenure not only represented Davidic pretensions but also canceled out the rival claims to territorial autonomy of other bedouin groups within or adjacent to the territory.

The prime agricultural products of David's kingdom were wheat, barley, and in particular the produce of perennials, oil and wine. This is what was traded out into Mediterranean countries by the Mycenaeans, then later by the Phoenicians under their treaty with Israel, and finally by the Assyrians when they took over Israel. David's house was established first in Judah. He controlled some oil and wine, though not nearly enough to establish a major commodity trade. We know that he did not trade through Egypt, and there is no evidence that he traded through Philistia. But he did control pastoral regions whose prime product in terms of a commodity was wool. The special relationship between David and the Phoenician rulers can be understood in terms of the supply of wool that he furnished to the Tyrians for dyeing and export. Tyre in fact became a great trading center through dealing in fabrics dyed with its distinctive and highly valued purple dye. David's role in this trade probably fueled the growth of his household economy.

David did not at first envision a regional nation-state. Economically, there was no regional kingdom to capture. That David continued to rule in Hebron for seven years after the death of Saul indicates that he did not set out to become a Middle Eastern monarch with power over the arable in Palestine. Attempts to control the arable of highland Palestine were of no lasting benefit to Saul, so how would they benefit David? He went another route. Rather than basing his household economy on the quicksand of immediate dominion over highland arable, he based it on control of the margins and the pastoral product, chiefly wool. By exporting wool and other products, he became a Middle Eastern monarch with considerable wealth. He expanded this power into dominion over the southern highland and lowland arable as well, eventually becoming the lord of many lowland lords, some of whom became his palace guard. Only then did he move to control all the highland.

---

and its immediate extensions and applied primarily to the territory claimed by Saul, somewhat redefined. It could in fact be argued that the role of J as "nationalist" is closer to (though not the same as) the spiritual clerical ideal betrayed, as described by Julien Benda in *The Treason of the Intellectuals (La Trahison des Clercs)* (New York: William Morrow, 1928), than to the "clerk's" role in fostering what we know today as nationalism.

David took the booty of the Amalekites—their produce and goods—and turned it over not to his bedouin allies, the likes of Abram, but to a group of farmers located in towns along the eastern and southeastern margins of Judah, where the Judahite highlands merge into the Judahite desert to the east. The names of these towns are listed in 1 Samuel 30. By doing this, he created allies along this border, enhancing the pastoral produce of farmers epitomized by Nabal and thereby increasing their participation in the state economy. He had done away with Nabal and married Nabal's wife, and now he himself owned major sheep estates in this region.[15]

Why did David not build a temple? The answer lies in the purpose of a temple, which was to represent the rule of the earthly monarch. Baal, or in the case of Solomon's temple, Yahweh, was the projection into the sky of the earthly monarch who held sovereignty over the territorial arable, which was the basis of monarchic power. The monarch could distribute and redistribute the arable, channeling the product of the arable into interregional, inter-urban commerce to his own benefit. David did not build a temple because he did not rule such a political economy in the highland heartland.[16] It is possible he could not have built a temple even had he wanted to. More likely, given the weakness of his direct control over his rivals in the highlands, he preferred to emphasize the illegitimacy of a temple and the taxes it implied in order to discourage anyone else from building or rebuilding one in opposition to his rule.[17]

Whatever popularity David's household and its cult enjoyed was based on the circumstance that his ownership of the state was largely free of dependence on the arable and perennial produce of the highland heartland of his kingdom. If he was liked, it was because he was at first able to lighten the taxes on peasant produce and labor. He was a populist who did everything he could to create an integrated Palestinian autonomy governed from the highland.[18] The only way he could bring about such an anoma-

15. Hans-Jürgen Zobel, "Beiträge zur Geschichte Gross-Judas in früh- und vordavidischer Zeit," in *Supplements to Vetus Testamentum* 28 (1975); cf. below p. 296 n. 11.·

16. He did, however, have a dual administration, supporting a private army that functioned as his bodyguard and his own private priest, Zadok, who may have come from a village south of Hebron, in the area that was so important for David's rise to power over Judah. See Saul Olyan, "Zadok's Origins and the Tribal Politics of David," *Journal of Biblical Literature* 101 (1982): 177–93.

17. See the suggestion by Carol Meyers that later in his career David did initiate the building of a temple, "David as Temple Builder," in *Ancient Israelite Religion*, ed. Miller, 357–76. Whichever was David's intent, Meyers's delineation of David's building of his empire is an excellent and useful summary.

18. David's populism became increasingly ideological as time went on. The disregard of his villagers' identities evidenced by J is indicative of how David was in fact able to rule with little popular support. Note the conclusion of P. Kyle McCarter, Jr.: "He seems to have had no popular support at all except, perhaps, in Gilead" (*Interpretation* 40 [1986]: 128). David's apologia in 1 Samuel 16—2 Samuel 5 appears at first to illustrate David's popularity. What it

lous situation was to generate political allegiance among disparate high-land peasantry through their clan heads. He was attempting to create an autonomous political entity that would normally be unstable in terms of the patterns of Palestinian history, and he succeeded for a moment. It is precisely because this was so unusual in Palestinian history that J came to play the role it did in the ideology of Palestine.

J is a world history that formed the basis of a cult. It is essentially a cult myth like those known to have been associated with temples in other societies of the period. World histories were not only household histories but cultic histories because there was no division between the political and the religious spheres of life. Religion was integral to politics.

Just as David projected a bedouin national identity rather than a peasant national identity in his world history, he established a tent cult rather than a temple cult. The fact that the state religion is represented as a non-temple cult in J is additional evidence that it was the royal cult document of David, not Solomon, for as buider of a temple Solomon would have had no immediate requirement for such an anti-temple document. Given that his cult was indistinguishable to all intents and purposes from the cult of Baal, if Solomon had overseen the composition of a fresh history as the basis of his cult, it would have been a temple myth of the kind that we have in the Baal cycle or the Babylonian *Enuma elish*.

The best example of what was probably a common myth of Baal, the divine equivalent of a state monarch, comes from Ugarit, a Late Bronze Syrian city-state on the Mediterranean coast, north of Beirut and Tripoli.[19] The Ugaritic myth of Baal begins with a threat from the god Sea, representing political and ecological chaos, against the assembly of the gods. The young warrior Baal is to be turned over to Sea by Baal's father El, the divine equivalent of a tribal sheikh. El agrees. Baal's craftsman Kothar, however, provides him with two magic clubs, and with these he drives away Sea and destroys him. On the basis of this victory and the introduction of a secure political order, Baal has Kothar design and build for him his "house," that is, his palace, the temple, the center of his political economy and the state of Ugarit. This palace has a window, which allows Baal the new king to thunder from the sky and thus bring on the clouds and rainy season to fructify the fertile lands of the realm. In time, after Baal has fathered sons

---

and the history of Absalom's revolt in 2 Samuel 13–20 actually show, however, is that the Saulide faction was persistent in Palestine long after Saul's death and that David was never able to override the endemic factionalism of Palestinian politics. It was leaders of popular forces, like Joab, Abiathar, Absalom, and Sheba, who were made to take the blame in David's court propaganda for acts of David that were potentially unpopular.

19. For translations, see James B. Pritchard, *Ancient Near Eastern Texts Relating to the Old Testament*, 2d ed. (Princeton: Princeton University Press, 1955), 129–42; and Michael D. Coogan, *Stories from Ancient Canaan* (Philadelphia: Westminster Press, 1978), 75–115.

and daughters, the agents of a second adversary, Death, sneak in, apparently through this same cloudy window. They demand that Baal submit to Death. Baal descends to the Underworld and is swallowed by Death. His sister and wife Anat goes down to his rescue, and after splitting, winnowing, burning, grinding, and sowing Death—as though he were, paradoxically, mere seed—Baal revives and nature is restored.

Like the *Enuma elish*, this Ugaritic myth is a narrative explaining how events in the unseen yet powerfully influential sky and underworld led to the establishment of the visible royal cults at the center of their respective political economies. J, as a narrative explaining the establishment of a visible royal cult, is remarkably different from the myth of Baal. Yet there are also similarities. It is probable, though failing more examples unprovable, that J belongs to the same underlying genre as the myth of Baal. J transforms the cosmic struggles of Baal with Sea and Death and reverses their meaning in reference to royalty, albeit foreign royalty. In J, Death is introduced rather than dispelled by the forebear of kings, when Cain the first builder of the city murders his brother. And Sea, while divided as in the narrative of Baal, becomes the means of killing the king of Egypt: the king succumbs to Sea rather than Sea to the king. Since J legitimates a non-temple cult, it also makes something quite different of the adversaries of the cult-founding god. In J, the divine protagonist Yahweh looks more like El than Baal.[20]

We may surmise, then, from known parallels that the royal temple cult of Solomon would have had a narrative document to accompany it. Either J is that document or it was completely lost.

It is unlikely that Solomon could have disposed of the cult world history of the founder of his dynasty. Moreover, although as a Baal-like king he would not have had a document exactly like J composed from scratch, once in existence it was not necessarily a bother to him. Not only could he live with it, he could also use it. Solomon was eager to present his reign as a reign of peace and justice to the heads of what is known to have been a widely dissatisfied populace. The ideological means by which he supported his establishment included the kind of presentation seen in parts of the description of his reign in 1 Kings 3—10, as well as the ideology of the dynastic temple itself. The purpose of this ideology was in part to try to keep the conflicts inherent in Solomonic social relations off the national agenda.[21] As one critic puts it, "Ideology is the negation of the inverted

20. See Frank Moore Cross, *Canaanite Myth and Hebrew Epic* (Cambridge: Harvard University Press, 1973), 1–194.

21. See Keith W. Whitelam, "The Symbols of Power: Aspects of Royal Propaganda in the United Monarchy," *Biblical Archaeologist* 49 (1986): 166–73.

character of social relations in reality."[22] But the critic goes on: "To be effective, though, it has to negate that negation." Ideology should include a denial of itself. This denial was provided for the Solomonic court in part by J. The cult world history adopted from David's court by the Solomonic court, J, denied the basic character of Solomon's cult, at the same time, paradoxically, that Solomon's priesthood and their descendants for over three hundred years could insist that the cult referred to in J was theirs. The criterion to which Solomon resorted as underlying this paradox was nationalism, the overriding social value in J. Outside of Judah this ploy was short-lived: at the death of Solomon most of Israel rejected Solomon's cult and successfully revolted against the house of David, taking Solomon to be J's pharaoh come back. This interpretation is the basis of E's adaptation of J. When the house of David made a renewed political appeal to Israelites in the seventh century B.C.E., after the fall of Israel, in the time of Hezekiah and Josiah, it was necessary to reestablish the legitimacy of the temple in Jerusalem as a national institution on a new basis. This necessity led eventually to the writing of the other great foundation history in the Bible that fictionalizes the premonarchic period, the Deuteronomistic History (D).

22. Jorge Larrain, *The Concept of Ideology* (London: Hutchinson, 1979), 211.

7

A Question of Prerogatives

(Genesis 2:4a—3:24)

At the time Yahweh, a god, made earth and sky—before there was any fruit-bearing tree in the field, or even grain-producing grass in the field had come up, since Yahweh, a god, had not yet made it rain on the earth, and there was no human to do the necessary cultivating of the ground, though a stream was coming up from the earth and moistening the whole surface of the ground—at that time Yahweh, a god, formed the human out of dirt from the ground, blew into its nostrils life-breath, and the human turned into a living being.

Then Yahweh, a god, planted a garden to the east and set there the human he had formed. Out of the ground Yahweh, a god, made to grow every tree enjoyable for seeing and good for eating, and the tree of life deep within the garden, and the tree of knowing good and evil. A river flows from Eden to water the garden. There it divides and becomes four branches. The name of the first is the Pishon. It is the one that winds through the whole land of Havilah, where there is gold. The gold of that land is good. It also has bdellium and lapis lazuli. The name of the second river is the Gihon. It is the one that winds through the whole land of Kush. The name of the third river is the Tigris. It is the one that flows east of Asshur. As for the fourth river, that is the Euphrates. The garden was well watered.

When Yahweh, a god, had taken the human and placed it in the garden of Eden to cultivate and guard it, Yahweh, a god, gave the human this order: "You may eat from any tree in the garden, but you may not eat from the tree of knowing good and evil. If you ever eat from it, you will die."

Then Yahweh, a god, thought, "It is not good for the human to be by itself. I will make for it a help corresponding to it." So Yahweh, a god, formed from the ground all the animals of the fields and all the birds of the sky and brought each in turn to the human to see what it would call it. Whatever the human called each living being, that was its name. So the human named all the domestic beasts and birds of the sky and all the animals of the fields. But the human failed to discover a help corresponding to it.

So Yahweh, a god, cast a deep sleep upon the human, and while it was asleep he took out one of its chops and closed up the place with flesh. Then Yahweh, a god, built the chop he had taken from the human into a woman. When he brought it to the human, the human said, "This, finally, is bone of my bone and flesh of my flesh.

42

Let this be called woman, since this was taken from a man." (Thus a man now leaves his father and mother and, he cleaving to his woman, they become a kinship unit.)

Though the two of them—the human and his woman—were naked, they were not embarrassed. However, the snake, more naked and clever than all the animals of the fields Yahweh, a god, had made, said to the woman, "It's true that God said you may not eat from any of the trees of the garden...."

The woman interrupted and said to the snake, "Of course we may eat fruit from the trees of the garden. It's just fruit from the trees deep within the garden that God said, 'You may not eat of it, and don't even touch it, lest you die.'"

The snake said to the woman, "You won't in fact die. It's just that God knows that the moment you two eat of it, your eyes will open and you will have become like gods by knowing good and evil."

The woman could see that the tree was good for eating, desirable to the eyes, and enjoyable for attention, so she plucked one of its fruit and started to eat, and gave some also to her man next to her, and he ate, too. Immediately the eyes of both of them opened and they knew, for the first time, they were naked. So they knit together fig leaves and made for themselves genital coverings.

Later, hearing the sound of Yahweh, a god, strolling in the garden in the cool of the late afternoon, the human and his woman hid from Yahweh, a god, among the trees of the garden. Yahweh, a god, summoned the human: "Where are you?"

He said, "When I heard you in the garden, I was afraid, since I was naked, so I hid."

"Who disclosed to you that you were naked? Have you gone and eaten from the tree I ordered you not to eat from?"

"The woman you put with me," the human said, "when she gave me fruit from the tree, I ate it."

Yahweh, a god, said to the woman, "What is this you have done?"

The woman said, "The snake beguiled me, so I ate."

Yahweh, a god, said to the snake, "Because you have done this,

> More cursed are you than all the beasts,
>> Than all the animals of the fields;
> Upon your belly you shall go,
>> And dirt you shall eat your whole life long.
> I shall place enmity between you and the woman,
>> And between your offspring and hers;
> They will [...] you on the head,
>> And you will [...] them on the heel."

To the woman he said,

> "I shall make great your pain in pregnancy,
>> And in pain you shall give birth to children.
> Yet toward your man will your urge continue,
>> And he shall be your master."

And to the human he said, "Because you listened to your woman and ate from the tree I ordered you not to eat from,

> Cursed is the ground on your account,
>> In pain you will eat from it your whole life long.
> Thorns and thistles will come up for you,
>> And you will eat of the grass of the field,
>> And in the sweat of your brow you will eat bread.
> Until you return to the ground,
>> Since you were taken from it,
> For dirt you are,
>> And to dirt you shall return."

The human named his wife Hawwah (Eve), since she became the mother of all the living. Yahweh, a god, made for the human and his wife garments out of skins and clothed them with these. Then Yahweh, a god, said, "The human has become like one of us [gods], able to know good and evil. So, lest he put his hand out and grab also from the tree of life and eat and live forever . . ."—Yahweh, a god, put him out of the garden of Eden to work the ground from which he was taken. When he had ejected the human, he stationed to the east of the garden of Eden the hybrid beasts and the waving sword of flame to guard the way to the tree of life.

J's history begins with a story of the creation of human beings. Similar stories in analogous texts from the Middle East are basically about the understanding of labor in the state, especially the relation between the ruler and the laborer. J's story is not primarily fact or fiction but a narrative way of showing the court's understanding of the labor of the inhabitants of the kingdom. This concern is central to J's history, which climaxes with Israel being defined as those who are released from slavery in Egypt and the God of the kingdom being defined as the one who releases them.

The slavery from which Israel were delivered was not what we perhaps most commonly think of as slavery.[1] The Hebrew word *mas* denotes corvée (in the Americas, *repartimiento* or *catequil*), which was a taxation in work, whereby a percentage of a town's or village's population was conscripted into hard labor on behalf of the ruler, usually in "public" building projects or on rulers' estates, without pay.[2] In the feudal context it was the feudal lord who often assessed a tax in labor. In the ancient Near East the sovereign power as well often made the assessment. In Egypt in the New Kingdom period, it was possible for Palestinians to be drafted from as far away as Palestine.[3] Corvée meant sovereignty over labor.

1. For an outstanding delineation of forms of labor exploitation and how they relate to historical social relations of interest to Americans, see Marvin Harris, *Patterns of Race in the Americas* (New York: W. W. Norton, 1974).

2. I. Mendelsohn, "On Corvée Labor in Ancient Canaan and Israel," *Bulletin of the American Schools of Oriental Research* 167 (1962): 31–35.

3. Donald B. Redford, "Studies in Relations Between Palestine and Egypt During the First Millennium B.C.: 1. The Taxation System of Solomon," in *Studies on the Ancient Palestinian World*, ed. J. W. Wevers and D. B. Redford (Toronto: University of Toronto Press, 1972), 149–50.

Corvée is absolutely central to J's history. What is commonly referred to as the "exodus" is the focal point of the history, not simply one more dramatic incident along the way. This deliverance of corvée laborers makes the point that Yahweh does not tolerate Egyptian corvée. The killing of the king of Egypt and the firstborn, which is an annulment of the power of the great power Egypt over its smaller neighbor's workers, takes place on the occasion of this deliverance from corvée. J introduces this corvée, from which the people will be delivered at the climax of the history, right at the outset of the history. This is the point of beginning with the creation of the ·human workers.

Two Akkadian texts are of particular value in interpreting J's history of the workers in the garden.[4] The *Enuma elish*, the Babylonian story of how Marduk created the world, and the *Atra-hasis*, the Babylonian flood story, have both been known for some time, although the *Atra-hasis* was not well understood until the 1960s because before then the text was available only in fragmentary form. The part of the three-tablet *Atra-hasis* that was previously most familiar is the story of the flood from the beginning of the third tablet, which had been adopted into the Gilgamesh epic and is therefore virtually identical to the eleventh tablet of Gilgamesh, known and compared with the biblical flood story since about 1875.

The *Atra-hasis* dates back at least to the time of Hammurabi in the Old Babylonian period, which is the Middle Bronze Age, around the eighteenth to the seventeenth century B.C.E. Our knowledge of the *Enuma elish* comes from tablets from Assurbanipal's library, which is Neo-Assyrian, late seventh century B.C.E. There are earlier fragments of the epic from the Late Bronze Age and Early Iron period, which was late second millennium B.C.E, so that we know the *Enuma elish* is extremely old. Linguistic analysis shows that the *Enuma elish* and the *Atra-hasis* were originally written at about the same time. Fragments of Gilgamesh were found in Late Bronze Palestine, in Megiddo.

Even if the writer of J was not trained in cuneiform (although it is possible that he was), he lived and wrote in a context where only shortly before the court of David emerged, the royal court of Late Bronze and Early Iron Jerusalem was manned by scribes who had done their training in Akkadian cuneiform by copying texts like these. When David took over the court in Jerusalem, his scribes inherited these traditions of the creation which predated J's own history perhaps by as much as eight hundred years.[5]

4. Comparisons between the beginning of Genesis and Mesopotamian lore go back at least as far as the Jewish historian Josephus in the first century C.E. They were of course greatly improved by the discovery of cuneiform documents beginning in the mid-nineteenth century.

5. A recent discussion of traditional motifs in Genesis 2—3 and of their literary and social

The *Enuma elish* is the story of the adventures of Marduk, who was the god of Old Babylon. When the world was created it had a center. For the Babylonians this center was the earthly palace of Marduk, which was equivalent to the temple of Babylon and parallel to the palace of the king of Babylon. In the ancient world, the god was the king projected into the sky. As in the Ugaritic myth of Baal, the state was legitimated by the temple, which was the palace of the king in its transcendent dimensions. This image of the king writ large then fed back into the common conception of what kingship implied. The story of the creation of human beings that emanated from Marduk's earthly palace reflected the origin and character of human beings from the perspective of the king's palace. The story is not the story of the creation of the world; it is the story of the creation of the Babylonian state, told as if the state were the world. It is not a universally applicable document but relates the creation of that world in which the perspective from which it is told, the palace perspective, was dominant.

The story is the story of the defeat of chaotic forces, which are represented by the personified sea. It is in two parts. The first concerns the defeat of Apsu, who represents the freshwater deep—chaos in terms of the waters directly beneath the earth. The second concerns the defeat of Tiamat, who is the personification of the salt waters of the cosmos and of severe ecological disorder. When Marduk defeats Apsu and then Tiamat, he creates Babylonian law and order.

Apsu and Tiamat are the divine parents of many of the gods, who personify the elements of the world (except for those elements created later by Marduk).[6] The parents are disrupted by the gods they have created, who make a lot of noise. The disruption is a characterization of the kind of disorder that typically threatens the state. Apsu and Tiamat determine to destroy these gods, so the gods gather together and appoint one of their number, Ea, to do battle with Apsu. Ea is in many ways comparable to El in the Syrian and Palestinian pantheon. Ea defeats Apsu and upon his corpse constructs his abode, where, with his wife Damkina, he fathers Marduk. So

background is provided by Howard N. Wallace, *The Eden Narrative* (Atlanta: Scholars Press, 1985). For the availability of cuneiform literature in Palestine, see W. L. Moran, "The Syrian Scribe of the Jerusalem Amarna Letters," in *Unity and Diversity*, ed. H. Goedicke and J. J. M. Roberts (Baltimore: Johns Hopkins University Press, 1975), 146–66, esp. 155–56; and Yohanan Aharoni, *The Archaeology of the Land of Israel* (Philadelphia: Westminster Press, 1982), 142, 145. Note the cautions expressed by Wilfred G. Lambert, "A New Look at the Babylonian Background of Genesis," *Journal of Theological Studies* 16 (1965): 287–300; and Thomas C. Hartman, "Some Thoughts on the Sumerian King List and Genesis 5 and 11B," *Journal of Biblical Literature* 91 (1972): 25–32.

6. Translations given here are mainly from James B. Pritchard, *Ancient Near Eastern Texts Relating to the Old Testament*, 2d ed. (Princeton: Princeton University Press, 1955), 60–72; and Alexander Heidel, *The Babylonian Genesis*, 2d ed. (Chicago: University of Chicago Press, 1951).

Marduk is born as a result of the defeat of the impending disorder and death.

Tiamat is incensed at the killing of Apsu and threatens the gods further. They turn to the son of Ea, Marduk, who does battle with Tiamat. Having defeated Tiamat, Marduk creates the world out of Tiamat's corpse.

After creating the world, Marduk hears that the gods are complaining about all the work they have to do. His heart prompts him to an ingenious plan, which he conveys to Ea: "Blood will I form and cause bone to be, then I will set up *lullu:* human shall be its name. Upon the human shall the services of the gods be imposed that they may be at rest." Humans are to be created to do the work formerly required of the worker gods in order "that the gods may rest." A new set of sweating workers is to replace the first sweaters so that the sub-gods can take it easy. Henceforth "humans" shall work so "gods" can rest.

Ea suggests to Marduk that the humans be created out of the god who fomented the strife: "Let a brother of theirs be delivered up. Let him be destroyed and humans be fashioned. Let the great gods assemble hither. Let the guilty one be delivered up and let them be established." Marduk assembles the gods, ordering them kindly and giving them instructions. The gods pay attention to the words as the king addresses the worker gods. "Verily the former thing which we declared unto you has come true about Tiamat. I speak the truth under oath by myself. Who was it that created the strife and caused Tiamat to revolt and prepare for battle? Let him who created the strife be delivered up. I will make him bear his punishment; you all be at rest." The worker gods decide to turn over the ringleader of the rebellion. "They bound him and held him before Ea. Punishment they afflicted upon him by cutting his blood. With his blood they created human beings. Ea imposed the work of the gods upon them and set the gods free." So the ringleader of the movement was executed and a new set of workers created out of him. Humans are made out of the blood of the ringleader of the workers' rebellion. That is why humans must work.

The gods say to Marduk, "Now, O lord, who established our freedom from compulsory labor, what shall be the sign of our gratitude before you? Come let us make something whose name shall be called sanctuary. It shall be a dwelling for our rest at night. Come, let us repose therein." So the whole of Babylon is portrayed as essentially a temple complex for the gods, the resting place of the ones who have been put at rest because they no longer have to do the work that the human workers now do for them.

The king of Babylon and the ruling elite of the royal court conceived of themselves as akin to gods. In the world of work, rulers were gods. While it was the lot of the peasants to till the arable in sweaty toil, and to give up much of their produce in taxes, fees, and fines, the work of the elite was the nonsweaty service of the gods of the state. In other words, the ruling elite enjoyed their comfort. Their work was symbolic (and sometimes military) work. Archaeologists have discovered representations of the king doing the service of the gods. Mesopotamian kings had themselves modeled in clay bearing the *shupshikku* basket (the corvée worker's basket of dirt).[7] These kings did not actually work, but just symbolized work, much the way elected officials do when they turn over a shovelful of dirt at groundbreaking ceremonies.

The *Atra-hasis,* the other great creation myth from Mesopotamia, begins with the words, "Once upon a time, when the gods as men bore the work, when they carried the *shupshikku* [the basket of dirt]."[8] The *Atra-hasis* is therefore also about how human beings came to do the work that once upon a time the gods did. It continues, "The toil of the gods was great. The work was heavy. The distress was much." This is a description of corvée labor. The seven great Anunakki gods are making the Igigi, the lesser gods, suffer under this heavy toil. Their father Anu is king, while their counselor is the lord Enlil (analogous to Marduk). Their chamberlain is Ninurta, and their sheriff (the one in charge of the corvée) is Enugi.

In due course the Igigi gods convene a workers' meeting and come in force to state their grievances to Enlil.[9] Enlil puts them off long enough for Ea (also called Enki) to come up with an idea of how to deal with this revolt. "Ea opened his mouth and addressed the gods. What are we accusing them of? Their work was heavy, the distress much. Every day . . . the lamentation was heavy. . . . While Belet-ili, the birth goddess, is present, let her create *lullu* [humans]. Let the human bear the yoke of work. Let the birth goddess create *lullu.* Let the human bear the toil of the gods." They summon and suggest to the goddess, midwife of the gods, "Wise Mami, you are the birth goddess, creatress of humankind. Create *lullu* that they may bear the yoke. Let them bear the yoke assigned by Enlil, the lord of the earth, and let humans carry the toil of the gods." Nintu replies, "It's not possible for me to make things. Skill lies with Enki since he can cleanse

7. See, e.g., the representation of Ur-Nanshe, king of Lagash, carrying a dirt-filled basket for building a temple, now in the Louvre (Samuel Noah Kramer, *The Sumerians* [Chicago: University of Chicago Press, 1963] photos following p. 64), and of Assurbanipal carrying a basket for rebuilding the temple Esangila in Babylon, now in the British Museum (James B. Pritchard, *The Ancient Near East in Pictures Relating to the Old Testament* [Princeton: Princeton University Press, 1954], no. 450).

8. The translations and much of the interpretation given here are based on Wilfred G. Lambert and A. R. Millard, *Atra-Hasīs: The Babylonian Story of the Flood* (Oxford: Clarendon Press, 1969); and W. L. Moran, "The Creation of Man in Atrahasis I 192–248," *Bulletin of the American Schools of Oriental Research* 200 (1970): 48–56.

9. Robert A. Oden, Jr., "Divine Aspirations in Atrahasis and in Genesis 1—11," *Zeitschrift für die alttestamentliche Wissenschaft* 93 (1981): 197–216.

everything. Let him give me the clay that I may make it. By me alone he cannot be fashioned. For Enki alone there's a task at hand. He alone can purify everything. The clay he must give me that I myself may fashion."

Enki decides that the ringleader of the rebellion should be slaughtered. "Let Nintu mix the clay with his flesh and his blood. Let the god himself, the leader of the rebellion, and humans be mixed together in the clay. For all days to come let's hear the drum. In the flesh of the god the ghost shall remain. Let her inform him while alive of his token, and, so that there shall be no forgetting, the ghost shall remain." The ghost of the god is represented in the sound of the drum; as long as humans are alive, the drum—the heart—beats as a token of the one from whom we are made. So we are made from a god, but that god was the ringleader of the suppressed rebellious worker gods. This is the meaning of our heartbeat, which beats harder the harder we work, so that the more it hurts the less we'll be tempted to rebel. This is the point of the Mesopotamian texts explaining the creation of humans.[10]

A third text from the ancient Near East that bears directly on the oppression of Israel's descendants described by J in Exod. 1:8–12 is the Egyptian text entitled "Are Humans Created Equal in Opportunity?"[11] In this text the purpose of creation is to still evil. "I did four good deeds," the god says. "I made the four winds that every one might breathe thereof like their fellow in their time. I made the great inundation that the poor person might have rights therein like the great person." (We shall see that the "flood" in J leads to rain agriculture, which is a freer form of agriculture than the irrigation agriculture prior to the flood.) "I made every one like their fellow. I did not command that they do evil, but it was their hearts which violated what I said. I made their hearts to cease from forgetting the rest in order that divine offerings might be given to the gods of the gnomes." The god created a fear of death in human beings so that they would sacrifice to the gods. "I brought into being the four gods from my sweat, while humans are the tears of my eye." We don't know what the four gods are, but we know that four is a pun on sweat and that humans is a pun on tears. This is from the Middle Kingdom, roughly contemporaneous with the Old Babylonian Mesopotamian texts, and once again we see that humans are conceived of as created to sweat for the gods.

Another Sumerian tradition from the same period has been published under the title "In Praise of the Ax." But the ax is not an ax, it is a hoe, a tool for digging, as in a work gang. The text says, "When Enlil [the lord]

---

10. It is hardly accurate, therefore, to label such texts simply "creation texts" without reference to what system exactly is being created; the same holds for biblical texts such as Genesis 1—3.

11. Pritchard, *Ancient Near Eastern Texts*, 7–8.

had made the fitting shine out ... he hastened to make heaven and earth separate, so that the seed should spring from the land, so that Uzumua[12] should cause first humans to spring forth. He put the furrow in the ground at Nippur [a Sumerian city]. He set the hoe there and day broke. He set working assignments, stretched out his hand to the *shupshikku* and praised the hoe and brought it into Uzumua. He put the first of humanity into the furrow. Enlil looked with favor on the Sumerians, made the Sumerian people grasp the hoe."[13] In other words, Enlil created the earth, put the sky in place, the ground, the seed, and now he needed a worker. So he created the hoe, and workers to till with it. Thus the world was in order. This is a description of state-run, highly organized labor in which the peasants do sweaty toil so that the elite may enjoy their comforts.

When J relates his story of the creation of human beings, he does so at the beginning of a history in which the very character of the god of the Davidic state is that of deliverer of the Israelites from precisely that work for which in Mesopotamian tradition human beings were created. In the tradition to which J is responding, corvée is not merely a curse inflicted late in human history but rather integral to the created order itself: peasants and bedouin slaves are lesser beings expressly created to carry the corvée basket. J contradicts, therefore, the usual state-temple view. He rebuts the Mesopotamian—and no doubt typical Palestinian—tradition's under-standing of humans. In J's history, sweaty labor is not inherent in the created order. The human in the garden is a sweatless figure, a "royal" figure. When sweaty toil is introduced later, in the curse, it is not corvée but good, honest agricultural work at one's own plot. From the perspective of the Davidic court, humans are not created for corvée, though it might have to be tolerated for the sake of avoiding Egyptian corvée. Indications are that well before the end of his reign David instituted corvée in Israel and appointed a certain Adoram chief over the corvée gangs (2 Sam. 20:24; RSV: "forced labor" is corvée).

It is significant that, unlike the Mesopotamian myths of creation and P's creation story in Genesis 1, J's history does not begin with the characteristic subduing of the waters. Rather, J has relocated the waters at the focal point of the story, which is commonly known as the exodus, reinterpreting the mythic defeat of the waters in terms of the conquering of pharaoh.

J's history opens with the planting of a garden. The Garden of Eden is not just any garden, but the private, enclosed formal garden, whose entrance

---

12. Sumerian *uzu-mu-a* means roughly the place "that lets flesh 'grow.'"

13. G. Pettinato, *Das altorientalische Menschenbild und die sumerischen und akkadischen Schöp-fungsmythen* (Heidelberg: Carl Winter, 1971), 31, 82–85; see also Thorkild Jacobsen, *Toward the Image of Tammuz and Other Essays on Mesopotamian History and Culture*, ed. W. L. Moran (Cambridge: Harvard University Press, 1970), 111–14.

was small enough to be blocked by a flashing sword, belonging to an urban elite ruler. Its main element is the orchard. It is irrigated by rivers and intensively farmed with perennials, whose harvest, to judge from Mesopotamian and Greek parallels, is nonseasonal.[14] Without rain, there are no seasons. Evidence for such gardens goes back at least as far as the twenty-first century B.C.E. At that time Urnammu the ruler of Ur in Mesopotamia composed the following: "For An, king of the gods, his master, Urnammu, King of Ur, a sublime orchard-garden erected here; a throne dais, a place of purity, he built here for him." The valley east of the city wall of monarchic Jerusalem also contained a royal garden; it may have gone back to the time of David.[15]

In J's time, areas that produced food in this form were typically held in freehold tenure. Freehold was passed from person to person through inheritance by kin, the son inheriting from the father in a sexual-based inheritance. This is why the two thematic tracks of production and reproduction are so intertwined throughout J's history. In J's conception, the discovery of sexuality in the garden will be the basis for the passing on of this kind of land in town and village, whereas the arable outside the garden was commonly held in collective tenure under the state system and was shared and taxed on a collective basis. Collective tenure has a direct relation to the village as a socioeconomic unit and the place of the village in the state as a taxable unit. It is quite different from the inheritance of the garden, which did not have this relation to the state. Normally the state merely maintained a limit on the heritability of freehold property in order to enhance the transferability and hence efficiency of arable.

The history begins when Yahweh, a god, created the earth and the sky. The RSV uses the expression "the Lord God," which is misleading because it is printed almost exactly as the translation of the common Hebrew expression *adonai Yahweh* ("the Lord Yahweh") is printed. J uses the uncommon expression "Yahweh, a god" only during the first seven generations, to mark them as a unit of time. In J, as in E and P, the various labels for the divinity serve to structure time.[16] It is important to retain J's "Yahweh, a god," because it focuses attention on the distinction between the categories of divine and human, raising the issue of what are the prerogatives of gods and the prerogatives of humans. The first prerogative

14. The nonfruit trees in the garden were evergreen, according to Ezek. 31:8–9.

15. See A. Leo Oppenheim, "On Royal Gardens in Mesopotamia," *Journal of Near Eastern Studies* 24 (1965): 328–33; and Emily Vermeule, *Aspects of Death in Early Greek Art and Poetry* (Berkeley and Los Angeles: University of California Press, 1979), 191–92.

16. It is erroneous to say that the different strands use different names for God. All four strands use both Yahweh and *elohim,* God. J, E, and P all use both these designations in such a way as to structure time. The strands differ in the structuring of time, not in their use of the designations for divinity.

portrayed by the story is that of creating human beings, which, since a god performs it, is a divine prerogative. The issue is raised in anticipation of the creation of Cain by the first humans, who thereby arrogate what had hitherto been a divine prerogative.

As the curtain rises and we are shown the set, we view a rainless scene. Without rain, it is necessary to utilize irrigation for agriculture. Although irrigation also occurred in Palestine, the models for this description of the set come from Mesopotamian irrigation agriculture, and the humans created in these models were created to work this agriculture. Such a highly developed system required a form of political and economic organization in which labor was directed by the central state.

This rainless scene is set before there was any "shrub of the field or *esev* of the field." Shrub and *esev* ("grass" or "grain") denote two distinctive kinds of plants raised in two types of agriculture. (Again, the RSV is misleading.) The picture is of fruit-bearing trees in orchards on the one hand and extensive grain agriculture on the other—the perennial and the annual. The setting thus reflects the major issues to be dealt with in the story. Both the perennial and the annual are introduced here because the history is to proceed from within the garden to outside the garden—from orchard to arable, perennial to annual. To begin with, however, the ground was arid. At first there was no agriculture of either type.

In this period when there were no human beings to work the ground, an *ed*—a word whose meaning is uncertain—emerged continuously from beneath the ground, out of the underworld, to water the face of the ground.[17] The RSV's "mist" is a possibility. Perhaps "flow" or "cosmic stream"[18] would be a better guess. This stream must have originated in whatever source gave rise to the rivers that irrigated the garden.

The god Yahweh formed the first human being from dirt (not "dust"), shaping moist dirt as a potter might shape clay. There is a wordplay between Adam and *adama* ("ground") which anticipates human labor in tillage of the arable. Yahweh intended this creature to be his worker, the one who would perform anticipated mild tasks of tending. This human became a living creature when the god breathed breath into its nostrils. (At this point it had no awareness of gender, so we shall refer to it with the

17. What is clear is that it initiates a compound wordplay, important for the first two generations and beyond, consisting of *ed*, whose meaning is uncertain, *adama*, meaning "ground," *adam*, meaning "human," and *dam*, meaning "blood, murder."

18. M. Saebo, "Die hebräischen Nomina *'ed* und *'ed*—Zwei sumerisch-akkadische Fremdwörter?" *Studia Theologica* 24 (1970): 130–41; P. Kyle McCarter, "The River Ordeal in Israelite Literature," *Harvard Theological Review* 66 (1973): 403–12.

neuter pronoun.) A human being, in J's view, is dirt that breathes—every human being, including landowner, priest, and king.[19]

The next thing Yahweh did was to plant a formal, perennial pleasure orchard to the east, an allusion to the Mesopotamian valley in some mythic dawn of history. J probably assumed that human beings originated in this region, because he was telling his story in terms of the Mesopotamian creation tradition. Egyptian creation texts come from the Middle Kingdom period, but not from the New Kingdom. When the New Kingdom ruled Palestine, the language used between Egypt and Palestine was Akkadian. So even though the Davidic court bureaucracy may have had an Egyptian element, its scribal tradition was Akkadian and its training was therefore in terms of Mesopotamian texts of creation. Note that Cain wandered in the east and that Abram also came from the east, specifically from Ur in Mesopotamia. J was derivative at the beginning of his history, drawing heavily upon Mesopotamian sources.

Land, water, and labor—the elements of food production—having been provided, the human was placed in the garden to work it. Now, there are different kinds of work, and the story goes on to make it clear that this was not hard labor. The RSV misses the point in Gen. 2:15 when it renders the Hebrew *avad,* meaning "work," as "till." This is an entirely different concept from "till" in Gen. 2:5, which refers to the hard, sweaty labor required to till arable. In Mesopotamian tradition the gardener of the god is the king, and the king doesn't do hard manual labor. The human whom Yahweh placed in his garden did not sweat in his work until the curse was instituted.

The rivers that irrigated the orchard[20] were characterized by their sources and the lands into which they flowed, which were lands of extraordinary wealth—a confirmation that the gardener was a royal personage who was familiar with gold and precious stones (Ezek. 28:13), not a peasant who would have no experience of such treasures.

"Eden" is sometimes thought by interpreters to refer to the steppe, because Sumerian *edin* and Akkadian *edinu* mean steppe land. Although it is possible that this is the case, the ancient historian makes nothing of this association but does make a great deal of the meaning of the apparent Hebrew root of the name Eden. This root, and hence the garden's name,

19. Delbert R. Hillers, "Dust: Some Aspects of Old Testament Imagery," in *Love and Death in the Ancient Near East,* ed. J. H. Marks and R. M. Good (Guilford, Conn.: Four Quarters, 1987), 105–9. On the first human being as a royal figure, consult the recent discussion and bibliography of Nicolas Wyatt, "Interpreting the Creation and Fall Story in Genesis 2—3," *Zeitschrift für die alttestamentliche Wissenschaft* 93 (1981): 14–21; "When Adam Delved: The Meaning of Genesis III 23," *Vetus Testamentum* 38 (1988): 117–22.

20. Making it a "watered garden," as in Isa. 58:11 and Jer. 31:12.

refers to luxuriance and connotes pleasure and voluptuousness,[21] specifically of a sexual nature.[22] This will be important as the story unfolds, for it is in this garden that the heterosexuality that is the basis of sexual pleasure and reproduction will be discovered.

The human is placed in the garden not only to work it but to "keep" it. This word has frequently been interpreted in the light of the Protestant work ethic, in the sense of upkeep; but the Hebrew *shamar* means to watch, to guard. The word implies that inside the garden is civilized, while disorder threatens outside the garden. This garden is like a meticulously pruned baroque French garden. It is an oasis of order, epitomizing and projecting royal order which exists in a world of threat. In the parallel literature the nature of this threat is clear: humans must be taught to maintain their orderly work routines and not join those rebels outside the state-controlled "garden" who threaten the system. The scribal historian is perhaps suggesting that under the Davidic state the people do not suffer the evil constraints of typical royal order. If the Egyptians ruled them, they would; but David rules them and has released them from those oppressive constraints. The creation of David's realm is therefore akin to, though not identical with, the original creation: all people were created to work in relative ease in David's royal "garden," his territory. In J's world view, human beings, including workers, were meant to enjoy harmony, ease, peace, and prosperity. The human was a "king."[23]

Next Yahweh gave a command to the human creature, granting it permission to eat of all the trees of the garden except the tree of knowing good and evil. When the human ate of this tree of knowing, it would die. The implication is that if it never ate of this tree, it would never know anything. It would live, presumably, with a vague awareness only of a perpetual present.

Knowing refers to the development of human history, which implies a consciousness of the consequences of one's actions and therefore awareness of past, present, and future. The awareness that past, present, and future are different from each other produces a sense of consequence from the past and the capacity to imagine the possibilities of the future. So far as we know, humans are unique among living creatures in having this awareness. If the fruit had not been eaten, then the life of the human might be

21. Compare the Latin Vulgate translation *paradisus voluptatis*.

22. A recently discovered Assyrian and Aramaic bilingual inscription equates the Assyrian expression "who *enriches* the regions" with Aramaic *ʿdn*. Since the enriching is in abundance of food, it is likely that this root is related to the Hebrew root from which Eden gets its name. See A. R. Millard and P. Bordreuil, "A Statue from Syria with Assyrian and Aramaic Inscriptions," *Biblical Archaeologist* 45 (1982): 135–41.

23. See Manfred Hutter, "Adam als Gärtner und König (Gen. 2, 8.15)," *Biblische Zeitschrift* 30 (1986): 258–62.

characterized as good in some limited sense, but not human as we normally understand it. There would have been no human history, which is a combination of, and a struggle between, the good and the bad.[24]

There is a wordplay on the word "know." Not only does it refer to awareness of past, present, and future, it is also a word that will be used throughout the J narrative to connote sexual intercourse and all that this stands for in the wake of Cain's act of murder.[25] It is significant that human history as conceived by J, involving the awareness of consequences and possibilities, starts with Adam's "knowing" Eve, generating the first offspring and thereby giving rise to the history of the world. A third meaning of knowing is political. In this sense it refers to the history of good and bad, in which David's rule exists to enhance the good over the bad. If life is a mixture of good and bad, then the political claim of J is that the rule of David is meant to discriminate between the good and the bad, promoting the good and keeping out the bad.[26]

So a further differentiation between the categories of the divine and the human has been introduced. Humans were not intended to create other humans or to have the capacity for knowing. Not only do gods have the ability to create humans, they are also able to know (the source of the ability to create). The god knows, and the god can tell the difference between good and bad. What J is bringing out is that our consciousness of history is a divine consciousness. Because it is divine, it brings with it a powerful tendency to presumption.

The human that Yahweh had made was, like Yahweh himself, a male, though the creature was unaware of its maleness. There is evidence that the name Yahweh is based on an epithet of the Palestinian god El, and that Yahweh is simply a version of El. In Syrian and Palestinian mythology, El was a prodigiously virile old man who had vigorous intercourse with several goddesses. None of these goddesses plays any explicit role in J, and they played only a minor role if any at all in the cults of Israelite Palestine.[27] Their absence, however, does not prevent J from alluding to them. It was the prerogative of Yahweh, a god, to create a human. But the human was to

24. Compare the concise statement of the double bind the humans would be in by Norman K. Gottwald, *The Hebrew Bible: A Socio-Literary Introduction* (Philadelphia: Fortress Press, 1985), 331–32.

25. The term "know" is not the usual way to refer to sexual intercourse in Hebrew. J himself also uses "to lie with," and contemporaneous documents from David's court employ the usual "go into." J uses "know" in order to combine several related meanings in one term.

26. The father both of David's royal priest Zadok and of the chief of his Cretan and Philistine mercenary palace guard was named Jehoiada, meaning "Yahweh knows."

27. See Jeffrey H. Tigay, *You Shall Have No Other Gods: Israelite Religion in the Light of Hebrew Inscriptions* (Atlanta: Scholars Press, 1987).

be alone, without a corresponding female, lest it arrogate to itself the divine prerogative of reproduction.

As Yahweh assessed the human's situation, he decided that it was not, after all, good for the human to be alone. The solution was to make for it a "help corresponding to it." The Hebrew word rendered "help" means "helpfulness," not "helper." In J's conception, Yahweh initially had no intention of creating a second human with a different gender, and J therefore represents this creature as another "it," a "helpfulness" or "assistance" equivalent to the first creature; hence he uses an abstract term rather than a personal term. The expression "corresponding to it" means simply as like it as possible, without necessarily being another "human."[28]

Yahweh proceeded to attempt to create a creature that would be sufficiently similar to the first to provide this helpfulness. He assumed that the best way to create such a creature was to use the same method of production. He would make this second creature out of dirt the same way he made the first. He brought his various attempts one by one to the human to see what it would name them. The degree of likeness would be represented by the names, of course, and the human was left to decide how alike Yahweh's creatures were to itself and to name them accordingly. Yahweh formed the first new creature out of dirt and brought it to the original creature, who named it, let us say, "sheep." "Sheep" and "human" do not sound at all alike, so this new creature did not correspond, and Yahweh had to try again. This time, when the new dirt creature was presented to him, the human named it, we might imagine, "giraffe." The sound of the name tells us that it, too, failed to correspond. And so forth. In this way Yahweh "accidentally" formed from dirt the entire animal kingdom, ominously populating his world of plants with an entirely different class of creature, whose members reproduce themselves almost exclusively by mating, two by two. In J's view, animals came into being as Yahweh attempted but repeatedly failed to provide a helpfulness for his masterpiece worker. When finally none of all the creatures that now make up the animal world was found to correspond to the human, the god was forced to try a different method of creating a helpfulness for the human.

Since the first human was a male like Yahweh himself, the god decided to make a second human, this time female in the likeness of a goddess. Yahweh built the second human from a part taken out of the first. Although this second human did not correspond perfectly, it was close enough for the first human to recognize its own kind. *Ish* and *ishsha*—"man" and "woman"—were close enough, and neither yet realized the consequence of the remaining slight difference. Both were entirely un-

28. Marsha M. Wilfong, "Genesis 2:18–24," *Interpretation* 42 (1988): 58–63.

aware of their sexual differentiation at this point in time, and Yahweh intended that they remain this way, that they not "know." They were to enjoy a mutual helpfulness but not to engage in the divine prerogative of creating other humans. That the introduction of heterosexuality was an afterthought of the god is also evident from the fact that Yahweh first brought the animals he created to the human to see if they would solve the problem of its being alone, and clearly there was no sexual purpose in this.

What J is addressing is how the creator god, intending good, initiated, again "accidentally," a mechanism that resulted in a historical sequence by which evil would be introduced into the world through the creatures' eating of the fruit of knowing. As it turned out, the correspondence between the two humans did have a sexual connotation, despite Yahweh's attempts to avoid this by first creating creatures that were other than human to be a helpfulness, then by denying the humans the capacity for knowing. Indeed the term "corresponding to it" suggests a face-to-face correspondence and hence alludes to the practice of copulating face to face, distinctive of humans.

The first human said of the second that it was "bone of my bone and flesh of my flesh." This is a Hebrew idiom for kinship. In anticipation of the kinship that would prevail in the human race, Yahweh took a chop—not a rib, but a chunk of flesh and bone—from Adam's side, almost in desperation in an attempt to get beyond the impasse of having created thirty-seven thousand species of animals without hitting on the right combination. Out of this chop, Yahweh built the second human: *ishsha*, for "this one was taken from *ish*."[29]

Ish and *ishsha* refer not to sexuality per se (in contrast to P's *zakar* and *neqebah*, "male" and "female") but to the social relation between the man and the woman as husband and wife. The creature *adam* has itself become something quite different, as different as the words *ish* and *adam*, with the creation of *ishsha*. When they described themselves as *ish* and *ishsha*, there was more to what they were saying than they knew at this point, because they had not yet eaten of the fruit of knowing. The social implications of male and female would be revealed only in the eating of the fruit, which would make actual the latent possibilities. Had they not eaten of the fruit, the possibility of mating and mating's entire social context would have

29. As often pointed out, there is no necessary correlation between gender and grammatical gender. Objects and ideas in the abstract are usually referred to as "feminine." That Hebrew *zot* ("this") is "feminine" does not in itself mean that the second human was aware of being female. Similarly, even though *adam* is "masculine" in gender, the first human was an "it" just like the second, until both ate fruit from the tree of knowing. The "feminine" *zot* also hearkens back to the animals, which are all referred to in the "feminine." It may be of interest to note that in grammatical *form* the Hebrew word for "fathers" is feminine and the word for "women" is masculine.

remained latent. The two creatures simply would never have recognized what exactly it was that was different about them. This is what J means Yahweh originally intended. The guarantee of productivity supplied by divine intercourse and embodied in royal temple institutions in neighboring kingdoms was to be addressed at the focal points of landownership and food distribution rather than intrinsic fecundity. As far as is known, this may indeed represent something of a departure from the norm in courtly literature. It certainly had a profound influence on the character of the Scripture that eventually coalesced around J. Marriage eventuates in the narrative, as well it might on the narrative's own terms: marriage is, after all, among other things a matter of politics and economics. In David's world, the family meant government. As one historian comments, "Insofar as the text reflects on the relation of the sexes, its concern is with the political dynamics of power, control, and autonomy."[30]

At this point in the story a new character is introduced, the snake, which paradoxically was not known to reproduce by mating but simply to live forever. It was thus "more clever" than all the other animals that Yahweh had made. There is a wordplay on the word "clever," which also means "naked." The snake was not only more clever but more naked than other creatures. Mythologically, it was a symbol of life because it had learned the trick of living forever, which was to shed its clothing (skin) periodically. There was no reason for the humans to believe they couldn't live forever too, and the snake assured them they could. Indeed, the snake asserted the god knew that by eating the forbidden fruit they too would become like the gods, with the capacity for knowing good and bad. It was the chance of being like a god that attracted the woman, as can be seen from what she says when she creates her first creature.

How was the woman able to recognize that the fruit was good, not bad, when she didn't yet have the ability to know? The key is the difference between knowing and seeing. She could see, but she couldn't yet know. She had a limited ability to discriminate, perhaps akin to that of a very young child, although not with a sense of the consequences. J takes an upper-class view that seeing rather than hunger, including visualizing in the mind's eye, is the root of appetite, or the impulse of anticipation, whether for food, sex, love, violence, or indeed all "good and bad," every truth and lie—hence the repeated references here, at the beginning of the history of good and bad, to seeing and eyes. Seeing precedes knowing. Throughout his history, J will present seeing good and good seeing, as he understands these, as standards for judging seeing bad and bad seeing.

When the first humans ate of the tree of knowing good and bad, they

---

30. Walter Brueggemann, *Genesis* (Atlanta: John Knox Press, 1982), 42.

became aware for the first time that they were heterosexual. Embarrassed, they wove fig leaves, which are shaped like genitalia, into vegetal garments to cover their naked reproductive parts. Before, J has said, they were naked but not embarrassed. Now they were embarrassed, since now they knew what humans know that induces them to wear clothes. When the man and the woman cover themselves, it signifies that they have a sense of shame, therefore of guilt, and therefore the capacity to know and respond to a sense of right and wrong, good and bad. By clothing themselves, they acknowledge their discovery of the capacity to do wrong. Henceforth for J, nakedness will signify the lack of such a sense of shame, the failure to acknowledge the capacity to do wrong,[31] represented by the nakedness of the snake.

As the evening breeze came up, the divine owner of the pleasure garden strolled through his garden looking for his gardeners, who had hidden out of their embarrassment based on that knowing which only gods are supposed to do. When the god called out to them, the male answered that he had hidden because he was afraid. This was the first moment of fear the humans had experienced, since fear is not possible without the ability, through knowing, to anticipate the future. There was no fear of death until this capacity to imagine was awakened in them. The fear of death is a distinctive feature of the consciousness of human beings, not found in other creatures: only humans can fear in a way that goes beyond the instinctive. Indeed, this threat of nonbeing is the basis of civilization and its discontents.[32] The fear of death is, paradoxically, what lies behind the act of murder, which will be the hallmark of Cain and his descendants, for it is an attempt to forestall one's own death. The issue here is not the origin of individual sinfulness but of evil in the world and human beings' complicity in the structures of culture that perpetuate it, including the distribution of food which allows some to live sumptuously while others are consigned to premature death—an arrangement tantamount to murder, in J's view.

The man blamed the woman whom Yahweh had "put" with him. The RSV has "whom thou gavest to be with me," which may suggest to some that J has an ideology of the subordination of women, an interpretation of

31. The importance of the sexual element in the genesis of the superego, as opposed to the authority-power element in the initiation and perpetuation of the superego, is stressed by Edward V. Stein, *Guilt: Theory and Therapy* (Philadelphia: Westminster Press, 1968).

32. For this concept, see Ernest Becker, *The Denial of Death* (New York: Free Press, Macmillan Co., 1973); and Francisco José Moreno, *Between Faith and Reason: An Approach to Individual and Social Psychology* (New York: New York University Press, 1977). The basic theme of the Mesopotamian Gilgamesh narrative is closely related. For a recent attempt to integrate social psychological factors in the analysis of the capitalist equivalent of what J is referring to, see Robert L. Heilbroner, *The Nature and Logic of Capitalism* (New York: W. W. Norton, 1985), esp. chap. 2 ("The Drive to Amass Capital").

Hebrew *nathan* that is beside the point J is making. While J comes from a patriarchal society in which women were dominated and so assumes the bases of the male supremicist syndrome, he is not here attempting to say that the woman was given to the man as a possession, merely that she was put with him. The issue is not the social relationship between man as dominant and woman as dominated; they were two equivalent human creatures which were meant to be dominated by Yahweh. What J is interested in is that they represent, in their "labor," two thematic tracks: the socioeconomic, food-growing, soil-oriented track; and the reproductive, property-inheritance, domestic economy track.

Through the garden story, J establishes a framework for his history which encompasses a single system, both material and symbolic. Everything that follows will fall within this system. The court's domestic economy is the political economy of the state, and all of this is conceived of as a single network of meaning in the ideological context we are seeking to understand. For us, sex is one thing and politics another, but not in the Bible. In the Bible, sexuality is conceived of in broad terms spanning all the way from the sexual act itself to the extended family as its result, to the extended family's political-economic behavior.

For instance, 2 Sam. 3:6–10 describes the fundamental conflict between the royal households of Saul and David. In the patriarchal context, the purpose of having a wife was to have a son, which enabled one to maintain a continuity between the male ruler of the dominion and the successor. Abner, the commander-in-chief over the armies of Saul and effective head of the house of Saul, made himself strong in the house of Saul during this war. Saul had a concubine, whom Abner attempted to make his own. Saul's son, heir, and successor, Ishbaal (Ishbosheth), said to Abner, "Why have you had intercourse with my father's concubine?" This made Abner angry. Abner's infringement upon Saul's concubine was a power move. If one could have intercourse with a ruler's wife or concubine, one moved into that person's power place. Abner changed houses, going over to David and making it possible for David to rule Israel, over an incident having to do with the claim to power implied in a sexual relationship with Saul's concubine. Sexual relations have powerful consequences, in David's world and ours.

The same theme is evident in the marriages that David made in his rise to power[33] and literarily in 2 Samuel 11 and its sequel, from a contemporary Solomonic document. The story of the succession from David to Solomon begins with David and Bathsheba. David's taking of Bathsheba and murder

33. See Jon D. Levenson and Baruch Halpern, "The Political Import of David's Marriages," *Journal of Biblical Literature* 99 (1980): 507–18.

of Uriah is the story of the legitimacy of Solomon. His legitimacy begins not when he wins out over Adonijah but in the story of the child of David and Bathsheba which died. This child is in essence a sacrifice, an atonement, a recompense that releases Solomon from the symbolic meaning of David's sexual and murderous acts of power.

Recall too that Absalom took out the concubines of his father and had intercourse with them in public view when he took over Jerusalem (2 Sam. 16:20–22). Absalom's rule is defined in terms of his intercourse with his father's concubines.

The story of Abishag the Shunammite (1 Kings 1:1–4) illustrates the same symbol system in two ways. First, it shows that David's rule was effective only as long as he could get an erection. Second, in 1 Kings 2:13–25 Adonijah asked for Abishag in the face of Solomon. This is parallel to Abner's asking for Saul's concubine in the face of Ishbaal. Sexual potency is a symbol of political power.

The Bible lists at least seven wives and seventeen sons for David. Solomon had seven hundred wives and three hundred mistresses. Yet his son Rehoboam, when he was forced to assert his rule over a rebellious populace appealing for a reduction in their corvée duties (1 Kings 12:4; RSV: "hard service"), made the inordinate boast, "My little one is thicker than my father's loins." Rehoboam's "little one" was his erect phallus. The RSV's "little finger" is entirely incorrect; "middle finger" would have been a better English translation. Here is the issue of the garden sharply epitomized: royal sex and the imposition of corvée go hand in hand. (The Assyrian king Assurbanipal describes in one detailed text left from his reign how he had the harem of his palace, called his "house of sovereignty," enlarged and rebuilt by a crew of captive bedouin corvée workers, "amidst gladness and rejoicing." Next to it was a garden of Eden: "A great park," says Assurbanipal, "of all kinds of fruit trees I planted at its sides.")[34] Since in J's view corvée is to be negated, so, according to Yahweh's intent at creation, is royal sex not to be a possibility. Once again, the starting point for understanding the story of the garden is to see its connection to the exodus. Though humans were not created for corvée work according to J, they got themselves into corvée work through a sequence of events that began with their coming to know themselves as sexual. Consistent with his initial purpose, Yahweh determines to get them out of Egyptian corvée at the climactic moment of J's history.

Of the two psalms said to come from Solomon, Psalm 72 and Psalm 127, Psalm 127 is a treatment of this motif. "Who builds a house builds in vain

---

34. See D. D. Luckenbill, *Ancient Records of Assyria and Babylon* (Chicago: University of Chicago Press, 1927), 2:321–23.

unless Yahweh builds it" (v. 1). This is not speaking of individual homes but of the household of those in power, and of the state and dynastic temple they built in Jerusalem. "Unless Yahweh watches over the city, the watchman stays awake in vain" (v. 1). The engendered household and the city are parallel. This parallel is repeated by the sage Ben Sira later in the biblical period: "Children and city make a name last" (Ecclus. 40:19). Psalm 127 is regarded by the writer who assigned authorship to the psalms as a composition of the son of the king, the one who defines the dominion as a dynastic dominion. The dominion remains within the household if the son inherits from the father.

Psalm 127 goes on to say, "Sons are a heritage from Yahweh, the fruit of the womb a reward. Like arrows in the hand of a warrior are the sons of one's youth. Happy is the man who has his quiver full of strong sons. He shall not be put to shame when they drive his enemies from the gate" (vv. 3–5). Sons are the measure of the inviolability of the city. It was characteristic for ruling families to be large. There were both local wives and those at a distance. The local wives produced indigenous sons who became the chief subrulers—the heads of the military and chief warriors, prefects, magistrates, and counselors. When they were loyal to the monarch, they were a great asset. When that kinship bond exists, it is the closest of political bonds, also signified in Hebrew by the word translated "know." But the kinship bond can also fall apart, and Psalm 133, for example, is about the avoidance of that kind of fragmentation of brothers.

Local sons produced a local ruling network which assisted the ruling family within its territory of dominion. The foreign alliances extended the political-economic network. These were political alliances as well as trade alliances. They encompassed not only the exchange of goods but military agreements, arrangements for the return of defectors, the refusal to harbor politically disaffected elements, and the like.

All of this is based on what we would define as kinship. In J as in the rest of the Bible, however, it all falls within the framework of a single system.[35] The garden story treats the origin of this system. We see it played out immediately in what is essentially a royal act of murder, committed by the one who was born of this sex-to-kin-to-power system. J's history portrays a form of royal sexual behavior which it rejects. In J, the evil Canaanite and Egyptian royalties, which descend from Cain, the firstborn son, are opposed by David's good royalty.

J addresses this material and symbolic system of production and re-

---

35. See the discussion of Adam, Eve, Cain, sex, and power in terms of "erotics" in Enrique Dussel, *Philosophy of Liberation* (Maryknoll, N.Y.: Orbis Books, 1985), 78–87. For the representation of power in general, see David Cannadine and Simon Price, eds., *Rituals of Royalty: Power and Ceremonial in Traditional Societies* (Cambridge: Cambridge University Press, 1987).

production in the curses that Yahweh pronounces on the humans. Until now, labor (from Heb.: *avad*, "work") had been painless; now it would be toilsome and painful. The curse of the woman was to labor in domestic reproduction, producing human beings through painful childbirth. The woman was also told, "To your man will be your desire and he will rule you." This refers specifically to the woman's tie to the man in the sexual act and does not mean that he was to determine every aspect of her life, as it has so often been taken to mean. She was to be bound to her husband by her sexual impulses. Again, the patriarchal bias of this view is not at issue. The expression "rule you" in the context of this curse refers to the man's privilege of keeping his wife pregnant and in the pains of pregnancy and childbirth, a condition that governs her life. It is the whole sex-to-kin-to-power realm that is in view here—reproduction, the extended family, kith and kin—as opposed to the male's role in the production of food and goods. Of course the man is also tied to the woman, but his pains are not caused by the woman as hers are by him. In line with J's schematization of the reproductive track in relation to the woman and the productive track in relation to the man, the man's pains are caused by the ground.

The curse of the man was to labor for the political-economic system, producing food from the arable by sweaty toil in tillage in place of the leisurely work of plucking fruit at will from the perennials of the orchard. Gone were the days of resting in the heat of the day and getting up in the cool of the evening breeze to prune a few branches, pluck an orange, peel and eat it with no sweat. In Hebrew, the man's pain is identical to the woman's.

The man now named his wife. Etymologically, the Hebrew *hawwa*, Eve, means "snake." J interprets this word to mean "mother of all living," perhaps because the snake had disclosed the means of creating life. This is the last of the many interrelated reasons J selected the snake to play its role in the orchard. Humans, who are to die as individuals, can live forever only through reproducing themselves in offspring. In mythology the snake often tells a half-truth. So also does J's snake. Humans will die when they eat of the tree of knowing, but the human species will live for generation after generation because the discovery of heterosexuality unleashes the human capacity for reproduction. It is in this way that the woman triumphs over the snake, which has perhaps nipped her heel (a more likely translation than "bruised") and injected the poison of death into the human species. Her ability to reproduce alleviates the harm done to humanity by the snake's half-truth.[36]

36. The christological reference frequently seen in this statement is of course a much later interpretation, entirely foreign to J's history. For the influence of this text on Western culture, see Elaine Pagels, *Adam, Eve, and the Serpent* (New York: Random House, 1988).

Yahweh made for the man and his woman cloaks of skin and dressed them. To interpret this as an act of grace, as many do, is to read back into the passage, where it does not belong, the Protestant notion of sin and grace. The cloaks of skin should be understood in terms of J's narrative, in which they carry a dual significance. The first refers back to the belief that the snake was immortal because it took its skin off. To mark the mortality that had overtaken the humans, and to enclose the presumption inherent in human reproduction, Yahweh reversed the snake's cleverness and put skins on them. The second related meaning of the skins is that prior to this point the two humans had lived as if asexual like plants. (In the world of the author, plants bore a fruit with a seed in it; there was no awareness of pollination by bees.) By eating of the tree of knowing, the humans had moved into the class of animals, which reproduce sexually. They had given themselves a covering of plants, but Yahweh gave them instead a covering of animals to signify that they had changed from creatures that the god could clone into mating creatures that could reproduce themselves. Henceforth uncovered pudenda were to be disallowed.[37]

Now that the humans had gained the capacity for knowing, like the gods, Yahweh drove them away from the garden of perennials to work the ground from which they had been taken. Hybrid beasts of some kind and a flashing sword, switching back and forth, guarded the tree of living,[38] whose fruit if eaten would complete the humans' transformation into gods, powerful *and* deathless. With knowledge, they were merely powerful. The death of the powerful will be the only way to prevent the tax in labor called corvée.

37. For an additional attempt to go beyond the simple theological interpretation of this clothing, see Robert A. Oden, Jr., *The Bible Without Theology: The Theological Tradition and Alternatives to It* (San Francisco: Harper & Row, 1987), 92–105.

38. The literature on the tree of life is extensive and complements the understanding of J suggested here. See Helmer Ringgren, *Religions of the Ancient Near East* (Philadelphia: Westminster Press, 1973), 78–79; and Bruce Vawter, *On Genesis: A New Reading* (Garden City, N.Y.: Doubleday & Co., 1977), 68.

8

Of Gods and Humans

(Genesis 4:1–17)

The human knew Eve his wife, and she got pregnant and bore Cain with these words: "I have gotten a man as though I were a god."[1]

Later she went on to bear his brother Abel. Abel was a shepherd of the flock, and Cain was a tiller of the ground. At the end of the year, Cain brought an offering to Yahweh from the fruit of the ground, while Abel brought from the young lambs of his flock and from their fat. Yahweh regarded Abel and his offering, but Cain and his offering he did not regard. So Cain became very angry and his face fell.

Yahweh said to Cain, "Why have you become angry, and why has your face fallen? Whether the ground bears well or not, sin is a crouching demon at the entrance. Its desire is for you, but you must master it."

Cain said to Abel his brother. . . . When they were in the field, Cain rose up against Abel his brother and murdered him.

Yahweh said to Cain, "Where is Abel your brother?"

He said, "I do not know. Am I my brother's watchman?"

And he said, "What have you done? The sound of the howling blood of your brother comes to me from the ground. Thus cursed are you more than the ground and from the ground, which opened its mouth to take the blood of your brother from your hand. If you work the ground, it will no longer give its strength to you. You will be a roaming wanderer in the earth."

Cain said to Yahweh, "My punishment is too great to bear. Since you have now banished me from off the face of the ground, and I am hidden from your face and your judicial grace and become a roaming wanderer in the earth, anyone who finds me may kill me."

---

1. The text says "Yahweh," which is translated "the Lord," but the Septuagint has *elohim,* meaning "a god." The Masoretic texts that form the basis of our Hebrew Bible date from considerably later than the Greek Septuagint. At times the Greek text preserves an older and more original reading than the Masoretic text. As previously observed, in P and E the history of the world is structured according to generations and the major divisions of the history are signified by the way in which God is named. The same is the case with J. There is a seven-generational scheme in J, and only with the birth of Enosh did people first use the name Yahweh. The few times people referred to God in speech in the first seven generations, they used the word *elohim,* with the exception in the Masoretic text of this statement by Eve. In this case the Greek Old Testament clearly preserves the original text.

Yahweh said to him, "In that case, if anyone kills Cain, Cain shall be avenged sevenfold."

And Yahweh put a sign on Cain so that anyone who found him would not attack him. Then Cain went out from Yahweh's presence and settled in the land of Nod east of Eden.

When Adam knew Eve, she became pregnant and gave birth to Cain. Then she named him, using these words: "I have *gotten* a man as though I were a god." The writer gives us an etymology of the name Cain, taking it to come from the word *qanah*. *Qanah* has a variety of meanings, including acquire, beget, produce, create, procreate, buy—all of which are best covered by the English word "get."[2] Cain's name means first of all, therefore, that the two humans created by God had themselves, like God, created a human. A name such as this tells all: Cain means that humans presume to act like gods.[3]

Qanah is the closest word in Hebrew to what we mean when we say in English "to capitalize." One Hebrew common noun from this verb means a wide variety of things—cattle, sheep and goats, possessions—but its root meaning is "capital." It is most frequently used to mean cattle (in this book we will usually translate it as "livestock"), and our English word cattle is itself a derivative of the word "capital." Cain's name, as etymologized by J, signifies that he will initiate the history of acquisition. We are not talking about capital formation in the capitalist sense; rather, we use it in the root sense of property by which more property can be acquired. Hence both seed and sheep are capital.

Cain *(Qain)* is also a Hebrew word meaning smith or metalworker.[4] The metalworkers were bedouin-like. They were tinkers, similar to gypsies.[5]

---

2. J uses the word in the fifteenth generation to refer to the creation of the sky and the earth. The Canaanite goddess Asherah was known by the epithet *qnyt ilm* ("begetter of the divines").

3. The Hebrew of Gen. 4:1 says literally "with" God. The same expression occurs later in a very significant J passage, Exod. 20:23: "You shall not make gods of silver to be *with* me." The "with" in this passage is the meaning of "with" in Eve's statement. The humans had become like gods, knowing good and evil, and the implication is that they were not to make humans with God, in other words, as one of the god kind. The RSV's "with the help of" is hardly supportable. See the comments of John C. L. Gibson, *Genesis*, Volume 1 (Philadelphia: Westminster Press, 1981), 143: "Not for [Eve] the thought of [God] alone giving life (2:7). She can do it too. She is in fact setting an example of defiance which Cain himself is later to follow, when he takes away life, something that was also the sole prerogative of God (Job 1:21)." For a full discussion of "with" in this passage, see Claus Westermann, *Genesis 1—11: A Commentary* (Minneapolis: Augsburg Publishing House, 1984), 290–92. This volume, together with the later two volumes of Westermann's commentary in translation (1985, 1986), serves as an invaluable resource for further study of matters of detail in Genesis.

4. See Peter Klemm, "Kain und die Kainiten," *Zeitschrift für Theologie und Kirche* 78 (1981): 391–408.

5. See Frank Frick, "The Rechabites Reconsidered," *Journal of Biblical Literature* 90 (1971): 279–87.

Their skills were necessary for the use of metals, which were essential to the culture that Cain founded, and it was therefore essential from the point of view of urban rulers that they be incorporated into the framework of urban society.[6] In the Palestine of David's day, these people, known as the Cainites (usually written Kenites), were apparently not fully integrated and needed to be subdued.[7] The tribal form of bedouin societies is expressed in a hierarchy of status. Among modern bedouin, smiths are at the bottom of the social hierarchy, along with slaves. In Muslim tradition, the bedouin and the blacksmiths were created at the same time. If this tradition is ancient, it may have much to do with why J should portray Cain as the "smith."[8] Herding bedouin typically regarded themselves as socially superior to tribes of smiths and looked down on them. J's defamation of the Kenites is in part the obverse of his favorable portrayal of the strong bedouin of the Negev whose favor he wished to cultivate. One historian believes that "evidence favors considering Hebron a major Kenite shrine city. . . . The anointing of Absalom was probably performed by Kenite groups."[9] If this historian is correct, the sharp denigration of Cain and the Cainites in J is furthermore a direct reflection of David's takeover of Hebron and, depending on when J was written, of David's suppression of his son Absalom's revolt. David's apologia has him doing battle against the Kenites much as he did against the Amalekites.

The smith in the Canaanite myth of state temple construction was Kothar-wa-Hasis. Kothar was indispensable in helping Baal, like Marduk, defeat the sea of chaos, as he made Baal's weapons for him; and he singlehandedly constructed Baal's temple. It can be no accident that J, writing for a king who could not or would not have a temple built, makes the firstborn human a smith who is a murderer. J persistently contrasts a proper earthen altar cult with an improper temple cult. J's characterization of the smith is his first clear allusion to that contrast.

Cain, of course, is the first city builder. His city probably included a temple. Both murder and city-building are dealt with schematically in the history, so that it is not possible to understand fully what the birth of Cain means until we have seen the history of Enoch, Lemek, Ham, Canaan, and

---

6. In the ancient Sumerian King List, the smith king comes near the end rather than as in J near the beginning. See James B. Pritchard, *Ancient Near Eastern Texts Relating to the Old Testament*, 2d ed. (Princeton: Princeton University Press, 1955), 266.

7. See the discussion in R. J. Forbes, *Studies in Ancient Technology* (Leiden: E. J. Brill, 1971), 8: 70–77, 88–89, and 94–95; and J. F. A. Sawyer, "Cain and Hephaestus: Possible Relics of Metalworking Traditions in Genesis 4," *Abr-Nahrain* 24 (1986): 155–66.

8. Daniel Bates and Amal Rassam, *Peoples and Cultures of the Middle East* (Englewood Cliffs, N.J.: Prentice-Hall, 1983), 263–64.

9. Cf. Saul Olyan, "Zadok's Origins and the Tribal Politics of David," *Journal of Biblical Literature* 101 (1982): 177–93. See the reflection of this distinction in 1 Sam. 15:6.

Egypt right through to the end of the entire history. In fact, we will not even know what Adam and Eve—Cain's parents—are all about until the full history has unfolded.

Following the birth of Cain, Eve bore Cain's brother, whose name was Abel (Heb.: *Hebel*). *Hebel* means "breath of air" or mere "breath." It is the word translated "vanity" that occurs some thirty times in Ecclesiastes. It signifies the shortness and futility of Abel's life.[10]

Cain and Abel were two sons of Adam engaged in two facets of agriculture in an agrarian village setting with a mixed economy. The village family planted grain and also had a few sheep and goats. Sheepherding was the lesser job in the village, a considerably lower status job. Abel was a shepherd, herding sheep and goats, while Cain as the elder son went into the same kind of work as his father, farming the land. What is portrayed is a typical village situation in which the younger son did the shepherding.

"In the course of time" (RSV, at Gen. 4:3) fails to indicate when the following action takes place. The Hebrew means "at the end of the year"[11] and refers to the harvest season at the end of the agricultural year. At this time, then, Cain brought an offering for Yahweh from the fruit of the ground, while Abel brought of the first fruit of his flock. Yahweh regarded[12] Abel and his offering but not Cain and his offering.

J does not say why Yahweh regarded one and not the other. The reason becomes apparent only as the history moves to its climax, reflecting the tension in David's day between Israel and Egypt. This tension is addressed in J's history in terms of the life and fortunes of the bedouin along the Egyptian border. We have seen that J projects for Israel a bedouin identity. The bedouin were predominantly shepherds, whereas the Cainites in Egypt lived by working the ground. In other words, later on in J's history Cain reappears, as it were, as the Egyptians, and Abel as the bedouin descendants of Jacob. When at that time Yahweh chooses the bedouin as opposed to the Egyptians, the implication of his choice of Abel over Cain at last becomes clear.

None of this is known, however, during the second generation. At that time Yahweh's choice appears whimsical. One of the characteristic ex-

10. Etymologically, *Hebel* is not a Hebrew name but is related to the Akkadian word *aplu*, meaning "heir." This happens to make a nice pun in English with the Hebrew meaning "air." We have already seen that the setting is in the east, in Mesopotamia, and that the writer is responding to an Akkadian tradition. Although Abel is murdered by Cain, the line of those who replace him in the story—Seth, Shem, and Abram—will become heirs to the land of the sons of Cain. This suggests that J might indeed have intended a double meaning.

11. Literally "at the end of the days." Hebrew *yamin* ("days") refers here to a year. Because the rain-based seasons have yet to be established in J's history, he refers to the harvest in vague but unmistakable language.

12. The same word occurs in J in Exod. 5:9, "Let heavier work be laid upon the men that they may labor at it and *pay* no *regard* to lying words" (RSV).

pressions of J is "to find favor in the eyes of." This expression captures the divine royal prerogative. Why was Noah, for example, the sole member of the eighth generation to survive the flood? Because he found favor with Yahweh. Yahweh is a god, and as such has divine prerogatives not granted to humans.

We shall see repeatedly in J's history that Yahweh has a distinct dislike for firstborn sons because they are the result of humans usurping the divine prerogative of creating. The firstborn son was the main heir of the property, and in the case of royalty the heir of the dominion. Dominion tended to be self-aggrandizing, often culminating in corvée. Ultimately we will hear Yahweh say, "Israel my firstborn son, *whom I have created*," in the story of the deliverance of the corvée workers. Yahweh could not tolerate humans creating.

Cain became very angry and his face fell. A person looks into the eyes of a person who is loved but will not face a person who is hated. Even today we say, "I cannot face such and such a person." The imagery of Cain's fallen face, therefore, depicts the breakdown of their brotherly relationship and everything this portends. The theme of conflict between brothers will occur again and again in J.

It is not the simple difference between shepherd and farmer that is prefigured here, but the dynamic between the elder and the younger, and between what will develop into a cursed line and a blessed line, the one becoming the city-dwelling and farming Egyptians and Canaanites, the other the sheepherding bedouin descendants of Jacob (though it would be inappropriate to regard Abel as bedouin). In J, all of the successful brothers are not firstborn sons but younger brothers—Isaac, Jacob, Joseph, Ephraim, Moses, and ultimately by implication David (who is not only a younger brother but the usurper of the kingdom).

Yahweh said to Cain, "Why are you angry? Why has your face fallen? Is it not the case that whether it [the ground] bears well or it does not bear well, sin is a crouching demon at the entrance? Its desire is for you, but you must control it." The temptation was to the specific sin of murder. The murderer was the firstborn whose status had been passed over, even though his lands produced perfectly well. So there wasn't a motivation of economic jealousy to this murder; the murderer was not poorer than the murdered. Rather, as an elite scribe J characterizes evil as tied to the usurping of the divine prerogative of creating.

J has a very different understanding from the common notion that the garden story is the history of what has come to be known doctrinally as the "fall." For J, sin means murder within a social context and all that contributes to it and flows from it in J's history. The RSV translation "sin is crouching at the door" (Gen. 4:7) is simply wrong. It abstracts and generalizes sin. Sin is grammatically feminine, while *rovetz* ("the croucher") is masculine. The sin talked about here is pictured as a demon. As with any demon at the door, you need to do something to ward it off, whether mental or magical, like putting up a little plaque or wearing a blue amulet. You have to watch out. When you go in and out the door, you take precautions. In J, sin is not a universal condition or a general set of undesirable behaviors but a specific act of injustice to be warded off.[13] Sin is resistible.[14] J is a highly ideological document which conceives the purpose of the Davidic realm as overcoming evil and counteracting the curse with blessing.

Cain said to Abel his brother, "Let's go to the field." And when they were in the field, working together, Cain attacked his brother and murdered him. Eve's "I have created a man" has been extended to an implied "If I can make a man, I may kill a man." There is no way to hear this incident and be too horrified. The full effect of this event is not felt until the deliverance of the bedouin corvée slaves from Egypt, when Cain's act of injustice and the comparable and consequent injustices perpetuated by his descendants are righted by Moses' killing of the Egyptian taskmaster and Yahweh's slaying of pharaoh's firstborn son and all the firstborn of Egypt.

J is presenting a theodicy, or defense of God's rightness, in which Yahweh did not cause the evil conditions in the world. J's theodicy does not simply rescue God's justice. It offers to explain the nature of evil, which J portrays not as intrinsic to the created order but as emerging in a historical dynamic and therefore rectifiable. J wants his readers to understand that there is nothing inherent in the created order to prevent the emergence of a genuine universal peace centered on the Davidic state. Humans living under the Davidic kingdom were not doomed. History holds out the possibility of the triumph of right. There is a struggle against evil which can be successful. The right can prevail over the wrong. J's optimism is confirmed by his historical scheme, whereby he begins each phase of his history, each new set of seven generations, with a great protagonist. (By contrast P, composed in exile, ends each phase of history, marked by sets of ten generations, with the same protagonists.) Ultimately J's optimism reflects the upward mobility of the Davidic court and allied Judahite leadership.

Yahweh said to Cain, "Where is Abel your brother?" To this, Cain replied, "I don't know." Yahweh sounded as if he didn't know either. We

---

13. Within three hundred years prior to David, and probably less as well, the linguistic equivalent of *rovetz* in Hebrew had the meaning of the commissioner or overseer who represented Egyptian power in various localities in Palestine at that time.

14. The phrase "its desire is for you" makes sin attracted to humans about as humans are sexually attracted to each other; compare Gen. 4:7 with Gen. 3:16.

found the same in the garden, when he asked Adam, "Where are you?" The point is that he did know. This is a foil to the human beings who "know" but who don't know. The compounded irony of this remark is that Cain said, "I don't know."

"Am I the watcher of my brother?" asks Cain. He was already exhibiting the consciousness of the one who would later build the city, which would exploit the peasantry for its own ends. To this, Yahweh responded, "What have you done? The voice of the blood of your brother is crying to me from the ground. As a consequence, cursed are you away from the ground, which has opened its mouth to take the blood of your brother from your hand." The flow of Abel's blood into the ground recalls the creation of humans, *adam*, who are ruddy because they are made out of red earth, *adama*. This is not clay, but the red soil of Palestine. Now a third play on this word is introduced: *damim*, the plural of *dam*, denoting blood or murder.

When the "descendants" of Abel (Israel) are rescued from the descendants of Cain (Egypt), they are led by one who kills a descendant of Cain (Moses). Yahweh then kills the firstborn and the pharaoh descendant of Cain. Through this parallel J is asserting that Egyptian corvée is tantamount to murder. This analysis of corvée is confirmed by the measure-for-measure response in the climax of the story. J's "cultural history" (see chapter 9) is a cultural history of social murder, murder itself of course being culturally defined.

Yahweh told Cain, "If you work the ground, it will not again give its strength to you. But a roaming wanderer you will be in the earth."[15] Cain replied, "My wrong is too great to bear. You having driven me this day from the face of the ground, I, now hidden from your eye, become a wanderer. What if someone should find me? He will kill me." This is a reference to simple blood vengeance, which is a bit surprising because Cain and Abel were in the same family. Why does J raise the issue of blood vengeance at this point? Under normal circumstances Palestine was a highly factionalized society.[16] One of the prerequisites for national solidarity was the suppression of fraternal and tribal conflict.[17] J's solution to the fissioning of

15. It is probable that this banishment reflects the application of a bedouin-like solution to the problem of revenge. The most common result of murder among bedouin is, according to one acclaimed study, the voluntary exile of the murderer or his expulsion. See Emrys L. Peters, "Some Structural Aspects of the Feud Among the Camel-Herding Bedouin of Cyrenaica," *Africa* 37 (1967): 261–81.

16. The constant feuding in Palestine is discussed in many accounts from late Ottoman Palestine. A good example is E. A. Finn, *Palestine Exploration Fund Quarterly* 10 (1879): 33–48, 72–87.

17. The cities of refuge (Num. 35:6–34; Deut. 19:4–13; Joshua 20), an institution that probably goes back to David's time, if not before, were a part of the administrative attempt to deal with fraternal and tribal conflict.

paternal interest groups will be elaborated in terms of a succession of reconciliations, the main one being the reconciliation of Joseph's brothers with Joseph through the agency of Judah. This culminating reversal of Cain's murder of Abel leads directly to the deliverance of the corvée slaves. The great foil of the deliverance story is the reconciliation of the bedouin brothers, and their immediate descendants represent an identity of reconciliation and solidarity projected onto the whole of Israel, standing united against Egypt.

J deals with this issue within the bedouin context not only because it is a bedouin identity that he is projecting onto Israel but also because of the critical character of fraternal alliances among the bedouin. The brother who wished to leave the group had a much harder time leaving the village than leaving the tribe: the tribe was more easily fissionable than the village. Even more than village society, the strength of the bedouin group was based on fraternal alliance. It was this that enabled bedouin to become wealthy. Bedouin society could readily expand and hence had the means to capitalize on the maintenance of fraternal alliance, whereas the village could not expand in the same way and thus could not capitalize on the maintenance of the fraternal interest group nearly as dramatically. An alliance among several brothers who had sons, with each of those sons shepherding a lot of sheep, created a pooled economic power that made possible expansion of the territory in which they were able to shepherd those sheep. So the clan leader had aegis over an expanding fraternal interest group, whose productivity expanded as the group expanded. Thus there was a direct connection between sons, power, sheep, and wealth. The picture of Israel as twelve sons who were all allied and reconciled with one another is schematic and an extraordinary representation of national unity. It warned any villagers within earshot to tone down their squabbles, gang wars, and vendettas. So Israel becomes a great band through capitalization. Again we see that reproduction and production went hand in hand.

Yahweh declared that if anyone killed Cain, he would be avenged seven times over, and he put a mark on Cain so that anyone who found him would not smite him. The mark of Cain constitutes an extraordinary protection of the murderer. You cannot make a policy that blood vengeance is disallowed; that isn't the way Palestinian society works. But this extreme way of expressing the protection of the murderer points to the intent of the Davidic court that Israelite not kill Israelite in the endless chain of vengeance.

How was blood vengeance at the village level exercised? Partly through the creation of vertical alliances that reached all the way up into the upper echelons of society and that could be taken advantage of by outside powers. Palestinian politics were aristocratic politics. Blood vengeance had its aristocratic counterpart in conflict among the elite. The villagers were clients of the aristocrats. The aristocrats would take care of them and use their political support for their actions.

David's was not the only dominant family, and in order to present himself as the single ruling house David needed to override aristocratic conflict. J's way of doing this was to portray Israel as needing to join together in the face of an external enemy. What the Davidic court was aiming at was complementary opposition: groups join together to the extent that they confront a common enemy. Such a notion was required to help counteract the imperial propensity to divide and rule. It was a power move on the part of a dominant aristocratic family. The prime direct referent was the vengeance of the house of Saul, which was David's worst political problem. He ended up murdering the disaffected of the house of Saul himself because he couldn't convince them they shouldn't take vengeance.[18]

So Cain went forth from Yahweh and dwelt in the land of Nod, or "wandering," east of Eden. He "knew" his wife and she gave birth to Enoch (Hebrew: Henok). Cain now became a city builder. The term is generic, like farmer or shepherd. He named the city after his son. The root of Enoch means "to consecrate at the founding of." It is a root that we find in the word Hanukkah, which is the festival of the reconsecration of the temple after the abomination of desolation was removed from it in the time of the Maccabees. The city consisted typically of the palace, which housed the royal bureaucracy and the military; the temple, representing the economic system and its religious legitimation; and the prime grain-storage facility. This was consecrated, or sacralized. So the name Enoch is an allusion to the sacral legitimation of the institution of the city in its schematic form.

We come now to the basic schemas of the J history, which thus far we have presented in narrative form. What follows is a formal, closely constructed, schematic history.

---

18. 2 Samuel 23. The situation of Cain and Abel is much like that of the two brothers described in 2 Sam. 14:5–7. Not only does this story appeal to David's sensibilities, but in other instances narrated in documents from David's court he goes out of his way to avoid taking personal revenge against the enemies of his rule. For a valuable discussion of vengeance in the Bible, see George E. Mendenhall, *The Tenth Generation* (Baltimore: Johns Hopkins University Press, 1973), 69–104.

9

A Royal Way of Thinking

(Genesis 4:18–26)

Cain knew his wife, and she got pregnant and bore Henok. Cain then became a city builder, and he used his son's name Henok for the city. To Henok was born Irad. Irad fathered Mehuya'el. Mehuya'el fathered Metusha'el. Metusha'el fathered Lemek.

Lemek took for himself two wives. The name of the first was Adah, and the name of the second was Silla. Adah bore Yabal. He was the ancestor of all who lived in tents with large estates, flocks, and herds. The name of his brother was Yubal. He was the ancestor of all who play string and reed instruments. Silla also bore children. She bore Tubal-qain, the one who whets every instrument of bronze and iron, and the sister of Tubal-qain, Na'mah.

> Lemek said to his wives,
> "Adah and Silla, hear my voice;
>   Wives of Lemek, give ear to my words.
> I have killed a man for my bruise,
>   A boy for my injury.
> If Cain is avenged seven times over,
>   For Lemek it will be seventy-seven."

The first human, Adam, again knew his wife, and she bore a son and named him Seth with these words, "For God has given me other seed in place of Abel, since Cain murdered him."

To Seth also there was born a son. He named him Enosh. At that time humans began to invoke Yahweh by name.

J's history of the world covers twenty-two generations, as can be seen on the chart on page 76. His main chronological device was not years but generations, which for him is the succession of sons. The generations come in three sets of seven. Seven was a common traditional number, but it figures distinctively in J. This distinctiveness can be seen by contrasting J with P, for whom seven is also important, such as in the seven-day week, but for whom ten and six are especially significant. In addition to sets of

74

seven generations, J has seven animals of each kind going onto the ark, seven plagues in Egypt, Balak sacrificing seven times, and so forth.

The second schematization in J is in terms of curse and blessing. Fourteen generations are characterized by the curse, which is God's response to humans' usurping of divine prerogatives for themselves. The disorder created by the curse limits humans' ability to exploit the prerogatives they have seized. Beginning with the fifteenth generation, there follow seven generations in which blessing is introduced into the world to counteract the curse. The prime element of the blessing is the grant of land, which is not fulfilled, however, until the issue of corvée and royal consciousness can be brought into conjunction with it. Pharaoh makes a land grant to the bedouin descendants of Abram in the eighteenth generation but reneges on that grant, leaving the bedouin in jeopardy of corvée. It is to resolve this jeopardy that Yahweh acts to fulfill the grant, leading the twenty-second generation to establish the Davidic kingdom as a sovereign state at the beginning of the fourth set of generations. Adam, Noah, Abram, and finally all Israel, are the protagonists of the generations of new beginnings—the first, eighth, fifteenth, and twenty-second generations.

The three columns show how J schematically represents agriculture, city culture, and herding culture. Following the murder and the building of the city, agriculture essentially drops out of the picture until the completion of the scheme in the twenty-second generation, the period of David's Israel. In the chart, the sons of Cain in the left-hand column represent urban, royal culture.[1] When this culture is wiped out in a great downpour, the line is reestablished in Ham, whose sons are, among others, Cush (Mesopotamia, the region of the great city builders of Genesis 11), Canaan (whose city culture will be displaced by the grant of land to Israel), and Egypt (whose building of food-storage cities is the purpose of corvée). The right-hand column is that of the herders, the key figure being Abram, who as a herder is the successor of Abel. This line is portrayed in terms of bedouin culture.[2] It is a schematic representation, using the Hebrew expression *ro'eh tson*, which can refer both to the village and to the bedouin shepherd.

---

1. Cf. Robert R. Wilson, *Genealogy and History in the Biblical World* (New Haven, Conn.: Yale University Press, 1977), 138–58. The early Sumerian King List lists eight kings in succession before the Flood. See James B. Pritchard, *Ancient Near Eastern Texts Relating to the Old Testament*, 2d ed. (Princeton: Princeton University Press, 1955), 265. A late text from Uruk, representing early tradition, lists seven kings in succession before the Flood. It is quite likely that this tradition lies behind J's scheme of seven-generation periods of history, even though the numbers seven, eight, nine, and ten are all attested. See J. Van Dijk, *Vorläufige Berichte über die Ausgrabungen in Uruk-Warka* 18 (1962): 44–60.

2. See B. Oded, "The Table of Nations (Genesis 10)—A Socio-Cultural Approach," *Zeitschrift für die alttestamentliche Wissenschaft* 98 (1986): 14–31.

GENEALOGY AND CULTURE IN J   vs. Gen 5 (P's account)

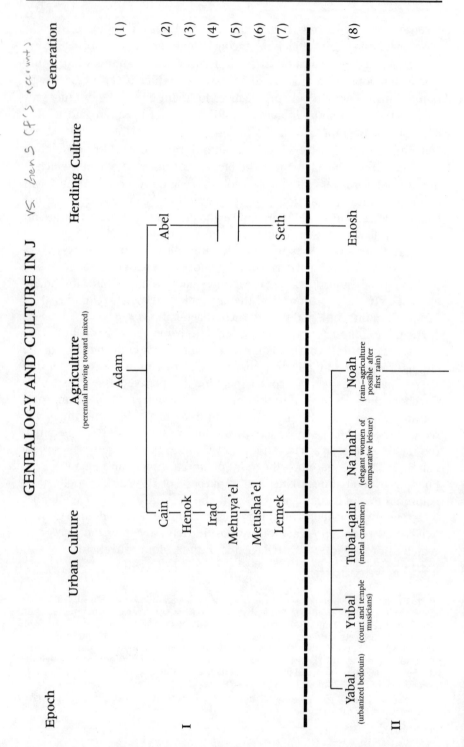

Epoch	Urban Culture	Agriculture (perennial moving toward mixed)	Herding Culture	Generation
		Adam		(1)
			Abel	(2)
	Cain			(3)
	Henok			(4)
	Irad			(5)
	Mehuya'el			(6)
	Metusha'el		Seth	(6)
	Lemek			(7)
I	Yabal (urbanized bedouin) / Yubal (court and temple musicians) / Tubal-qain (metal craftsmen) / Na'mah (elegant women of comparative leisure)	Noah (rain–agriculture possible after first rain)	Enosh	(8)
II				

Fantasy | Realism

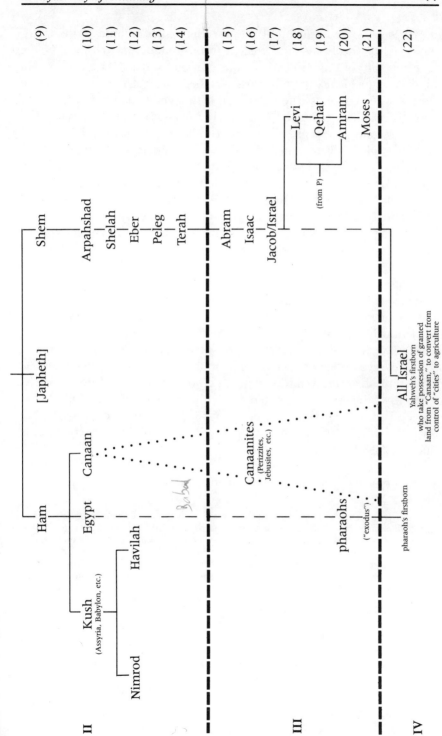

(9) Shem

(10) Arpahshad
(11) Shelah
(12) Eber
(13) Peleg
(14) Terah

(15) Abram
(16) Isaac
(17) Jacob/Israel
(18) Levi
(19) Qehat
(20) Amram
(21) Moses

(22)

(from P)

[Japheth]

Ham

Canaan

Egypt

Kush
(Assyria, Babylon, etc.)

Havilah

Nimrod

Canaanites
(Perizzites,
Jebusites, etc.)

Babel

pharaohs

("exodus")

All Israel
Yahweh's firstborn
who take possession of granted
land from "Canaan," to convert from
control of "cities" to agriculture

pharaoh's firstborn

II

III

IV

The ideal is the agricultural column, the center column of the chart, which is the ideal of Adam, created from ground, and the ideal of the redeemability of Cain and Abel as reconciled brothers. This ideal is not fulfilled in the history itself, because it is the history of a dynamic between the two outer columns. The restoration of the center column is assumed to be achievable only with all Israel taking possession of the land in the twenty-second generation under the conditions of the Davidic state.[3] J conceives of this generation as restoring the original coherence of the creation and utilizing a mixed agriculture that capitalizes on the beneficial historical developments such as those introduced with Noah. There is no history of Joshua and the Judges in J; they may have been organized and placed by the Deuteronomist. The story of J goes directly from the blessing of Balaam to the generation of David. This sounds strange to us because we are familiar with the Bible as it is, but there was no such Bible when J wrote.[4]

Having scanned J's schematization, we now take a closer look at Cain's immediate descendants.[5] Cain's son Henok (Enoch) had a son Irad, whose name contains the word *ir*, meaning the temple-palace-grain-storage center denoted by the word "city." So there is an obvious connection between Cain as the original city builder and his son and grandson, Henok and Irad.

In the seventh generation of this line we encounter the name Lemek. This name has no Semitic etymology, no cognates, and no parallels, whereas all the names encountered so far have been perfectly good Semitic names. Lemek is a made-up, or nonce, word.[6] It is a thinly disguised cipher for Hebrew *melek*, meaning "king," which contains the same consonants but in a different order.

Lemek has two wives, which may be viewed as an elite prerogative. Both wives, Adah and Silla, have Semitic names. Adah bears two children, Yabal

---

3. Such a scheme did not originate with J. It is reminiscent of the common ancient Sumerian distinction between "town and pasture" in Mesopotamian tradition, a usage attested as late as the Amarna letters in the fourteenth century B.C.E. (EA 306:30). See William W. Hallo, "Antediluvian Cities," *Journal of Cuneiform Studies* 23 (1970): 58. It is possible that Hebrew itself continues this tradition in the opposition of "city" and "open field" in passages such as Deut. 28:16, where the pair occurs together with several other sets of oppositions.

4. In Iron Age Greece, the history of culture was likewise tied to cult jurisdiction and the critique of labor in Hesiod's *Works and Days*, most accessible in Richmond Lattimore, trans., *Hesiod* (Ann Arbor, Mich.: University of Michigan Press, 1972), 15–117. The closest we can come to a Phoenician equivalent of J is the work of Sanchuniathon preserved in fragments in Philo of Byblos; see Harold W. Attridge and Robert A. Oden, Jr., *Philo of Byblos: The Phoenician History* (Washington, D.C.: Catholic Biblical Association of America, 1981).

5. The realization that royal culture traces back to Cain occurs at least as early as St. Augustine at the end of the fourth century C.E.

6. Some scholars suggest the name may be derived from the Akkadian Lamgu, but this does not fit the history of J. The name is better understood as a reference to the kings of the city culture.

and Yubal. These two names and that of another child, Tubal-qain (Tubal-Cain), are built on forms of *yabal,* which means "to produce." This can be interpreted as the consequence of *qanah,* getting. If *qanah* alludes to the capital function, *yabal* refers to the productive function. The last male in the line, Tubal-qain, combines the final set of names with the first of the line, Cain, to tie the first set of seven generations together.

Yabal was the father of "the estated one of the tent and capital," as it is put in the Hebrew text. The capital referred to here is that of flocks and herds. This son was not the urban elite ruler but was of the tent, movable. He was the urban bedouin sheikh, the bedouin leader who had become so wealthy he could buy urban property and become influential in urban politics. Cain produced offspring who, like the banished Cain, were not attached to the ground and who were therefore movable. The Hebrew reader or hearer would easily connect *miqneh* with *qanah.* So in the first male we have a connection with the folk etymology of Cain, while in the last male we shall see that we have the historical etymology of Cain, which is "smith."

Yubal was a wielder of the stringed instrument and of the reed instrument—the harp and the pipe. This is a reference to the court musician, who could move from court to court as necessity dictated or opportunities arose.

The first of Silla's children was Tubal-qain, who was the whetter of all instruments of bronze and iron—specifically the smith, fulfilling the smith connotation of Cain's name. The other of Silla's children was a woman, Naʿmah, which means "beautiful." The sharpest way to define Naʿmah is in terms of Naʿman, the king of Aram, who was cured of his leprosy (2 Kings 6). The name means "elegantly handsome," in contrast to the fact that he contracted leprosy. Naʿmah is the elegant woman described in the cursing of urban culture in Deut. 28:56 and Isa. 3:16–24. She is the elite daughter, who is a link in the chain of political alliances and completes the genealogical picture through her political implications in marriage alliances.[7]

Lemek was a king who presumably ruled for many years and no doubt did many important things, but J chooses to tell about only one thing: he killed a lad and bragged to his wives about it. He told his wives, "Hear my voice, wives of Lemek; give ear to my word." He was boastful. This is the extension of Eve's statement that she, like a god, had created a man. Not only had Eve usurped the prerogative of creating a man, and not only did Cain carry out his assumed right to kill a man, but Eve and Cain's descend-

---

7. In the next generation, Naʿmah was the name of the Ammonite princess, wife of Solomon, who became the mother of the third ruler of the house of David, Rehoboam (1 Kings 14:21, 31). For a Phoenician parallel to J's sociocultural scheme, see Attridge and Oden, *Philo of Byblos,* 40–47; Hallo, "Antediluvian Cities," 57–67, esp. 63–65.

ant Lemek even boasted that he possessed that right, to his wives, and in inordinate measure.

"I have killed a man for my bruise, a boy for my injury," he said. This is the only place in the Bible where *ish* and *yeled* are in parallelism, and J conveys a double-entendre by means of this parallelism. *Ish* implies maturity, *yeled* immaturity. The young men who advised Rehoboam to resist the appeals of the northerners are called his *yeladim* ("lads").[8] The implication is that Lemek was murdering a political upstart who was becoming his opponent—his Absalom, as it were. But *ish* can also be taken not as referring to maturity but simply to a man, with *yeled* qualifying *ish* to show that he was a young male at that, alluding back to Eve's comment, "I have created a man." This emphasizes the youthfulness of Lemek's victim in order to draw out the utter illegitimacy of the act. The picture is of the strongest man in the society killing one of the weakest men in society, a mere boy.

The overarching issue is the power to kill. How can one human think he or she has the right to kill another human? The answer is that if you think you can make them, then you think you have the right to kill them. Lemek's address to his wives continues the sex-power connection, for he tells them that he has power to kill. When this young lad offended him, Lemek manifested the attitude of the city-dwelling ruling elite by killing him.

The excess of Lemek's act is pointed to in the statement, "If Cain is avenged seven times, then Lemek seventy-seven times." This is a stock motif of royal excess. The *lex talionis*, the law of an eye for an eye and a tooth for a tooth, was a limiting law that stated the limits of retribution. We think of it as a cruel law, but its purpose was to reduce excessive retribution. An avenger might be tempted to kill ten members of a village in retribution for the crimes of one of its villagers. The *lex talionis* counteracts this kind of excess, permitting at most only one for one.

City culture emerged from Yahweh's attempt to dampen the revenge element by putting a protective mark on Cain. By this point in the story, revenge has instead gone rampant. Royal culture is supposed to suppress endemic revenge. In this exposé of royal urban culture, urban culture is exposed as the worst fosterer of revenge of all. The line of Cain and Ham is the foil to the line of Abram, Israel, Judah, and David. The king himself fosters excessive revenge in the foil. Contrast David's gracious treatment of his opponent in 1 Samuel, which portrays him as just a poor man caught in the middle who never did anything as bad as Lemek. He did everything

8. Patrick D. Miller, "*Yeled* in the Song of Lamech," *Journal of Biblical Literature* 85 (1966): 477–78.

possible to avoid laying hands not only on Saul but any of his kin or supporters. He had them killed only when they resisted.

Adam and Eve lived a long time in this history. Now, in the seventh generation, Eve again bore a son and named him Seth. Reflecting on the victimization of Abel, she concluded, "God has given me other seed in place of Abel." ("Given" in Hebrew sounds like Seth.) In other words, parallel to the birth of Lemek in the Cain line, there is a new birth to replace Abel. Cain stands for the ruler, Abel stands for the ruled. Eve reflected analytically on the meaning of the ruled and concluded that human beings don't control their lives. They don't manage life and death, as was presumed in her first statement that she, like a god, had created a man. She acknowledged that it was God who had given her this replacement for Abel: "God has given me . . . ." She had reached a new level of consciousness.

Seth bore a son and named him Enosh, whose name means the same as Adam's. The implication is that this is a new kind of man, the first human to be born in this new consciousness and the first in the eighth generation. J marks the beginning of the second set of seven generations by telling us that it was at this time that humans began to use the name Yahweh.

In the ninth generation of the genealogy in Genesis 5, from P, we encounter another Lemek, who is the son of Seth, the son of Adam (Gen. 5:25). Lemek in J was the son of Cain. In P's understanding of the genealogies of Cain and Seth, these two Lemeks are two different individuals. Noah is made the son of a Lemek (Gen. 5:28–29) in P's genealogy of Seth. As far as is known, J did not have a genealogy of Seth. If in J also Noah was the son of Lemek, the likelihood is that this Lemek was the son of Cain, making Noah[9] the eighth generation descendant of Cain.

9. Gen. 5:29 is a fragment of J embedded in P's genealogy of Seth.

10

The Beginning of Rain Agriculture

(Genesis 5:29; 6:1—10:7, parts)

Lemek fathered a son and named him Noah with these words, "This one will console us from our work and from the pain of our hands from the ground which Yahweh cursed."

As humans began to increase on the face of the ground, and daughters were born to them, the sons of the gods saw that the daughters of the humans were good. So they took for themselves as wives any they happened to choose.

Yahweh said, "My wind will not ... with humans forever. Since they are just flesh, their lifetime shall be no more than 120 years."

At that time there were big military elite men on earth, since after the sons of the gods had intercourse with the daughters of the humans, they bore sons to them. These sons were the perennial urban military elite, the men of name.

Yahweh saw that the evil of humanity on earth was great, and every formation of the devices of their minds was nothing but perpetual evil. So Yahweh regretted he had made humanity on earth and was pained in his mind. So Yahweh said, "I will erase the humans I created from off the surface of the ground, from the humans to the beasts, insects, and birds of the sky, for I regret that I made them."

Noah, however, found favor in the eyes of Yahweh. Yahweh said to Noah, "Enter, you and your entire household, the giant houseboat, since it is you I graciously look upon as the just man in this generation. Of all the clean beasts take for yourself seven of each kind, males and their mates (three pairs plus one for sacrifice), and of the beasts that are not clean take two of each kind, a male and its mate. Also of the birds of the sky, seven of each kind to keep alive their offspring over the surface of the whole earth, because in seven days I will cause rain to fall on the earth for forty days and nights, and I will wipe out all that subsists from off the surface of the ground."

Noah did everything Yahweh ordered him to. Noah, his sons, his wife, and his sons' wives with him entered the giant houseboat. The assigned number of clean beasts, unclean beasts, birds, and insects entered the houseboat with Noah.

When seven days were up and it began to pour on the earth for forty days and nights, Yahweh shut Noah in. The water increased and lifted the giant houseboat, and it rose above the earth. As everything on the dry land which had the breath of life in its nostrils died, Yahweh wiped out all that subsisted on the surface of the ground, human beings, beasts, insects, and the birds of the sky. While everything was wiped out from the earth, Noah and whoever and whatever were with him in the houseboat were left.

The sky cleared, and the waters gradually receded off the earth. At the end of forty days Noah opened the window he had made in the houseboat and let a dove loose to see whether the waters had lessened from off the surface of the ground. When the dove failed to find a resting place for the bottom of its foot, it returned to Noah in the houseboat. He put out his hand and received it and brought it into the houseboat. He waited another seven days, and again let loose the dove from the houseboat. When the dove returned to him that evening with an olive sprig in its bill, Noah knew that the waters had lessened from off the earth. He waited another seven days and let the dove go, and it didn't come back. Noah removed a cover from the houseboat and saw that the surface of the ground was dry. Noah, his sons, his wife, and his sons' wives came out of the houseboat.

Noah built an altar to Yahweh. He took one of every kind of clean beast and clean bird and offered them as total sacrifices upon the altar. When Yahweh smelled their delicious aroma, he thought to himself, "Never again will I derogate the ground on account of humans. Even if the formation of the minds of humans is so evil, I will never again kill all the living as I have just done. Henceforth each year on earth will consist of sowing and harvest, cold and heat, and late summer and early fall—these will not cease."

The sons of Noah who came out of the houseboat were Shem, Ham, and Jepeth. Ham became the father of Canaan. Noah, a man of the ground, planted the first vineyard. When he drank some wine, he became drunk and ended up lying uncovered inside his tent. Ham, destined to be Canaan's father, saw his father Noah naked and told his two brothers outside. Shem and Jepeth took a coat, placed it on their shoulders, walked backward, and covered their naked father. Since they faced out, they did not see their father naked. Noah awoke from his wine-induced stupor and knew what his second son had done to him. "Cursed is Canaan," he swore, "an utter slave will he be to his brothers." Then he added, "Blessed is Yahweh the god of Shem; let Canaan be their slave."

(The sons of Ham were Cush, Egypt, Put, and Canaan. The sons of Cush were Seba, Havilah, Sabtah, Raamah, and Sabteca. The sons of Raamah were Sheba and Dedan.)

Lemek fathered a son, who joined the eighth generation, and called his name Noah, of whom he said, "This one will *console*[1] us from our work and from the pain of our hands from the ground which Yahweh cursed." As indicated by the genealogical chart, Noah was a brother of the urban culture people. J takes his name to mean "alleviation" or "easement," a direct reference to his chief significance in J's scheme. Although Noah is generally associated primarily with what is commonly known as the "flood," in J this is secondary to his role as the one who introduces rain agriculture. While P makes much of the flood, in J the story of the "flood"

1. J understands Hebrew *yanahem* to allude to Noah's Hebrew name, Noh.

is brief and should more properly be referred to as the great downpour, in line with J's term for it, *geshem*. The significance of this downpour comes from its being the first rain in history. J tells us that at the conclusion of the downpour Yahweh instituted the seasons, which points to the seasonal character of the rainfall in Palestine being established in the eighth generation. Seasonal rains made possible the cultivation of the perennial, such as the vine, outside the original pleasure orchard.[2] The ground had been cursed so that men would hurt. For agriculture to continue outside the garden, Cain had to build a city that controlled irrigation of the grain fields and agriculture to the east—and, with the later birth of Egypt, to the west. This state-run irrigation system was constructed with the sweat of the peasantry and existed for seven generations. Now, in the eighth generation, at the start of a new set of seven generations, Noah's life would bring an alleviation of the pain of laboring for highly organized state-run agriculture.[3] Viticulture, the culture of the grapevine, is a less demanding form of agriculture in terms not of the seasonal activity but of the degree of backbreaking work and of peasants' relative control over the product. Plowing and harvesting are extremely arduous tasks, for which there is no equivalent in viticulture once the vineyard is planted.[4] A further meaning of the alleviation pointed to in Noah's name is that the wine from the grapes has a relaxing and restorative effect. The main alleviation wrought by Noah's rain-dependent vineyard, however, is the producer's hold on his land. Whereas arable was invariably under the ownership of the state, vineyards were held in freehold, the property of the individual, representing a security of possession not known to humanity to this point. (Compare 1 Kings 21:1–3; Micah 4:1–4.)

Noah does not, however, escape the association with royalty indicated by his having Lemek for his father. Grapevines have always figured prominently in the production of the lands in the vicinity of Hebron, David's first royal capital. The distinctive abundance of Hebron's grape production is noted in literary references all the way from J (Num. 13:22–24) to the nineteenth century.[5] Wine from grapes figured as a significant royal export

2. "For the land which you are entering to take possession of is not like the land of Egypt, from which you have come, where you sowed your seed and watered it with your feet, like a green garden; but the land which you are going over to possess is a land ... which drinks water by the rain from the sky" (Deut. 11:10–11).

3. Noah is placed beneath Adam in our genealogical chart, as both are concerned with perennials.

4. In recent times Palestinian peasants have been observed plowing in their vineyards periodically. For the work that vineyards involved, see Oded Borowski, *Agriculture in Iron Age Israel* (Winona Lake, Ind.: Eisenbrauns, 1987), 102–14.

5. C. Warren, "Hebron," in *A Dictionary of the Bible*, ed. J. Hastings (Edinburgh: T. & T. Clark, 1899), 2:339: "Luxuriant vineyards still clothe the hills and vales, and produce some of the best grapes in Palestine, and groves of olive and fruit trees abound." See also Yehuda Karmon, "Changes in the Urban Geography of Hebron During the Nineteenth Century," in *Studies on Palestine During the Ottoman Period*, ed. M. Ma'oz (Jerusalem: Magnes Press, 1975), 70–85.

product in pre-Islamic Palestine, and in nearly all periods as a characteristic component of royal conspicuous consumption. Most important, Noah is equivalent to the Mesopotamian flood survivor Atrahasis, who was without qualification a king.[6]

Following the birth of Noah, J describes conditions in the seventh and eighth generations, which J takes for rampant miscegenation of the divine and the human, a violation of the categorical distinction between creator and creature. Observing this miscegenation, Yahweh stated that his *ruach* (wind, or spirit) would not "strive," as the RSV ventures to translate, with humanity forever. The meaning of the Hebrew word used in this statement is not known, but the general sense of the passage is clear.

In those times the *nephilim* were in the earth. *Nephilim* means something like the "fallen ones," but they are not fallen in the sense of fallen down. More likely they are prostrate in leisure, like the elite in Amos 6:1–6. The verb "fall" occasionally means "encamp" or "spread out," as in Gen. 25:18 (see the RSV footnote), or like the Midianites and the Amalekites in Judg. 7:12. The RSV renders the Hebrew *nephilim* with the traditional "giants," following the comparison made in Num. 13:32–33. This is only part of its meaning. The *nephilim* are giants in the sense of mythically domineering figures of the past. This is elaborated at the beginning of the Deuteronomistic History with a political meaning like J's: according to D, the defendants of the kingdoms of Moab and Ammon were giants like the Anakim, who in turn were derived from the *nephilim* (Deut. 2:10, 21; Num. 13:33).

In fact, military elites tended to be considerably larger than the average of the population they dominated. In J's conception, three of these giant Anakim ruled vine-rich Hebron prior to David. The conjunction of the drowning of the forebears of Hebron's giant rulers with the invention of the vineyard so important to Hebron's agriculture, both as a result of the first great downpour, is no coincidence. These are the two main elements that J himself adds to the traditional urban history of the "flood" which he closely follows as his literary source, and they are a direct mirroring of David's capture of royal sovereignty over Hebron. As agriculture implies settlement, the ease of rain agriculture represented by the vine in J makes a subtle appeal to the bedouin elite in J's audience to ally themselves with David's state and, with other upwardly mobile followers of David, to enjoy the benefits of landownership allocated by David in Hebron, where viticulture was the primary source of agricultural wealth.

J is interested in more than the size of these men; he is also interested in what he characterizes as their *shem* ("name"). The significance of such a

6. Wilfred G. Lambert and A. R. Millard, *Atra-Hasis: The Babylonian Story of the Flood* (Oxford: Oxford University Press, 1969), 9–10.

"name" can be seen from 2 Chron. 26:8: "The Ammonites also gave tribute to Uzziah, and his fame *(shem)* extended to the border of Egypt, for he became very strong." Then the writer adds, "In Jerusalem he made engines, invented by skillful men, to be on the towers and the corners, to shoot arrows and great stones. And his fame *(shem)* spread far, for he was marvelously helped, till he was strong" (2 Chron. 26:15).

The divine sons had intercourse with the human daughters, who bore children called *gibborim*. The term signifies great warriors—what J calls men of "name" (RSV: "men of renown"). This is a reference to infamous warrior groups, or warrior classes. They were famous because they were able, possessing the self-made character of those who confuse the categories of divine and human. This is the actualization of Eve's first reproductive consciousness, at the birth of Cain, in a new form, the miscegenizing form—as though Eve had had intercourse with Yahweh himself.

Yahweh saw that the evil of humanity in the earth was great, so that the formation of the devices of their minds was evil perpetually. The key word here is *yetzer* ("formation"), because Yahweh takes this *yetzer* as the arrogation of his prerogative to create human beings, as he had "formed" *(yatzar)* the first human being. The *first* act of God was *yatzar,* to form something out of the dirt. Now these male lesser gods and human daughters were, like Yahweh, engaging in their own conception.

J tells us that Yahweh was pained in his own mind. He had imposed pain *(etzev)* upon the human beings; now these humans were making their own equivalent of his creation, and this was causing Yahweh pain *(etzev).* The pain lay in the violation of the distinction between god and human. So Yahweh formulated another plan: as the divine one, he would reject the imposition of this pain upon himself by the human abrogation of this category distinction.

J's history is not fatalistic, not predetermined, but one that unfolds, with Yahweh responding to historical developments. In modern terms, Yahweh is the God of the process theologian.[7] It lies within the historical process to counteract evil. There is no *deus ex machina* to remove evil. J is dealing with history as we know history in its reality, and his conception of Yahweh is that of a god who can feel—a compassionate god—who both affects and is affected by history. This will be the god who will be moved to deliver the bedouin from corvée labor in Egypt. He is not a god who simply hears the cry of these entrapped bedouin and cleanly intervenes, as in E or P, but he is the god who in J says, "I *know* their pain." God's passion is distinctive of

7. The experimental, catch-up quality of J's Yahweh was captured remarkably in Marcus Connelly's play *The Green Pastures* (1930) and the film based on it produced by an all-black company in the 1930s. Both were adapted in turn from Roark Bradford, *Ol' Man Adam an' His Chillun* (1928).

and essential to J's theology. It will be reiterated at that arch moment in the twenty-first generation when Yahweh goes to the one who killed the slave driver and says to him, "Moses, I know your pain." God's capacity to know pain is revealed first in the eighth generation.

Like the pain Yahweh felt in the time of Noah, the pain felt by the bedouin slaves was that created by pharaoh's abrogation of this same category distinction between divine and human. Pharaoh posed as god, just as Eve and Adam posed as god in naming Cain, and just as Cain posed as god in killing Abel. Pharaoh said, "I know not Yahweh. Who is Yahweh?" Pharaoh "knew" procreation and power but knew neither Yahweh nor pain. He would have to be taught.

Yahweh had intended through the birth of Noah to bring consolation to humanity. Now he regretted making humanity. There is a play on Noah's name here. Literally, Yahweh "consoled" himself with Noah. Although he regretted making humanity, he had found one human being to keep. "I will erase humanity whom I have created from off the surface of the ground, for I regret that I made them," Yahweh concluded. But Noah found favor.

No reason is given for why Noah was favored by Yahweh. In J, Yahweh's choice appears quite arbitrary. P, on the other hand, explains that he was a righteous man. In fact, in J Noah as a son of Lemek was potentially a dubious character, and he fathered Ham, another dubious character. There was nothing special about Noah before Yahweh picked him out. Yahweh is a god and can act as he pleases in sovereign arbitrariness. This arbitrariness serves to highlight the nonarbitrary selection of Moses later on, when Yahweh had one very good reason for his selection.

J's history is first and foremost the history of Yahweh. What J knows about Yahweh, he knows through all that Yahweh creates in the course of time. This history of how Yahweh continues to create in history is J's way of knowing who Yahweh is and what Yahweh stands for and against. We shall see that for humans to bless is most specifically to acknowledge Yahweh as the creator, whereas in the cursed generations humans themselves had initiated godlike creative acts. Noah and Abram represent windows, as it were, for glimpsing the character of Yahweh. Just as Noah found favor, we shall see that Abram became wealthy—not because he was a great man or righteous but because he was blessed by Yahweh. As the Hebrew expresses it, his name was made great by Yahweh rather than by himself. These key figures in J's history are described not for themselves but for what they reveal about Yahweh, David's state god.

If in his account of the creation of humans J departed somewhat from the Mesopotamian scribal tradition that the Davidic court had inherited, in his account of the great downpour he was beholden to that tradition. Indeed, parts of the tradition were so well known that J simply transferred them into Hebrew with very little change. In the traditions on which J drew, the flood story is the story of the creation of order. The flood stands for sociopolitical disorder. There are parallels between the *Atra-hasis* and J's story of the downpour, and at some points the two stories are almost identical. The social connotation of the flood in the *Atra-hasis* is that the peasants rebel as the flood washes up. J does not develop this theme in his story of the great downpour but saves it for the twenty-first generation and the "flood" at the Sup Sea.

Another repeated and essential theme of J's history is introduced when Noah builds an altar. This is the first altar to be built. Its construction occurs in the first generation of the second set of seven. When J brings us to Sinai to give us the stipulations of the cult, the prime stipulation will be, "You shall build an earthen altar"—as the ancestors did—rather than a temple and monumental altar. This is where the altar theme is headed.

Noah took the animals he had rescued and sacrificed from them. Yahweh savored this meal, then remarked, "I won't cause a destruction like this again, even if the formation *(yetzer)* of the minds of humans is so evil." Having created rain, Yahweh needed to impose some limits on rain if it wasn't to destroy all humans again. His scheme was that "all the days of the earth [each year on earth] will consist of sowing and harvest [fall and spring], cold and heat [winter and summer, or the wet and dry seasons], and late summer and early fall [the end of the dry season and the beginning of the rainy season]." This list of pairs focuses on the pattern of rains in Palestine. This controlled pattern is the primary outcome of the episode of the disastrous downpour.

Taking advantage of the seasons, Noah planted a vineyard. The RSV's translation of Gen. 9:20 is inadequate. Noah was not the first tiller of the soil, Adam was. The passage should be translated, "Noah, as a man of the ground, was the first one to plant a vineyard."[8]

Noah lay naked in his tent, and Ham, by accident but in line with his being the first son of Noah the descendant of Cain, "saw" his father's nakedness. (Wine in the ancient Mediterranean world was believed to enhance male virility.)[9] Although the incident was accidental, like previous accidents we have encountered in J it had profound implications. The motif of seeing nakedness takes us back to when Adam and Eve saw their nakedness, the consequence of which was the birth of Cain and the beginning of human history with its mixture of good and bad.

The first consequence of this new seeing is that the ninth generation,

8. This is a hendiadys in Hebrew. The New American Bible translates correctly. The idiom can be identified because it occurs elsewhere in J.

9. H. Hirsch Cohen presents the evidence in *The Drunkenness of Noah* (University, Ala.: University of Alabama Press, 1974).

paralleling the second generation, recapitulates the lines of Cain and Abel. The line of Cain is continued in the line of Ham, through Canaan and his brothers. (The reestablishment of urban kingship following the flood is found in many Mesopotamian traditions.) The incident also has implications that will not come to the fore until the story of Sodom and Gomorrah in the fifteenth generation; only then will we understand fully what Ham did.

Yahweh pronounced a curse upon Canaan because Ham saw his father's nakedness. The name Canaan may be a textual corruption, or an emendation by a later editor who wished for the purposes of his own time to focus on the Canaanites in Palestine, since one would expect the cursed son of Noah to be Ham, Canaan's father, the one who saw his father naked.[10] If in the original version of J it was Ham who was cursed, the Canaanites would be included along with Ham's other descendants. Canaan was to be the servant or slave of Israel. J typically uses "Canaan" to refer to greater Palestine's ruling classes.[11] In J's own time, the "Canaanites" or Palestinian urbanites did indeed function as the servants of the Davidic state, and there is evidence of Hamites serving the Davidic state. Uriah the Hittite, one of David's military leaders, was one of them. The Philistines, themselves Hamites, also served David. In fact, the main corps of David's palace guard and private army was "Hamite." The prophecy anticipates the reversal of the Canaanite role, which has been that of the elite, under Davidic rule. In all likelihood it also anticipates the climactic moment in the history when the Egyptians, also descendants of Ham, become Israel's servants.

In the Noah story in J there is a direct line from the rain, to the seasons, to the vineyard, to the drunkenness of Noah, to the cursing of Ham or Canaan. Noah should be seen as the son of Lemek because the story is not so much the story of the birth of Shem but of the birth of Ham and of the continuing of the cursed line of Cain through the cursing of Ham or Canaan (much as the Jonah story is not the story of the whale, which is a necessary incidental to the story, but is the story of the prophet).

There are sets of three in the generations of the sons, but J does not develop the relevance of all of the sons. While Shem and Ham are developed, Jepeth is not. Similarly, Cush and Canaan are developed, while Put is

---

10. A further textual corruption may be present in the appearance of the term *elohim* in this prophecy, since it is not normally used in this way in the J strand. Alternatively, the statement may belong to another strand.

11. This conception of "Canaanite" is quite different from that of D (Deuteronomy to 2 Kings), where the Canaanites form a nation in opposition to Israel. Canaanite appears to have meant basically Syro-Palestinian urban noble or trader; in the Bible, several different meanings have grown out of this one. There is no linguistic connection whatever between Canaan and Cain.

left unexplained. Cush, which here is Mesopotamia, together with Canaan and Egypt, is essential to the history.

The sons of Ham and Cush are given in P lists. It is assumed that P was here summarizing information in J material which was then discarded. The sons of Cush are listed as Seba, Havilah, Sabtah, Raamah, and Sabteca. Raamah's sons are Sheba and Dedan. These are all trading localities. For instance, Havilah, one of the places to which the rivers of the garden in Genesis 2 flow, has already been characterized as a land of precious stones, while Sheba and Dedan were on the route to the fertile lands and wealthy states of southern Arabia. Since these states may not have formed before the ninth or eighth century B.C.E., some of these specific names may have been added by P.

11

East of Eden

(Genesis 10:8—11:9)

Cush fathered Nimrod. He was the first armed warrior in the earth [in the second era]. He was a hunting warrior in the presence of Yahweh. (Therefore the saying goes, "A hunting warrior the likes of Nimrod in the presence of Yahweh.") The chief cities of his royal sovereignty were Babylon, Erech, Akkad, and Kalneh in the land of Shinar. From that land he went forth to Asshur and built Nineveh, Rehoboth-Ir, Calah, and Resen between Nineveh and Calah,[1] being the great city.

Egypt fathered the Ludim, the Anamim, the Lehabim, the Naphtuhim, the Patrusim, the Casluhim, and the Caphtorim, from whom the Philistines sprang.

Canaan fathered Sidon, his firstborn, and Heth; and the Jebusites, the Amorites, the Girgashites, the Hivites, the Arkites, the Sinites, the Arvadites, the Zemarites, and the Hamatites. Afterward the Canaanite groupings spread out so that the Canaanite borders extended from Sidon through Gerar to Gaza, over to Sodom, Gomorrah, Admah, and Zeboiim, as far as Lasha.

To Shem also, the oldest brother of Jepeth and the ancestor of all the sons of Eber, were sons born. The sons of Shem were Elam, Asshur, Arpachshad, Lud, and Aram. The sons of Aram were Uz, Hul, Gether, and Mash. Arpachshad fathered Shelah, and Shelah fathered Eber. To Eber two sons were born. The name of the first was Peleg, for in his time the earth divided; the name of his brother was Yoqtan. Yoqtan fathered Almodad, Shelep, Hazarmawet, Yerah, Hadoram, Uzal, Diqlah, Obal, Abima'el, Sheba, Ophir, Havilah, and Yobab. (Peleg fathered Terah.)

At that time the whole earth had one language and one set of words. As they migrated eastward, they found a valley in the land of Shinar and settled there. There they said to one another, "Come, let us make clay bricks and prepare a fire for hardening them." The bricks were their stone, and for mortar they used bitumen. They said, "Come, let us build a great city-tower, with its top in the sky, that we may make for ourselves a name, lest we be scattered over the face of the whole earth."

Yahweh came down to see the great city-tower that the humans were building. Yahweh said, "If as one people with one language for all of them they have started to do this, nothing will stop them from whatever they presume to do. Come, let us

---

1. Calah may be a later addition. See E. Lipiński, "Nimrod et Assur," *Revue Biblique* 73 (1966): 89.

go down and there confuse their language, so they won't be able to understand what each other is saying." So Yahweh scattered them from there over the face of the whole earth, and they stopped building the city. (Thus it is called Babylon, because there Yahweh confused the speech of the whole earth.) This was the way Yahweh scattered them over the face of the whole earth.

Cush bore Nimrod, who was the first one to be a *gibbor* in the earth. The Hebrew means "armed warrior," and we have already encountered it in Gen. 6:4. *Gibbor* and "man of name" are synonymous. Nimrod is not the first mighty warrior in the history but the first in the new set of seven generations, in the line of Cain, following the annihilation by the great downpour.

We are told that Nimrod was a hunter. What J refers to is not simply the origin of hunting, as if these were primitive peoples.[2] Nimrod should be understood in terms of several famous friezes from the Neo-Assyrian period in which the Assyrian king is shown in his ritual hunt. This is an urban royal motif and shows the connection between Assyrian royal violence as expressed in the hunt and the exercise of power. The Assyrians actually captured lions, tigers, and leopards, setting them loose for the king to hunt as an act of power.[3] (Lions existed in the Near East until the nineteenth century.) The Egyptian version of this practice was known in southern Palestine in the Late Bronze Age, when Palestine was under Egyptian suzerainty. A Late Bronze scarab, or beetle-shaped seal, discovered recently at the site of the ancient city of Lachish shows a pharaoh aiming his arrow at a lion in a thicket. A second, inscribed scarab, also from Lachish, describes how Pharaoh Amenhotep III, who ruled in the fourteenth century B.C.E., hunted one hundred and two lions during the first ten years of his reign.[4] This is not a motif limited to the ancient world. The royal hunt has been a ritual expression of royal prerogative and power through the ages.[5] The stories of Robin Hood poaching the king's deer in Sherwood Forest relate directly to this motif, and the fox hunt in which the

2. In P, the killing of animals for food occurs in the tenth generation, and the reference to Nimrod in J is coincidentally also in this generation. But in P, hunting is a matter of diet and begins when humans begin to eat meat in addition to plants. Diet is not what J is referring to.

3. A. Leo Oppenheim, *Ancient Mesopotamia: Portrait of a Dead Civilization* (Chicago: University of Chicago Press, 1964), 46; Pauline Albenda, "Lions on Assyrian Wall Reliefs," *Journal of the Ancient Near Eastern Society of Columbia University* 6 (1974): 1–27; and idem, "Landscape Bas-Reliefs in the *Bit-Hilani* of Ashurbanipal (Part 2)," *Bulletin of the American Schools of Oriental Research* 225 (1972): 29–48.

4. David Ussishkin, "Lachish: Key to the Israelite Conquest of Canaan?" *Biblical Archaeology Review* 13:1 (January/February, 1987): 18–39. The first scarab appears on p. 30, the second on p. 26.

5. See John K. Anderson, *Hunting in the Ancient World* (Berkeley and Los Angeles: University of California Press, 1985).

English gentry still participate is a vestige of this elite ritual act. The point of the royal hunt is that as the king destroys the lion, so he will destroy his human enemies. This is the significance of Nimrod the mighty warrior hunter.

Nimrod reigned over the cities of Babel, Erech, and Akkad in the land of Mesopotamia. From that land he went forth to Assyria and built Nineveh, Rehoboth-Ir, Calah, and Resen. Rehoboth-Ir means "the wide places of a city," which connotes an expansive city. J also uses the expression "the great city," which is a motif that will be picked up immediately after the listing of the generations is complete, in Genesis 11. Just as Cain built the first city, the sons of Ham continued to build cities. J wants to convey the image of the line of Cain as all city dwellers who have no nonirrigation agriculture.

J has two great imperial foils to the Davidic state, one being Mesopotamia and the other Egypt. These were the two great historical threats to Palestinian political autonomy. Structurally, J focuses on Mesopotamia in the second set of generations, the eighth through the fourteenth generation. Beginning with the fifteenth generation, at the outset of the third set of generations, he will switch the focus to Egypt.

Canaan bore Sidon and Heth, the ancestor of the Hittites. The Hittites were a significant people in terms of political economy, but they are subsumed under the Canaanites because of their relatively subsidiary role by the time we come to the period of David in the tenth century. Recall that Uriah in the service of David was a son of Heth, the son of Canaan.

A list of peoples is now subsumed under Canaan, greater Palestine's ruling classes. It is a cosmopolitan grouping, a fair characterization of Palestinian urban society, which typically consisted of many outsider types—which is why it is not appropriate to characterize even Canaanite urban society as a single social or culturally uniform entity. The urban Canaanite often had allegiances to an ethnic identity quite apart from his elite social identity in Palestine.

The line of Shem brings us to the fourteenth generation, by which time the building of many large cities resulted in the attempt to build one colossal city. It is in this generation that the events of Gen. 11:1–9 occur. J begins by observing that the whole earth spoke one language.[6] This episode deals with a standard tradition in the ancient world, of a king

6. We do not know whether "the whole earth" refers to all humanity or to all the Canaanites. J has told us in Gen. 10:18–19 that the Canaanites were scattered over the whole of the land of Palestine, and the beginning of Genesis 11 may be a reference to this. The motif of the confounding of a common human language has now also been discovered in cuneiform literature, from the Ur III period about 2000 B.C.E.; see Samuel Noah Kramer, "The 'Babel of Tongues': A Sumerian Version," *Journal of the American Oriental Society* 88 (1968): 108–11.

leading his people to build a temple-tower. An early example of this from the Ur III period is from the Sumerian king Gudea. When Gudea wished to build the temple of Ningirsu, the city ruler gave directions to the population of his city as to a single man, and Lagash, the city in which the temple of Ningirsu was built, followed him unanimously like the children of one mother, as he put it.[7]

So the tradition of building the great city-temple contains the motif of the unanimity of behavior, which is what is behind the motif of all humanity sharing a common language and joining in this enterprise. J wants readers to understand that all humanity are affected by the intent of the Cushites— the Mesopotamians—who have already been portrayed as building great cities. Now they build with a vengeance, the greatest city of all, as J characteristically takes Nimrod's city-building to the extreme, forcing Yahweh to make some extreme response as he did with the great rain.

Within this scene there are the rulers and the ruled, though the latter are partially invisible. There are the taskmasters and the workers, just as there will be when the Egyptians build their grain-storage cities in the twenty-first generation, seven generations after this building effort of the fourteenth generation. The masses are forced to do this work on behalf of the name-making sons of Ham.

While the story of Yahweh's opposition to the building of the great temple-tower undercuts the unanimity projected by royalty upon the people of the realm or empire, its greatest significance is that it prepares the ground for the primary cultic law of J and David, which is opposed to the city-temple and portrays the cult as utilizing an earthen or fieldstone altar.

They were building a city-tower, for which there are two models in the ancient world of J's time. Within the Palestinian context it was the stone-built urban citadel tower, which was generally a temple-tower. The citadel tower served as the main fortress for a city population. Archaeologists have unearthed an apparent good Late Bronze example of such a temple-tower at Shechem, in the region covered by the highland heartland of David's kingdom. A Palestinian would have known the Shechemite example, as evidenced by Judges 9, the story of Abimelech of Shechem, a king. One of the features of Shechem is what is referred to as a *migdal*, or tower.[8] The

7. A. Falkenstein and W. von Soden, *Sumerische und Akkadische Hymnen und Gebete* (Zurich and Stuttgart: Artemis, 1953), 150.

8. Judg. 9:46–52. See G. Ernest Wright, *Shechem: The Biography of a Biblical City* (New York: McGraw-Hill, 1965), 94–97, 120–21; Yohanan Aharoni, *The Archaeology of the Land of Israel* (Philadelphia: Westminster Press, 1982), 110–11, 124–25; William G. Dever, "The Contribution of Archaeology to the Study of Canaanite and Early Israelite Religion," in *Ancient Israelite Religion: Essays in Honor of Frank Moore Cross*, ed. P. D. Miller, Jr., et al. (Philadelphia: Fortress Press, 1987), 209–47, esp. 231–33; and the chart in Volkmar Fritz, "Conquest or Settlement? The Early Iron Age in Palestine," *Biblical Archaeologist* 50 (1987): 89.

biblical story of "premonarchic" Shechem thus actually makes reference to a modest version of this structure.[9]

The more important model is the literary-historical Mesopotamian scribal source motif of the clay-brick ziggurat. There is a considerable amount of information in the scribal documents of the period based on this motif.

The temple-tower that the fourteenth-generation humans were building was an urban shrine of a particular kind. This was the earthly home or way station of the deity. The Hebrew expression for this structure is *ir umigdal,* which reads literally "a city and a tower" or "a city and a great one." The expression is a hendiadys, meaning a great tower-city.[10] *Ir* can also be taken in its meaning of temple precinct and the whole phrase translated temple-tower. Or it could mean great city. We have been encountering the *ir,* or city, motif ever since Cain built the first city. The temple is a feature of the city. City, temple, palace, and grain-storage facility are all typically related in a single urban complex. *Ir umigdal* refers specifically to the temple character of the city, the fortress that served as the prime architectural representation of the power of urban humanity throughout the agrarian era.[11] *Ir umigdal* might well be translated as a city crowned by a temple-tower.[12]

The humans say, "Come, let us build a great city-tower, that we may make for ourselves a name *(shem)."* J has made a great deal of naming and the significance of names as part of his treatment of the meaning of reproduction. This motif began when the first human named all the animals and then the woman; it continued with the woman naming Cain and Enosh, with Cain naming his firstborn son and the city he built by the same name, and with other namings. To make or have a name means among other things to have offspring, to engage in reproduction, and to gain fame through other acts of power as well. Beginning with the sons of Noah, there existed a man and then a genealogy whose name was "Name," Shem and

9. For the association of power, towers, and name, compare again the description of King Uzziah in 2 Chron. 26:8, 15: "Uzziah's name spread to the border of Egypt, for he became very strong and built towers in Jerusalem . . . and fortified them. . . . In Jerusalem he made engines to be on the towers and corners, to shoot arrows and large stones. His name spread far."

10. The RSV translates "a city, and a tower" (Gen. 11:4) and "the city and the tower" (Gen. 11:5), both times missing the point of the single meaning of the combined expression.

11. In the generation after David, Solomon heavily fortified the most vulnerable side of Jerusalem, its north side, by having his palace and dynastic temple built there.

12. The building of the temple-tower in the fourteenth generation climaxes the set of cities and temples built following the subsiding of the flood. In the myths of temple-building, the temple is invariably built following the defeat of the sea. The bronze sea in Solomon's temple is a symbol of this sequence.

his descendants. The descendants of Shem joined those attempting to "make their own name" by building the great city-tower.

The language of the building of the city-tower in J is similar to the language used for the building of Babylon in the *Enuma elish*. It speaks of a house with its foundations in both earth and sky. What is being described is a great tower that binds heaven and earth. It is not only the house of the god but the avenue from sky to earth, the architectonic center of the earth, the pillar of the world through which the divine reaches down into the human. It is the Babylonian equivalent of Bethel ("temple of God") in Gen. 28:12–13, containing, according to the conception of the supplement by E, a great palatial stairway that joins the world of the gods with the world of humans. Another name for this place was *esangil*, meaning the house with its head lifted, with its head in the sky (RSV: "its top in the heavens"). These are generic conceptions for the great temple-city at the capital of the state, of which there are many examples in ancient literature.

The annals of Sennacherib contain an account of improvements in his capital Nineveh:

A piece of land 340 cubits on the side, 289 cubits on the front, out of the bed of the Khosr River in the plain about the city I measured off according to plan. To the plot of the former palace terrace I added it, and *raised* the whole of it to the height of 190 units. *I raised its head....* Those palaces all around the large palace I beautified to the astonishment of all nations. *I raised aloft its head.* "The palace temple that does not have a rival," I called its name. In a favorable month, a propitious day, with the aid of the master builders and the wisdom of the priests, I built its foundations of mountain limestone. *I raised its head,* its foundation as well as its walls. I constructed it entirely of mountain limestone. I raised it up mountain high. Two irrigation ditches I dug around its sides and encircled it with a garden of abundance and orchards. With luxurious plantations I surrounded its sides.[13]

What is described is the temple citadel palace of the god, which is the archetype of the king's palace. Such structures were normally surrounded with the equivalent of the garden of Eden. It is an attempt to reinstitute the urban basis for the garden of Eden culture.

Even earlier, in Sumerian building inscriptions, the builder or restorer of the temple was referred to as "the man who built such and such temple." For providing the temple's expenses, including the personnel, the king was

13. D. D. Luckenbill, *The Annals of Sennacherib* (Chicago: University of Chicago, 1924), 105–6, 110–11, 137. Compare this description of Hammurabi's thirty-sixth year of rule: "He restored the temple 'The Pride of the Hero' and built the temple tower, the mighty abode of Zababa and Inanna, whose top is in the sky, and thus he greatly increased the glamor of Zababa as well as Inanna in a pious manner." See James B. Pritchard, *Ancient Near Eastern Texts Relating to the Old Testament,* 2d ed. (Princeton: Princeton University Press, 1955), 270.

styled *sangush*, "the one who raised the head" of such and such temple. In other words, this was a distinctively royal activity. The raising of the head into the sky alludes back to the miscegenation of Genesis 6, with both the miscegenation and the raising of the temple's head into the sky constituting in J's view a violation of the distinction between divine and human.

In the *Enuma elish*, the Babylonian epic describing the creation of the Babylonian state, the raising of the city-tower to the sky is spoken about in exactly the same terms.[14] Says the *Enuma elish*: "The first year they made its bricks. When the second year had arrived, as for *esangila*, 'the house with its head raised high,' the counterpart of Apsu [the subterranean depths], they raised high its head." When the temple was completed, and its lands and workers created, the gods then pronounced the fifty names of Marduk in order, thus in effect making a name for him. The making of Marduk's name brings to a conclusion the building of the Mesopotamian equivalent of the *ir umigdal* in J's history.

In the *Odyssey*, book XI, which describes Odysseus's journey to the underworld, Odysseus relates:

After her I saw Iphimedeia, wife of Aloeus, but she told me how she had been joined in love with Poseidon and borne two sons to him [a reference to miscegenation, though in this tradition it has a meaning different from J's], Otos like a god, and the far-famed Ephialtes. And these were the tallest men the grain-giving earth has brought forth ever, and the handsomest by far, after famous Orion. When they were only nine years old [these two giant famed men of a union of gods and humans] they measured nine cubits across, but in height they grew to nine fathoms, and even made threats against the immortal gods on Olympus, that they would carry the turmoil of battle with all its many sorrows against them. And were minded to pile Ossa on Olympus and above Ossa Pelion of the trembling leaves, to climb the sky.

They were building mount upon mount at the site of the temple Olympus. "Surely they would have carried it out if they had come to maturity, but the son of Zeus whom Leto with auburn hair had borne him, Apollo, killed them both, before ever the down gathered below their temples, or on their chins the beards had blossomed."[15] This is the Homeric parallel to J's *ir umigdal*.

As already pointed out, Ben Sira in the second century B.C.E. observed, "A birth and a city make a name last" (Ecclus. 40:19). The significance of

14. For a complete and well-illustrated study of the "Tower of Babylon" and its political significance, see Evelyn Klengel-Brandt, *Der Turm von Babylon: Legende und Geschichte eines Bauwerkes* (Leipzig: Koehler und Amelang, 1982).

15. *The Odyssey of Homer*, trans. Richmond Lattimore (New York: Harper & Row, 1965), 176.

the building of the tower to make a name is summed up in this single line of courtly wisdom concerning what a name implies. The next line of this quotation reads, "The firstborn of the beasts and the plantings cause a name to sprout." The first line refers to human reproduction and the city, as in Psalm 127, while agricultural productivity is separated into the second line. The whole motif of sex and city begins with the creation of the woman, for which the verb *banah* ("build") is used.[16] There is in J's ear the association of *banah* and *ben*, building and children, as in Psalm 127. The *bn* combination runs through this story. The word for bricks is *laben*, a third like-sounding term. This gives a new meaning to *banah*, namely, the clay brick used to build the imperial cities of Mesopotamia and Egypt, which are a symbol of the dynastic household that has been built through reproduction. That's why this brick-building motif fits with J's history. East and West, Mesopotamia and Egypt, are portrayed in terms of building great brick cities, even though they don't fit the immediate highland Palestinian mode of stone building.

---

16. Gen. 2:22 (RSV: "made"). In Eastern Mediterranean Semitic tradition the creator god El is known as *bny bnwt*, and in the creator Ea/Enki's Sumerian epithet *nu–dim–mud*, *mud* is the equivalent of *banah*.

12

A New Approach

(Genesis 11:27—13:18)

(Terah fathered Abram, Nahor, and Haran, and Haran fathered Lot.) Haran died before Terah his father, in the land of his birth and kinship base and network, Ur of the Chaldeans. Then Abram and Nahor took wives for themselves. The name of Abram's wife was Sarai, and the name of Nahor's wife was Milkah the daughter of Haran the father of Milkah and the father of Yiskah. Sarai was childless: she had no child.

So Yahweh said to Abram, "Go from your land, your birthplace and kinship base, and your father's household, to the land I will point out to you, that I may make you into a great nation, that I may bless you and make great your name. And so be a blessing that I might bless those who bless you and curse those who derogate you, that you might be the means of blessing for all the kinship groupings of the ground."

Abram went as Yahweh told him to, and Lot went with him. They came to Canaan, and Abram passed through the land as far as the shrine of Shechem, the oak of Moreh. The Canaanites were then in the land. There Yahweh appeared to Abram and said, "To your descendants I will give this land." So Abram built there an altar to Yahweh, who had appeared to him.

From there he moved on to the hill country east of Bethel and pitched his tent with Bethel on the west and Ai on the east. There he again built an altar to Yahweh and invoked Yahweh by name. Then Abram journeyed by stages in the direction of the Negev.

There was a famine in the land, so Abram went down to Egypt to reside there temporarily, since the famine was severe in the land. As he approached Egypt, he said to Sarai his wife, "I know that you are a beautiful-looking woman. When the Egyptians look at you, they will say, 'She is his wife,' and kill me and let you live. So say you are my sister, so that I can benefit on your account and my life may be spared for your sake." When Abram entered Egypt, the Egyptians looked at the woman, since she was so beautiful. When pharaoh's courtiers saw her, they praised her to pharaoh. So she was taken into pharaoh's household. In the meantime Abram benefited on her account: he received flocks and herds, male and female slaves, male and female asses, and camels. But Yahweh struck pharaoh with severe plagues, and his household as well, because of Sarai, Abram's wife. So pharaoh

99

summoned Abram and said, "What have you done to me? Why didn't you tell me she was your wife? Why did you say, 'She is my sister,' so that I took her as my wife? Here, then, is your wife. Take her and go." Pharaoh gave men orders concerning him, and they sent him off with his wife and all he had gotten.

From Egypt Abram went up to the Negev, with his wife and all he had gotten, and with Lot. Since Abram was now extremely rich in cattle, silver, and gold, he proceeded by stages to Bethel, to the shrine where his tent was earlier, between Bethel and Ai, to the place where the altar he had made earlier was. There Abram invoked Yahweh by name.

Lot, who had gone with Abram, also had flocks, herds, and tents, and a dispute arose between the herders of Abram's cattle and the herders of Lot's cattle. The Canaanites and the Perizzites were at that time the local landowners. Abram said to Lot, "Let there be no strife between me and you, or between my herders and yours, for as men we are brothers. The whole earth lies before you. Why not separate from me? If you prefer the left, I will take the right. If you prefer the right, I will take the left." Lot surveyed the view and saw how well watered the entire lower Jordan basin was—before Yahweh had devastated Sodom and Gomorrah—like Yahweh's own garden, or like Egypt, as far as Zoar. So Lot chose for himself the whole lower Jordan basin and set off toward the east. In this way the brothers separated. Abram settled in the land of Canaan, and Lot settled among the cities of the basin, pitching his tents just outside Sodom.

The men of Sodom were extremely evil and sinful to Yahweh, but Yahweh made the following pronouncement to Abram, after Lot had separated from him: "Lift your eyes and see, from where you are, to the north, south, east, and west. The whole land you can see I will give to you, and to your descendants in perpetuity. And I shall make your descendants like the dirt of the earth: if anyone could count the specks of dirt, then your descendants could be counted, too. Proceed to traverse the length and breadth of the land, for to you I will give it." So Abram decamped and went and settled at the oaks of Mamre by Hebron, and there built an altar to Yahweh.

With the genealogy of Shem completed in the story of the city-tower, the Bible's first history has come to the beginning of a new era. This new era, stretching from the fifteenth to the twenty-first generation, will receive far more development than either preceding era.

Historians have long noticed a difference between the history before the fifteenth generation and the history that commences with the fifteenth generation. The usual designation of the first fourteen generations is the primeval history, by which is meant a history that is mythic rather than realistic. Beginning with the fifteenth generation, the history is generally regarded as realistic. Such a distinction mattered little to J. It is our intention to treat the whole of J's history as fantasy that addresses historical issues in the reign of David. While J's history points to the historical conditions of the Davidic kingdom, the history draws its images from traditional sources. So far in his history J has made much use of mostly

Mesopotamian traditions, which are known from cuneiform copies of literature copied and studied in the scribal workplaces of cities throughout the ancient Near East. J's sources up to this point might therefore be categorized as urban literature. From now on, the main traditional source of J's material will be traditions characteristic of the bedouin of south-western Palestine. Historians generally label the traditional sources of these later generations "saga." While some of these traditions may go back in part to the lengthy period of the spread of village settlement under the direction of bedouin and others, the reason J employs bedouin traditions is not primarily that bedouin played a role in the emergence of the highland settlements that became village Israel but rather that bedouin played a role in the emergence and maintenance of David's state.

The fifteenth generation is the era of Abram, the son of Terah, the son of Shem. J says little about this family, but what he does tell us relates directly to the issues we have been dealing with all along. There are apparently three brothers—Abram, Nahor, and Haran. Ur of the Chaldees is described by a term usually translated "the land of their birth," but is perhaps more relevantly to be understood to mean the land of their "bearing," the land of their secure place within the system of reproduction and kin. There Abram and Nahor have taken wives. Abram's wife is named Sarai; Nahor's wife is Milkah. Milkah, like Lemek, contains the root for royalty and means "queen." Sarai means "noble" or "royal one."[1] The royal connotation of these names indicates that J intends to explore in depth a new meaning of urban royal culture as it is expressed through the reproductive system. This should not mislead us into understanding Abram and Sarai simply as urban royal figures. Like all sons of Shem, and particularly the children of Abram, including Israel himself and his descendants until the twenty-second generation, Abram and Sarai were pastoral nomads or bedouin. There is an ambiguity in Abram's name, which means "the father is high." Is the high father Abram himself, father-to-be; or is it Yahweh, the creator and hence father of his human creatures? This question more than any other overarches the whole of the history of the fifteenth generation.

As Yahweh has reacted to or interacted with his creatures during the preceding fourteen generations, history in general has been evil. J represents these first fourteen generations schematically as the time of the curse, involving hardship, social stratification, and rule by inordinate force.

Now, in the fifteenth generation, Yahweh adopts a fresh approach to his creatures, an approach diametrically opposed to the curse. He "blesses" one individual and intends that as all other creatures bless this one, they

---

1. Sarai is often translated "princess," but the difference between the wives' names is not to be emphasized. In Hebrew poetic diction, the two roots appear in parallelism to signify the simple idea of royalty or aristocracy.

too shall be blessed. The history of evil will then eventually be transformed by a history of good. Evil will not disappear. Human beings will forever bear the curses and the tragic heritage of the first fourteen generations. But history will be ameliorated. Humans will have the opportunity, by acknowledging the blessing of Abram and his heirs, through will and action to make life better in the political, economic, social, and religious arenas as J understood them.

The transformation of history that begins here is signaled by Abram's leaving a place called "Ur of the Chaldees" (Ur in Mesopotamia). Given J's propensity to derive meaning from names at important junctures in the history, one is not surprised that he makes direct allusion to the curse (*arur*): the blessed human being leaves the land and the era of the curse behind. The journey from Mesopotamia is not the seasonal nomadic wandering over the family's territory but a migration from one place to another. Provincial peoples elsewhere are known to have thought of themselves as having migrated from a cultural center to the periphery where they live. Abram's migration from Mesopotamia may, however, have as much to do with J's adoption of the Akkadian concept of early humanity as with a common Israelite sense of cultural derivation.

Where Abram was to migrate is not immediately explained. He ended up walking all the way to Egypt, but several incidents of note occurred along the way, one of which proved to be the turning point of the whole history: on the way Yahweh blessed Abram.[2] The terms of the blessing are important enough to examine closely. Abram was to go from his land and from his secure place within the reproductive and kinship culture of his homeland, and from the house of his father (all three of these phrases—land, birthplace, house—are essentially synonymous and reinforce each other),[3] to the land that Yahweh would show him, in order that Yahweh might make him into a great nation and that he might bless him by making great his name. As the one blessed by Yahweh, Abram himself would in turn become a blessing: Yahweh would bless those who blessed him and curse those who despised him,[4] that he might be the means of blessing for all the

2. Although it is an important matter, we do not present an abstract definition of curse and blessing. Our preferred approach would be to define curse in relation to blessing, and blessing in terms of the specific ways in which it is fulfilled. This approach is not meant to confuse the meaning of the specific curses of the first fourteen generations but to enable us to focus on the dialectic of curse and blessing as schematized by J.

3. The expression "the house of my father" occurs twice in the Amarna letters from the king of Jerusalem to the pharaoh in the fourteenth century B.C.E. (EA 286:9–13; 288:14) to mean rule or dominion in an inheritance: "Look, it wasn't my father or mother who put me in this place, but the powerful hand of (you) the king has led me into the house of my father."

4. The emphasis is on blessing; cursing is merely its counterpart. See Patrick D. Miller, "Syntax and Theology in Genesis XII 3a," *Vetus Testamentum* 34 (1984): 472–75. Miller's point is confirmed by the way Balak's curse must yield of necessity to Balaam's blessing at the conclusion of J.

families of the ground. The terms of the blessing—the birth of a male heir, the growth of the blessed individual into a great nation, and residence within a given territory—correspond directly to the major issues raised in the history of the first fourteen generations.[5] Those issues are given a new cast, set in a new framework, and assigned a new meaning in the fifteenth generation.

The contrast with the preceding history is obvious. It is a simple contrast, and we must not allow the several terms of the blessing to cause us to lose sight of it. In the fourteenth generation, the descendants of Shem worked to make their own name. In the fifteenth generation, Abram, a son of Shem, is arbitrarily selected by Yahweh and instructed to remove himself from his reproductive and productive context, from the household of his father, the whole context in which he would bear offspring. Yahweh intends to make Abram's name great away from this context so that it will be clear that Yahweh did it and not Abram himself. Here the word "name" has all the meanings that have become known to us from the history to this point: progeny, power, fame.

The history, readdressing in so many ways the issue of procreation in this new generation, reveals to us a striking circumstance: the wife of Abram was childless.[6] J has painstakingly related how X bore Y, Y bore Z, and so forth, to set us up for the surprise that the birth of Abram's son Isaac will be initiated by Yahweh, not Abram. Abram thus neither builds a city nor creates for himself offspring through his wife Sarai. This is the contrast that separates the men of name in the fourteenth generation from the man of name in the fifteenth, the generations of the curses from the first generation of the blessing.[7]

Abram's independence from his father's reproductive and productive context reflects David's own rise to power with diminishing assistance from his immediate kin. Some of his brothers are said to have joined him in his early banditry. Perhaps these were younger brothers like himself. His increasing dependence on his mercenary palace guard headed by Benaiah from southwestern Judah (the Kerethites and Pelethites) and his willingness to shift blame to his sister's nephew Joab, the head of his people's militia, show that he became what he was in the beginning—self-reliant and beholden to no one, except Yahweh. When he did support relatives, as

5. The royal basis of the elements of this pivotal blessing is splendidly laid out on the basis of both biblical and other ancient Near Eastern parallels by Eberhard Ruprecht, "Der traditions-geschichtliche Hintergrund der einzelnen Elemente von Genesis XII 2–3," *Vetus Testamentum* 29 (1979): 444–64.

6. Today in our cultural context we would say the couple, not the wife, was childless. This is not the cultural assumption of J.

7. The similar but not identical expression addressed to David in 2 Sam. 7:9 has often been compared.

when he appointed his apparent stepson Amasa after the revolt of Absalom, it was for particular political reasons, in this case to regain the loyalty of a Calebite in Hebron.

The meaning of Yahweh's declaration that those who bless Abram will be blessed is directly related to this central issue of just who it is that makes Abram's name great. The unfolding of the history will make it clear that for others to bless Abram will mean for them to acknowledge that the greatness of Abram's name is a creation of Yahweh. The conception is essentially identical to the royal blessing of prosperity and justice stemming from royal progeny and extending to "all nations" contained in Ps. 72:17: "May [the king's] name be forever, may his name have increase before the sun; may [all nations] gain blessing by him, and all nations call him fortunate."

Abram's migration to Egypt was broken by a stop midway through the northern Palestinian highland at Shechem. Here Yahweh appeared to Abram and pronounced a momentous and ominous grant: "To your descendants I will give this land." As David's scribe describes it, this grant was nothing less than the historical basis of the house of David's presumption to rule the mountains of Palestine and the surrounding territory. J tells us that Abram was in the land of the Canaanites at this point on his journey, in the heart of northern country later of great interest to J in the person of Joseph. The potential conflict between Abram's descendants and the Canaanites anticipated by Yahweh's pronouncement never actually took place, because in J's conception the two groups did not occupy the same places, with a few exceptions. The Canaanites, children of Ham and hence urbanites like the children of Cain, lived in cities and not throughout the land itself. The description of David's capture of his own Canaanite capital, Jerusalem, makes little of armed hostilities between the two groups (2 Sam. 5:6–8). The close contact did produce tension, but the elaboration of this tension is limited in J to stories such as the rape of Dinah in Genesis 34.

The point of the grant of the Canaanites' land to Abram is thus not necessarily the quasi-national conflict between Canaanites and Israelites (as it is in D) but rather the issue that grows as the history proceeds at length before the grant is actually consummated: when and how will Abram's descendants inherit this grant? This question comes to dominate the history at the point where Abram's descendants become comfortably settled on land granted to them by the king of Egypt and it therefore becomes questionable whether Yahweh's grant made here at Shechem will ever be fulfilled. In other words, the issue is developed more in terms of a Hamite royal prerogative—the granting of land in Egypt—exercised contrary to Yahweh's blessing, than in terms of a conflict between Abram's descendants and the city-dwelling Canaanites of Palestine.

J states that Yahweh appeared to Abram. The different strands of the

Tetrateuch, written as they are in different historical contexts and therefore from different theological perspectives, describe the presence of God in their own distinctive ways. In J, Yahweh typically appears in the presence of someone. He looks like a man. The narrator will sometimes even refer to him as a man or a genie.[8] The distinctiveness of J's description becomes clear when it is compared with E and P. In E, God typically appears at a distance, in visions or dreams, or through an intermediary such as a messenger or a prophet. In P, God appears most characteristically in the presence of the cloud of smoke that forms over the sacrificial altar of the tabernacle described in detail by P.

As Noah had done at the beginning of the second set of generations, so Abram, at the beginning of this third set of seven generations, built an altar to Yahweh. J's history of the world is told in relation to the cult of the Davidic state. It is a cult of the simple altar and emphatically not a temple cult, and hence the building of this altar by the first blessed individual becomes an essential paradigm for the good cult. As Yahweh through the land grant begins to make Abram's name great, the contrast to the building of the great temple-tower at Babel, analogous to the Late Bronze tower at Shechem, for making a name in the preceding generation is striking. This all-important contrast is immediately reinforced by the story that frames Abram's journey to Egypt and back, the building of a second altar near Bethel and his return there.[9]

Bethel lay along the highland ridge farther south than Shechem and slightly north of Jerusalem, itself straddling the same ridge. By the time of David, Bethel had already for several generations played a significant role in the history of the peoples who under David became known as Israel. It was apparently one of the primary highland sanctuary towns prior to the formation of the Davidic state. After the secession of Israel from the house of David, following the death of Solomon, it again became the primary sanctuary of non-Davidic Israel. Given the modesty of David's state cult, it is not likely that Bethel served as Israel's principal sanctuary during this entire period.

It may be symbolic that Abram built his second altar between Bethel and Ai rather than at Bethel itself. J is anxious to describe the cult of the house of David as a non-temple cult. Bethel, as we have already noted, means "temple of god," and having Abram build his altar in Bethel would have

---

8. The RSV uses the word "angel." This word has come to denote created beings of a supernatural character. What is intended by the Hebrew text of J is not a being separate from Yahweh but a popular and accessible representation of Yahweh—his genie.

9. The opposition to temple-building and favoring of pilgrimage presented through the contrast between the temple-tower and Abram's altar is discussed by Jack R. Lundbom, "Abraham and David in the Theology of the Yahwist," in *The Word of the Lord Shall Go Forth*, ed. C. L. Meyers and M. O'Connor (Winona Lake, Ind.: Eisenbrauns, 1983), 203–9.

been a good way to root a temple cult in the history of Abram. But J intended the opposite: David's non-temple cult of the land is grounded in the history of Abram's altar in the countryside, away from the "temple of God."[10]

The individual stories of Abram correspond nearly one for one with the main stories of the preceding generations. J schematically reverses each main event in the cursed generations through the events in Abram's generation:

Adam and Eve in the garden	Abram and Sarai in Egypt
Cain and Abel	Abram and Lot
Cities and kings from Cain to Lemek	Abram and the kings of Sodom and Salem
Miscegenation of gods and humans	Birth of Isaac initiated by Yahweh, a god
Ham sees Noah's nakedness	Hagar sees herself pregnant
Noah is drunk and "knows"	Lot's daughters get Lot drunk, but what his daughters do he does not "know"
The city-tower, the "big one"	Lot escapes Sodom, fleeing to the city Mits'ar, the "little one"

Abram and Sarai's relationship while in Egypt is, for J, a reversal of Adam and Eve as *ish* and *ishsha*, man and wife, and hence of the relationship that produced Cain. Their story has to be read not just at the level of what happens but also at the level of the words that are used. "Say you are my sister," Abram instructed Sarai. You can often tell what a story is about by the point that is repeated at the beginning and the end. At the end of the story, pharaoh speaks, returning to the conversation at the beginning of the story: "She is not your sister, Abram, she is your wife." They were man and woman, but Abram said, in effect, "We are not man and woman." Why did he say this?

One should relate this incident as clearly as possible to the issues already posed by J rather than psychologize the story, trying to explore what was going through Abram's mind, how Sarai felt about this abuse, or any of a number of other obvious concerns that would occur to a reader of this incident in our modern cultural context. Abram's statement was in response to being confronted with the typical behavior of the sons of Cain and Ham. Abram had no food. He was dependent upon the king of Egypt, who was the son of Ham and heir to Cain's royal cultural line. He was not only dependent, he was in dire jeopardy. Like any royal "son of Cain," the king of Egypt could kill him and take his wife. This is the Lemek mentality

---

10. Abram traveled on the main road between Shechem, Bethel, and Hebron, and from there to the Negev. All these are important highland cities. Abram is not a petty shepherd but a big sheikh, destined to get bigger. He had urban connections, building an altar outside each city: his settlements were adjunct to city culture.

dramatized. Abram knew that this man had the power to kill him and take his wife. J wants his readers to see him as one who says, "If such a mentality is a consequence of the human claim to the man-woman relationship, then I will reverse that claim." Instead of seizing conjugal rights as did Adam and Eve, Abram gave up these rights. (The chance that pharaoh might make Sarai pregnant J probably rules out because of her childlessness.)

The king of Egypt as a son of Ham had perpetrated completely unjustifiable behavior, in terms of the values represented in J, by seizing Abram's wife. So Yahweh attacked pharaoh and his "house"—a term that encompasses his family, his household, his estate, his dominion, his inheritance, his power base, his power. (Pharaoh means "great house" in Egyptian.)

The reversal of the man-woman implications of the history of the first generation led to a substantiation of the blessing. Abram became magnificently wealthy. J is anxious to portray those whom he wishes to project as the prime ancestors of Israel as no poor peasants, for as David's scribe he would prefer both bedouin and peasants to believe that they will prosper under David's rule. The prosperity comes, furthermore, from abroad, not through oppression at home.

This is the first of many examples of positive irony in J. Those who follow in the line of Cain and Ham will in the history of the blessing eventually participate in the blessing, constrained by Yahweh as projected by this optimistic, upwardly mobile narrator. Thus this king of Egypt, a prefigurement of the pharaoh who subjects the children of Israel to corvée, ends up pronouncing Abram and Sarai man and wife and sending them off with the equivalent of a stupendous wedding gift. The man-woman relationship has been given a new meaning in the history of humanity.

Abram departed from Egypt, traversed Sinai, and entered the Negev. With him, J tells us, he had his wife and all who belonged to him, including Lot his nephew (or, as the text will say, his "brother"). Abram, J repeats, was "very rich in livestock, silver, and gold." The word for livestock is *miqneh,* the word that means capital. Recall that in J's view it is based on the same root as the name Cain. Abram's history portrays an alternative history of amassing wealth, a way of blessing that contradicts the way of Cain and Ham. Hence it is justifiable.

It is not by accident that J stresses the great wealth of Abram at just this point. In terms of the correspondence between the history of Abram and the history of the first fourteen generations, we have come to the story of Cain and Abel. Cain and Abel's conflict grew out of their common wealth. The fact that they both prospered not only did not prevent their conflict but could even be said to have led to it. The question in the reader's mind at this point must be, Will not Abram murder Lot as Cain murdered Abel, and if not, how will he avoid it?

Lot was also very wealthy with *miqneh*. Their capital (flocks and herds) expanded so successfully that the land available to them ran out. Their herdsmen began to fight with each other. This was not simply a fight over scarce resources, in this case grazing. The expansion of the brothers' capital had brought them to the critical point of the fissioning of the social unit. In sociological terms, this represents the possibility of the creation of a competing and hostile group. A harmonious large and strong herding band is threatened in its success with fragmentation. Such bands have a propensity for fissioning.[11] How will this fissioning result in continued alliance rather than hostility?

The answer is: through Abram's deference, the reverse of Cain's jealousy. "As men we are brothers," said Abram. The Hebrew expression puts the emphasis on brothers. "We can't fight." Abram recognized that if there was to be fission in the extended family, it should be fission on peaceable, not hostile, terms. The nephew-uncle relationship was not so important; what mattered was the avoidance of hostility between brothers. Two parties to a treaty were brothers, if not blood brothers, and this reversed the fratricide of the second generation.

Abram offered his "brother" the first choice of the best land. Yahweh's response to this deference was to give precise definition to the grant of land referred to in his earlier oath to Abram. Abram's descendants would receive the length and breadth of Palestine visible from the heights of Bethel at nearly three thousand feet. Lot selected land to the southeast—land "now," in David's time, occupied by the Dead Sea. In Abram's time, prior to the destruction of Sodom, this was luxuriously well watered land, so lush that J could compare it only with Eden—"like the garden of Yahweh." In this "garden" the men of Sodom lived a nonheterosexual life, like Adam and Eve in the earliest garden.

After making the grant of land to Abram at Bethel, Yahweh concluded, "I shall make your seed like the dirt of the earth, which, were it able to be counted, your seed would equal in number." One of the primary values of the bedouin tribe, especially from the point of view of the head of the tribe, is the unlimited increase in the tribe and its resources, along with the avoidance as much and as long as possible of any breakup in the tribe.

We have already discussed the value to J and the Davidic court of a reduction in blood feud in the kingdom. Here, in the reversal of the Cain-Abel story, we can recognize J's adoption of this primary nomadic value as

11. See the summary in Karen E. Paige and Jeffery M. Paige, *The Politics of Reproductive Ritual* (Berkeley and Los Angeles: University of California Press, 1981), 126–39.

the vehicle by which he will treat positively the avoidance of blood feud. ✓ The theme of the reconciliation of brothers in conflict is introduced here in a way that allows us to see its basis in specifically bedouin culture.

Abram then moved to Hebron. It is said that the city of Hebron was founded in the Late Bronze Age (Num. 13:22). This is not confirmable, because it is not possible to excavate most of Hebron since the present-day city is built directly over previous cities at the site. However, highland cities like Hebron tend to be few in number and stable over a long period of time. The persistence of urban sites in the highland contrasts with the variability of urban sites in the lowlands. Thus from at least the Late Bronze Age until the present, the main cities of the central Palestine mountains have been Shechem in the north, Jerusalem in the center, and Hebron in the south. Hebron lies on the edge of a marginal area of settlement in Palestine, where the shifting line of settlement (toward and away from arid lands) represents the degree of political organization at any given time. It is thus a center for both village and bedouin culture, and these two cultures have met each other there in an urban setting since the founding of the city. David's monarchic dominion was founded at Hebron partly as a result of the close relationship between agrarian and bedouin factors in his rise to power.

Abram built an altar to Yahweh at Hebron, which henceforth served as the primary place of the blessed human being. This feature of Abram's history links Abram directly to the founding of the monarchic dominion of the house of David in Hebron. This comparison has often led to the identification of Abram with David, but such an identification is not correct. David was not bedouin. The issue is the projection of a bedouin "national" identity upon the Davidic kingdom, which was at least 80 percent non-bedouin. The story we are about to read makes the first portrayal so far in J of a genuinely David-like figure.

13

Two Kinds of Royalty

(Genesis 14:1—15:6)

When Amraphel was king of Shinar, Aryok the king of Ellasar, Kedarlaomer the king of Elam, and Tidal the king of Goyim, they made war against Bera the king of Sodom, Birsha the king of Gomorrah, Shinab the king of Admah, Shemeber the king of Zeboyim, and the king of Bela (that is, Zoar). The latter five kings joined forces in the Valley of Siddim (what is now the Salt Sea [or Dead Sea]). For twelve years they had been subject to Kedarlaomer. In the thirteenth year they had rebelled. In the fourteenth year, Kedarlaomer and the kings with him had come and defeated the Rephaim at Ashteroth-Qarnayim, the Zuzim at Ham, the Emim at Sheweh-Qiryatayim, and the Horites in the mountains of Seir, as far as El-Paran on the edge of the desert. Then they had turned around and come back to En-Mishpat (that is, Qadesh) and subdued the entire territory of the Amalekites, as well as the Amorites settled in Hazazon-Tamar. At this point, as indicated, the king of Sodom, the king of Gomorrah, the king of Admah, the king of Zeboyim, and the king of Bela (Zoar) marched out and drew up battle lines against them in the Valley of Siddim: against Kedarlaomer the king of Elam, Tidal the king of Goyim, Amraphel the king of Shinar, and Aryok the king of Ellasar—these four kings against the five.

Now the Valley of Siddim had bitumen pits everywhere. When the kings of Sodom and Gomorrah fled, they fell into these. The survivors fled to the hills. The victors took all the possessions of Sodom and Gomorrah and all their food and went off. And they took Lot, Abram's nephew, and his possessions, since he was settled at Sodom, and went off.

A fugitive came and reported to Abram as potential head of a mercenary band, while he was encamped by the oaks of Mamre the Amorite, the brother of Eshkol and Aner, who were in league with Abram. When Abram heard that his brother had been taken captive, he drew out his forces and made pursuit as far as Dan. He and his men split up against them by night, attacked them, and pursued them to Hobah north of Damascus. He brought back all the possessions of the cities, and Lot his brother and his possessions he brought back as well, along with the women and the other captives.

At his return from defeating Kedarlaomer and the kings with him, the king of Sodom went out to meet him in the Valley of Shaweh (that is, the King's Valley).

But suddenly Malkitsedeq, the king of Salem, brought out bread and wine. As he

110

was a priest of El Elyon, God Most High, he greeted Abram with a blessing in these words, "Blessed be Abram by El Elyon, maker of sky and earth, and blessed be El Elyon, who has delivered your enemies into your hand," and gave him a tenth of everything.

The king of Sodom said to Abram, "You give me the people and keep the goods."

But Abram said to the king of Sodom, "I hereby swear by Yahweh, El Elyon, maker of sky and earth, that I would not take a thread or a sandal thong or anything that is yours, lest you should say, 'I have made Abram rich.' Nothing for me except what my lads have consumed, and the share of the men who went with me—Aner, Eshkol, and Mamre, let them take their share."

Afterward Yahweh said to Abram, "Don't worry. I am your protector, and your reward will be very great."

Abram said, "Lord Yahweh, what are you going to give me, considering that I go on 'stripped'? You have not given me offspring, and a son of my household (not my own) is now destined to become my heir."

Yahweh's response went as follows: "This one is not to be your heir, but one who will come forth from your loins will be your heir."

Yahweh led him outside and said, "Look at the sky and count the stars, if you can count them. Thus will be your descendants."

In trusting Yahweh, he considered it his right.

This is our first major passage that is not commonly ascribed to the J source.[1] From Abram on, J mentions many specific places and names. Historians have been inclined to seek out factual correspondences to these, and this passage has been treated almost exclusively in terms of what precise place and time it refers to rather than its relation to the rest of J.[2] When it is treated in relation to J as a whole, one can begin to recognize the thoroughly J-like character of this incident. The vocabulary, style, and point of view all indicate the J source, though our attention will focus mainly on the point of view.

For fourteen years, during the fifteenth generation of humanity, one of the eastern kings had held the Canaanite kings in subjection. The Canaanite kings now rebelled, and the eastern kings came to put down the rebellion. Four kings from the East (Shinar), presumably kin to the likes of Babylon, did battle with five kings from the region settled by Lot in Canaan.[3] This conflict is between sons of Ham.

The kings of the East defeated the Canaanite kings, who fled into the mountains surrounding their territory. Some of them fell into bitumen pits.

1. Many critical commentaries discuss the supposed difficulties of the source analysis of this passage.

2. This is well illustrated in the commentaries, where one can find this passage assigned to every age of biblical history from the Middle Bronze to the fourth century B.C.E.

3. One of these kings is named Tidal. He is said to be king of Goyim, which means "nations." This is possibly one of J's generic characters, a king whose name signifies kings with nations in general.

What on earth could that refer to? We need only change the question slightly to find its answer. Sodom and Gomorrah represent urban royal culture. What does bitumen have to do with urban royal culture?

The only way J could talk about the region lying at the foot of the Dead Sea, which in David's time was a barren wasteland as it is today, as a Canaanite region was to identify the cities that marked it, since the Canaanites lived only in cities. Apart from these cities, the region was used for bedouin herding as well as for bitumen gathering and mining for interurban trade. The foot of the Dead Sea contains significant asphaltic deposits, and bitumen was probably the main trade item originating in this area. Bitumen had many uses in antiquity, particularly prior to the classical period. Much of the bitumen used in Mesopotamia and Egypt was exported from this area. It served as a bonding element in the clay-and-vegetable bricks that were used in buildings for the elite;[4] as a waterproofing agent, as in drainpipes, bathrooms, urban pools, embankments, dikes, and shipping containers; and for road building, specifically for roads used for ritual purposes, not general all-purpose roads.

Equally significant was the location of the five Canaanite cities. Sodom was the main city in the southeastern region of the area that David came to control. Gerar, Hebron, Sodom, and Beersheba are where J concentrates his stories, spreading his attention all along this area of which Sodom was a part. The Dead Sea represented an effective barrier between east and west in southern Palestine. It is no accident that one of the three main highland cities, Jerusalem, was located on exactly the same latitude as the upper end of the Dead Sea. Nor is it an accident that J's interest focuses on cities in the barren area parallel to the foot of the Dead Sea, which were the exchange points of trade going east and west in Palestine. Hence the geopolitical and economic importance of this region to the house of David went beyond the fact that it lay in that marginal region skirting the whole southern end of Judah, where David rose to power, and included also its strategic location in terms of east-west exchange. The picture of the kings of this region falling into bitumen pits is a way of drawing attention to these significances.

Victorious, the eastern kings seized the goods of the Canaanite kings and headed north. They captured Lot and his goods, taking him with them. This capture brought Abram into the drama. Abram acted out the generic role of the bedouin ally of the urban elite, who in this case had a direct

---

4. "In general practice. . . , the use of burnt bricks [with bitumen] [was] confined to the construction of palaces, temples and the like." "To the Babylonians . . . [bricks bonded with asphalt] represented something which men referred to as a symbol of stability." R. J. Forbes, *Studies in Ancient Technology,* 2d ed. (Leiden: E. J. Brill, 1964), 1: 67–74.

familial interest in reversing the outcome of the battle.[5] He overtook the kings north of Damascus, another trade center, defeated them, and returned with the stolen goods and folk to the region of the Canaanite kings at the foot of what was to become the Dead Sea.

When he arrived, two kings came out to meet him. One of them was the king of Sodom, whose name was Bera. In Hebrew, Bera means roughly "with evil," or simply "evil." The king of Gomorrah's name, Birsha, means roughly "with wickedness," or "wickedness." The characterization inherent in these names fits with J's characterization of the sons of Cain and Ham and does not surprise us. In the era of the curse, royal consciousness was epitomized by Lemek's assumption of the prerogative to murder and by his failure, implied in the contrast between himself and Seth, to "know" Yahweh. J wishes to show that a style of kingship quite different from that of the Hamitic line of Babylonian and Egyptian kings is possible.

The second king we have not yet encountered. His name is Malkitsedeq, roughly "the king is just,"[6] and he comes from the city of Salem, which is related to *shalom*—"justice and prosperity"—and stands unmistakably for Jerusalem, the eventual capital of the Davidic monarchy.[7] The kings met, we are told, in the *King's* Valley: precisely here we are to discover the two possible alternative natures of kings. To do so, we must listen carefully to what they said and what Abram said to them in return.[8]

5. Abram is said to have gathered together a force of 318 men. This time the specificity of the narrative is to be attributed not to J but to someone who revised the narrative in the time of the priestly writer or later (the Hebrew phrase translated "born in his house," Gen. 14:14, is a P expression). The number 318 is the numerical value of the letters added up in the name Eliezer in Genesis 15. This is a typical example of the later changes in the text. Eliezer means "my God is a help," so the 318 men are Abram's help.

6. In one Ugaritic text, the king of Ugarit is styled *b'l ṣdq*, the "just lord," and in another the king of Egypt is called *mlk ṣdq*, the "just king." These texts come from only three centuries or so before David. The root *ṣdq* is a common element in names ("ṣ" stands for "ts"). Nevertheless, its use for pharaoh is especially interesting considering the ultimate contrast in J between pharaoh and the king of Jerusalem, here styled as the just king. See Keith W. Whitelam, *The Just King* (Sheffield, Eng.: JSOT Press, 1980); and P. Bordreuil, "Les récentes découvertes épigraphiques," in *Ugarit in Retrospect*, ed. G. D. Young (Winona Lake, Ind.: Eisenbrauns, 1981), 47.

7. In the fourteenth-century B.C.E. cuneiform letters from Palestine to Egypt, Jerusalem is written *u-ru-sa-lim*, possibly a learned double-entendre, as *uru* can also mean "city," thus "city of Salim (Salem)." In Ps. 76:2, Salem is synonymous with Zion.

8. It might be asked whether Malkitsedeq is a son of Ham. It is possible that J intended to separate Malkitsedeq from that category precisely by means of the awkward way, to our sensibilities, in which he is introduced: he comes out of nowhere. The situation, however, is ambiguous, and it is not clear to what extent J wanted to address the issue in these terms. Later on in his history he will characterize the population of the Davidic territory more generally in terms of peoples all apparently descended from Ham, including the Jebusites associated with Jerusalem. A king of Jerusalem named in the Deuteronomistic accounts of the time of Joshua was named Adonitsedeq, "the lord is just." The similarity between this name and Malkitsedeq is obvious, but the exact reason for the similarity is not.

Both kings were eager to address Abram. The king of Sodom approached him first, but the king of Salem apparently got ahead of him and was the first to speak. "Blessed be Abram," he announced. Our minds leap back to Yahweh's oath, "I will bless those who bless you," where "bless" means to recognize the role of Yahweh in a person's success and prosperity. Hence we are interested to know the god in whose name Malkitsedeq blessed Abram. "Blessed be Abram by El Elyon." The god was El Elyon, El the Exalted, characterized further as the "maker of sky and earth." "Maker" is Hebrew *qoneh*, formed from the same root from which J derives the name Cain. In other words, Malkitsedeq attributed to this god, in a way consistent with the values embodied in J, the whole of the act of creation, the converse of the meaning of Eve's pronouncement, "I have created. . . ." The exact identity of this god comes out only in Abram's response to the king of Sodom, which we must anticipate to understand the point fully: "I have sworn by Yahweh, El Elyon. . . ." It turns out that Abram took El Elyon generically to mean "the exalted god," Yahweh, and so heard Malkitsedeq's response as though he had said, "Yahweh bless you . . . and blessed be Yahweh who has delivered your enemies into your hand."

Nearly every English translation of Gen. 14:20 says that Abram gave Malkitsedeq a tenth of everything. For Malkitsedeq to be blessed with a tenth of Abram's goods in return for blessing Abram may seem appropriate to modern readers, but this is not an accurate rendering of the Hebrew at all. The Hebrew says only, "He gave him a tenth of everything." Who gave whom a tenth? Malkitsedeq was the king, and Abram in this situation something like a mercenary servant. We only need to ask ourselves what would be the likely exchange in this kind of situation to realize that it was Malkitsedeq who gave Abram a tenth, as payment for his services, of what Abram had brought back. The exchange between Abram and the king of Sodom makes it clear that the king rewarding Abram is the point. Furthermore, just this point links this story with what follows immediately as Abram continued to wonder when his full award from Yahweh, going back to Yahweh's oath, would be fulfilled. The reason the passage has been misunderstood is that Abram is the protagonist and will be the benefactor. But the spotlight isn't on him in this narrative. Abram was the occasion for the shining of the spotlight on first one king and then the other, so as to focus on precisely what distinguished them.

By this time the king of Sodom had worked his way into the spotlight. "You give me the people and keep the goods," he said. A very generous offer, but how different from Malkitsedeq's pronouncement. There was no blessing, no mention of Yahweh. This is the difference between a just king and an evil king. The one blessed Abram in the name of Yahweh, the other did not. Abram's response makes clear that this is precisely the distinction:

"I hereby swear by Yahweh, El Elyon, maker of sky and earth, that I would not take a thread or a sandal thong or anything that is yours, lest you should say, 'I have made Abram rich.' " The statement "I have made Abram rich" is the exact opposite of "blessed be Abram by El Elyon who created." It denies the role of Yahweh in an individual's success in the same manner as Eve's "I have created. . . ."

In these kings, J is representing the polarity between "evil" (Sodom) and "just" (Jeru-Salem) kingship. The portrayal of the just king is the portrayal of David. Malkitsedeq in this narrative anticipates David. The acknowledgment of Yahweh in the mouth of Malkitsedeq is an encapsulation of the Davidic court's projection of the national god. The just king for J is not any king in general who attributes his prosperity to a god, but *the* king—David—who attributes Davidic prosperity to the Davidic national god. J is nationalist, not prophetic.[9] The Davidic kingdom is the just kingdom, whereas all other empires are evil. No son of Ham will ever make this attribution of his success to god, only sons of Shem.[10]

The literary analysis of Genesis 15 is debated.[11] There are one or two indications in the beginning of the chapter that remind critics of the E strand (the mention of "vision" and the statement "fear not"). Beginning with v. 7, much if not all of the chapter is quite uncharacteristic of J.[12] Because of the difficulties in the literary analysis, it is preferable to take a minimalist approach and interpret the parts of Gen. 15:1–6 that fit well with the construction put on J so far. This includes most of this passage, with the exception of a few phrases in the first two verses.

Abram had declined the compensation offered by the king of Sodom. But in direct continuation with his fair expectation of compensation in

9. As P. Kyle McCarter, Jr., comments, "Apologetic writing presents unfavorable circumstances forthrightly in order to cast a favorable light on them by a variety of literary means." See *Interpretation* 35 (1981): 360 n. 12, and *II Samuel*, Anchor Bible (Garden City, N.Y.: Doubleday & Co., 1984), 13–16. In actuality David did not live up to the royal ideal of J. Just to take J's prime issue of corvée as an example, David was not against corvée, as his treatment of the Ammonites in 2 Sam. 12:31 shows, and he probably instituted it in Israel as well. There are good literary reasons for not regarding 2 Sam. 20:24—"and Adoram was in charge of corvée"—as coming late in David's reign. J characteristically describes a disreputable trait of royalty and then defuses its reference to David by tying it polemically to a son of Cain or Ham, particularly Egypt.

10. Pharaoh, a son of Ham, will bless Moses, but only temporarily.

11. In some ways the most interesting treatment of the latter part of the chapter is by John Van Seters, who interprets the whole chapter as a mélange of types brought together at a late period. Cf. John Van Seters, *Abraham in History and Tradition* (New Haven, Conn.: Yale University Press, 1975), 249–78.

12. Critics have rather widely taken the last verse of the chapter, describing the extent of the land grant to Abram, as the clearest statement of J's notion of the Solomonic empire. When J is interpreted as Solomonic, as it usually is, there is perhaps some justification for such an analysis; if J is Davidic, as is indicated here, there is little reason to regard Gen. 15:18–21 as necessarily J.

return for services, he turned to Yahweh to ask about the fulfillment of the god's oath regarding offspring. Given his expanding wealth, it was natural that he should be concerned about an heir. "What will you give me, considering that I continue 'stripped'?" he pressed. "You have not given me an heir, and a son of the household [not my own] is now destined to become my heir." Yahweh's response was: "This one is not to be your heir, but one who will come forth from you will be your heir." Yahweh led him out into the night and invited him to count the stars, if possible. "So many will be your descendants," he assured him.

What was Abram's response? Notwithstanding a slight awkwardness in the syntax of what follows, Gen. 15:6 tells us that Abram trusted Yahweh's reiteration of his oath because he regarded the promise of "name," or progeny, as his right. For those familiar with the writings of Paul in the New Testament, this translation of Gen. 15:6 will look strange indeed. In order to interpret the J source, however, one has to bracket prior under- standings, including those made in later parts of Scripture, so as to under- stand what a particular phrase, line, or story meant in an earlier context.

It is no accident that this brief section of Abram's history concludes with the word "right" in reference to Abram's progeny, since the main point of the whole history of the birth of Isaac is the rightness of it. Indeed, it is the perceived rightness, since Abram regarded Yahweh's fulfillment of the oath concerning an heir to be "right." The distinctive element of Malkitsedeq's name—ṣedeq (meaning "right" and "just")—becomes the key term for understanding the second half of the history of Abram, which relates the birth of Isaac.

14

A Birth That Meets with Approval

(Genesis 16:1–15; 18:1—19:38; 21:1–2a)

Abram's wife Sarai had borne him no children. She had, however, an Egyptian slave named Hagar. So Sarai said to Abram, "Since Yahweh has prevented me from bearing children, have intercourse with my slave. Perhaps I shall be 'built' from her."

Abram heeded Sarai. Sarai the wife of Abram took Hagar her Egyptian slave and gave her to Abram her man as wife. He had intercourse with Hagar and she got pregnant. When she saw she was pregnant, she looked on her mistress Sarai with disdain.

Sarai said to Abram, "The violence done me be upon you. I put my slave in your lap, and when she sees she's pregnant, she ends up disdaining me. Let Yahweh judge between us."

Abram said to Sarai, "Here is your slave back. Do to her what you want."

Sarai abused Hagar, and she fled from her. Yahweh's genie found her by a spring in the desert, the spring on the way to Shur, and asked her, "Hagar, slave of Sarai, where have you come from and where are you going?"

She answered, "I am running away from Sarai my mistress."

The genie of Yahweh said to her, "Return to your mistress and submit to her." And the genie of Yahweh said to her, "I will make your descendants so numerous they will be too many to count." And the genie added, "You are pregnant. When you give birth to a son, name him Ishmael, since Yahweh heard your affliction. He will be a wild ass of a man, and his hand will be on everything and the hand of everyone on him, and he will encamp before all his brothers."

Hagar named the Yahweh-genie talking to her: "You are El Ro'i, God of My Seeing," since she said, "Have I even seen here after the one who sees me?" (Thus the well is called Beer-Lahai-Ro'i, between Qadesh and Bered.)

Hagar bore Abram a son, and Abram named his son whom Hagar bore Ishmael.

Yahweh appeared to Abram at the oaks of Mamre. Abram was sitting at the entrance of his tent during the heat of midday when he looked up and saw three men standing by him. When he saw them, he ran from the tent entrance to meet them. Bowing to the ground, he said, "If I have found favor in your sight, do not go on past your servant without stopping. Let some water be brought, and wash your feet, and then rest yourselves under the tree. Let me get a bit of bread so you can sustain yourselves. Afterward you can pass on. Surely for this reason you arrived in the first place."

They said, "Very well, do as you have indicated."

So Abram hastened into the tent to Sarai and said, "Quick. A large bowl of fine flour. Knead it and make bread loaves." Running to the herd, Abram took a calf, tender and good, and gave it to the boy, who quickly prepared it. Then he took curds and milk together with the calf which had been prepared, and set these before them. He stood by to serve them under the tree while they ate.

They said to him, "Where is Sarai your wife?"

He said, "In the tent."

One of them said, "When I return to you about the living time, as I shall, Sarai your wife will have a son."

Now Sarai was listening at the entrance of the tent, which was behind him. Abram and Sarai were old, having arrived in their years, and Sarai had ceased to menstruate. Still, Sarai "laughed" inside and thought, "After my wearing out, have I had sexual pleasure, with my master being old?"

Yahweh said to Abram, "Why has Sarai laughed, thinking 'Shall I truly bear a child when I am old?' Is a matter too wonderful for Yahweh to accomplish? I will return to you at the right time, about the living time, and Sarai will have a son."

Sarai dissembled, "I did not laugh," because she was afraid.

But Yahweh said, "You did so laugh."

The men got up from there and looked down toward Sodom before them. Abram was walking with them to see them on their way. Yahweh was thinking, "Am I covering up from Abram what I am doing? After all, Abram is to become a great and mighty nation through whom all nations of the earth are to be blessed, since I have known him precisely in order that he might give instruction to his offspring and his house who inherit him, that they might keep the way of Yahweh and perform justice."

Then Yahweh said, "The cry of injustice of Sodom and Gomorrah is indeed great, and their sin is exceedingly grave. Let me go down and see whether they act completely according to the cry that is coming to me, or whether not—let me know."

While the men turned and went on in the direction of Sodom, Yahweh remained standing in front of Abram. Abram came up and said, "Are you really going to sweep away the innocent with the guilty? Perhaps there are fifty just men in the city. Will you then sweep it away? Will you not forgive it on account of the fifty just men in its midst? On no account would you want to do such a thing, killing the just with the wicked, and treating the just and the wicked alike. On no account would you do that. Is the judge of the whole world not going to do justice?"

Yahweh said, "If I find in Sodom fifty righteous men, in the midst of the city, then I will forgive the whole place for their sake."

Abram answered, "Here I am presuming to speak to my lord, even though I am dirt and ashes, but what if there are five less then fifty righteous men? Will you destroy the whole city because of the five?"

Yahweh said, "I will not destroy it if I find forty-five there."

Abram spoke again to him. "What if only forty are found there?"

Yahweh said, "I will not do it for the sake of the forty."

Then Abram said, "Let my lord not get angry if I keep asking, but what if you find only thirty there?"

"I won't do it if I find thirty there."

"I presume again to speak to my lord, but what if there are only twenty?"

"I will not destroy it for the sake of the twenty."

"Now let my lord not get angry if I speak this one more time, but what if there are ten there?"

"I will not destroy it," said Yahweh, "for the sake of the ten."

Yahweh went on when he had completed speaking to Abram, while Abram returned home.

The two genies arrived at Sodom in the evening. Lot, sitting at the gate of Sodom, saw them and arose to meet them. Bowing his face to the earth, he said, "Welcome, my lords. Come aside to your servant's house to spend the night. Wash your feet, and in the morning go your way."

"No," they said, "we will spend the night in the street."

He urged them greatly, however, and so they turned aside to his place and came into his house. Lot prepared for them a meal. He baked flat cakes, and they ate.

Before the genies went to bed, the men of Sodom, both young and old, every last one, surrounded the house. They called to Lot, "Where are the men who came to you tonight? Send them out to us so we can know them." Lot went out to them and stood in the entrance, closing the door behind him.

"Do not act wickedly, my brothers. I have two daughters who have not known a man. Let me bring them out to you, and do to them as you wish, only do not do anything to these men, for they have come under the shelter of my roof."

"Stand back," they said. "First this guy comes as an immigrant, and then he presumes to judge. We will do worse to you than to them."

They pushed hard against the man, against Lot, almost pushing in the door behind him. The men inside put out their hands and brought Lot in to them inside the house and shut the door. The men at the entrance of the house they struck with blindness, from the youngest to the oldest, so that they became exhausted trying to find the entrance.

The men inside said to Lot, "Does anyone else here belong to you? Son-in-law, sons, daughters, anyone you have in the city, take them out of the place, for we are about to destroy this place, since the cry of their injustice is great in the presence of Yahweh, and Yahweh has sent us to destroy it." Lot went out and spoke to his sons-in-law who had taken his daughters in marriage.

"Get out of this place," he said to them, "for Yahweh is about to destroy the city." But the sons-in-law thought he was laughing.

As dawn broke, the genies urged Lot, "Take your wife and your two daughters who are here, or you will be swept away in the punishment of the city." When he hesitated, the men grabbed his hand and the hands of his wife and two daughters, since Yahweh had mercy on him, and took him out and set him outside the city.

When they had taken them outside, one of them said, "Flee for your life. Do not look back, and do not stop anywhere in the basin. Flee for the hills, lest you be swept away."

"No, my lords," Lot said to them. "Your servant has found favor in your eyes such that you have done me a great favor and saved my life. But I am not able to flee to the hills. The disaster will overtake me and I will die. Look, this city right here is near enough to flee to, and it is a little one. Let me escape there. It is little. There my life will be spared."

"I grant your request," he said to him. "I grant you also this request, that I will not overthrow the city you have referred to. Escape there quickly, for I won't be able to do anything until you get there." (Thus the name of the city is Zoar.)

The sun was fully out by the time Lot arrived at Zoar. By raining down upon Sodom and Gomorrah sulphurous fire from the sky, Yahweh overthrew these cities and the entire basin and all the inhabitants of the cities and all the plants of the ground. Lot's wife looked back and became a pillar of salt.

Abram went up in the morning to the place where he had stood in the presence of Yahweh and looked down toward Sodom and Gomorrah and the whole area of the basin. There he saw a column of smoke going up from the earth like a column of smoke from a furnace.

Lot went up east from Zoar and settled in the hill country with his two daughters, since he was afraid to stay settled in Zoar. He dwelt in a cave with his two daughters. The older said to the younger, "Since our father is old, and there is not a man in the world to come to us in the manner of the whole world, let's make our father drink wine and lie with him, that we may give birth to offspring from our father."

So they made their father drink wine that night. The older then went in and slept with her father. He did not know, however, when she lay down or when she got up.

The next day, the older said to the younger, "Yesterday I lay with my father. Let's make him drink wine tonight, too, and you go in and lie with him, so that we may give birth to offspring from our father."

So they gave their father wine to drink that night also. Then the younger went and lay with him, but again he did not know when she lay down and when she got up.

The two daughters of Lot got pregnant by their father. The older bore a son and named him Moab. He is the father of the Moabites to this day. The younger also gave birth to a son and named him Ben-ammi. He is the father of the Ammonites to this day.

Abram traveled from there by stages to the Negev. There Yahweh, having attended to Sarai according to his very word, did to Sarai as he had spoken, and she became pregnant. Sarai bore a son for Abram and named the son who had been born to him, whom Sarai had borne to him, Isaac.

Later on it was reported to Abram that "Milkah has given birth, too, to sons for Nahor: Uz his firstborn son, Buz his brother, Qemu'el the father of Aram, Kesed, Hazo, Pildash, Yidlap, and Betuel." Betuel became the father of Rebekkah. These were the eight children of Milkah and Nahor the brother of Abram.

Abram had a mistress whose name was Reumah. She gave birth also to Tebah, Gaham, Tahash, and Ma'kah.

Having shown us how Abram attributed to Yahweh his success in terms of the theme of production, J now turns to the parallel theme of Abram's and Sarai's reproduction. The story of Hagar, the story of the visit of the three men, and the story of Sodom and Gomorrah are all interconnected with the birth of Isaac—the overarching theme of the whole of Abram's history. How can the consciousness of man and woman that led to the birth of Cain and his cursed line be reversed? The birth of Isaac will make it possible for human beings to reproduce for the first time with Yahweh's blessing.

J addresses first the legitimacy of a woman's sexual presumption. Sarai had a slave. Sarai said to her husband, "Sleep with my slave. Perhaps I shall be built from her." Of course, what Sarai said is not good English idiom. But it is important to be aware that Sarai used the word "build," which goes back to Yahweh's "building" the first woman in the garden and the repeated "building" of dynastic houses that has occurred in connection with procreation. Once again J takes advantage of the similarity between the Hebrew words "build" and "child" or "son."

Abram accepted the suggestion, and Sarai gave her slave Hagar to him. Surrogate motherhood was an accepted practice for J. Hagar became pregnant and—just as Adam and Eve saw their genitals, and Ham saw Noah's genitals—Hagar, an Egyptian and therefore a descendant of Ham, "saw" that she was pregnant. She took pride in her pregnancy—excessive pride. She looked at her unpregnant owner Sarai, who by right was above her, and saw herself as better and higher.

The modern reader will immediately notice that the historian here is playing two sets of oppositions off against each other. One is the distinction between a pregnant woman and an unpregnant woman, as a way of addressing the issue of procreativity; the other is the distinction between owner and slave. The second distinction would be a perfectly good way of addressing the issue of the culture of productivity and social justice. Indeed, it is precisely the distinction that J chooses for dealing with these all-important issues: the history as a whole climaxes with Yahweh's release of the king of Egypt's slaves. Here, however, this issue is overridden for the time being by the first distinction. Our historian wants to pinpoint the issue of justifiable human procreativity. To our sensibilities, the second issue really ought always to take precedence. Again, for the sake of interpretation, it is necessary to adopt momentarily a different set of assumptions and expectations.

Sarai complained to Abram: "The violence done me be upon you." This is strong language. It is tantamount to a complaint of injustice. "I gave you my slave," Sarai and the historian repeat, "she saw she was pregnant, and I was slighted in her sight. May Yahweh judge between us." Sarai's charge defines Hagar's attitude as unjust. In the cultural expectations of the narrative, Sarai was within her right. She, not Hagar, was the wronged party.

Sarai drove Hagar away. Out in the wasteland, on her way back to Egypt,

Yahweh's genie found Hagar by a spring. The genie sent her back to her owner. "Submit beneath her hand," he instructed her. "I shall greatly increase your seed." The Hebrew expression recalls the curse of Eve: "I shall greatly increase your painful pregnancy." The curse is transformed for this woman, who in her pregnancy must submit to the mastery of Sarai. "When you bear your son, name him Ishmael, for"—here the historian gives his etymology of the name—"Yahweh has heard your affliction."[1] There are hints of what is to come in Exodus, where Yahweh will hear the affliction of Abram's descendants through Isaac.

At the point that her unjustified pride had been punctured by being cast out into the wasteland, Hagar had *seen* Yahweh in the form of his genie. This was the turning point in her history. "And she named the Yahweh who was speaking to her, 'You are El Ro'i [God of Seeing],' for she said, 'Have I even this far out seen the one who sees me?'" To make sure we don't miss the point, the narrator says it once again: "Therefore the spring is named 'to the living one who sees me.'" Usually Yahweh *hears* the affliction of those who cry out in the right. Here, Sarai in her right has "afflicted" Hagar, and Yahweh has instructed Hagar to return to Sarai and allow herself "to be afflicted" (the literal meaning of the Hebrew) beneath Sarai's hand. The historian does not intend the meaning of Ishmael's name to reverse what we have already said about Sarai's right and the un-justifiability of Hagar's pride in her pregnancy. The conclusion of this section of the history is not that Yahweh delivers the righteous, the conclusion that we look for and that would be the case if Hagar were the wronged party. Rather, the point is that Yahweh delivered Hagar *once she saw Yahweh instead of her own pregnancy.* It was her acknowledgment of Yahweh as the source of blessing and her abandoning of her presumption that was her redemption.

Under what circumstances can the woman's procreativity be made valid in the fifteenth generation? Can pregnancy and birth happen and evil be avoided—a combination that has not happened in the previous fourteen generations? Pregnancy is validated, J's history suggests, when understood in juxtaposition to the negation of presumption and pride like that of Hagar. Hagar's haughtiness is the recapitulation of Eve's presumption. Here it is negated and hence narratively neutralized. The humbling of the pregnant one redeems her creative capacity and puts it ultimately in the service of the cultural column of Abel, Seth, and Shem, rather than of royal culture.

J gives us a hint of what is to come later in the history when he says that

1. The change favored by many translators to "God has answered you" in place of "your affliction" does not seem likely.

Ishmael was to become a "human onager," or wild desert ass. The exact meaning of the next phrase—"his hand will be on or against everything or everyone, and the hand of all will be on or against him"—is unclear, but it seems to refer to the Ishmaelites as bedouin traders or raiders, who in expressing their parentage travel through Palestine between Syria and Egypt.[2] No doubt J is alluding particularly to the role of the Ishmaelites in taking Joseph to Egypt, an essential step in the saving of Abram's descendants in the generations of both Joseph and Moses.

J's history then explains the kinship relation with Israel of kingdoms to the east. Through their prominence in the history of Jacob, Aram and Edom are made more important than Ammon and Moab. Kinship in this context refers to political and economic relationship. One can suppose that Aram to the northeast and Edom to the southeast were of particular importance to the house of David. Edom may have been the most important of all, and this is not surprising, since it was adjacent to the marginal lands to the south which were important to the rise of the house of David.

The historian turns now to the conception of Abram and Sarai's son, Isaac. Isaac is short for "Isaac-el" (Heb.: *yitshaq-el*), which has the meaning "God laughs," as is often indicated in textual footnotes. The Hebrew word means more than simply laughter, however. It refers also to sexual play, foreplay, or intercourse. This is its meaning in Gen. 26:8, where the RSV translates the verb as "fondling." Isaac's name therefore might be more accurately translated or interpreted as "God engages in sex." To understand its full meaning in the context of the Davidic court we must turn to Psalm 2, usually regarded as a psalm of the Davidic or Solomonic cult.

Psalm 2 represents the right of the Davidic emperor. "The kings of the earth set themselves against Yahweh and his king. . . . Now therefore, O kings, be wise; be warned, O rulers of the earth; submit yourselves to Yahweh in fear." This was the position of David at the height of his power and of his son Solomon, but of no other Davidic king in anywhere near the same way. How is the position of the king defined in this short psalm? "He who is enthroned in the heavens *laughs*" and speaks in his terror: "I have set my king on Zion. . . . You are my son, today *I have begotten you*. Ask me and I will make the nations your possession." This is the royal meaning of Isaac, "God laughs": the house of David in its dynastic and imperial form is heir itself to the dominion of none other than Yahweh, the creator of the nations. Isaac's name within a royal context means that the king is godlike, the son of god, born of god, a divine offspring.[3] The issue is the authority of

---

2. See Israel Eph'al, "'Ishmael' and 'Arab(s)': A Transformation of Ethnological Terms," *Journal of Near Eastern Studies* 35 (1976): 225–35.

3. For a Middle Assyrian treatment of this motif, see Peter Machinist, "Literature as Politics: The Tukulti-Ninurta Epic and the Bible," *Catholic Biblical Quarterly* 38 (1976): 465–68.

the king to be lord of the nations in a domineering sense, and that authority is portrayed in the birth of the king in terms of God laughing. Of course, for J Isaac is not this imperial scion. The point is that J presents the heir as the opposite of its model or foil in the hymnic version of imperialism in his attempt to suggest that David's dominion is benign.

The royal significance of Isaac's name is similar to the significance of Cain's name. Cain's name means "I am godlike," and the consequence is cities and royal rule. In fact, Isaac's name is even more explicitly royal. But J is about to describe this birth in such a way that the royal meanings of the firstborn son in the blessed set of generations will not go in the direction that Cain's went.

Three men visited Abram at midday in the heat, one of whom was Yahweh. Two of these men would later visit Sodom, and the two visits are meant to be read in relation to each other. The men's visit to Abram and Sarai is set in contrast to their visit to Sodom. Right and wrong are defined in terms of the hospitality paid to the stranger or the lack thereof.[4] Abram and Sarai showed effusive hospitality. Having prepared a fantastic meal, Abram placed it before his visitors and stood next to them beneath the tree while they ate. Then the dialogue began, and we listen carefully.

Yahweh said to Abram, "Where is Sarai your wife?" This is an appallingly rude question. Although it is a practice among bedouin who meet each other to ask about the well-being of each other's families, without referring directly to a wife or a child, nevertheless, to inquire pointedly or at length about another's wife is a grave offense tantamount to asking to have intercourse with her. While Abram's and Sarai's hospitality to the men is virtually all that happens on the surface in the first part of this narrative, the Hebrew idiom of hospitality and the idiom of sexuality are largely congruent. This makes the talk about Abram's wife *and* her childbearing all the more striking and out of place. Abram played the perfect host and maintained his equanimity, replying, "She is in the tent." The sexual connotation of Yahweh's inquiry about Sarai was confirmed when Yahweh said, "When I return to you about the living time,[5] Sarai your wife will have a son."[6]

Sarai, we are told, was listening at the entrance of the tent, which was behind Yahweh. The historian explains parenthetically but importantly that both Abram and Sarai were old, that they had entered their years and that "a way like the woman has ceased with respect to Sarai"—that is, she

---

4. The same device is used to contrast David's Bethlehem and Saul's Gibeah in the pro-Davidic narrative in Judg. 19:1–28.

5. The precise meaning of "the living time" is not known.

6. This point is explained also by David Bakan in *And They Took Themselves Wives* (San Francisco: Harper & Row, 1980), 108–25.

had ceased to menstruate and could no longer become pregnant by her husband. Hearing Yahweh's remark, Sarai laughed inside herself. The RSV translates the last phrase "to herself." This is incorrect. The Hebrew *qereb*, "midst" or "inside," means womb in J in Gen. 25:22; "to herself" would have been expressed in Hebrew by another phrase, "to her heart," which J will use shortly in Gen. 24:25. And after all, "laugh," the basis of the name of this son to be born, is a loaded word. While "laughing," Sarai thought to herself, "After my wearing out, have I had sexual pleasure, with my master being old?" The RSV and many other translations employ the future tense—"shall I have pleasure?" This is grammatically incorrect and misses the point altogether: Sarai had just experienced sexual pleasure in her midst, inside herself. The word translated sexual pleasure is *edna,* a form of exactly the same word as *eden,* Eden, the name of the garden where the man and the woman first "knew."

Yahweh said to Abram, "Why is this? Sarai laughed, thinking 'Shall I truly bear a child when I am old?' " He continued, "Is a matter too wonderful for Yahweh?" Here again the RSV gives an inadequate translation. The appropriate rendering is found in the RSV footnote: not "too hard" but "too wonderful." Furthermore, "wonderful" refers not simply to just any wonder but specifically to the wonder of birth, as can be seen by comparing a number of other uses of the Hebrew term in the Bible. This then is one more statement of Yahweh's creative prerogative, going back to the original creation of the first human beings. Hence Yahweh's next statement: "I will return to you at the right time, about the living time, and Sarai will have a son." This repeated phrase frames the main conversation so far, setting it off as a unit and specifying its primary meaning: through Yahweh's agency, Sarai will have a son. It is typical of Hebrew composition or rhetoric to set off a unit of narrative or conversation by repeating the beginning and end—an inclusio (or framing construction). The subject of the repeated phrases often reveals the main subject of the unit so enclosed. In the case of the present narrative, the dialogue continues beyond the enclosed unit and focuses our attention even more directly on the term "laugh." In this way the narrative reinforces the significance of the name Isaac in relation to Yahweh's interaction with Sarai.

Fearful, Sarai dissembled: "I did not laugh." Yahweh, without having seen or heard her, retorted, "No, you did laugh." By now it's clear that the Hebrew *tsahaq* is rich with meaning. It must be stressed that such words simply have no single English word that can represent their meaning. Although the word "laugh" can be used to stand for *tsahaq,* it does not adequately translate it. Thus each time the word "laugh" is encountered, it is important to recall the full meaning of the term so represented.

The whole narrative of the birth of Isaac refers not only to the birth of the firstborn in the second generation but even more specifically to the next narrative in the sequence of recapitulation, the history of miscegenation of gods and humans in Gen. 6:1–4. The solution, as it were, to the problem of the royal consciousness of creating heirs is furnished by having Yahweh, a god, impregnate Sarai and so provide Abram an heir. Isaac had a divine father and a human mother, just like the men of name in that earlier generation. But in this case, in the generations of the blessing, the whole history points without qualification to the primacy of Yahweh. It is Yahweh who creates for Abram a name, with all that implies.

We have seen that the birth of Abram and Sarai's firstborn of the sixteenth generation (which is the second generation in J's third set of generations) constitutes a reversal of the birth of Cain, the firstborn of the second generation in the first set of generations. Each event in the narrative of the birth of Isaac has its own clear reference back to an incident from the history of the second set of seven generations, which spanned from Noah to the building of the temple-tower. But just as Abram and Lot's reversal of the strife between Cain and Abel precedes the reversal of the birth of Cain by the birth of Isaac, so the sequence of reversals does not follow strictly and discretely the sequence of incidents in the second set of seven generations. Rather than referring back to the previous history in strict sequence, the narrator makes various references, throughout the course of recounting the conception of Isaac, to the history of the first fourteen generations—all under the umbrella of the recapitulation of the issue of humans' usurping of the divine right of creating other humans.

All the incidents involving the birth of Isaac occur under the rubric of the justifiability of procreation. However, the fact that Yahweh had visited Abram and in effect cuckolded his very gracious host by impregnating Sarai gave Yahweh some pause. J now takes up the justifiability of Yahweh's actions. The issue of justice spans the remainder of the Isaac narrative up to the actual birth of Isaac.

The key issue in the pair of narratives in Genesis 18 and 19:1–28 is *tsedaqah* ("justice")—that is, what is right and just in terms of hospitality and sexual relations. Yahweh's impregnating Sarai is tantamount to adultery. Yahweh is now in the same position vis-à-vis Abram and Sarai that pharaoh was at the beginning of the history of Abram, when he took Abram's wife. This parallel helps reinforce the point that J wants to bring out for the history as a whole. Yahweh's impregnating Sarai was, on the face of it, not only an unjust act, it was a royal unjust act. And although it solved the problem posed by Adam's knowing Eve—Abram and Sarai would have a son without Abram's knowing Sarai—it needed to be justified. That is, it must be defined as an act that is *tsedaqah*, right, rather than *rasha*, wrong.

Yahweh could not justify what he had done by direct means, so the history must justify it for him indirectly. This is done by means of the typical Hebrew conception of comparative justice: something was right if it could be contrasted to something that was less right. Or, in other words, something was just, without qualification, if it could be shown to be more just than something else. In Hebrew rhetoric, comparative right made for absolute right. Such a notion is illustrated by Ezek. 16:48–58, where Jerusalem's sins are compared with those of Sodom and Samaria. "You, Jerusalem, have made your sisters Sodom and Samaria righteous [not "appear righteous," as in the RSV] by all the abominations which you have committed." An example from J is Gen. 38:26, where Tamar's acquittal is based on the greater wrong of Judah. The greater evil that J uses to justify Yahweh's sexual wrong with Sarai is the greater sexual wrong of the inhabitants of Sodom and Gomorrah.

The comparison between Yahweh and the Sodomites is made in terms of the Hebrew expression "to know" someone, which of course for J goes back ultimately to the knowledge acquired by the man and the woman in the garden. Yahweh "knows" Sarai, but the key phrase for Abram's history is found in Gen. 18:19, "For I have *known*[7] Abram." Here "know" refers to Yahweh's oath of blessing in Gen. 12:1–3 and has the same meaning as in Exod. 1:8: "A new king arose over Egypt who did not *know* Joseph." "Know" in these contexts means to establish or maintain a contractual relationship based on production, such as land tenure, or on reproduction, such as having an heir. In this case it is both. Yahweh has known Abram, as he says, for the sake of the performance of justice, in departure from generations of injustice. But in the process of carrying out this contractual relationship, Yahweh himself, by knowing Abram's wife for the purpose of generating an heir, committed an act of injustice. In order to justify his knowing Abram not only by granting him land but also through this unjust relationship with Sarai, Yahweh found another example of a man knowing a man that was more unjust—the men of Sodom knowing another man in gang rape.

J's use of the motif of homosexual knowing should be allowed to unfold within the context of the history, uncolored by a person's preconceptions or understandings of the rights or wrongs of homosexuality. That J's history of the homosexuality of the Sodomites is fantasy is evident from the fact there are no nonhomosexual Canaanites in his history of the fifteenth generation. The wrong or injustice of the Sodomites had already been indicated and confirmed well before this point in J's history. They were Canaanites

---

7. The RSV's "chosen" is an attempt to convey this nuance of "known," relegated to a footnote in the RSV translation.

and hence were descended through the column of cursed urbanite culture (Gen. 10:6, 19). As sons of Ham, their homosexuality was doubtless derived in part from the homosexual implications of Ham's seeing his father's nakedness. J has already said unequivocally that the men of Sodom were wicked, great sinners (Gen. 13:13). Their king's name, Birsha, contained within it the word "wrong" or injustice. What was their wrong? They did not know Yahweh, either in terms of production or reproduction. Their king did not recognize or "know" Yahweh's role in his acquiring wealth, and now they do not recognize or "know" Yahweh even as they strive brutally to know him.

In J's time, urban society was patriarchal. Outwardly, publicly, it was an all-male society; the visible actors were almost exclusively male. J is able to characterize Canaanite society (urban Palestinian society) in the extreme form of an all-male homosexual society because there was typically an excess of males in Palestinian urban society, so that many men simply had no opportunity to marry or establish a family. There are many stories in the Bible about urban lords, themselves often with many wives or mistresses, who have an inordinate number of sons and hardly any daughters. This pattern may well point to a skewing of demography by the practice of female infanticide. Sons were valued because of their military and economic role in society. In other words, J in his characteristic manner takes a social feature of urban society to an extreme in order to use it as a foil.

J's assumption that homosexuality is wrong grew out of the strong emphasis among the highland generations prior to David on reproduction, an emphasis that fit and was even important to the expansion of population in a previously much less populated highland. This widespread cultural assumption reinforced the normal reproductive bias of elite urban culture. J not only scorns homosexuality but he caricatures the worst features of royal culture in these terms. In characterizing urban society as unjust, he selects a particularly vicious and despicable form of sexual behavior, rape, which was no doubt a feature of Palestinian urban society.

The men arose, went off, came to a high point, and gazed down upon the lush plain of Sodom. Abram went with the men to see them off. On the way, Yahweh was thinking to himself, "Am I covering up from Abram what I am doing? After all, Abram is to become a great and mighty nation through whom all nations of the earth are to be blessed, since I have known him precisely in order that he might give instruction to his children and his house who inherit him, that they might keep the way of Yahweh and perform justice." The word "justice" here translates the word we have usually translated by "right," the word that has occurred in the name Malkitsedeq and in Abram's claim to the right of having an heir, and is about to occur in reference to the innocent *(tsaddiqim)* of Sodom. J's basic concern is to characterize the just king; so now, Yahweh is concerned that, just as the way of Yahweh is to be taught as just, Yahweh may disclose his action here (of impregnating Sarai) as just.[8]

At this point our historian sets the stage for a dialogue between Yahweh and Abram by composing a series of disjunctive clauses in Hebrew, clauses that do not themselves advance the narrative in progress but explain the circumstances of the narrative. They tell the reader what he or she needs to know. The dialogue immediately reveals Yahweh's ploy for representing himself as just. Yahweh said, "The cry of injustice of Sodom and Gomorrah is indeed great, and their sin is exceedingly grave. [J has used the term "sin" only twice before, once in reference to the men of Sodom and once—the only place where he characterizes sin—in reference to Cain's murder, and appears to regard sin as social violence.] Let me go down and see whether completely they do according to the cry that is coming to me, or whether not—let me know." This is an awkward translation awkwardly said because the two key words come at the end of two separate clauses, namely, "completely" and "know." Why does Yahweh want to "know" how "complete" the Sodomites' wrong is? The answer comes in the subsequent dialogue between Abram and Yahweh.

As the men proceeded on their journey to Sodom, Abram approached Yahweh in deference and questioned him: "Are you really going to sweep away the innocent[9] with the guilty? Perhaps there are fifty just men in the city. Will you then sweep it away? Will you not forgive it on account of the fifty just men in its midst? On no account would you want to do such a thing, killing the just with the wicked, and treating the just and the wicked alike. On no account would you do that. Is the judge of the whole world not going to do justice?" This is a lengthy speech for J.[10] Abram indeed put Yahweh on the spot, and yet he played right into Yahweh's hands.

---

8. The reader who is following with an English translation can notice that Yahweh's statement actually goes on, ". . . and justice [the translator used English "righteousness" to represent what we have translated "justice"]; so that the Lord may bring to Abram what he has promised him." It is likely, though not certain, that this is an addition to J. It is a bit more pleonastic than is expected of J and includes the phrase "righteousness and justice" (RSV) that occurs only one other time in the Bible, in Proverbs (the usual phrase is "justice and righteousness"). It is not possible to be certain about this analysis, as with so much of trying to discern J. The reason in this case for even discerning the indications of such a secondary addition is to recognize J's emphasis on the term *tsedeq* and its meaning in the whole narrative.

9. Hebrew *tsaddiq*, from the same root as "just." Innocence and guilt are always defined in relation to each other. In this narrative, the behavior of the Sodomites has been defined as wicked. Hence the innocent are not intrinsically just or righteous, only in contrast to the Sodomites.

10. Many interpreters regard it as secondary to J for just this reason. See Joseph Blenkinsopp, "Abraham and the Righteousness of Sodom," *Journal of Semitic Studies* 33 (1982): 119–32, for a recent interpretation of this section of J as a "midrash" on original J.

Our historian makes so much of Yahweh's dialogue with Abram over the precise number of righteous people in Sodom because the way in which the injustice of the Sodomites is proven is not through the quality of their behavior, which is a simple wrongness, but through its quantity in terms of the involvement of the complete city. The question is not how wrong but how many. The precision of judgment concerning justice has been quantified. The narrative reason for this kind of precision is to detract from any kind of a qualitative judgment. It displaces the question of whether it was fair to characterize the Sodomites in this way. Abram himself would be enlisted as a party to the precise definition of an act—the destruction of the Sodomites—that would justify his own cuckolding. As the one who had been cuckolded, he would be the one to define the terms of the justification.

At the end of the dialogue, the narrator concludes that Yahweh walked off when he had completed speaking to Abram. In Hebrew, it is not usual to make such a statement as the narrator does concerning Yahweh completing his dialogue with Abram. J concludes the dialogue by actually saying it was complete in order to form an inclusio and to draw attention once again to the degree of "completeness," which after all has been the subject of the dialogue.

The two genies arrived at Sodom in the evening. Lot offered them hospitality just as Abram had. J now exploits in full the congruent set of terminologies and images that hospitality shares with sexuality. The extreme hospitality of Abram in Genesis 18 is contrasted with the extreme lack of hospitality of Sodom. This contrast was first signaled in the story of the encounter of the king of Salem with the king of Sodom in Genesis 14, where the one was hospitable and the other was not. Yahweh's genies were received in Sodom with an inhospitality and injustice that was as despicable as Abram's hospitality was gracious.

The narrator wants his readers to draw the conclusion that hospitality is harder to find in the urban context than in the villages and tents. It is a generic phenomenon that hospitality in Palestine was more available in the village. Every village had an assigned guest house in which a guest was welcome to stay for three nights. A parallel to the lack of hospitality in Sodom can be found in Judges 19, where, in a pro-David, anti-Saul narrative, a Levite and his concubine, having just enjoyed abundant hospitality in Bethlehem, like Yahweh here, pass by Jerusalem looking for a place to stay at night. They conclude that Jerusalem, being a city and non-Israelite as well, would treat them cruelly rather than offering them hospitality, so they pass by and end up in Gibeah, a small town, where one would expect hospitality. The point the anti-Saul author wants to make is ironic: the town, destined to be Saul's capital, was inhospitable; if only they had stopped in Jerusalem, which was to become David's capital!

The two genies had found in Lot their first innocent person, who together with themselves made three so far. The sexual innuendos of the language of hospitality do not long lie latent. As the men were about to turn in, "the men of the city, the men of Sodom, both young and old, all the people, every last one"—J does not pass up an opportunity to remind us that he is talking about a city, laying great stress on quantity—"surrounded Lot's house." Bent on gang rape, they wanted to "know" the genies, who appeared as men to them. The men of Sodom wanting to "know" the genies was the same as their wanting to "know" Yahweh and hence the reverse of Yahweh "knowing" Sarai and knowing Abram. Once again the historian emphasizes the connection between seeing and knowing: the genies smote the men with blindness so that they were unable to "see" and therefore unable to "know."

There seems to be a wordplay between *tsahaq* ("laugh") and *tsaʿaq* ("cry out"). Sarai's and Yahweh's laughter is to be contrasted with the cry from the Sodomites. As the latter was unjust, so the former was just. This wordplay comes to its climax as the genies and Lot attempt to persuade Lot's sons-in-law to depart with them. While the cry of the Sodomites rises, the sons-in-law take Lot to be what the RSV misleadingly translates "jesting." The Hebrew is once again *tsahaq* ("laughing"). The sons-in-law imagine Lot to be making a pass at them. Hence the two Sodomites who had the best chance of being innocent turned out to be just like the rest. Altogether then there were only six innocents—Lot, his wife, his two daughters, and two genies—and none of the men of Sodom. The city's wrong was complete.

Lot did not simply escape. The two men instructed him to flee to the hills. Lot preferred to flee to a city which is called *mitsʿar* ("little one"), and named *Tsoʿar*, or Zoar, from the same Hebrew root. The form of "little one" is identical to the form of the word "great one" that is half of the expression "city and great one" which we have usually translated "a city and a tower" or "city-tower." This episode is the reversal of the story of that great city of the fourteenth generation in Shinar, Babylon. In Abram's generation, the first blessed generation, the "city" is partially redeemed from the curse, for David himself is a city dweller.

The pillar of salt refers to a natural resource of the Dead Sea area controlled by David in his rise. Like tar, it would have been among the significant trade products of David's kingdom. In addition, the removal of Lot's wife is a precondition of the story of the birth of the Moabites and the Ammonites, with its emphasis on Lot not knowing. Lot having only daughters mirrors the Sodomites consisting of only men. Lot's loss of his wife mirrors his daughters' loss of their husbands.

The connection with Ham now comes full circle. Fearful of residing in Zoar, Lot and his two daughters took to a cave. There, the daughters devised a way to become pregnant. They made their father drunk, and while he slept they lay with him. This incident of course is the reversal of Noah lying drunk in his tent. In this case, no one "saw" anything, and—as is repeated—Lot did not "know." The children of Lot, cousins of Abram, were the Moabites and the Ammonites, two nations to the east subdued and ruled by David. They were under Israel's rule because they were born of incest, while Israel was born of a god. The result of incest though they may be, they were redeemed by the repetition of the phrase "Lot did not know." Before the birth of Isaac, all births were still problematic. But since their father did not know—just as Abram did not know Sarai and did not know that he had been replaced—their birth, like Isaac's, was validated in the narrative.

Of course, Isaac had not yet been born. This event the historian saves to the very end of Abram's special history, to enclose all that has led up to it. It occurs in Gen. 21:1. Genesis 20 is almost entirely an insertion from E, as is most of Genesis 21 and 22, and Genesis 23 is apparently entirely from P. Although much about the composition of the combined histories of J and E remains unclear, it seems that E's stories of Abram are largely modeled on J's and collected toward the end of that block. When studying J, the modern reader must pay particular attention to bracketing stories in the Bible that were simply not a part of J.

As might be expected, our historian phrases the description of the birth of Isaac carefully, in view of its cause. "Yahweh attended to[11] Sarai according to his very word, and Yahweh did to Sarai just as he had spoken, and she became pregnant." What is so noticeably missing in this account is the formula, "And Abram knew his wife." Sarai bore for Abram a son and he was duly named Isaac. The naming in J is not actually available in the biblical text; it has been replaced by P's phrasing.

11. The Hebrew word has many meanings in English. The RSV's "visited" is one of them, but to the reader unfamiliar with the broad ambiguity of the Hebrew term that translation is misleading. Yahweh did not simply visit Sarai at this stage, and this is not a reference to his visit with the two genies to the tent of Abram and Sarai.

15

"Make Me a Match"

(Genesis 24:1—25:11)

Since Abram was old and had entered his years, and Yahweh had blessed Abram with everything, Abram said to his slave, the senior slave of his household, who had charge of all his possessions, "Place your hand under my thigh, so that I can have you swear by Yahweh, the god of the sky and the god of the earth, that you will not take a woman for my son from the daughters of the Canaanites in whose midst I am settled, but that you will go instead to my land, the land of my birth and kinship base, to take a wife for my son Isaac."

The slave said to him, "Perhaps the woman will not be willing to follow me to this land. Should I then take your son back to the land from which you came?"

"Watch out," Abram said, "that you don't take my son there. Yahweh, the god of the sky, who took me from my father's household and from the land of my birth and kinship base, and who spoke to me and swore to me, 'To your offspring I will grant this land,' he will send his genie before you, and you will get a wife for my son from there. If the woman is unwilling to follow you, then you will be released from this oath of mine. But in no case shall you take my son back there."

The slave placed his hand beneath the thigh of Abram his master and swore to him according to the specified terms. The slave then took ten of his master's camels and went, and with a full array of goods from his master in his charge, he set off toward Aram to the northeast, toward the city of Nahor.

Outside the city, by the spring, he made the camels kneel down. It was evening, the time when women came out to draw water. He said, "Yahweh, god of my master Abram, give me good fortune today and so be kind to my master Abram. Here I am standing by the spring, while the daughters of the men of the city come out to draw water. If I say to a girl, 'Lower your jug that I may drink,' and she says, 'Have a drink, and let me give water to your camels as well,' let her be the one you have decided upon for your servant Isaac, and through her I will know that you have been kind to my master."

Before he had finished speaking, Rebekkah, who had been born to Betuel, the son of Milkah, the wife of Nahor, the brother of Abram, came out with her jug on her shoulder. The girl was beautiful to look at, a virgin, whom no man had known. She came down to the spring and filled her jug and started back up. The slave ran to meet her and said, "Give me, if you would, a sip of water from your jug."

She said, "Have a drink, my lord," and quickly she lowered her jug with her hand and gave him a drink. When she had finished letting him drink, she said, "Let me draw water for your camels as well, until they have finished drinking." Quickly she emptied her jug into the trough and ran back to the well to draw water. She drew water for all of his camels.

During this time, the man watched her in silence, waiting to know whether Yahweh had made his journey successful or not. When the camels had finished drinking, the man took a gold ring weighing half a shekel and fastened it on her nose, and two gold bracelets weighing ten shekels, which he placed on her wrists. He then said, "Whose daughter are you? Tell me. And is there room for us to spend the night in your father's house?"

She said, "I am the daughter of Betuel, the son of Milkah, whom she bore to Nahor. There is straw and much fodder at our house, as well as a place to spend the night."

The man bowed and worshiped Yahweh and said, "Blessed is Yahweh the god of my master Abram, who has not abandoned his kindness and his faithfulness to my master. As for me, Yahweh has led me in my journey directly to the household of the brothers of my master."

The girl ran and told her mother's household about these events. Now Rebekkah had a brother named Laban. Laban ran to the man outside at the spring. When he saw the nose ring and the bracelets on his sister's wrists, and when he heard his sister Rebekkah's words, "Thus the man said to me," he went to the man. He was standing by his camels at the spring.

Laban said, "Come, blessed of Yahweh. Why are you standing outside when I have made the house ready, including a place for your camels?"

The man went to the house. His camels were unloaded, straw and fodder were provided for them, and water was brought for washing his feet and those of the men who were with him. When food was placed before him, he said, "I will not eat until I have told my errand."

He said, "Tell it, then."

So he began, "I am the slave of Abram. Yahweh blessed my master so abundantly that he has become a great man. He gave him flocks and herds, silver and gold, male and female slaves, and camels and asses. My master's wife Sarai bore a son for my master in her old age, and he has given to him everything that he has. My master has put me under this oath: 'You shall not take a wife for my son from the daughters of the Canaanites, in whose land I am settled. You shall go instead to my father's household, to my own relatives, and there take a wife for my son.' I said to my master, 'Perhaps the woman will not follow me.' He said to me, 'Yahweh, in whose presence I have walked these many years, will send his genie with you, and he will make your journey successful. You will take a wife for my son from my relatives and from my father's household. Then you will be released from my sanction. And if you go to my relatives and they do let you have one of their daughters, then also you will be released from my sanction.'

"So I arrived today at the spring. I said, 'Yahweh, the god of my master Abram, if you would make successful my journey which I am now engaged in, while I stand here by the spring, if I should say to a girl coming out to draw water, "Give me a bit of water from your jug to drink," and she should say to me, "Take a drink, and let me draw water for your camels, too," let that be the woman Yahweh has decided for the son of my master.' Before I was finished speaking to myself, Rebekkah came out with her jug on her shoulder, went down to the spring and drew water. I said to her, 'Give me a drink.' She hurried to bring her jug down from her shoulder and said, 'Take a drink, and let me water your camels as well.' I drank, and she also gave my camels water.

"I asked her, 'Whose daughter are you?' And she said, 'The daughter of Betuel the son of Nahor, whom Milkah bore for him.' I fastened a ring on her nose and bracelets on her wrists. I bowed down and worshiped Yahweh and blessed Yahweh the god of my master Abram, who had led me on the true road to get the daughter of the brother of my master for his son.

"If therefore you are willing to show truth and kindness to my master, tell me. If not, tell me that, too, so that I can do what I have to do."

Laban and Betuel answered, "This matter has come from Yahweh. We cannot say anything to you either good or bad. Here is Rebekkah, ready for you. Take her and go, and let her become the wife of the son of your master, as Yahweh has said."

When Abram's slave heard their words, he bowed to the earth before Yahweh. The slave brought out things of silver and gold, along with clothing, and gave them to Rebekkah. And he gave gifts to her brother and her mother.

When he and the men who were with him had had their fill of food and drink, they spent the night. In the morning they got up and said, "Let us go to my master."

Her brother and mother said, "Let the girl stay with us ten or so days. After that she can go."

He said to them, "Don't delay me, now that Yahweh has made my journey successful. Let me go so that I can go back to my master."

They said, "Let us call the girl and ask her herself."

They called Rebekkah and said to her, "Do you want to go with this man?"

She said, "I want to go with him."

So they sent Rebekkah their sister and her nurse along with Abram's slave and his men. They blessed Rebekkah with these words:

"Our sister are you;
  Become thousands of myriads,
And may your offspring
  Take possession of the gate of their enemies."

Then Rebekkah and her attendants mounted the camels and followed the man. So the slave took Rebekkah and went.

Meanwhile Isaac had gone from Beer-lahay-ro'i and was now settled in the Negev. Isaac had gone a ways out from the camp to urinate, when he looked up and saw camels coming toward him. Rebekkah looked up and saw Isaac and dismounted from her camel. She said to the slave, "Who is that man over there walking across the field to meet us?"

The slave said, "He is my master."

So she took her veil and covered herself.

The servant recounted to Isaac all that he had done. Isaac brought her into his tent to Sarai his mother. He took Rebekkah and she became his wife. Isaac loved her and found solace after his mother.

Abram himself took another wife, whose name was Qeturah. She bore him

Zimran, Yoqshan, Medan, Midian, Yishbaq, and Shuh. Yoqshan became the father of Sheba and Dedan, and the sons of Dedan were the Asshurim, the Letushim, and the Leummim. The sons of Midian were Ephah, Epher, Henok, Abida, and Elda'ah. All these were the descendants of Qeturah. Abram gave everything he had to Isaac. To the sons of his mistresses Abram gave gifts and, while he was still alive, sent them away from Isaac his son to the east, to the land of the east. Isaac settled in Beer-lahay-ro'i.

Compared with Abram and Jacob, Isaac receives scant attention from the Davidic historian.[1] Isaac, however, does not die until well into Jacob's story, which continues up to the end of Genesis.[2] Although little is said about him after his son Jacob leaves home as a young man, everything about Jacob pertains to his conflict with Esau, and that conflict to the inheritance of Isaac, a question that will come to a head with Isaac's death.

The sequence of the narrative is patterned after the history of the first fourteen generations, especially as these are recapitulated in the history of Abram. The birth of Isaac's sons and the purchase of the birthright correspond to the blessing of Abram with offspring and greatness. Then the history of Isaac refers in sequence to Abram's calling his wife his sister, the struggle of the shepherds of Abram and Lot, and Abram's peaceable encounter with the king who blessed him.

The theme of the reproductive system which is primary in the history of the birth of Isaac continues without a break into Isaac's history as the

---

1. In this century it has generally been assumed either that the available traditions about Isaac were in fact more scanty or that the historian composed most of what is said about Isaac as transitional filler material between Abram and Jacob. The critical interpretation of the section about Isaac has leaned in the direction of tradition history: the Isaac traditions derive from a separate source or cycle associated with the sanctuary of Beersheba and have been inserted here secondarily by J, coincident upon a loose conception of chronology. The useful aspect of this theory is that it reminds us that the traditional sources for the historian were not simply disembodied or universal traditions of pastoralists but traditions that are likely to have been closely associated with important points of bedouin congregation and exchange. Whatever the traditional source of the material relating directly to Isaac (again of bedouin character), if it ever was told separately from the stories of Jacob, it has been fully integrated by J into this part of his history.

2. The conception of the nation of Israel in terms of their unilineal descent from Abram should not be taken as the "natural" way of describing the nation's early history in terms of its genealogy. As Marvin Harris points out, "The greater the intensity of agricultural production, the greater the likelihood of unilineality. Sibs and lineages reflect a growing concern with claims for and counterclaims against permanent forms of property and wealth. It is a travesty of the evolutionary process leading to social stratification and the state to picture unilinear descent groups as functioning to enhance solidarity when in fact they are the tangible expression of a growing lack of solidarity caused by the struggle over increasingly rare resources" (*Cultural Materialism: The Struggle for a Science of Culture* [New York: Random House, 1979], 176). Although Harris is here concerned with long-range historical processes, his observation nevertheless suggests that the form of the genealogy of Israel and his sons in J reflects the overall intensification of production in Israel that accompanied David's monarchic consolidation of extensive holdings, in the highlands as well as far beyond.

historian jumps from the birth of Isaac to his marriage. How will the firstborn of the first blessed man and woman come to have his own wife? Or, how will marriage be redeemed in this generation as birth had been in the previous generation? In view of this thematic continuity, J explains the genealogy of the woman who is to become Isaac's wife. This is the meaning of the brief section regarding Abram's brother, nephews, and nieces in Gen. 22:20–24, where we are told that Nahor and Milkah bore Betuel, who bore Rebekkah.

The history of Isaac introduces a type of narrative that we have not yet encountered. These are the kinds of stories told by shepherds and bedouin. Consequently the stories tend not only to be lengthier than the sagalike history of Abram but they also tend to deal with more typically bedouin circumstances and incidents; they only convey their specific J meanings in terms of how they fit within the wider framework of the overall history.

This can be seen clearly in the narrative of the discovery of Isaac's wife. By the standards of our historian, it is a lengthy, even repetitious, narrative that makes just one essential point in terms of J's specific interests: Yahweh selected Isaac's wife. Yet the story of how Isaac acquired his wife is by itself one-fourth as long as everything that has gone before! Our historian is far more patient to make his points through this kind of narrative and does not mind letting the narrative expand and be itself in terms of its traditional source. This new character of the historian's narrative continues from this point to the end of his history. It is the main reason the whole history has the length it does, when to all intents and purposes J has set forth his main points in only a fourth of the history and will add little to them besides elaboration. The remaining three-fourths of the history he reserves for illustrative material drawn from bedouin sources. This elaboration serves an important purpose, however. Even though J has represented Abram as a bedouin, he has not yet effectively represented Israelite national identity as bedouin—he has done more constructing of narrative than borrowing of narrative up until this point. From this point on, he incorporates an expansive bedouin tradition so that this definition of national identity can be given full play.

Abram sent his servant to acquire for Isaac a wife who was not a Canaanite but rather a member of the family. Yahweh selected this wife. The repetitiveness of the story allows the narrator to reiterate the main point. First the story is narrated, next the servant retells the whole story, then the punch line comes at the conclusion of this double telling of the story as Laban and Betuel respond, "The matter *(dabar)* has come from Yahweh. We cannot speak to you evil or good; take Rebekkah ... as Yahweh has spoken *(dibber)*." J makes the point that unlike the divine males who at an earlier time "took for themselves wives of all whom they chose," Isaac's wife was chosen by Yahweh, and Isaac neither saw her nor was present. Indeed, unlike Eve, who both saw that the tree was good and then saw her nakedness and her man's, when Isaac and Rebekkah first met each other, Rebekkah's face, the historian is careful to point out, was covered.

Just as childbirth was redeemed in the fifteenth generation, in the sixteenth generation the redemption of the choice of wife brought with it the redemption of the kinship network. The narrative repeats the point that Isaac was to take to wife a person from the house of his father, the reproductive context of which Abram had been heir and which he had abandoned. The kinship network, whose validity was bracketed in the history of Abram, has now been redeemed from the negative connotation that it bore in the first fourteen generations.

Isaac occupied the territory at Beer-lahay-ro'i. That's where Ishmael was born. Ishmael presumably was not displaced—that story would surely have been told—but simply replaced. Ishmael will reappear. For now, all we are told is that Isaac was sociopolitically like the Ishmaelites in terms of the social niche he occupied. This is what happened during the rise and early monarchy of David.

Our historian takes great interest in the condition of the lands of southern Palestine. He is about to tell a lengthy narrative concerning the relationship between Jacob and Esau, who were Israel and Edom. Before he does that, however, he explains that after Sarai's death, Abram remarried and bore many more children. His wife was Qeturah, which is nearly identical to the Hebrew term "incense." The children born included Midian, Dedan, and Sheba, referring directly to trading peoples and lands to the south of the Negev, into northern and southern Arabia. The main trade items from this direction were the incenses, frankincense, and myrrh. These children Abram displaced to the east in order to allow his son Isaac full room and sway in the prime productive region of the northern Negev, toward the Philistine plain. The main interest for J was the political and economic importance of areas to the south and southeast. There David first rose to power. From there would come many of his best fighters and probably all of his personal palace guard.

16

A Younger Son Prevails

(Genesis 25:21—26:33)

Isaac entreated Yahweh for his wife, as she was childless. Yahweh heard his entreaty, and Rebekkah his wife became pregnant. The children were crushing each other in her womb, so she said something like, "If this is the way it is, who needs it?"

She went to consult Yahweh, who said to her,

> "There are two nations in your womb,
> And two peoples shall separate from within you.
> One people will be stronger than the other,
> And the older will serve the younger."

When her time to deliver came, she was found to be bearing twins. The first came out all ruddy, and like a hairy mantle all over. They named him Esau. Afterward his brother came out, with his hand holding onto the heel of Esau. They named him Jacob.

The two lads grew up, Esau becoming an expert hunter, a man of the field, and Jacob being a naive man, who stayed around the tents. Isaac loved Esau, because he liked game, while Rebekkah loved Jacob.

Once Jacob was boiling lentil stew, when Esau came from the field famished and said to Jacob, "Give me some of this red pottage to gulp down, since I'm famished." (Thus his name is Edom.)

Jacob said, "Sell me your birthright, then."

Esau said, "Okay. I'm on the point of dying, so what good would my birthright do me?"

Jacob said, "Swear to me right now."

So he swore to him, and sold his birthright to Jacob under oath. When Jacob had given Esau bread and lentil stew, he ate and drank and got up and went. That's·how Esau despised his birthright.

There was a famine in the land, different from the earlier famine that occurred in the time of Abram. Isaac traveled to Abimelek, the king of the Philistines, in Gerar. Yahweh appeared to him and said, "Don't go down to Egypt. Camp in this land wherever I tell you, and stay in this land as an immigrant. I will bless you, and by giving to you and your descendants all these lands, I will keep the oath I swore to

Abram your father. I will make your descendants as numerous as the stars of the sky, and I shall grant to your descendants all these lands. Through your descendants shall all the nations of the earth procure blessing for themselves."

Isaac settled in Gerar. When the men of that place asked concerning his wife, he said, "She is my sister," for he was afraid to say, "My wife," lest the men of the place kill him for Rebekkah, because she was beautiful. When Isaac had been there for some time, Abimelek, the king of the Philistines, looked down from his window and saw Isaac laughing with Rebekkah his wife. Abimelek summoned Isaac and said, "She's your wife. How could you say, 'She's my sister'?"

Isaac said to him, "Because I thought I might lose my life on her account."

Abimelek said, "What have you done to us? In no time at all, someone in my court would have lain with your wife, and you would have brought guilt upon us."

Abimelek ordered his court, "Anyone touching this man or his wife shall be executed."

Isaac sowed a crop in that region and reaped a hundredfold that year. In this way Yahweh blessed him, and the man became greater and greater all the time, until he was exceedingly great. He possessed such capital in flocks and herds, and such a great staff of slaves, that the Philistines envied him. All the wells that had been dug by the servants of Abram his father, the Philistines stopped up by filling them with dirt. Abimelek said to Isaac, "Go away from us, for you have become too strong and numerous for us."

So Isaac went from there and made his camp settlement in the Wadi Gerar. Isaac redug the wells that were dug in the days of Abram his father and that the Philistines had stopped up after Abram died, and gave them the same names which his father had given them. Isaac's servants dug around the wadi and found there a well fed by a spring. The shepherds of Gerar argued, however, with the shepherds of Isaac, "The water belongs to us." So they named the well Eseq, Contention, because they had contended with him.

They dug another well, but they argued over that one, too, and named it Sitnah, Enmity.

He moved on from there and dug yet another well, which they did not quarrel about. He named it Rehoboth, Space, saying, "Finally Yahweh has given us enough space to flourish in the land."

From there Isaac went up to Beersheba. There he built an altar and called on the name of Yahweh. Then he pitched his tent there. Isaac's servants dug a well there. Abimelek came to him from Gerar with Ahuzzat his bedouin agent and Pikol the commander of his forces. Isaac said to them, "Why have you come to me, since you hate me and have driven me away from you?"

They said, "We have seen without a doubt that Yahweh is with you. We thought there ought to be a sworn agreement between us, so let's make a covenant with you. Hence we would like to make a covenant with you. You will not do any evil to us just as we have not molested you and done only good for you by letting you go in peace. You are the blessed of Yahweh."

He prepared for them a feast, and they ate and drank. The next morning they took oaths between them. Then Isaac sent them on their way and they went in peace. On that very day Isaac's servants came and reported to him concerning the well they had been digging: "We have found water." So they named it Shiba. (Thus the name of the city is Beersheba to this day.)

Rebekkah, like Sarai, was childless. As heir of the first blessed pair, Isaac rightly turned to the creator of human beings to plead his case for a child. Yahweh acceded. J tells us that the children were crushing each other in Rebekkah's womb. The narrative contains a bit of humor—albeit with an element of dire pain—that might be missed. The Hebrew is not entirely clear, but Rebekkah said something to the effect that, "If this is the way it is, who needs it!" Having inquired of Yahweh, she was told, "There are two nations in your womb." (Jacob stands for Israel, Esau for Edom, Israel's neighbor as seen particularly from the Judahite point of view.) The humor occurs at the nonmetaphorical level: a woman with two nations in her womb would indeed be having a problem pregnancy. J's history of Jacob is mildly but distinctively humorous, and that narrative character begins to quicken here.

It is not surprising that Jacob and Esau fought each other in the womb, for that was to be the theme of much of their history, as it was of Cain and Abel. Similarly, it is not surprising that, Esau the elder having emerged first, Jacob followed instantly after, grasping hold of his heel. "Jacob" sounds like "heel" in Hebrew. As Esau said, "Is he not rightly named Jacob? For he has 'heeled' [RSV: "supplanted"] me these two times" (Gen. 27:36). Jacob's name refers directly to two pivotal acts in his life: he would first take Esau's birthright, then his blessing. Esau is described as "red" in a pun on his other name, Edom, and "hairy" in a pun on the name of the mountainous region of Edom, Se'ir. Not for the first time has our historian crowded a great deal of etymologizing into a brief section of his history.

The history of Abram had dealt thoroughly with the historical implications of the critique implied in the history of Adam and Eve. The history of Jacob deals thoroughly with the historical implications of the critique implied in the history of Cain and Abel. The two brothers Cain and Abel struggled to the death. In the fifteenth generation, the brothers Abram and Lot were able through the deference of Abram to avoid repeating that history. Not only is the story of Jacob based on that theme, the story of Joseph is based on it too. J's history of the seventeenth to the twentieth generation comprises a full third of his total history, and the one overriding point of this entire third is the reconciliation of brothers in the form of two great reversals of the brotherly struggle of Cain and Abel—first the nations Israel and Edom in the south of Palestine, then the constituent groups of the nation Israel itself. National harmony was an essential component of the success of the Davidic regime. Solomon's failure either to communicate or to maintain that harmony played a primary role in the collapse of the regime at his death.

Even before the two sons were born, their mother Rebekkah learned that the younger would prevail over the older. Here for the first time J makes a point that is basic to this entire third of his history concerning Jacob, Judah, and Joseph: the younger prevailed over the older—Abel, as it were, over Cain. This represents a profound and powerful overturning of the social norm—not necessarily an overturning that never occurred. J chooses not only to emphasize the overturning but also to make it the basis of an important redefinition: royal dominion is epitomized as the prevailing of the younger brothers Jacob and Joseph. J undoubtedly chose this way of making his point because of the tradition in David's court that David was a younger son. If the norm of primogeniture were weakened, and its violation sanctioned by the court, it would mean that the king himself could exercise a broader prerogative within the resulting looser social framework. The king could make assignments of inheritances.

Yahweh's intent that the younger should prevail upset normal cultural expectations and was bound to cause tension and conflict. As soon as Jacob purchased Esau's birthright, Isaac's death became a pivotal moment toward which the story must move. Hence at the beginning of the story of the theft of the blessing, Isaac is heard saying, "I do not know the day of my death." The importance of this unknown moment is confirmed by Esau's resolution, at the conclusion of the story of the brothers in Beersheba, to murder Jacob upon the death of his father.

When Jacob is first introduced to us, he is called an *'ish tam,* an innocent or naive man. On the surface of the story this refers to his being raised among the women in the tents, unlike his older brother, who was a hunter. But Jacob was far from either innocent or naive, as the historian is on the verge of unveiling. He is described as "boiling lentil stew." The Hebrew means more, for the words approximate an expression meaning "he was excessively presumptuous."

Esau is called a skillful hunter in the RSV. The Hebrew is "a man who knows . . ."—a man knowing the hunt. Jacob is called a man who is naive, the one who does not know. (RSV's "quiet man" misses the point.) The irony of this contrasting characterization of the brothers is in line with J's themes. The man who knew was the man over whom the man who did not know would prevail. The naive man was not naive at all, but J ironically covers Jacob's craftiness with this term in order to highlight at the beginning the basic theological issue behind the blessing of Jacob, which is whether Yahweh or Jacob accomplished Jacob's blessing.

For many modern readers, Jacob seems wily and even dishonest. That his blessing is inextricably linked to his character as the tricky one, the deceiver, the liar (which J in the words of Esau takes to be the meaning of the name Jacob), thus represents a moral problem. How can this individual represent the uprightness and nobleness that one assumes the eponymous ancestor of nothing less than Israel would possess? The standards of uprightness that the modern reader brings to the narrative are inappropriate, however, and a different interpretation of these aspects of his character is necessary.

The issue our historian addresses through the story of Jacob is how is it possible to reconcile Yahweh's prerogative of blessing with the prerogatives assumed by active and opportunistic persons for whom it is wisdom that God helps those who help themselves. Jacob was able, and hence able to get for himself. Jacob was resourceful, and hence able to provide where provision seemed absent. Jacob was cunning, able to fall back on his own intellect and craft to accomplish his ends. And yet, Jacob was "blessed." Till now, to be blessed has meant that one has received of Yahweh in contrast to the self-made character of pre-blessing humanity. Now our historian wishes to incorporate the resourcefulness of human beings into the blessing—the resourcefulness and even self-made character of the Davidic state. The character of Jacob represents the character of Israel, and in particular of its monarch David.

The history of Jacob is structured in three main parts, each of which consists of two separate incidents. The blessing of Jacob involves his acquisition of family and flocks—the twin themes of reproduction and production. This was preceded and followed by the explicit blessing of Yahweh. In this way the counterpoint between the two themes of the blessing of Yahweh and the resourcefulness of the man is dramatized. So the structure of Jacob's history is directly related to J's primary interest in divine as opposed to human prerogatives.

Through Esau's statement—"first he takes my birthright *(bekor)*, then he takes my blessing *(berakah)"*—J defines the main action of the first part of Jacob's history. A sizable block of history, however, comes between the incidents of the birthright and the blessing: while Jacob is growing up, the history of his father is told.

A famine occurred. And just in case we are slow to make the connection with the famine early in the history of Abram, J makes it for us, proceeding to tell us how that which happened to Abram happened in nearly the same way to Isaac. Yahweh appeared to Isaac, however, and instructed him not to go to Egypt but to the Philistine land of Gerar because, as he explained, "I am going to grant you all these lands." Gerar[1] is J's way of referring to the

---

1. Victor H. Matthews, "The Wells of Gerar," *Biblical Archaeologist* 49 (1986): 118–26.

region about Ziklag, where David was lord of the lands under Philistine aegis.

We have seen the important role the Philistines played in both the rise of the house of David and its maintenance in power. David was at peace with the Philistine lords of the coastal lowland. This all-important melding of powers is represented in J in the treaty between Abimelek and Isaac. The basis of that treaty is tied directly into one of the chief themes of J's history by means of the climactic words of Abimelek: "You are now the blessed of Yahweh." Abimelek had fulfilled the terms of Yahweh's original oath to Abram, and what must follow, though J does not elaborate on it, was the mutual prosperity of Isaac and the Philistines.

This is a different view of the Philistines from that presented in the history of David's rise to power, as indicated by the document incorporated into 1 Samuel and the beginning of 2 Samuel. There, the Philistines are represented as the opponents of Israel. David's association with them requires apology when mentioned and is otherwise played down. The history of the rise of David makes the point that David, although he had been a Philistine vassal and had fought on the side of the Philistine forces, played no role in the Philistines' defeat and killing of Saul, nor did he use the Philistines to support his rise to power in a cynical maneuver against the majority of the Israelites whom he came to rule. J chose to ignore entirely this apologetic point. The history of the rise of David was forced, for the sake of this apology, to grant the hostile intent of the Philistines against the Israelites and to treat the Philistines collectively as the chief enemy of the Israelites, as though they always acted in unison. J makes a different point entirely, and an important point it is: Egypt was the chief enemy of the Israelites, and hence the Philistines became Israel's allies. The two documents—the rise of David and J's history—have different purposes, and the contradiction in their portrayal of the Philistines is avoided by J's fictional device of removing Isaac's treaty with them to a time in past history. These Philistines, headed by a man whose name includes the word *melek* ("king"), were Hamites, and thus it is quite striking that they are treated as benignly as they are. They should be no better than the Canaanites or the Egyptians. Clearly the compatibility that came about between Isaac and the Philistines is a measure of the importance to the court of David of conceiving of the Philistines as friendly allies.

Indeed, an inherent uprightness of the Philistine king is disclosed at an early stage. One distinctive feature of Isaac's ruse regarding Rebekkah is the way in which Abimelek himself discovered their true relationship. Looking down from his window, Abimelek saw Isaac "laughing" with Rebekkah and knew immediately that they were husband and wife. Nothing less than the name *(tsahaq)* of this first legitimately born human being is used as the occasion for portraying the uprightness of the king of the Philistines. This is remarkable indeed.

Like Abram, Isaac became wealthy and powerful. In the land of the Philistines, his increased power led to inevitable conflict. Like Abram and Lot, Isaac separated, gradually, from the Philistines. This distance, however, was not sufficient to overcome all hostility. When Isaac and his company had gone as far as Beersheba and dug there yet another well, Abimelek traveled out with his commander and chief state representative to the bedouin tribes to negotiate a satisfactory settlement. They reached an agreement: Abimelek pronounced Isaac blessed, and, to prove the effectiveness of the settlement, Isaac's men thereupon found water in the well. This incident concludes with the naming of Beersheba, a bedouin center of importance to David whose etiology, or origin, has just been explained.

The separation of Isaac from Abimelek and their eventual agreement comes where it does for a good reason. Sandwiched between the purchase of the birthright and the theft of the blessing, it prefigures the essential part of the history of Jacob and Esau. Isaac's adventures with Abimelek can be considered a micro-version of Jacob's adventures with Laban. They focus attention on the eventual outcome of reconciliation. Jacob, like Isaac, would be forced to take refuge in a foreign land: for Isaac, Gerar; for Jacob, Aram. In both cases, Yahweh appeared at the beginning and the end of their sojourn. The three main episodes of Isaac's history correspond to the three main episodes of Jacob's life with Laban. A marital sexual impropriety was committed, which sowed the seeds of potential conflict. Isaac became prosperous in Gerar, as Jacob would become prosperous in Aram, and in both cases the prosperity led to distancing. Isaac became wealthy, then his shepherds began to dig wells and had to dig them farther and farther away as his prosperity increased. A parallel course of events would take place with Jacob and Laban: Laban would say that Jacob could have all of a particular kind of sheep, and Jacob would remove these sheep to a distance in order to keep the two flocks separate. Just as Isaac was accosted by Abimelek, if not pursued, Laban would hurry after Jacob and eventually make an agreement with him. From the ideological point of view, it is noteworthy that this prime example of an international tie of importance to the Davidic monarchy is made congruent with or equivalent to the alliance with the Philistines. Like Abram and Lot, Isaac and Abimelek remained separate. Similarly, Jacob and Esau were to remain separate, and the lands to which they would journey are about to be specified by the blessings respectively of Jacob and Esau.

17

A Self-Made Man

(Genesis 27:1—33:17, parts)

When Isaac was old and his eyesight was failing, he called Esau his older son and said to him, "Son."

And he said, "Yes."

He said, "I am old, and I do not know how long I have before I die. So take your things, your quiver and bow, and go out into the field and hunt me some game. Then prepare for me a tasty dish the way I like, and bring it to me to eat, so I can give you a robust blessing before I die."

Rebekkah overheard what Isaac said to Esau his son. While Esau went out into the field to hunt game to bring back, she said to Jacob her son, "I have heard your father say to Esau your brother, 'Bring me some game and make it into a tasty dish for me to eat so I can bless you in Yahweh's presence before I die.' So listen to me, my son, to what I am about to order you to do. Go to the flock and get me two choice kids so that I can make them into a tasty dish for your father the way he likes. Then take that to your father for him to eat, so that he will bless you before he dies."

Jacob said to Rebekkah his mother, "But my brother Esau is a hairy man, and I am a smooth man. What if my father feels me? He will think I am making fun of him, and I will bring on myself a curse instead of a blessing."

His mother said to him, "Let the curse be on me, my son. Just listen to me and go get the kids for me."

So he went and got them and brought them to his mother, and his mother made them into a tasty dish the way his father liked. Then Rebekkah took the finest garments of Esau her older son that were in her charge in the house, and put them on Jacob her younger son. The skins of the two kids she put on his wrists and hands, and over the smooth parts of his neck. Into the hands of her son Jacob she placed the tasty dish and the bread she had made, and he brought them to his father.

He said, "Father."

And he said, "Yes. Who are you, my son?"

Jacob said to his father, "I am Esau, your firstborn son. I have done as you told me to. Sit up and eat the game I have prepared so that you may give me a robust blessing."

Isaac said to his son, "You certainly have come back quickly, my son."

He said, "Yahweh your god put success in my way."

Isaac said to Jacob, "Come closer so that I can touch you, my son. Is this really my son Esau, or not?"

Jacob got closer to Isaac his father, and he touched him and said, "The voice is the voice of Jacob, but the hands are the hands of Esau."

So he did not recognize him, for his hands were like the hairy hands of Esau his brother. So he blessed him. Then he said, "Are you really my son Esau?"

He said, "Yes, I am."

He said, "Push the game dish closer toward me so I can eat, my son, so I may give you a robust blessing."

Jacob pushed it closer to him, and he ate. Then he brought him wine and he drank. Isaac his father then said to him, "Come closer and let me kiss you, my son."

He came closer and he kissed him. He smelled the odor of the garments and blessed him and said, "The smell of my son is like the smell of a field that Yahweh has blessed.

> May God[1] give you of the dew of the sky,
>   and of the fatness of the earth,
>   and abundance of grain and wine.
> May peoples serve you,
>   may folk bow down to you.
> Be master to your brothers,
>   and let them bow before you,
>   and let the sons of your mother bow before you.
> Let those who curse you be cursed,
>   and those who bless you be blessed."

When Isaac had finished blessing Jacob, at just the moment Jacob went out from the presence of Isaac his father, Esau his brother got back from his hunt. He also prepared a tasty dish and brought it to his father and said to his father, "Let my father sit up and eat of the game of his son, that he might give me a robust blessing."

Isaac his father said to him, "Who are you?"

He said, "I am your son, your firstborn son Esau."

Isaac trembled mightily and said, "Who, then, was the one who hunted game and brought it to me and I ate it all up before you arrived, and whom I blessed, and who is then indeed blessed?"

When Esau heard the words of his father, he cried out in bitter distress and said to his father, "Bless me also, my father!"

His father said, "Your brother has come in deceit and taken your blessing."

Esau said, "Is he not well named Jacob, since he has tricked me these two times, first by taking my birthright and now by taking my blessing? Haven't you saved a blessing for me?"

Isaac answered Esau, "I have made him master over you, and all his brothers I assigned to him as servants. I have undergirded him with grain and wine. What then can I do for you, my son?"

---

1. The reason for "God" instead of "Yahweh" is not clear.

Esau said to his father, "Do you have only one blessing, father? Bless me, me also, father." And Esau began to weep loudly.

Then Isaac his father responded to him,

> "From the fat of the earth will be your settlement,
>   and from the dew of the sky above.
> By your sword shall you live,
>   and your brother you shall serve.
> To the extent you are unsettled,
>   you shall tear his yoke off your neck."

So Esau despised Jacob for the blessing with which his father had blessed him. Esau said to himself, "When the days for mourning my father arrive, I will kill Jacob my brother."

These words of Esau her older son were reported to Rebekkah. She sent for Jacob her younger son and said to him, "Esau your brother consoles himself with the intent to kill you. Listen to me, my son. Flee to Laban my brother in Haran. Stay with him for a few years, until the wrath of your brother subsides and he forgets what you did to him. Then I will send to get you back from there. Why should I be bereaved of both of you in a single day?"

In J's conception of history, the basic orders are overturned. In the seventeenth generation, the generation of Esau and Jacob, the relationship of inheritance governed by sonship is called into question in a new form. The story of how Jacob, the younger son, came to inherit the birthright and blessing reflects important elements in David's own rise in power.

Favoring Jacob, Rebekkah instigated a plot to have the primary blessing conferred upon this favored son instead of on Esau, to whom it belonged by prior birth. Jacob was not, however, an unwilling participant. This is clear from the historian's use of a wordplay in Gen. 27:11, which the RSV captures well when it translates, "I am a smooth man." Like our English word "smooth," the Hebrew can mean slippery or deceptive and refers not only to Jacob's smooth skin but to his wily character. This is a good example of the ambiguous diction featured in J's history of Jacob. The narrator emphasizes the theme of blessing both here and later on in the story.

Jacob's theft of the blessing is told in terms of a ruse well known to shepherds. If a ewe twins, she is rarely able to nurse both lambs. Without the shepherd's intervention, one of the lambs would die. On the other hand, many ewes will bear one lamb and that lamb will die. In any flock at lambing time there will usually be several unnursed lambs and several ewes without lambs. In order to present a motherless lamb to a lambless ewe, the shepherd skins a ewe's dead lamb, clothes one of the twin lambs in its skin, and presents it to the lambless ewe. The skin and odor of the dead lamb almost always fool the lambless ewe into thinking that the twin lamb is her own lamb, and she proceeds to nurse the lamb and adopt it as her own. Anyone hearing the story of Jacob's theft of the blessing in its original cultural context would have recognized this motif immediately. Perhaps the most striking thing about the use of the motif is the way in which it casts Isaac in the role of the ewe. It is likely that this feature of the story is related as a counterpart to the emphasis on the active, "shepherd's" role of Jacob's mother. Isaac is portrayed as a hapless fool, tricked out of conferring his paternal blessing on his rightful and favorite heir. It is not for Isaac to bless his posterity, for Yahweh has already selected Jacob. All that Isaac can do is confirm, as with his choice of wife, Yahweh's prior choice.

Isaac's blessing of Jacob was a blessing of agricultural plenty, the service of other nations, and the subordination of his brother. The blessing concluded by repeating the conclusion of the blessing of Abram: cursed be everyone who curses you and blessed be everyone who blesses you. When Esau returned, he too requested a blessing. Isaac, shocked at being deceived, made a valiant attempt to repeat his blessing. He repeated the phrases "of the dew of heaven" and "of the fatness of the earth" in lines that sound nearly identical to the blessing of Jacob, but this time they came out with a different meaning altogether. Esau was to dwell in a land not of agricultural plenty but in the land of Edom, a land where pastoral richness exceeded agricultural richness. He was to live the life of the armed band, subordinate to his brother (the nation of Israel).[2] J's history will conclude with a reiteration of this baleful blessing.

As she had suggested the theft of the blessing, it was Rebekkah who now suggested that Jacob should visit his relatives on her side.[3] Rebekkah's suggestion appears at first to be an imitation of Abram's sending to Aram to get a wife for Isaac, but the situation has reversed itself. In the case of Isaac getting a wife, Rebekkah was Isaac's first cousin once removed on his father's side. Leah and Rachel, on the other hand, were most directly Jacob's first cousins on his mother's side. This is the way the relationship is described almost every time it is mentioned.[4]

2. The meaning of the last line of the blessing of Esau is somewhat disputed. It is widely taken to refer to the event described in 1 Kings 11:14–22, when the crown prince of Edom rebelled against the house of David and took refuge in Egypt. In fact, this association has been one of the pillars of the argument for dating J in the time of Solomon (even toward the end of his reign). It is unlikely that the Hebrew term translated "break loose" in the RSV has that meaning. Instead, it appears to mean "to be unsettled, restless, wandering," and to represent a concept much like the concept of wandering applied to Cain. The reference is primarily to the predominant Edomite mode of life. This nuance is confirmed by Jer. 2:31, in which Yahweh complains "Am I a desert, that you must say, 'We have moved on'" (New American Bible). Other passages containing this verb can be understood similarly, although it has to be admitted that the verb is somewhat obscure.

3. No direct reason is given for this suggestion in J. Isaac's agreement with the proposal is from P.

4. See, e.g., Gen. 27:43; 28:2; 29:10, 12, and 13. Gen 29:12 is a most telling case, as there Jacob gives himself a matronym, an extremely rare occurrence in Hebrew.

There are indications that this was felt to be slightly odd. We don't clearly know the rules or expectations that governed kinship and marriage among either the bedouin or the peasants of Palestine in early Israel, but the two other examples of cousin marriage of significance to this story—Isaac's marriage to Rebekkah and Esau's to Mahlat—were both on the father's side. Further, there is an incident in Gen. 29:5 that would be quite easy to pass over. Jacob inquired about his kinsman Laban. Rather than saying to the Aramean shepherds, "Do you know my uncle on my mother's side?" he said, "Do you know my second cousin on my father's side?" Or at least that is the relationship he was referring to when he said, "Laban, son of Nahor." Though there are examples of such, it is not common in Hebrew to use the grandfather in a patronym in this way. To these shepherds Jacob obscured his maternal kinship to Laban in favor of his far more distant paternal kinship. This incident confirms that Rebekkah's plan of matrilateral cousin marriage went against custom, and this oddity serves to emphasize further Jacob's special and peculiar connection to his mother. This emphasis with eponymous Israel reflects a notable peculiarity of David's rise over historical Israel. Rather than relying on his older brothers for political connections, David bypassed them for the most part[5] in favor of the connections available through his sisters and sororal nephews.[6]

With Esau and Isaac thoroughly alienated by the younger son Jacob's presumption, Jacob's inheritance of the blessing, birthright or not, became problematic. The tension was resolved when Rebekkah sent Jacob away from his father's land, ironically setting him on a career that led eventually to his acquiring a huge wealth quite apart from the wealth represented by the birthright. It is difficult not to be reminded of David. The resolution of fraternal conflict that arose from Yahweh's plan to favor the younger is made possible in a household sphere of action that entirely bypasses the basic patrilineal and patrilateral sphere. We have come to expect such reversals in the history of the blessed generations.

Jacob departed from Beersheba and traveled toward Haran. At sunset he stopped at the local shrine to spend the night. As he lay down in that place, there was Yahweh standing next to him. He said, "I am Yahweh, the god of Abram your father and the god of Isaac. The land you are lying on I will give to you and to your

5. Though see 1 Sam. 22:1.

6. For a structural analysis of kinship relations in Genesis, see Mara E. Donaldson, "Kinship Theory in the Patriarchal Narratives: The Case of the Barren Wife," *Journal of the American Academy of Religion* 49 (1981): 77–87; Terry J. Prewitt, "Kinship Structures and the Genesis Genealogies," *Journal of Near Eastern Studies* 40 (1981): 87–98; Robert A. Oden, Jr., "Jacob as Father, Husband, and Nephew: Kinship Studies and the Patriarchal Narratives," *Journal of Biblical Literature* 102 (1983): 189–205; and idem, *The Bible Without Theology: The Theological Tradition and Alternatives to It* (San Francisco: Harper & Row, 1987), 106–30.

offspring. Your offspring shall be like the dirt of the earth in numbers. You shall burst out to the west, east, north, and south. All the clans of the ground will find blessing through you and through your offspring. I will watch over you everywhere you go and bring you back to this ground. I will not abandon you until I have done everything I have told you."

Jacob said, "Surely Yahweh was at this site, and I did not know." He named that place Beth-El, although formerly the name of the city was Luz.

Jacob departed and resumed his journey to the land of the easterners. He saw, and there was a well in the open country. Three flocks of sheep and goats were lying next to it, for flocks were regularly watered from that well. A great stone lay over the mouth of the well. Only when all the shepherds were gathered there did they roll the stone off the mouth of the well and water their flocks. Then they returned the stone to its place over the mouth of the well.

Jacob said to them, "My brothers, where are you from?"

They said, "We are from Haran."

He said to them, "Do you know Laban, the son of Nahor?"

They said, "We know him."

He said to them, "Is he all right?"

They said, "He's fine."

At just this point, Rachel his daughter arrived with her flock.

He said, "There is still much daylight left. This is no time for gathering in the livestock. Water the flocks, then go and continue pasturing them."

They said, "We cannot do that until all the shepherds have gathered to roll away the stone from the mouth of the well and water the flocks."

As he continued to talk with them, Rachel arrived with her father's flock, since she was the family shepherd. As soon as Jacob saw Rachel the daughter of Laban his mother's brother, and the flock of Laban his mother's brother, Jacob went up, rolled away the stone from the mouth of the well, and watered the flock of Laban his mother's brother. Jacob then kissed Rachel in greeting and wept aloud. Jacob told Rachel that he was her father's kinsman, the son of Rebekkah. She ran and told her father. When Laban heard the news about Jacob, his sister's son, he ran to meet him. He embraced him and kissed him and brought him back to his house. When Jacob had recounted all that had happened, Laban said to him, "Surely you are my bone and my flesh."

When he had stayed with him for a month, Laban said to Jacob, "Even if you are a kinsman of mine, should you work for me for nothing? Name your wages."

Now Laban had two daughters. The older was named Leah and the younger Rachel. Leah had delicate eyes, but Rachel was beautiful of form and beautiful of appearance. Jacob had fallen in love with Rachel, so he said, "Let me work for you for seven years for Rachel your younger daughter."

Laban said, "It is better for me to give her to you than to another man. Stay with me."

So Jacob worked for Rachel seven years, but they seemed to him like only a few, since he loved her.

Jacob said to Laban, "Give me my wife, since my years of work are complete, so that I can have intercourse with her."

Laban got all the men of that place together and put on a feast. That evening he took his daughter Leah and brought her to him. He had intercourse with her. Laban gave his slave Zilpah to his daughter Leah as her slave. In the morning it was obvious it was Leah.

Jacob said to Laban, "What is this you have done to me? Did I not work for you for Rachel? Why have you deceived me?"

Laban said, "Giving the younger daughter in marriage prior to the older daughter is not done here. Complete another seven years, and Rachel will be given to you as well, for the work you will do for me for seven more years."

So Jacob did it and completed these seven years. Laban then gave him Rachel his daughter as well. Laban gave his slave Bilhah to his daughter Rachel as her slave. Jacob then had intercourse with Rachel also. He loved Rachel more than Leah, and so had been willing to work for him another seven years.

When Yahweh saw that Leah was less loved, he opened her womb, while Rachel was childless. Leah became pregnant and bore a son and named him Reuben, since she said, "Yahweh has seen my affliction, and now my husband will love me." She got pregnant again and bore a son and said, "Yahweh has heard that I am less loved and given me this one as well." So she named him Simeon. She got pregnant again and bore a son and said, "This time my husband will become attached to me, for I have borne him three sons." Therefore she named him Levi. She got pregnant again and bore a son and said, "This time I will give thanks to Yahweh." So she named him Judah. Then she stopped bearing.

When Rachel saw that she bore Jacob no children, she gave him Bilhah her slave as wife. Jacob had intercourse with Bilhah, and she got pregnant and bore a son to Jacob. Rachel said [. . .] and therefore named him Dan. Then Rachel's slave again became pregnant and bore a second son to Jacob. Rachel said [. . .] and named him Naphtali.

When Leah saw that she had stopped bearing, she took her slave Zilpah and gave her to Jacob as wife. Zilpah, Leah's slave, bore Jacob a son. Leah said, "What good luck," and named him Gad. Zilpah, Leah's slave, bore a second son to Jacob, and Leah said, "What good fortune, so my girlfriends have called me fortunate," and she named him Asher.

During the wheat harvest, Reuben went out and found some mandrakes in the open field. He brought these to his mother Leah. Rachel said to Leah, "Give me some of your son's mandrakes."

Leah said to Rachel, "Was it not enough for you to take away my husband, that you should also take my son's mandrakes?"

Rachel said, "In that case, let him lie with you tonight in exchange for your son's mandrakes."

When Jacob came in from the field in the evening, Leah went out to meet him and said to him, "Come in and sleep with me, for I have hired you with my son's mandrakes." So he slept with her that night. She got pregnant and bore Jacob a fifth son, saying, "[Yahweh] has given me my wage, since I gave my slave to my man." So she named him Issachar. Leah got pregnant again and bore a sixth son to Jacob and said, "This time my husband will honor me, because I have borne him six sons." She therefore named him Zebulun. Afterward she bore a daughter and named her Dinah.

[Rachel bore a son] and named him Joseph, saying, "Yahweh has added another son for me."

On the way to Haran, Jacob stopped to spend the night at a place that was to become the primary Israelite shrine, Bethel. The most famous element of this story, the "ladder" (actually stairway) to the sky with "angels" (messengers) ascending and descending upon it, was contributed by E. In J's history, just as Jacob was about to fall asleep, Yahweh appeared next to him. The wording and manner of Yahweh's appearance are usual for J. At just this point in the text, between the words "he lay down at that place" and "there was Yahweh standing next to him," E inserted the following words: "He dreamed and there was a stairway resting on the earth with its top reaching to the sky, and there were the messengers of god going up and down on it, and"—here E intended J's own words to be understood differently—"there was Yahweh stationed above it." (J's statement that "there was Yahweh standing next to him" can indeed have the meaning E wanted.) Then, in the original J, Yahweh reiterated the grant of land that had been made to his grandfather Abram, as well as the blessing of progeny, and promised his special protection. Jacob, either then or when he later awoke from sleep, made this thoroughly J-like pronouncement: "Surely Yahweh was at this site and I *did not know*." Having met Yahweh there, he named the place Bethel, or "house of God," in which "house" refers not simply to the sanctuary to be built there but to the household— Yahweh's household—under whose sponsorship Jacob was to acquire his wealth. J concludes with another allusion typical for his history of Jacob: the place used to be called Luz, which meant among other things "deception"—as anyone would have known.

Jacob's sojourn with Laban in Aram opens with the discovery of Rachel at the well, a common folklore motif here employed much like the discovery of Rebekkah by Abram's servant. With that comparison in mind, the question with respect to the reproduction theme is whether Jacob's behavior in choosing a wife differed in any way from the behavior of Abram's servant. As Rachel approached the well with her flocks, Jacob in his usual brusque and assertive manner "removed the stone" from the well to water her flocks. This removal of the stone was an act of great forwardness. The custom was for the well to be shared among several families and their flocks. In order that no one family and flock have an advantage at the well because they happened to have arrived first, all had to be present before it could be used. This was achieved by capping the well with a stone so heavy that it took everyone to lift it off. As the first of several instances of his mythic strength—J portrays Jacob as a Herakles-like figure, a strong man, using magical powers to achieve great feats, as will be especially evident in

his breeding of Laban's cattle—Jacob himself took the stone off. His forwardness in this act emphasizes that the self-made individual is now
included in the blessing. Having already been blessed by Yahweh, Jacob
himself chose Rachel at first sight.

As with everything in Jacob's story, his success was ambiguous and
ironic. His forwardness in choosing a wife was not to be immediately
rewarded. The historian draws out the ambiguity of Jacob's choosing as he
begins to elaborate on the interplay between Jacob's craftiness and Laban's
craftiness. Jacob lived with his maternal uncle for a month or so as a
worker. Eventually Laban proposed that Jacob should request some payment for his work. Laban presented him with a choice of one of his two
daughters. Jacob had met first and fallen in love with Rachel. He thought it
over. The eyes of Leah were delicate, but Rachel was "beautiful of form and
beautiful of appearance." Jacob chose the more beautiful one. The Hebrew
uses appearance to emphasize the sight of Rachel, in line with the historian's interest in man and woman seeing each other.

In Middle Eastern societies it was quite undesirable from the family's
point of view that a younger daughter should be married prior to an older
daughter. Laban would say this in nearly so many words later on, but at
this point he dissimulated: "It is better for me to give her to you than to
another man." He didn't say yes or no, so as not to be caught lying when he
replaced Rachel with Leah. In telling us that Jacob slept with Leah the
entire night of his wedding without realizing she was not Rachel, J is
reminding us of the replacement of Esau by Jacob. In a sense there is a
"righting" of the score: Jacob had happen to him what he did to Esau.

One of the several ways in which the historian ties together the many
otherwise separate episodes of his history is through like-sounding terms.
The seven-year periods of work imposed on Jacob were prepared for
narratively by the story emphasizing the origin of the place-name
Beersheba; for even though in J Beersheba is taken to mean "the well of
the oath" between Isaac and Abimelek, the term *sheba* in that name can
also mean seven. The number seven is the number most often chosen by J
for specific periods of time. We note too the parallel between the completion of fourteen generations prior to the first blessing of a human being and
the fourteen years that preceded the consummation of Jacob's marriage to
Rachel.

Although Jacob's forwardness was checked by his having to marry Leah
and wait for Rachel, in another sense he could do no wrong as a member of
the blessed family line: Leah became the mother of half of his twelve sons
and of his apparently sole daughter, and hence an important contributor to
the wealth of the household. She was also the mother of Judah, who—as

one might expect in a Judahite history—would play a crucial role among all the sons of Israel.

The issue of Jacob's forwardness continues into the story of the birth of his children. This is the main issue. The story of the births of Jacob's children is not simply a catalogue of births, names, and their meanings. Jacob loved Rachel more than Leah because she was younger and more beautiful, and he had worked for her a total of fourteen years, whereas he had worked only seven years for Leah. When Yahweh "saw" that Leah was the less preferred, he favored Leah himself, the elder having become the underdog. He made Leah fertile and Rachel infertile. And to make sure the point is not missed, our historian interprets the names of Leah's first sons in terms of this favor, even when the interpretation stretches what is otherwise an obvious meaning. For example, she named her first son Reuben. It is a typical name and like most sentence names in Hebrew makes some reference to the moment of birth. Reuben means "see the son." This is not the meaning that Leah gave it, however. For her, this son emphasized the favor that she had found in the sight of Yahweh. The god had seen her affliction. Similarly, whereas Simeon's name probably refers to a god's answering a request for a child, for Leah it meant that Yahweh had heard that she was less favored. The historical etymology of Levi is not fully clear, but it certainly does not mean what Leah said it meant. The birth of Judah, her fourth son, completed this first set of children, and she named him for her gratitude to Yahweh. Again, most historians do not take this to be the normally understood meaning of the name Judah.

Before Rachel eventually became pregnant, the slaves of the two sisters bore four children, and Leah three more, including Jacob's only named daughter, Dinah. Only then did Rachel become pregnant. She named her son Joseph, whose name for her meant "may Yahweh add for me another son." Joseph was a typical name of a younger son, and his name was to be fulfilled in the birth of Benjamin.

Leah is a parallel to Hagar in that she was not the one Jacob would have chosen to bear his firstborn son, even as Hagar was not the one Abram would have chosen. Just as there were two mothers for the children of Abram in whom J is most interested, so there were two mothers (and two slave consorts) for the children of Jacob. Like Hagar, Leah was favored by Yahweh with the birth of a child prior to the protagonist's favored wife. Of course, Hagar, although pregnant, was spurned by Yahweh for her pride over her pregnancy and was only fully favored when, out in the desert with no resources and at risk of perishing without bearing at all, she "saw" Yahweh. Our historian makes this link by having Reuben, whose name means for Leah "Yahweh saw," be the first of her sons. J dwells on the birth of the sons of Jacob to focus attention on the emergence of the Davidic nation Israel and the role of its component tribal parts, with which David was forced to live.

One might be tempted to regard this series of births and names as seemingly meaningless. But those ancient readers or hearers of J who identified with one of these sons would have paid particular attention if the name of his own supposed forebear had been related as closely to J's major themes as were Reuben, Simeon, Levi, and Judah. After all, it was to influence the behavior of these subjects of the Davidic kingdom that J constructed his fantastic history of the ancestors in the first place. Indeed, these names advertise loudly that David's policy toward the tribal heritage of Israel was to continue to be favorable.

The birth story of Jacob's children is the structural centerpiece of the history of Jacob. His struggle with Esau, his journey to Laban, and his work for Laban culminate in the births, which are followed by a reversal of these events: his work for himself, his journey from Laban, and his reconciliation with Esau.

After Rachel bore Joseph, Jacob said to Laban, "Let me go so that I can go back to my land and locale. Give me my wives and children for which I worked for you and let me go, for you know the work I have done for you."

Laban said to him, "If I have found favor in your eyes, I realize Yahweh has blessed me on your account. Name your wage, and I will give it to you."

Jacob said to him, "You know all the work I have done for you and what your livestock have become in my hands. However small what was yours was before I came along, it has burst out in multitude, and Yahweh has blessed you at my pace. But now, when am I going to do something for my own household?"

Laban said, "What shall I give you?"

Jacob said, "Don't give me anything. I will again pasture and keep your flock. Let me go through your whole flock today and set aside every spotted, patchy, and dark-brown sheep and every spotted and patchy goat, and let them be my pay. Tomorrow, let my right witness against me should there be added to my wages, to your knowledge, any animal that is not spotted or patched among the goats or spotted, patched, or dark brown among the sheep. It may be regarded as stolen property in my possession."

"Okay," said Laban, "let it be as you say."

That same day, Laban set aside the patchy and spotted goats and the spotted and patchy lambs, any that had white on them, and all the dark-brown lambs, and put them in his sons' charge. Then he put a three days' journey between himself and Jacob.

While Jacob was pasturing the rest of Laban's flock, Jacob got for himself still green branches of poplar, almond, and plane trees. He made white stripes in them by peeling off the bark of the branches. He fixed the branches he had peeled upright in the watering troughs so that they would be in front of the flocks that came to drink. Those that were in heat when they came to drink mated before the branches.

These sheep bore spotted and patchy sheep. Jacob set aside their lambs. Later Jacob turned the other sheep toward these spotted, patchy, and brown sheep now in Laban's flock, and so all by himself made for himself flocks which he did not put with Laban's flock. When the heartier sheep and goats were in heat, Jacob would set the branches in front of them in the troughs so they would be in heat by the branches. With the weaker sheep he did not set the branches. Thus the feeble sheep went to Laban, and the more hearty to Jacob. Thus the man burst out in extreme prosperity. He acquired many flocks, female and male slaves, and camels and asses.

Jacob heard that Laban's sons were saying, "Jacob has taken everything of our father. He has produced all this wealth from what belonged to our father."

Yahweh said to Jacob, "Return to the land of your fathers, and to your birthplace and kinship base."

Jacob arose and lifted his children and wives onto the camels and led off all the livestock he had gotten. When Laban had gone to shear his sheep, Jacob and all who were with him fled. He crossed the river and set his face toward the highlands of Gilead. Three days later it was reported to Laban that Jacob had fled. He took his kinsmen with him and chased after him for seven days. He finally overtook him in the highlands of Gilead. When Laban had caught up with Jacob, Jacob had pitched his tent in the highlands, and Laban and his kinsmen had pitched theirs in the highland as well.

Laban said to Jacob, "Why did you flee in secret? You have stolen from me and not reported it to me. I would have sent you off with shouting and singing, with music of tambourines and harps, but you went hurriedly off, because you had acquired a few shekels for your father's household."

Jacob answered Laban, "I was afraid because I thought you might steal your daughters back from me." Jacob was angry and argued with Laban and answered Laban, "What is my transgression? What is my sin, that you have chased after me?"

Laban answered Jacob, "The daughters are my daughters and the sons my sons. The sheep are my sheep, and everything you see belongs to me. And as for my daughters, what shall I do for them today, or for their children whom they have borne? Let's make a covenant, I and you, and let it be a witness between me and you."

Jacob said to his kinsmen, "Take stones." So they took stones and made them into a heap. They ate there by the heap.

Laban called it Yegar-Sahadutha, "Heap of Witness" in Aramaic. Jacob called it Gal-'Ed, "Heap of Witness" in Hebrew. Laban said, "This heap is a witness between me and you this day." That is why its name is "Heap of Witness." It is also called Mitspah, because he said, "May Yahweh keep watch between you and me, when we cannot see each other, that you do not oppress my daughters or take wives in their place." Laban said further to Jacob, "This heap which I have set up between me and you is a witness that I not pass beyond it to your side and you not pass beyond it to my side. May the god of Abram and Nahor judge between us."

Jacob swore to the treaty. Then he summoned his kinsmen to eat, and they ate and spent the night in the highlands. The next morning, Laban got up, kissed his sons and daughters, blessed them, and went on his way and returned home.

As soon as Rachel bore her first son, Jacob desired to depart. For him, the

sequence of events that began when he fell in love with Rachel had reached
its conclusion with the birth of her firstborn son. Laban, however, didn't
want him to go. Jacob spoke to Laban, emphasizing the work that he had
done for him and requesting leave. Laban's response draws the whole
episode under the rubric of J's theme of the blessing: "I realize[7] that
Yahweh has blessed me on your account. Name your wage and I will give it
to you." Jacob responded, "You know all the work I have done for you and
what your livestock have become in my hands. However small what was
yours was before me, it has burst out in multitude and Yahweh has blessed
you at my pace.[8] But now, when am I going to do something for my own
household?" J's interests have come thick and fast: livestock, burst out,
blessed, household. With the reproductive theme covered, the main theme
of the section to follow is clearly Jacob's provisioning of his household.
Now we are alerted to the overall issue of J's history of Jacob: whether it
was Yahweh or Jacob himself who produced this wealth. Laban responded,
"What shall I give you?" And Jacob answered, "Don't give me anything."
As when the kings of Sodom and Salem came to Abram, Jacob refused to
be the beneficiary of his kinsman.

It remained for Jacob, however, to cull out sheep and goats of a certain
kind. These are described by Hebrew terms that mean something like
spotted, patchy, and dark brown. Laban, wily as ever, agreed. But then he
had his men remove all such animals from the flocks. There is a clear
correspondence between Jacob's tricking Isaac when he stole Esau's blessing and Laban's tricking Jacob when he forced him to marry Leah. It is
likely that Laban's theft of sheep and goats that were properly Jacob's
corresponds with Jacob's other offense against Esau, his "purchase" (the
next thing to theft) of Esau's birthright. Because Jacob suffered Laban's
tricks, his tricks against his brother were neutralized. Laban's tricking Jacob
and putting him at serious disadvantage in each of the two major sections
of the history of Jacob in Aram also allows the historian to stress the ability
of Jacob to recover from such disadvantages by his own devices. Had the
trick worked, Jacob would have been left with nothing. Presumably he
would have continued to work for Laban.

But Jacob was up to the trick. During the mating season, he took
branches (the Hebrew means a staff) of three trees, partially stripped them,
and placed them before the mating sheep. When the ewes bore, their
lambs' markings matched the markings of the bark of the branches. The
three trees were the poplar, the plane tree, and the almond. The poplar's

7. The usual translation "divine" is possibly correct. Later we will make a few additional
observations regarding Joseph's ability "to divine."

8. The precise meaning of the last phrase is not certain. The best guess is that Yahweh has
blessed Laban gradually at the same rate as he has blessed Jacob.

bark is gray-green with patches of creamy white or gray, smooth but pitted with small dark diamond-shaped spots. This tree produced spotted lambs. The plane tree is related to the sycamore tree known in America. Its bark is greenish brown and sheds large rounded plates to leave yellow patches. The plane tree produced patchy lambs. The almond's bark is dark brown, nearly black. The almond produced dark-brown lambs. Jacob's method so far was magical.[9] J apparently also defined the method in terms of the common goals of selective breeding. Jacob selected the stronger of the flock for special breeding and left the weaker to Laban. The upshot of this episode was that Jacob had manipulated the reproduction of his flocks so as to create his own wealth.[10] He certainly owed nothing to Laban. Because Jacob was a blessed individual, his self-made character had prevailed, despite opposition.

Jacob had now become like Abram and Isaac, marvelously wealthy. Perhaps the most significant thing about Jacob's acquisition of his blessing is that, like Abram, he acquired his family and wealth away from his homeland, away from the supportive framework of his father's household, with the complete absence of a fraternal interest group that would normally have been required for the success of most individuals. This is another way of directing attention indirectly to Yahweh's role in the production of wealth, progeny, and power. The fraternal interest group is an essential component of the context of one's bearing. When Jacob left his father's household to journey to Aram, he was like Abram when he departed from his father's household. And like his grandfather Abram, Jacob heard Yahweh's grant of land reiterated at Bethel.

In the sixteenth generation, Isaac had received and benefited from Abram's blessing (though J narrates Yahweh's rather than Abram's blessing of Isaac). In the next generation, Jacob did not receive and benefit from Isaac's blessing, except by his own cunning. Thereby J highlights Jacob's dependence on Yahweh's support, signaled by Yahweh's opening pronouncement to the pregnant Rebekkah. Then, armed with the support of Yahweh's blessing, it is Jacob's own ability that brings about his success.

Yahweh instructed Jacob to return to "the land of your fathers, and to the

9. The text has become somewhat confused because of E's use of an alternative set of terms to supplement this narrative, followed by later mixing.

10. The development of white fleece was a result of two technological developments quickly increasing in importance during David's century, the advent of dyeing and the invention of sheep shears, especially the former. Laban assigned Jacob the lower value sheep, in terms of the commercial development of wool dyeing. Why Jacob settled for this arrangement in the long run is not made clear. It is likely that David contributed wool to the Tyrian woolens market; thus it is expected he would sanction breeding for white fleece. See Michael L. Ryder, *Sheep and Man* (London: Gerald Duckworth & Co., 1983); and idem, "The Evolution of the Fleece," *Scientific American* 256:1 (January 1987): 112–19.

whole context of your bearing"—the phrases come straight from the blessing of Abram. Jacob led away what J calls the *miqneh qinyano*, the livestock of his getting. The root *qanah*, known to us from the story of Cain, is used not once but twice. The heir of the blessing in this generation is a true "getter."

There is an interesting correspondence between Jacob's large family and his large flocks. It is not just that his large family made possible his large flocks, with his sons and daughter providing the necessary labor for keeping them. Rather, the correspondence is to be found in a feature of the family that Jacob had married into that is not usually noticed. Jacob had married, with respect to nomenclature, into a family of sheep. Rachel's name makes this obvious: it means ewe.[11] Leah's name most likely also designates some kind of sheep. It does not occur with this meaning in Hebrew but is closely related to the Ugaritic word *ll'u*, having to do with sheep. Laban's name marks him as a white ram, an image that is played on in this story of Jacob turning white sheep into spotted, patchy, and brown sheep. Seen in this way, Jacob ended up with two sets of flocks—humans and livestock.

Although the literary analysis of what follows is difficult, it appears that when Jacob departed, Laban followed after him, and that when the two met up with each other they concluded a peaceful agreement. Not only is this agreement in line with the agreement between Isaac and Abimelek, it also prefigures that between Jacob and Esau. One should not forget that by these individual actors J refers to the important neighbor states under David's dominion. Just as Abimelek stands for the Philistine rulers and Esau for the Edomite rulers, it is probable that Laban represents an Aramean ruler. The treaties between Isaac and Jacob and these people are most likely significant representations not only of the relations between David and his client kingdoms but also of the Israelite assumption that David's rule was benign and beneficial.[12] The Hebrew for "heap of witness" sounds like Gilead, the place where the treaty between Laban and Jacob was made, and the buffer zone between Israel and Aram.

It is difficult to know what portion of this section of the biblical story derives from J and what from E.[13] There are several definite indications of E material but little that would indicate what is definitely J. The treaty itself,

11. The Hebrew word in Rachel's name is used for "ewe" in, e.g., Gen. 31:38 and 32:15.

12. "The main issue of David's era was the contest between Zobah and Israel" (A. Malamat, in *The Biblical Archaeologist Reader 2*, ed. D. N. Freedman and E. F. Campbell, Jr. [Garden City, N.Y.: Doubleday & Co., 1964], 96).

13. The literary task is to distinguish in this episode lines that compare with Isaac's quarrel with Abimelek and his men in J (Gen. 27:17–33) from lines that compare with Abram's quarrel with Abimelek in E (Gen. 20:8–17). Our solution is only tentative.

marked by a heap of stones, appears to come from J's history not only because of the appropriate political implication mentioned in the previous paragraph but also because of a verbal allusion to the incident that had introduced him to Laban's family as Jacob departed from that family. Recall that Jacob presumptuously removed the stone from the well to water Rachel's flocks. In Hebrew the expression "removed the stone" sounds almost identical to the expression "heap of stones." This verbal similarity provides a framework to Jacob's sojourn in Aram and helps to confirm that the treaty described comes from J.

As Jacob went on his way, he sent messengers ahead to Esau his brother, to the land of Seir, the open country of Edom. He gave them this order: "Thus you shall say to my lord Esau, 'Thus your servant Jacob has said, "Having stayed with Laban and not left until now, I have come into possession of oxen, asses, sheep, and male and female slaves. I am sending this news to my lord to find favor with you."'"

The messengers returned to Jacob and said, "When we got to your brother Esau, he was already coming to meet you, with four hundred men with him."

Jacob was extremely frightened. He devised a plan for himself and divided the people with him, as well as the flocks, herds, and camels, into two camps. "If Esau should arrive at one camp and attack it," he was thinking, "at least the remaining camp would be left."

Then Jacob said, "O god of my father Abram and god of my father Isaac, O Yahweh, who said to me, 'Go back to your land, birthplace, and kinship base, that I may do good for you,' I am too small and young for all the acts of kindness and faithfulness you have done for your servant. With but my staff I crossed this Jordan. Now that I have become two camps, save me from the hand of my brother, from the hand of Esau, for I fear him, because he might come and attack me, with mothers and children. You did say, 'I will do good for you and make your offspring like the sand of the seashore, too many to count.'"

Jacob prepared to spend that night there. He took from what he had brought with him a gift for Esau his brother, consisting of two hundred she-goats and twenty he-goats, two hundred ewes and twenty rams, thirty milch camels and their young, forty cows and ten bulls, and twenty she-asses and ten he-asses. These he put in charge of his slaves, in separate sections, and said to his slaves, "Pass in front of me, but keep a space between the sections."

Then to the slave who was to head up this parade he said, "When my brother Esau runs into you and asks you, 'Whose slave are you? Where are you going? Who do these animals in front of you belong to?' say, 'To your servant Jacob—but they are a gift sent to my lord Esau. Also, he is right behind us.'"

He gave the same orders to the second slave in line, the third, and all those going along attending the sections: "This is what you should say to Esau when you find him. And say, 'Your servant Jacob is right behind us.'" Jacob was thinking, "I'll appease his face with a gift going ahead of my face. Then when I see his face, perhaps he will raise my face."

The gift passed ahead by him. While he spent the night in the remaining camp, he got up during the night and took his two wives, two slaves, and eleven boys and forded the Jabbok. After he had taken them and helped them ford the stream, and then had carried everything else belonging to him across, Jacob was left alone. A man wrestled with him until dawn came up. When he saw he would not prevail, he struck his groin, and Jacob's groin was wrenched while he wrestled with him.

He said, "Let me go, for it is dawn."

Jacob said, "I won't let you go unless you bless me."

He said to him, "What is your name?"

"Jacob."

He said, "No longer shall your name be Jacob, but Israel, for you have striven with gods and with men and prevailed."

Then Jacob asked, "Tell me your name."

He said, "Why on earth are you asking my name?"

That's the way he blessed him there.

Jacob named the place Penuel, the Face of God, with these words: "I have seen a god face to face and my life is saved."

The sun came up on him as he crossed at Penuel. He was limping because of his groin. (Thus the Israelites do not eat the groin tendon at the groin to this day, since he struck Jacob's groin in the groin tendon.)

Jacob lifted his eyes and saw none other than Esau coming, and with him four hundred men. He divided the boys between Leah and Rachel and the two slaves. He put the slaves and their children first, Leah and her children next, and Rachel and Joseph last. He passed before them and bowed to the ground seven times as he approached his brother. Esau ran to meet him. He embraced him and fell on his neck, kissing him in greeting and weeping. Then he looked up and saw the women and children. The slaves and their children approached and bowed down. Then Leah also with her children approached, and they bowed down. After them Joseph and Rachel approached and bowed down.

He said, "What were this whole camp of yours I just encountered?"

Jacob said, "It was for finding mercy in the eyes of my lord."

Esau said, "I already have a great deal. Keep what you have."

Jacob said, "No. If I have found mercy in your eyes, take my gift from my hand, for I have seen your face the same as seeing the face of a god, the way you have received me kindly. So take my blessing brought to you, for I have everything."

Jacob insisted with him, so he took it.

Esau said, "Let us break camp and go. I will travel at your side."

He said to him, "My lord knows the children are delicate, and the flocks and herds, now sucking young, weigh upon me. If they are overdriven even a day, the whole flock will die. Let my lord pass before his servant. I will proceed at the more gentle pace required by the task about me and by my children, until I get to my lord in Seir."

Esau said, "Let me appoint for you some of my men who are with me."

He said, "Why? Let me find favor in the sight of my lord."

That day, Esau set off on the way back to Seir. When Jacob had gotten as far as Succoth, he built there a house for himself, and for his livestock he made shelters. Therefore he named the place Succoth, Shelters.

Another example of the ambiguity that attends the attempt to distinguish

J from the combination of J and E in this section is provided by the Hebrew term translated by the RSV as "distressed" (Gen. 32:7). The word as vocalized in the Masoretic text of the Hebrew Bible means literally "to be in straits," or "to be in a tight spot." This would fit the picture apparently intended by E: Jacob was sandwiched between Esau in front of him and a somewhat hostile if partially mollified Laban behind him—the Laban of E. A different vocalization of the same consonants, a vocalization that might well have applied prior to the merging of E into the J history, would make the verb equivalent to the J term "formed," used to describe Yahweh's creation of the first human being and repeated in the expression "every imagination" and "imagination" (Gen. 6:5; 8:21) in reference to humans' usurping of Yahweh's creative prerogative. The J meaning would have been, "Jacob devised a plan for himself and divided the people and property. . . ." Just as once human beings presumed to create for themselves, so now, beginning with Jacob, they presumed to devise their own means of reconciliation. This is valid conduct, the historian suggests, within the family of the blessing.

Jacob devised a strategy to help himself in this difficult moment—a strategy for risk reduction. This initiates the great scene of fraternal reconciliation. If we think back to Abram and Lot, we recall an action of complete generosity, if not deferential abandon. Abram said to Lot, "You choose first and take whatever you want." Abram's reliance on Yahweh's blessing was complete. In contrast, Jacob did what he could to remain in control of both his possessions and his reconciliation with his brother. The eponymous hero of David's nation was resourceful and self-reliant to the point where one could wonder wherein lay the blessing of Yahweh. The history of Jacob is a history of commonplace reality in which resourcefulness is everything. Yet our historian is at pains to stress and to project a point about the commonplace: Israel's nationhood under David is nothing less than the doing of David's god.

Jacob divided his possessions into two groups, one of which was to survive, the other of which was to be a large gift to appease his brother. As he has done so often, J again makes use of the device of separating related incidents with an intervening incident that helps to explain them. Between the dividing of his possessions and the presentation of his gift to Esau, Jacob prayed to Yahweh much as Abram's servant did. Jacob's prayer apparently was modest, deferential in the extreme, giving all credit to Yahweh and none to himself. Yet what did he say? "With but my staff I crossed this Jordan" (Gen. 32:10). The word for staff is not the usual word but rather the word used by the historian for the tree limbs (Gen. 30:37; RSV: "rods") by which Jacob acquired for himself all his sheep and goats.

In other words, Jacob gave Yahweh credit with his statement while simultaneously withdrawing it with the words he used.

Our historian does not exhaust the allusion to the prayer of Abram's servant in this ambiguity. Whereas Yahweh up to this point in the history of Jacob had been only implicitly involved in reproduction and production, he was now explicitly called upon to make reconciliation possible. This is a genuine equivalent to the deference of Abram's servant in the matter of marriage. The prayer, however, was more for deliverance than for reconciliation.

Hedging his bets, Jacob now implemented the other aspect of his strategy by cutting out a generous offering for Esau. He arranged for Esau to encounter the gift in a gradual crescendo before encountering Jacob himself. By having his entire brood precede him, Jacob was true to his own self-effacing character—some would call it timorous, others perhaps cowardly. Having sent his offering before him, he brought his family across the Jabbok stream, apparently returning to the Gilead side to spend the night there alone.

But he was not alone. In fact, he had a rough night, spending dusk to near dawn wrestling with a man. The incident was not a dream and it did not manifest or affect Jacob's psyche in any way other than what is already clear from his previous history. There is no indication that Jacob's injury from the man was serious. Nothing is made of his momentary disability in any other part of his history.[14] What role does this incident play? It has more than one meaning, but one meaning is primary and obvious, given everything that has so far been said about J and about Jacob. Jacob forced this man, who of course was Yahweh's genie, to bless him. Now what made Jacob force the man to give him what had already been given him from the beginning of his story? This is the point of the history of Jacob: the eponymous ancestor of Israel does not rely on Yahweh alone but on Yahweh and himself or, better put, on himself and Yahweh.

Jacob refused to release the genie. "I won't let you go unless you bless me," he asserted. The genie inquired, "What is your name?" And Jacob said, "Jacob." The genie thereupon changed his name: "Your name is to be Israel, for you have striven with gods and with men and prevailed."[15] Then Jacob asked the genie to tell him his name. The genie was surprised: "Why on earth are you asking *my* name?" As descendant of the blessed Abram

14. It may be that the tendon henceforth made taboo has some reproductive association. What is clear is that the name of the tendon (Heb.: *gid hannasheh*) could be interpreted "the deceptive tendon," referring to Jacob's character.

15. This etymology by J is not in fact the original historical meaning of the name Israel, which meant something like "El commanded [the heavenly armies]." See Robert B. Coote, "The Meaning of the Name Israel," *Harvard Theological Review* 65 (1972): 137–42.

and possessor of the blessing, did Jacob intend to bless the genie? Such would be in character. His character notwithstanding, it turned out that Jacob did not make a name for himself but had his name made great by Yahweh (at least in a nominal way).

Throughout his history, J typifies a person through the use of terms related either to the person's name or to the person's conduct. Several words refer to Jacob's deceptive, resourceful conduct, not directly but connotatively or by means of a pun.[16] "Supplanted": this word comes from the same word as Jacob's name. It refers to "gain," as in Psalm 19: in keeping Yahweh's precepts there is "much gain" (RSV: "reward"), more than gold, even fine gold. The Jabbok that Jacob crosses is a pun on the same root. "Boiling pottage": the word connotes immoderate behavior (in Jacob's case, calculated immoderation). "Smooth man": Jacob was "slip-pery." "Luz/almond": the word connotes deception. "Plane": the word sounds like the one used to describe the snake in the garden as "crafty." "Hip": the word sounds like the one used by the woman in the pleasure orchard when she said that the snake "beguiled" her. Thus there are precedents in the narrative for the genie to change Jacob's name to "Israel," which, like the other terms in J's mind, refers to Jacob's slyness. In modern usage this incident lends itself to psychologizing and personalizing inter-pretations. But Jacob's personal character in no way changed at this mo-ment. Nor did our historian have any interest in psychologizing none other than the eponymous ancestor of the entire nation.

The historian now turns to the other meaning of this incident. Jacob's plan, in his own words, literally was "to cover his [Esau's] face with the offering going before my face and after I see his face perhaps he will raise my face." The historian has taken the idiom of faces raised in face-to-face communion (contrast Cain's fallen face) and has made much of it in reference to his theme of fraternal reconciliation. He makes this experience a foreshadowing and surety of Jacob's reconciliation with Esau: "Jacob named the place Face of God (Peni-el) with these words, 'I have seen a god face to face and my life is saved.'" Having seen a god face to face, there should be no problem seeing a man face to face, just as he had striven, in the words of the genie, with both gods and men.[17]

By the time Jacob was actually face to face with Esau, Esau had been able to imbibe the full magnitude of Jacob's wealth and generosity. As we did when Abram addressed Malkitsedeq and the king of Sodom, we will pay particular attention to the brothers' conversation. This is the moment toward which the history of Jacob has been moving from its inception.

16. See Gen. 27:36; 25:29; 27:11; 28:19; 30:37; 32:32.
17. The difference between the Hebrew Peniel and Penuel is insignificant.

Esau politely feigned ignorance, asking, "What is this train of yours I have encountered?" Jacob reiterated, "It is for finding mercy in the eyes of my lord [Esau]." To this, Esau responded, "I already have a great deal." He didn't need Jacob's gift, as Isaac's blessing was indeed a blessing. Jacob's response turned the tables: "If you favor me, receive my gift from my hand, for so I have seen your face as one sees the face of a god. If it pleases you, take my blessing which has been brought to you, for I have everything." Jacob insisted and Esau relented. What is most noticeable is that Jacob, unlike Abram with the kings, missed a unique opportunity to aver that what he had, he had from Yahweh. As everywhere in the history of Jacob (Israel-to-be), it is left to the reader and hearer of the history to furnish the full theological implications.[18]

As they prepared to move from the scene of their reconciliation, Jacob was understandably unwilling to anticipate these moves in direct language. It would have been quite inappropriate, if not dangerous, for him to raise once again the issue over which their struggle occurred in the first place. He said therefore that he would join Esau in Edom but pleaded that he could not keep pace with Esau, what with his large and frail retinue. Esau took off to Edom, the land of his blessing, while Jacob lingered behind, never in fact arriving in Edom but settling in Canaan, the land of his grant and blessing. In J's history, Esau became the Edomite nation and Jacob the Israelite nation, both of the time of David.

---

18. For a complementary literary perspective on Jacob, see Michael Fishbane, *Text and Texture: Close Readings of Selected Biblical Texts* (New York: Schocken Books, 1979), 40–62 (chap. 3: "The Jacob Cycle").

18

The Primacy of Judah

(Genesis 33:18—35:22, parts)

Jacob arrived peaceably at the city of Shechem, in the land of Canaan, and camped before the city. Dinah, the daughter Leah had borne to Jacob, went out to admire the daughters of the land. Shechem, the son of Hamor, the Hivite, the chief of the region, took her and lay with her and raped her. He became infatuated with Dinah, the daughter of Jacob. He fell in love with the girl and tried to make up to her for his rude behavior.

Shechem said to his father Hamor, "Get this girl for me for a wife."

Jacob heard that he had violated his daughter Dinah. With his sons out in the open country with his livestock, Jacob kept quiet until they got back. Shechem's father Hamor came out to Jacob to talk with him. When they heard, Jacob's sons came in from the open country and stood by. They were extremely angry that such an outrage had been committed against Israel, to force the daughter of Jacob to lie with him. Such a thing simply was not done.

But Hamor spoke with them in these words: "My son Shechem has fallen in love with your daughter. Give her to him as a wife. Intermarry with us. Give your daughters to us, and take our daughters for yourselves. Settle with us. The land is before you. Settle down, move about here, and buy property here."

Shechem said to her father and brothers, "Let me find favor in your eyes. Whatever you require of me, I will give it. No matter how great you make the bride price I must pay, I will give whatever you say. Only give me the girl as my wife."

The sons of Jacob answered Shechem and Hamor his father with guile, speaking in response to the violation of Dinah their sister. They said to them, "We are not able to do this thing, to give our sister to a man who still possesses his foreskin. That would be a disgrace for us. But we will agree with you on this condition: if you become like us, having every male among you circumcised, then we will give you our daughters and take your daughters for ourselves, and settle with you, and become with you one people. If you do not listen to us and circumcise yourselves, we will take our daughter and go."

Their words seemed good to Hamor and Shechem his son. The lad did not waste any time performing the requirement, since he had a great desire for Jacob's daughter, and he was the most important man of all his father's house. Hamor and his son Shechem went to the gate of their city and spoke to the men of the city. "As these men are peaceful with us," they said, "let them settle in the area and move about in it. Since the land is broad before them, let us take their daughters for our wives, and let us give to them our daughters. But the men will agree to settle with us to become a single people only on this condition, that all our males become circumcised as they are circumcised. Will not their livestock and property, all their animals, become ours? Let us come to an agreement with them, so that they will settle with us."

All men qualified to go out through the city gate heeded Hamor and Shechem his son, and all the males, all those qualified to go out through the city gate, became circumcised.

Three days later, while they were in pain, two of Jacob's sons, Simeon and Levi, the brothers of Dinah, each took his sword and went to the city without hindrance and killed all the males. When they had killed Hamor and Shechem his son by the sword, they took Dinah from Shechem's house and went off. Jacob's other sons came in over the corpses and looted the city for defiling their sister. They seized their flocks, herds, and asses, whatever was in the city or the open country. They took away all their wealth, their children, and their women, and looted everything in the houses.

Jacob said to Simeon and Levi, "You have irked me by making me stink among the city dwellers in these parts, among the Canaanites and the Perizzites. I am few enough that they could gather against me and attack and destroy me and my house."

But they said, "Should he be allowed to treat our sister like a harlot?"

Some way into the land they came to Ephrathah, where Rachel went into labor. She had a difficult labor. On the point of death, as she took her last breath, she named her son Ben-oni, "Son of my trouble." His father named him Benjamin. Rachel died and was buried on the road to Ephrathah (that is, Bethlehem).

Israel departed and pitched his tent beyond Migdal Eder. While Israel encamped in that area, Reuben went and lay with Bilhah his father's mistress, and Israel heard.

The main incidents that marked Jacob's journey from Aram to Palestine proper had occurred at Penuel, Succoth, and Shechem. These places were important cultural centers, either religious or commercial, in the northern part of the Davidic dominion. That J was particularly interested in Jacob's association with them is another indication that the writer of this history presumed the unity of the Davidic dominion centered in Jerusalem. Prior to the writing of J's history, Jacob as a traditional figure may have been more closely associated with what became after Solomon the northern kingdom of Israel. If this is so, then J's appropriation of traditions that were not directly tied into the history of either the family of David or of Judah must be understood as an attempt to project the unity of David's kingdom through the amalgamation of regional traditions.

J uses features of bedouin culture to refer to features of Davidic urban culture so as to remove them from the condemnation attached to Cain's line. One such feature is his description of what probably were in actuality

royal marriage alliances in terms of the marriages of his bedouin protagonists, especially Jacob himself. "Band societies rely on marriage ex-
changes to establish long-distance networks of kinspeople. Bands that
formed a completely closed breeding unit would be denied the mobility
and territorial flexibility that are essential to their subsistence strategy."[1]
This observation refers to hunter-gatherers, but it applies to nomads as
well. It also applies to urban society, and this coincidence is used by J.

While Jacob was settled in the vicinity of Shechem, the urban center of
the northern hill country, his daughter Dinah was accosted by the prime
youth of the city, the lord of Shechem, whose name was itself Shechem. (In
other words, he was the eponym of Shechem.) He stands of course for the
city of Shechem and for cities in general, and his behavior typifies the
behavior of people of the first fourteen generations and later lines who
were not yet included in the blessing. He was presumptuous, aggressive,
violent, cynical, and callous, epitomizing the behavior of the sons of Cain
and Ham. His strategy was to choose his own wife, rape her, and then
marry her in order to possess her family's property.[2] His behavior recapitulated the city and rape motifs in the history of Sodom. In order to give some
semblance of recompense for his unrectifiable behavior, he offered to pay
any price named as his marriage gift, and he held out to Jacob and his
family the advantages of intermarriage and the mutual inheritance of lands
in the vicinity of Shechem. Shechem's apparently generous motivation had
limits, however, ones that J signifies when he describes how Shechem later
explained to his fellow Shechemites that this would be a way of acquiring
Jacob's "cattle" and "property" (both words are formed from the root
qanah contained in Cain's name). Shechem's offer was unlikely to appeal to
Jacob, not only because of its intrinsic offensiveness but also because Jacob
had no reason to form an alliance with Canaanite city dwellers to acquire
land that had already been granted to him from the hand of Yahweh. The
association of Jacob's grandfather Abram (from whom Jacob inherited this
grant) with the region of Shechem went back to the beginning of this
blessed family's presence in Palestine when Abram first built his antiurban
altar at Shechem.

The bride price required by Jacob represents an appropriate retribution
for J, reversing the potency presumed by Shechem's behavior. The men of
Shechem were to be circumcised. Circumcision is harder on men than on
baby boys, and the men's penises were temporarily disabled. Jacob's pre-

---

1. Marvin Harris, *Culture, People, Nature: An Introduction to General Anthropology*, 3d ed.
(New York: Harper & Row, 1980), 267.

2. For an anthropological treatment tying this narrative to the earlier history of marriages
in J, see Julian A. Pitt-Rivers, *The Fate of Shechem or the Politics of Sex: Essays in the Anthropology
of the Mediterranean* (Cambridge: Cambridge University Press, 1977), 145–71.

scription, to test the fraternal loyalty of the Shechemites by means of circumcision, comes close to the historical function of this rite in the many societies in which it occurs,[3] but J's use of the motif is separate from this coincidence. Simeon and Levi had no intention of going along with the arrangement. Neither apparently did Jacob, since the historian characterizes him as full of "deceit" as well. In revenge for the rape of their sister, Simeon and Levi killed Shechem and his men and looted their city. Before he died, Jacob may have granted Shechem to Joseph (Gen. 48:21–22). In any case, the killing of the urban men of Shechem made room for the landowning northern elite who, loyal to David, replaced them.

The family seems excessively prolific in sons and poor in daughters, even for ancient times. There are specifically twelve brothers, because in combining his two kingdoms into one, David divided the people into twelve tribes, possibly in order to make one responsible for provisioning the court each month of the year, as his son Solomon did with his nontribal administrative districts. The predominance of sons is due to J's assumption, shared with his fellow men and probably women, that power and authority belonged to males.

The role of Simeon and Levi must be considered from a broader perspective. Recall that Leah bore six of Jacob's twelve sons and that the first four of these six were Reuben, Simeon, Levi, and Judah. The Davidic historian is of course particularly intent on eventually magnifying the role of Judah, ancestor of the land of David. Judah is to appear particularly righteous as the history unfolds. But he was the fourth and had three older brothers who ought properly to be more favored. How, then, did Jacob feel about these three older brothers? The attack on the Shechemites introduced a degree of animosity between Jacob and Simeon and Levi. Jacob was upset with his two sons. "You have irked me," he said to them, "by making me stink among the city dwellers in these parts. We are few enough that they could do away with us altogether." Immediately following this story comes what has always been regarded as a strange fragment regarding Reuben: "While Israel encamped in that area, Reuben went and lay with Bilhah his father's mistress, and Israel [Jacob] heard." Heard what? In Hebrew, the line comes to an abrupt stop. What did Jacob do? No one has ever been able to answer these questions—of no concern to our historian of course. All the historian needs to establish is that Jacob had reason to dislike Reuben. Since the relationship between Jacob and his first three sons had been disturbed, his favor shifted naturally to his fourth son Judah.

The disfavor of Reuben, Simeon (both historically contiguous with Ju-

---

3. Karen Ericksen Paige and Jeffery M. Paige, *The Politics of Reproductive Ritual* (Berkeley and Los Angeles: University of California Press, 1981), 122–66.

dah), and Levi clears the way for the history to develop as the history of Judah and Joseph. It then climaxes at the end of Jacob's life with Jacob's blessing of his sons (Genesis 49) in terms that reflect these earlier incidents. Reuben would not be preeminent, because he had invaded his father's bed. Simeon and Levi would be scattered in Israel because of their imprudent anger. Only when Jacob came to Judah did he pronounce a genuine blessing: "Your father's sons shall bow down before you" (Gen. 49:8). Nothing less than the preeminence of Judah in Israel, the basis of Davidic rule over all Israel, derived from these incidents involving the first three sons.

The material in the Bible immediately following the story of Shechem comes almost entirely from the E and P writers. For J to give out in favor of supplemental material from the other strands is characteristic of most of the main narrative blocks concerning the great ancestors. This pattern, seen already in the stories of Abram, applies as well to the stories of Jacob, Joseph, and Moses.

J places the birth of Benjamin, the son of Rachel and the brother of Joseph, at Bethlehem, David's birthplace. Historically, the territory of Benjamin began several miles north of Bethlehem. This displacement of Benjamin to the south at his birth probably signifies David's command over the heartland of Saul's kingdom. More important, it brings the birth of national Israel to its completion at the site of David's birth.[4]

In Gen. 35:21 Jacob is called "Israel" for the first time as a matter of course in the narrative. From this point on, the historian uses the name Israel instead of Jacob until his death. It might be thought that Israel would replace Jacob immediately following the scuffle at Penuel, or, as is usually said, that the name Israel is J's designation of Jacob in the block of material frequently referred to as the Joseph story. Both of these suggestions appear frequently in secondary scholarly literature, but neither is correct. The point that J makes by changing Jacob's name to Israel in his narrative at precisely this stage is political. The name Israel applies immediately upon the birth of his twelfth son, who completes the complement of the twelve-tribe unit ruled by David.

The burial of Isaac comes from the P writer (Gen. 35:22–29). The lack of tension evident in this episode is characteristic of P, but it can be assumed that it was similar in J.[5]

---

4. Gen. 35:16–20 is widely regarded as E. While the line "The midwife said to her, 'Don't be afraid—this one is a boy for you, too,'" from v. 17, and the whole of v. 20 are almost certainly E supplements, the incident probably comes from J.

5. Some of the genealogy of Edom in Genesis 36 is usually included in J.

19

West of Eden

(Genesis 37:1—41:56, parts)

We have come to what is often referred to as "the Joseph story." Contrary to the way many Old Testament "introductions" describe the latter part of Genesis, or to what one might first expect upon reading these chapters in their present form, there never existed in J a long story that could be described as the story of mainly Joseph, one that could stand by itself —an incorporated "court novelette."[1] It is best to regard the episodes that constitute the story of the reconciliation of the sons of Israel as the history of Judah and Joseph together. What we tend to think of as the whole history of Joseph is actually an interweaving of the histories of Judah and Joseph. It is the later additions from the E writer (the northern strand—where Judah plays no further role and Joseph is of primary importance) that tend to turn J's story into the story of Joseph alone.

It is often suggested that this story, in which the scene shifts to Egypt, is of a different type from the kind of traditional material contained in J's history of Abram, Isaac, and Jacob, which consists of stories associated with the lives and activities of Palestinian bedouin. But throughout the story, the traditions employed or imitated resemble the kinds of traditions prevalent among the bedouin, particularly of southern Palestine. The range of territory of these bedouin could extend as far west as Egypt. In times of particular distress or opportunity, they even made their way into the gaps, and sometimes the administrative hierarchy, of Egyptian society.[2] An important exception to this characterization of the traditional source of the material in the history of Judah and Joseph is the Egyptian "Story of Two

---

1. See, e.g., Gerhard von Rad, "The Joseph Narrative and Ancient Wisdom," in *The Problem of the Hexateuch and Other Essays* (New York: McGraw-Hill, 1966), 292–300.

2. This is extremely important in the context of the modern discussion of the Pentateuchal materials, which is influenced by a propensity of German form criticism to understate the common character of these traditions.

Brothers."[3] It contains an episode nearly identical to the story of Joseph being accused of attempted rape. It is possible that just as J had access to written cuneiform tradition while writing the first part of his history, here he had access to an Egyptian document. It is known that David's court bureaucracy was based on Syro-Egyptian practice.

Although the history pursues the theme of fraternal or national reconciliation throughout the story of the brothers' hatred of Joseph, their eventual reconciliation, and the death of Jacob, the history that begins here involves entities within what was to become Israel rather than addressing relationships between Israel and other national entities.

More specifically, the history addresses the perennial issue in Palestinian national politics: how the northern hill country, the mountain land of which Shechem was the traditional capital (the focal area of today's West Bank), was to be integrated effectively into the national whole. Shechem was neutralized. In other words, the traditional capital lost its position in favor of Jerusalem. Joseph, the father-to-be of the northern tribes Ephraim and Manasseh, represents this mountain land. The sons of Israel had little use for Joseph, this odd brother out, and sold him into slavery. In the process of recapitulating many of the incidents seen already in the history, the brothers were eventually reconciled, primarily through the agency of Judah (the home tribe of David).

At one level the issue behind the relationship between Judah and Joseph is the unity of the twelve tribes of the eighteenth generation, the tribes comprising the Davidic kingdom. What is being addressed is the unity of the nation of Israel ruled for the first time as a unity by David.[4] At another level the issue of the Judah and Joseph sagas is the issue of whose ruler will prevail, the ruler from the hill country of Judah or the ruler from the northern hill country. As subsequent history showed in the revolts against David of disaffected elements of the house of Saul, it was never fully resolved. Thus it was important for David's historian to address this as effectively as he could. The north, J claimed, owed its existence to Judah, the homeland and original kingdom of David. Benjamin, from which sprang the household of Saul, David's opponent in his rise, owed its existence to Judah, from which sprang the household of David. It is as

3. See the translation by John A. Wilson in James B. Pritchard, *Ancient Near Eastern Texts Relating to the Old Testament*, 2d ed. (Princeton: Princeton University Press, 1955), 23–25.

4. Many historians believe that David's rule represented a personal union of two separate and distinguishable kingdoms. See A. Alt, "The Formation of the Israelite State in Palestine," in *Essays on Old Testament History and Religion* (Garden City, N.Y.: Doubleday & Co., 1968), 223–309, esp. 282–83. Compare, however, the comments of J. Alberto Soggin in *Israelite and Judaean History*, ed. J. H. Hayes and J. M. Miller (London: SCM Press; Philadelphia: Westminster Press, 1977), 352–56.

though the homeland of the ruling family were assuring regions within the realm which were potentially disadvantaged by their coming late under David's rule that Judah in fact loved them much. The importance of the role of Judah is brought out not only by the way he contributed to national reconciliation but also by the way the history concentrates on the question of the rightness of Judah's acts. Our historian has a degree of interest in the rightness of Judah that matches or surpasses his interest in the rightness of Yahweh in the fifteenth generation.

The history of Joseph brings Egypt to front and center stage, where it remains for nearly the rest of J. (At this point we are slightly less than halfway through J.) As is clear from the disquiet in Solomon's reign, which led to the secession of Israel from the ruling house of David at Solomon's death, the northern hill country, as a result of its perennial independence from the rule of Jerusalem, was prone to make, through its local chieftains, warlords, and kings, separate alliances with the great powers of the Middle East such as Egypt. This tendency has prevailed throughout the agrarian era in Palestine. The link in J between the rule of Joseph (who represents the heartland of what later became the northern kingdom of Israel after Solomon) and Egypt hints at just the sort of collusion between Egypt and Shechem that led to the dissolution of the united kingdom a mere generation after David had unified it.

The shift in geographical focus to Egypt at this stage is not an accident. It is an important new development in the historian's crafting of his story of national reconciliation. As often happens, parties who differ may discover a common cause that brings them together in the opposition of some outside body or force. Anthropologists and historians sometimes refer to this phenomenon as complementary opposition. A common enemy strengthens internal cohesion. At just the moment, then, when the twelve sons of Israel are welded together in this history, the primary outside opponent enters the stage in order to reinforce and solidify the harmony effected by Judah. Having defined, in the history of the fifteenth to the seventeenth generation, the set of alliances and bonds that sealed the periphery of David's empire through a chain of lesser powers, the historian now begins his thorough characterization of the opposing empire, the superpower threat of David's time—against which they together must defend themselves. Having begun this characterization in the eighteenth generation, the first generation of the sons of Israel, the historian will bring it to its grand climax in the twenty-first, the generation of Moses. The proof of the comparative rightness of Judah vis-à-vis his brothers will gradually overflow into the comparison that comes to dominate the entire history—the wrong of Egypt vis-à-vis Israel. For it is ultimately Egypt's wrong that justifies the nationalism of J.

Joseph was pasturing the flocks with his brothers. He was just a lad at that time. Israel loved Joseph more than all his other sons and made for him a long-sleeved gown. His brothers saw that their father loved him more than his brothers. So they hated him so far as to be unable even to say hello to him.

His brothers went to pasture their father's flocks in Shechem. Israel said to Joseph, "Your brothers are pasturing in Shechem. I want to send you to them. Go, see how your brothers are doing and how the flocks are doing, and then bring me back word."

He sent him from the valley of Hebron. When he arrived near Shechem, a man found him wandering about in the open country. The man asked him, "What are you looking for?"

"I am looking for my brothers. Tell me where they are pasturing."

"They have moved on from here," the man said. "I heard them say, 'Let's go toward Dothan.'"

Joseph went after his brothers and found them in Dothan. Before he got too close to them, they plotted to kill him. When Joseph came up to his brothers, they stripped him of his gown, the long-sleeved gown that was on him. While they were seated eating, they looked up and saw an Ishmaelite caravan making its way from Gilead. Their camels were laden with gum, balsam, and myrrh, which they were on their way to take down to Egypt.

Judah said to his brothers, "What profit is there in it if we kill our brother and cover his blood? Let us sell him to the Ishmaelites so that our hand will not be on him. He is after all our brother and our flesh."

His brothers listened to him. They sold Joseph to the Ishmaelites for twenty pieces of silver, and the Ishmaelites took Joseph to Egypt.

They took Joseph's long-sleeved gown. They slaughtered a goat and dipped the long-sleeved gown in its blood. They sent some of their number ahead to bring the gown to their father. They said, "We found this. Recognize whether it is your son's long-sleeved gown."

He recognized it. "My son's long-sleeved gown! Joseph has been torn to pieces!"

He put on sackcloth, and mourned his son for many days. All his sons and daughters attempted to console him, but he refused to be consoled. "No, as a mourner I will go down to my son in the nether world." Thus did his father weep for him.

The history of Judah and Joseph begins with Joseph shepherding flocks with his brothers and develops initially in an episode that involves shepherding. As the major block of the history of Judah and Joseph concludes, the first episode of the next major block, regarding the condition of Israel's family in Egypt, similarly portrays Israel's family as sheepherders. The Egyptians, our historian then informs us, abominated sheepherders. This information takes us back once again to Cain and Abel and prepares us for the impending conflict. For J, as issues of sex and reproduction recede in prominence and issues of production and conflict come to the fore, the regular allusion to Abel as sheepherder becomes a device for relating one major section of the history to another, and the whole back to the first murder.

Israel loved Joseph more than his other sons. The composite text tells us that was because he was the son of his old age. That reason probably comes from P, whose text apparently has displaced J's at this point. Jacob's favoring of Joseph in J derives from his favoring of Rachel, and it is important not to be distracted from that awareness by the subsequent revision of J. For J, the whole crucial episode of Judah and Joseph stems from the contrast between Abram's servant (for Isaac) and Jacob in selecting a wife. Besides, P's explanation does not account for why Jacob preferred Joseph over Benjamin.

As a token of his favor, Israel gave Joseph a "long-sleeved gown."[5] His other sons took a profound dislike to their brother Joseph for that reason. Indeed, they determined to kill him. One time his brothers were shepherding in the vicinity of Shechem while his father and he were near Hebron. His father sent him to check up on his brothers, and his journey brought him to the region that eventually was to be granted to him and named after him. Failing to find his brothers at Shechem, he was found by an anonymous man, perhaps Yahweh, who informed him that his brothers had gone north to Dothan. This placed them at the edge of the northern hill country, adjacent to the Jezreel valley through which the primary trade and communication route between Egypt and the East ran.

When Joseph arrived at Dothan, his brothers saw their opportunity to murder him. They stripped him of his gown. Then they sat down to eat in preparation for the deed. While they were eating, an Ishmaelite caravan passed near, working its way west with a cargo of gum, balsam, and myrrh. This gave Judah an idea: "Why murder Joseph, when we could make some money off him and not be guilty of his murder?" The brothers agreed, and sold Joseph as a slave to the Ishmaelites in return for twenty pieces of silver. In a sense, then, Joseph owed his life to Judah. This did not completely exonerate Judah, however, for he was the brother who, to save Joseph, proposed that he be sold as a slave. The history of Judah and Joseph is the history of how this wrong of Judah was redeemed; all its main incidents contribute to this purpose.

The Ishmaelites, our historian states, took Joseph to Egypt. It makes sense that the Ishmaelite traders passed this way traveling back and forth between Aram and Egypt, since Ishmael's father was a son of Shem, as was Aram, and his mother a daughter of Ham, as was Egypt. Our historian

---

5. The translation is P. Kyle McCarter, Jr.'s, of the same Hebrew phrase in 2 Sam. 13:18, the only other place it occurs. See McCarter, *II Samuel*, Anchor Bible (Garden City, N.Y.: Doubleday & Co., 1984), 325–26. The storyteller makes Joseph's cloak a special one to draw attention to the importance of cloaks in linking the next several incidents.

probably regarded this trade as integral to Israel's prosperity as Ishmael was kin to Israel (great-uncle).

Our historian will resume the adventures of Joseph in due course by repeating his statement that Joseph was brought to Egypt. This repetition marks off a set of two stories having to do with the conduct and conscience of Judah. The first is about how the brothers used Joseph's gown to trick their father Israel. The second is about how Tamar, Judah's daughter-in- ⎣law, used the hem of Judah's cloak to trick Judah and to make him conscious of his lack of rightness.

The brothers took Joseph's gown, smeared it with goat's blood, brought it to their father and said, "We found this. Do you recognize it as your son's?" The key word in their statement is "recognize," as it is the most explicit verbal similarity between this story and its parallel, Judah's recognition of his wrong when he saw the hem of his gown. Israel recognized the gown and assumed that Joseph had been torn apart by a wild animal. Israel had had a trick played on him, and we almost expect him in some sly way to retaliate, to turn the tables on his sons and undo the evil that had occurred. But this was not the same old Israel. The historian has left behind the wily eponymous ancestor, the protagonist of the seventeenth generation. In moving to the eighteenth generation to deal with Israel's sons, particularly Judah and Joseph, he portrays Israel in the conventional role of the elder bedouin sheikh, lacking most of his earlier distinctive features. Israel grieved incessantly and refused to be consoled. While he grieved, the parallel story took place.[6]

At that time Judah went down and pitched his tent by a certain man of Adullam named Hirah. There Judah saw the daughter of a Canaanite named Shua. He married her and had intercourse with her. She got pregnant and bore a son, and he named him Er. Then she got pregnant again and bore a son and named him Onan. Then she bore yet another son and named him Shelah. It was in Kezib that she bore him.

Judah took a wife for his firstborn Er. Her name was Tamar. Er, the firstborn son of Judah, was evil in Yahweh's eyes, so Yahweh killed him.

Judah said to Onan, "Have intercourse with your brother's wife. Do your duty to her as brother-in-law, and establish offspring for your brother." Onan knew, however, that the offspring would not be his. Whenever he had intercourse with his brother's widow, therefore, he ejaculated onto the ground, so as not to contribute offspring to his brother. What he did was evil in Yahweh's eyes, so he killed him also.

Judah then said to his daughter-in-law Tamar, "Dwell as a widow in your father's

6. Genesis 38 is widely regarded as "out of place," under the erroneous assumption that in the supposed original novelette about Joseph, Genesis 39 followed directly on Genesis 37. For a recent summary of this discussion, see G. R. H. Wright, "The Positioning of Genesis 38," *Zeitschrift für die alttestamentliche Wissenschaft* 94 (1982): 523–29.

house until my son Shelah grows up." He was thinking, "I don't want him, too, to die like his brothers." Tamar went and stayed in the house of her father.

After some years, Judah's wife, the daughter of Shua, died. After his period of grief, Judah went up to Timnah, with Hirah the Adullamite his companion, to be with the sheepshearers. Someone reported to Tamar, "Your father-in-law has gone up to Timnah to shear his sheep." She took off her widow's clothes and covered herself with a veil. She then sat at the entrance to Enaim, on the way to Timnah. She saw that Shelah had grown up but that she had not been given to him as wife.

Judah saw her and, since she had covered her face, figured she was a prostitute. He went over to her on the way and, since he did not know she was his daughter-in-law, said, "Come, let me have intercourse with you."

She said, "What will you pay me for letting you have intercourse with me?"

"I will send you a kid from the flock."

She said, "You will have to leave a pledge until you send it."

"What pledge shall I give you?" he asked.

"Your seal, a part of the hem of your garment, and the staff in your hand."

He gave her these and had intercourse with her. She got pregnant. She went and removed her veil and put her widow's clothes back on. Judah sent the kid through his companion the Adullamite to get back his pledge from the woman. He did not, however, find her. He inquired of the men at the place where she was seen: "Where is the sacred prostitute, the one at the wayside in Enaim?"

They said, "There hasn't been any sacred prostitute here."

He went back to Judah and said, "I didn't find her, and even the men of the place said, 'There hasn't been any sacred prostitute here.'"

Judah said, "Let her keep them. We don't want to become a laughingstock. At least I sent her this kid, even though you couldn't find her."

About three months later, it was reported to Judah that "Tamar your daughter-in-law has been a harlot, and she has even gotten pregnant by her harlotry."

Judah said, "Bring her out and let her be burned."

As she was being brought out, she sent someone to say to her father-in-law, "I have become pregnant by the man to whom these belong. Recognize to whom this seal, hem, and staff belong."

Judah recognized them and said, "She is more right than I because I did not give her to Shelah my son." Thereafter he did not know her again.

The time for her delivery came, and she turned out to have twin sons in her womb. As she was giving birth, one stuck out his hand. The midwife took a scarlet thread and tied it around his wrist. She said, "This one came out first." When he pulled back his hand, suddenly his brother came all the way out. The midwife said, "What a breach you have made for yourself." Thus his name became Perets. Afterward his brother came out, with the scarlet thread on his wrist. His name became Zerah.

Judah went down into the foothills west of Hebron to a place called Adullam to spend some time with a man named Hirah. David had a base at Adullam (1 Sam. 22:1; 2 Sam. 23:13–17). There Judah saw the daughter of a Canaanite and married her. She bore him a son named Er. His name sounds like J's word for city (*ir*). It is also related to a number of like-sounding terms used in the culture of the time to refer to impotence and potency.[7] Of course, the pun on both city and potency is quite in line with J's depiction of the lines of Cain and Ham. Judah's wife then bore him a second son named Onan, whose name is another veiled reference to reproductive potency, and a third son named Shelah, whose name apparently makes him the "peaceable" one (the significance of the name is uncertain). Judah's wife bore these children in a place called Kezib, which, given the history of Jacob, we are not surprised to learn signifies a lie or deception.

Then Judah chose a wife for his firstborn son, Er. Her name was Tamar. The text says that Er was evil in the sight of Yahweh—he didn't like him—so he killed Er. Er was the firstborn of a Canaanite, possibly born in a place called deception, and the holder of a name that recalls the city-building lines of the cursed generations. Yahweh probably took Er as a presumptuous firstborn. In line with David's youth and his relation to his brothers as well as Saul's son Jonathan, the primacy of younger sons is a preoccupation of J. The sequel to the killing of Er reveals the importance of his implied reproductive presumption.

Judah instructed his next son, Onan, to take his brother's wife in levirate marriage.[8] The historian tells us that Onan "knew" (in J's phraseology the term could carry the full load of what Yahweh regarded as Onan's evil) that the offspring of his marriage would not be his heir but his brother's, so when he had intercourse with Tamar, he practiced *coitus interruptus*. What went through Onan's mind was the anxiety that his first son would not be his heir but Er's. Onan then would be merely uncle to the grandson of Judah in the direct line of inheritance. Yahweh regarded this attempt to control the reproduction of this family as evil and killed Onan too. What went through Yahweh's mind was Onan's presumption in trying to control the economic power passed on through reproduction. This is verified when Judah himself then tried to control it in order to save his youngest son, Shelah, and was thereby shown to be unjust.

Judah feared that if he sent Shelah to marry Tamar as he should have as a matter of course, he would lose him as well. (Presumably Judah did not know why his sons were dying.) So he sent Tamar back to her father's family with the agreement that when Shelah came of age, she could marry him. Apparently he had no intention of keeping this agreement. Eventually Judah's wife died, and he went off to spend time with his friend Hirah in

7. Charles H. Bowman and Robert B. Coote, "A Narrative Incantation for Snake Bite," *Ugarit-Forschungen* 12 (1980): 135–39.

8. Levirate marriage means marriage by the brother-in-law. In Hebrew law a man was required to marry the wife of his deceased brother. This institution is described in Deut. 25:5–10.

Timnah. This placed him in the vicinity of Tamar. When she found out that he was nearby, she disguised herself as a harlot on a way she knew Judah would take. Judah propositioned her, not recognizing her, since she had veiled her face. J informs us that "he did not know" that she was his daughter-in-law. Tamar knew that by this time Shelah had come of age but had not been given to her. The purpose of her trick was to try to acquire her rightful man, that is, the man that was hers by "right" in contrast to Judah's "wrong" in not giving him to her in order to save him from being killed by Yahweh. "What will you give me for lying with you?" Tamar asked. Judah said, "I will send you a goat." Tamar replied, "I'll do it if you give me security until you send the goat." When Judah inquired what the security should be, she said, "Your seal, a part of the hem of your garment,[9] and the staff in your hand." He gave her these securities, had intercourse with her, and made her pregnant. Then she went off and again put on her garments of widowhood. Judah sent the goat with his friend Hirah in order to recover his securities. Hirah couldn't find the harlot. When he got back, Judah said, "Well, at least I did send the goat, even though we couldn't find her. Let her keep the securities, lest we become a laughingstock."

Three months later Judah discovered that Tamar had become pregnant. He accused her of being a whore and called to have her brought out and executed. When she was found, she sent word to him that she could identify the man who had made her pregnant: "Just recognize to whom this seal, hem, and staff belong." Judah recognized them. The word "recognized" (repeated here) flashes back to the preceding story, which was also based on the recognition of a person's garment. The similarity would not be so striking were the following story, regarding the unjust accusation of Joseph, not also based on the recognition of a garment. All these garments are related to a sexual act[10] and allude to the clothing of the first man and woman in the garden. They appear here together as signs of the truth or untruth of an incident and point up the significance of trial and proof at this stage in the history. Then comes the key statement from Judah: "She is more right than I because I did not give to her Shelah my son." Judah did not know her again, the historian concludes. Judah's discovery and acknowledgment of his guilt, in view of the later development of his history with Joseph, seem to have gone a long way toward resolving his guilt for selling Joseph as a slave and tricking his father. His unrightness in presuming to protect his own youngest son had paved the way for his later right act of surety for the protection of Israel's youngest, Benjamin.

9. The word usually translated cord or cords here refers most likely to the hem of Jacob's garment. This proposal is based on the practice of using the hem of a person's garment as judicial proof attested in Akkadian texts.

10. Joseph's cloak is a mark of the favored status of Rachel in the eyes of Israel.

How did Judah become the just and loyal protagonist? Judah was tricked as he himself had joined in tricking his father Israel. Thus he alone among the brothers was punished, so to speak, by having to recognize the tokens in witness against himself. Then, in the following episode, Joseph would be proven more virtuous than Judah by refusing to lie with his master's wife.

The issue of Judah's justification *(tsedeq)* refers directly to the justification of the Davidic monarchy represented in the history first by the king named Malki*tsedeq* (the just king). It is a striking feature of J's history as Davidic propaganda that it gives so much attention to the legitimation of David's Judahite monarchy in relation to the northern hill country. Whereas we tend to think of biblical Israel as uniformly overlying the general region of Palestine, historically the northern and southern hill countries (Joseph and Judah) have typically existed as separate regions that have almost always fallen under different rulers or belonged to separate administrative districts. The divided kingdoms of Israel and Judah represent the norm for Palestine, while David's "unification" of these areas represents a historical anomaly that was fragile and insecure. It was not without reason that David's world historian devoted the effort he did to bringing these two historically separate regions into relation with each other by means of a narrative that joins them directly on the issue of Judah's justification.

Tamar bore twins. The first stuck his hand out, and the midwife tied a red string on his hand saying, "This one came out first." When he pulled back his hand, however, his brother popped out ahead of him "How you have burst forth for yourself," the midwife shouted, using the Hebrew word *perets* twice and naming him Perets. This is a common word in J, with strong connotations of prosperity and abundance. After he emerged from the womb, his older brother came out and was named Zerah. Once again the younger had prevailed over the older. In this case the younger, Perets, became the ancestor of David.[11] He is the last individual, with the exception of Caleb, that J deals with in the direct ancestry of the house of David.

Judah's sons by Tamar kept the inheritance of Judah, the ancestor of David, in the line of Shem rather than mixing it with the line of Canaan— through Judah's Canaanite wife—and hence Ham and Egypt. This is in contrast to Judah's actual political rivals Ephraim and Manasseh, who were half Egyptian, hence half Hamite, rather than pure Shemite.

When Joseph was brought down to Egypt, an Egyptian man bought him directly from the Ishmaelites who had brought him down there. Yahweh was with Joseph, and the man prospered. Joseph became a member of the household staff of his

11. That David was conceived as an offspring of incest is not too surprising. If the tradition that Ruth was his great-grandmother is accurate, there is incest on that side as well in J's conception, since Ruth descended from Moab. Evidence is that David married his sister Abigail. See Jon D. Levenson and Baruch Halpern, "The Political Import of David's Marriages," *Journal of Biblical Literature* 99 (1980): 507–18.

master, the Egyptian. When his master saw that Yahweh was with him and that everything he did Yahweh made a success, Joseph found favor in his eyes. He continued to serve him, until eventually he put him in charge of his household, putting everything he had in his hands. From the moment he put him in charge of his household and everything he had, Yahweh blessed the Egyptian's house on Joseph's account. The blessing of Yahweh was on everything he had, in both house and field. Having left everything he had in Joseph's hands, he gave no thought to Joseph, but only to the food he ate.

Joseph had a handsome body and was good-looking. After a time his master's wife began to take notice of Joseph. She said, "Lie with me."

He refused and said to his master's wife, "My master gives no thought to me regarding anything in the house. Everything he has he has placed in my hands. He is no greater in this house than I. He has withheld from me nothing but you, since you are his wife. How then should I do this great evil?"

As often as she spoke to Joseph, day after day, he refused to agree to lie beside her or with her. One such day he came into the house to perform his duties, and there were no other men of the house staff there in the house. She grabbed his cloak and said, "Lie with me."

He left his cloak in her hand and fled outside. When she saw that he had left his cloak in her hand and fled outside, she called to the men of her house and said to them, "See here. He has brought in a foreign slave to make sexual advances on us. He came in here to me to lie with me. I called out loudly, and when he heard me raise my voice and shout, he left his cloak here beside me and fled outside."

She set his cloak beside her until his master arrived back in the house. She told him the whole story. "The foreign slave you brought in for us came in and made sexual advances on me. When I raised my voice and shouted, he left his cloak beside me and fled outside."

When his master heard the story his wife related to him—"Your slave did such and such"—he became angry. Joseph's master took him and put him in the prison where the king's prisoners were confined.

Even while he was in prison, though, Yahweh was with Joseph. He channeled kindness toward him and made the chief jailer favorably disposed toward him. The chief jailer put Joseph in charge of all the prisoners in the prison. For everything anyone did there, he was the one to say so. The chief jailer paid no attention to anything under Joseph's charge, since Yahweh was with him, and everything he did Yahweh made successful.

[Joseph's administrative success in prison came to the attention of the king, who brought him out of prison to make better use of his skills in the king's court. There Joseph foresaw impending famine and advised the king on coping with it as follows:] "Let pharaoh have overseers appointed over the land, and divide the land of Egypt into five districts. During the seven years of plenty, let them gather in all the food of the coming good years and stockpile the grain under the hand of pharaoh, as food in the cities, and let it be guarded. The food will serve as official grainstores for the land during the seven years of famine that will be in the land of Egypt, and the land will not perish in the famine."

The plan seemed good to pharaoh and all his court. Pharaoh said to Joseph, "You will be in charge of my household. At your command shall all my court bustle about. By the throne alone shall I be greater than you." Then pharaoh said to Joseph, "See, I hereby set you over the whole land of Egypt." Pharaoh took his signet ring off his hand and put it on Joseph's hand. He had him dressed in garments made of fine Egyptian linen, and put a gold chain around his neck. He had him climb into the vizier's chariot, which became his, and as he rode by they shouted before him "Abrek!"

In placing him over the whole land of Egypt, pharaoh said to Joseph, "As pharaoh I hereby declare that without your approval no one in all Egypt may raise hand or foot." Pharaoh named Joseph Sapnat-pa'neh. He gave him as wife Asnat the daughter of Potipera', priest of On [Heliopolis]. Thus Joseph emerged in charge of the land of Egypt.

When Joseph had left pharaoh's presence, he traveled all over Egypt. During the seven years of plenty, as long as the land produced abundantly, he gathered all the food of the seven years in the land of Egypt and put food in the cities, putting the food from the lands around a particular city in that city. Joseph thus stockpiled grain in vast quantities, like the sands of the shore. Eventually he stopped keeping track of how much, since it had exceeded all reckoning.

The seven years of plenty in the land of Egypt came to an end, and the seven years of famine began to come, just as Joseph had said. Then while there was famine in all other lands, there was food in all the land of Egypt. When the famine hit the whole land of Egypt and the people cried out to pharaoh for food, pharaoh said to all Egypt, "Go to Joseph and do whatever he says to you." When the famine had spread over the whole land, Joseph opened the stores everywhere and sold grain to the Egyptians.

The historian now shifts the focus of the history back to Joseph. When Joseph was brought to Egypt by the Ishmaelites, he was purchased by an Egyptian (his name is not given in J). The historian emphasizes Yahweh's blessing on Joseph and in turn on the Egyptian. Indeed, the blessing of Yahweh was on everything that belonged to the Egyptian because of Joseph. We can assume that J conceives of all twelve brothers as bearers of the blessing, but it is the next to youngest brother, vulnerable and jeopardized—enslaved and then imprisoned—who stands out for special attention.

The narrative stresses Joseph's trustworthiness in the view of his master. This laid the groundwork for his next turn of fortune. Joseph was very handsome, being the son of a beautiful woman and well fed at his master's table. His master's wife made advances to Joseph, asking him to bed down with her. Reminding her of his master's trust in him, Joseph consistently rejected her advances. The master's wife pressed her request repeatedly. Eventually she did so when there was no one else in the house but Joseph and herself. This time when he said no, she grabbed him by his garment. In desperation, Joseph slipped out of his garment and fled out of the house. Left holding just his garment, the master's wife raised the alarm and accused Joseph of making sexual advances to her. (The word used by J for aggressive sexual advances here is our familiar "laugh." The RSV's "insult" misses the point.) She retained his garment as proof that he had attacked her. When her husband returned, he accepted the garment as sufficient proof of her right and Joseph's wrong. Being a highly placed servant of his king, he had Joseph incarcerated together with the rest of the royal prisoners. Joseph's refusal to succumb to the wiles and insistence of his master's wife represents the reversal in his case of the system of sex and power, elaborated most recently in the case of Judah. Joseph was innocent of the presumption that began back in the pleasure orchard of Eden. Thus his success was transparently Yahweh's doing.

Now begins a new cycle, in words that are reminiscent of Joseph's success in his master's household. The chief of prisoners, apparently in recognition of Joseph's administrative skills, placed him in charge of the rest of the prisoners. Whatever was done in that office, the historian explains, he did. Indeed his ability, based explicitly on Yahweh's assistance, led, as with his previous master, to the chief of prisoners' complete trust in him.

At this point in the biblical narrative come the famous dreams of Joseph, through which he found out about the impending great famine and managed to get out of prison. These dreams belong to E. Here more than perhaps anywhere else in the J history there seems to be a gap created by the insertion of E. When J resumes, Joseph is in the court of pharaoh advising him on arrangements for dealing with the famine. The question must now be asked as to how, in the material that is now missing from J, Joseph got from the king's prison to the king's court. We can only speculate, but the clues are to be found in what J tells us about Joseph. Joseph was a capable administrator and, as we are twice told, had the gift of "divination."[12] Whatever the last was, it provided him with the skill of clairvoyance. (The historian refers to this skill, as in the case of Jacob and Laban, unselfconsciously and without elaboration.) It is easy to imagine how Joseph's fortunes turned, and it would not have taken much narrative to place Joseph in pharaoh's court. Joseph having shown his administrative skill in prison, the king brought him out of prison to use his skill to better advantage, and once he was in court his ability to "divine" the future could be put to use immediately.

---

12. Most historians understand the word used here to refer to the observation of signs or the interpretation of omens, practices that were extremely common in the ancient Near East, including ancient Judah and Israel. From the point of view of the official practice represented in most of the biblical documents, these forms of divination were proscribed. The proscription is itself a measure of the presence of the practice. With the exception of J's uses of the term, which are probably the oldest in the Bible, in every other occurrence it is condemned. These include Lev. 19:26; Deut. 18:10; and 2 Kings 21:6. In 1 Kings 20:33, non-Israelites are described as following the practice without censure.

The main thrust of this section of the history of Judah and Joseph dealing with the fortunes of Joseph now emerges. To the king of Egypt Joseph proposed his plan for bringing the entire grain production of the nation under the control of pharaoh. This was a major service on behalf of the Egyptian crown for which Joseph would receive a great reward: when his family eventually joined him in Egypt, they would be granted extensive land use rights on the basis of Joseph's service to the king of Egypt.

J understood Joseph's plan as the origin of centralized food control in agrarian society. The plan was to have pharaoh "gather" (i.e., tax) grain from the peasantry during seven years of plenty in order to have sufficient supplies to dispense during the following seven years of dearth. The grain was to be heaped under pharaoh's control in the urban centers of the various regions of Egypt. This plan is usually perceived by modern readers not acquainted with lifelong poverty as an effective plan that would make it possible for the Egyptian people to survive the famine. In reality, it was the basis for the enslavement of the Egyptian people and a model for the oppressive system of socioeconomic exploitation that has characterized agrarian societies from the beginning and agricultural commodity producing societies until today.[13] Plans like Joseph's cause famines.

The historian emphasizes that Joseph's plan involved the storage of grain in the cities of Egypt—an allusion to the city system detailed early in J's history. This also foreshadows Joseph's family being impressed into corvée labor, building the central urban grain-storage facilities required by the king of Egypt for carrying out Joseph's original arrangement. In other words, the climax of J's history in Yahweh's rescue of these corvée workers is rooted in a part of the history that reaches back explicitly to the eighteenth generation and is bound inextricably with the history of that generation's fraternal accord.

Having heard and approved of Joseph's plan, pharaoh placed him as second in command over all Egypt. Joseph's elevation completed the cycle of his afflictions, and he remained at the pinnacle of Egyptian society until his death. Just as Joseph lost his first garment (his gift gown) and became a slave, and just as he lost his second garment (the garment he left in the hands of his master's wife) and went to prison, so he, having been placed over all Egypt, received a fine new garment from pharaoh. As he rode out

13. Susan George and Nigel Paige (*Food for Beginners* [London: Writers and Readers Publishing Cooperative Society, 1982], 16) describe the granary as "the embryo of the state." In ancient Morocco, they indicate, the same word meant both granary and government. See also Frances Moore Lappé and Joseph Collins, *Food First: Beyond the Myth of Scarcity*, rev. ed. (New York: Ballantine Books, 1979); Susan George, *How the Other Half Dies: The Real Reasons for World Hunger*, rev. ed. (New York: Penguin Books, 1977); John W. Warnock, *The Political Economy of Hunger* (New York: Methuen, 1987); and Keith Griffin, *World Hunger and the World Economy* (New York: Macmillan Co., 1987).

in the vizier's chariot, now his own, the Egyptians greeted him with an apparent salute *(abrek).* To J and his Hebrew-speaking audience this salute sounded as if it were the Hebrew word "bless" and summed up the completion of Joseph's fortunes.

Several elements in this narrative remind us of motifs seen previously. The younger son was favored by both his father and Yahweh. Forced to leave his homeland because of the hatred of his brothers, he acquired his fantastic wealth by the blessing of Yahweh alone. The similarity with Abram and Jacob is obvious.

This part of J's history has treated a cycle of extreme swings in the fortunes of Joseph. From being the favorite and favored son of his father, he entered Egypt as a slave. From this degraded state, he rose without much difficulty to be the head steward over a well-to-do Egyptian master's entire household. Unjustly charged with seducing his master's wife, he was thrown into the house where the prisoners of the king of Egypt were incarcerated. From there he rose by way of taking charge of the rest of the prisoners to being adviser to the king of Egypt and eventually to being completely in charge over the entire country of Egypt, second only to pharaoh himself. Not only has the amplitude of these waves of ups and downs increased, the variation serves to point up the guardianship of Yahweh over Joseph (or, as J would put it, Yahweh's blessing) in the face of repeated extreme hardship. J states this in so many words both times Joseph's fortunes changed for the better.

Joseph had rejected his master's wife, but now he accepted the daughter of the priest of On (Heliopolis). To the Hebrew ear, On sounds like "Vigor, Manhood." His two sons, Manasseh and Ephraim, would be half Egyptian. The Egyptian associations already described for the northern kingdom of Israel on the basis of Joseph's history were that much more cemented.

20

It's in the Bag

(Genesis 41:57—Exodus 1:8, parts)

At the end of seven years the famine began. The people of Egypt cried in distress to pharaoh for food, and pharaoh said to all Egypt, "Go to Joseph and do what he tells you." Joseph opened the stores and sold back the grain taken from the Egyptians. The more severe the famine became, the more the Egyptians resorted to the cities' supplies. Our historian leaves the history of Joseph's arrangements at this point to resume the history of Judah. When he resumes the history of Joseph's arrangements, he deals with the effect on the Egyptian peasantry of having to buy back the grain that had been taxed from them. Consistent with this interest, momentarily suspended, in the meaning of the purchase of grain, the historian re-introduces Joseph's brothers at the point where they proposed to go and purchase grain in Egypt.

As the famine got more severe in the land of Egypt, and the whole world came to Egypt to buy grain from Joseph, since the famine had become severe over the whole earth, the sons of Israel came with the throng to buy grain, as the famine affected the land of Canaan as well. Since Joseph was the dominant figure over the land, personally selling grain to all the people in the land, when Joseph's brothers came and bowed before him with their faces to the ground, Joseph saw his brothers and recognized them. He concealed his identity from them, however, and spoke harshly with them. "Where have you come from?"

They said, "From the land of Canaan, to buy food."

As Joseph recognized his brothers but it was clear they did not recognize him, he said to them, "You are spies. You have come here to see the nakedness of the land."

They said to him, "No, my lord. Your servants have come to buy food. We are all sons of one man, and we are honest. Your servants are not spies."

He said to them, "No! You have indeed come to see the nakedness of the land."

They said, "We your servants were twelve brothers, the sons of one man, in the land of Canaan. The youngest is with our father right now, and one is gone."

Joseph said to them, "It is just as I said: you are spies. You shall be tested in this way. By the life of pharaoh I swear you shall not leave here unless your youngest brother comes here. Send one of you to get your brother. The rest of you will be confined. In this way your words will be tested, whether the truth is with you. If not, by the life of pharaoh you are spies."

He kept them together in the guardhouse for three days. On the third day, Joseph said to them, "Do this if you want to live. If you are honest, go, take famine stores of grain back to your households. Then bring your youngest brother to me, in order to verify your claims and not die." They agreed to do it.

Joseph gave orders to have their containers filled with grain, but their silver returned to their individual sacks, and to provide them with provisions for the journey. These things were done for them. They loaded their asses with their bought grain and went from there. At that night's station, one of them opened his sack to give fodder to his ass and saw his silver right in the top of his bag. He said to his brothers, "My silver has been returned. It's right here in my bag." Their hearts sank.

When they got back to their father in the land of Canaan, they told him everything that had happened to them. "The man, the lord of the land, spoke with us harshly and put us under arrest as though we were there to spy out the land. We said to him, 'We are honest men, not spies. We are eleven brothers, the sons of our one father. One brother is gone, and the youngest is now with our father in the land of Canaan.' The man, the lord of the land, said to us, 'In this way shall I know that you are honest men: take famine stores of grain for your households, and go, bring your youngest brother to me, that I may know that you are not spies but honest men, and so may move freely in the land.' "

Israel said, "My son may not go down with you. His brother is dead, and he is the only one left. If some harm should come to him on the way you would be taking, you would send my gray head to the nether world in inconsolable grief."

The famine remained severe in the land. When they had finished the grain they had brought from Egypt, their father said to them, "Return and buy a little food for us."

Judah said to him, "The man solemnly warned us, 'You shall not see my face without your brother with you.' If you are prepared to send our brother with us, we will go down and buy food for you. If you are not prepared to send him, we will not go, for the man said, 'You shall not see my face without your brother with you.' "

Israel said, "Why did you do me this evil of telling the man you had another brother?"

They said, "The man asked about us and our birth and kin. He said, 'Is your father still alive? Do you have another brother?' So we told him whatever he wanted to know. How were we to know he would say, 'Bring your brother down?' "

Then Judah said to Israel his father, "Send the boy with me, so we can get going, and live and not die, we, you, and our children. I myself will stand surety for him. You can hold me responsible for him. If I do not bring him back to you and stand him before you, I may be counted as having sinned against you for the rest of my life. If we had not delayed, by now we could have returned twice."

Israel their father said to them, "If it must be so, do this. Take some of the products of the land in your containers, and take down a gift to the man, a bit of balm, honey, gum, myrrh, pistachios, and almonds. And take twice as much silver in your hands, since you have to take back the silver put back in the tops of your bags. Perhaps it was an oversight. And take your brother. Go ahead and return to the man."

The men took this gift, twice as much silver in their hands, and Benjamin, and went back down to Egypt. They stood in the presence of Joseph. Joseph saw Benjamin with them and said to his steward, "Bring the men into the palace. Have an animal slaughtered and prepared, as the men shall eat with me at midday."

The man did as Joseph said, and brought the men into Joseph's palace. The men became afraid when they were brought into Joseph's palace. They said, "It must be on account of the silver returned to our bags the first time that we are being brought in. They want to make it an issue against us in order to attack us and take us and make us slaves, and take our asses."

So they approached Joseph's steward and spoke to him at the entrance to the palace. They said, "My lord, earlier we came down to buy grain. On the way back home, when we got to the night station and opened our bags, there was each man's silver in the top of his bag—our silver, every shekel of it. We have now brought it back in our hands. We have brought down other silver in our hands for buying food. We did not know who put our silver in our bags."

He said, "It's okay. Don't worry. Your god must have given you a little treasure in your bags. Your silver comes to me."

Then the man brought the men into Joseph's palace. He arranged to have water brought and their feet washed, and fodder provided for their asses. They made ready their gift while waiting for Joseph's arrival at midday, for they had heard that they were to eat food there. When Joseph arrived at the palace, they brought to him the gift they had carried into the palace, and bowed before him to the ground.

Joseph asked them how they were, then said, "Is your old father you were telling about well? Is he still alive?"

"Your servant our father is well," they said, bowing deeply. "He is still alive."

Then he looked and saw his brother Benjamin, his own mother's son. "Is this your youngest brother you were telling me about?" Joseph moved quickly when his affection for his brother began to well up. On the verge of weeping, he slipped into a private room and wept there. After washing his face, he went back out and thereafter controlled himself.

He said, "Serve the meal." They served the meal to him by himself, to the brothers by themselves, and to the Egyptians eating at his table by themselves. Egyptians were not allowed to eat with foreigners, since it was abhorrent to them. When the brothers were seated before Joseph according to their ages, they looked at each other in amazement. As portions were brought from Joseph's table to them, Benjamin's portion turned out to be five times larger than that of the other brothers.

While they drank freely with him, he ordered his steward, "Fill the men's bags with as much food as they can carry, and put each man's silver in the top of his bag. And my goblet, the silver goblet, put in the top of the youngest one's bag, together with the silver he spent on grain." Joseph's orders were carried out.

At first light the next morning, the men were sent off with their asses. They had not gone out far from the city when Joseph said to his steward, "Get going and chase after the men. When you catch up with them, say to them, 'Why have you paid back evil for good? Is this [goblet] not what my lord drinks from and uses for divination? You have done evil by what you have done.' "

The steward caught up with them and said to them what Joseph had told him to. They said to him, "Why does my lord speak this way? Far be it from your servants to do any such thing. The silver we found in the tops of our bags we brought back to you from the land of Canaan. How then could we steal even silver or gold from your lord's palace? If anything stolen is found in the possession of any of your servants, then let him die, and we shall become my lord's slaves."

He said, "All right, it will be as you say. If anything is found with someone, he will be my slave, but the rest of you can go free."

Each man quickly put his bag on the ground and opened it up. He groped around in each man's bag, beginning with the oldest and finishing with the youngest. He found the goblet in Benjamin's bag. They tore their clothing. Each man reloaded his ass, and they returned to the city.

When Judah and his brothers arrived at Joseph's palace, Joseph was still there. They fell on the ground before him.

Joseph said, "What is this deed you have done? Do you not know that a man like me can discover things by divination?"

Judah said, "What can we say to my lord? How can we respond, and how can we possibly put ourselves in the right? We are hereby my lord's slaves, both we and the man in whose hands the goblet was found."

Joseph said, "Far be it from me to do this. Just the man in whose hands the goblet was found shall be my slave. As for the rest of you, go on up to your father in safety."

Judah came close to him and said, "I beg you, my lord, may your servant speak a word in the ears of my lord? Do not be angry with your servant—you are the equal of pharaoh. My lord asked his servants, 'Do you have a father or brother?' We did say, 'We have an elderly father, and there is a young boy. His brother is dead. He alone is left of his mother's sons, and his father loves him.' Then you said to your servants, 'Bring him down to me, so that I can set eyes on him.' We said to my lord, 'The boy is not able to leave his father. If he leaves his father, his father would die.' You said to your servants, 'If your youngest brother does not come down with you, you shall not again see my face.' When we went back up to your servant my father, we told him my lord's words.

"Our father said, 'Go back, buy some food for us.' But we said, 'We are not able to go down. If our youngest brother is with us, we can go down. We are not allowed to see the face of the man if our youngest brother is not with us.' Your servant my father said to us, 'You know that my wife bore me two sons. One left me, and I thought he must have been torn to pieces, and I haven't seen him since. And now you want to take this one from my presence as well. If any harm comes to him, you would send my gray head to the nether world in evil.'

"So if I should get back to your servant my father and the boy is not with us, whose life is bound to his life, when he sees the boy is gone he will die, and your servants will have sent the gray head of your servant our father to the nether world in inconsolable grief. Since, however, I your servant have gone surety for the boy with my father, by saying, 'If I do not bring him back to you, I may be counted as having sinned against my father for the rest of my life,' let then your servant stay behind as my lord's slave, and let the boy go back up with his brothers. How could I go back up to my father if the boy were not with me? I could not stand to see the evil that would come on my father."

Joseph could not control himself in the presence of his attendants. He shouted, "Have everyone get out of my presence." No one stayed with him there as Joseph made himself known to his brothers. Joseph said to his brothers, "Come close to me." They came close. He said, "I am Joseph your brother, whom you sold into Egypt. Now do not be pained, and do not be angry with yourselves for selling me to here. Hurry back up to my father and say to him, 'Come down to me. Do not wait. Settle in the land of Goshen and be near to me, you, your sons and grandsons, your flocks and herds, and everything you have. I will provide for you there, since there are still five years left of the famine, so that you and your household and everything that is yours are not dispossessed.' Your eyes, and the eyes of my brother Benjamin, can see that it is my command that is being spoken to you. Tell my father about my wealth and honor in Egypt, and about everything you have seen. And hurry and bring my father down here."

Then he fell on his brother Benjamin's neck and wept, while Benjamin wept on his neck.

Pharaoh said to Joseph, "Tell your brothers to do this: 'Load your animals and go to the land of Canaan. Get your father and your households and come back to me. I shall grant to you good land in Egypt, and you shall eat of the fat of the land.' Then give them these orders: 'Take carts for yourselves from the land of Egypt for your children and wives, and bring them with your father. When you come, don't be concerned about things you have to leave behind, since the best of all the land of Egypt will be yours.'"

The sons of Israel did as told. Joseph supplied them with carts as pharaoh ordered, along with provisions for the journey. He gave each man a fresh change of clothing. To Benjamin he gave three hundred pieces of silver and five changes of clothing. To his father he sent no less than ten asses loaded with the goods of Egypt and ten jennies loaded with grain, bread, and other staples for his father for the journey. As he sent his brothers on their way, he said, "Engage in no recriminations on the way."

[When they had returned to their father,] Israel said, "Enough. My son Joseph is still alive. I must go and see him before I die."

Israel decamped with everything he owned and went to Egypt. Israel had sent Judah ahead to Joseph so he could show him the way to Goshen. When they arrived in the land of Goshen, Joseph hitched up his chariot and went up to meet Israel his father in Goshen. When he saw him, he fell on his neck and wept on his neck steadily.

Israel said to Joseph, "At last I can die, now that I have seen your face, and that you are still alive."

Joseph said to his brothers and to his father's household, "Let me go and tell pharaoh, 'My brothers and father's household who were in the land of Canaan have come to me. The men are sheepherders, as they are men of livestock, and they have brought their flocks and herds and all they own.' When pharaoh calls for you and says, 'What is your work?' you can say, 'Your servants have been men of livestock from our youth till now, both we and our ancestors,' so you can settle in the land of Goshen, since all sheepherders are abhorrent to the Egyptians."

Joseph went and told pharaoh, "My father and my brothers, their flocks and herds and all that is theirs, have come from the land of Canaan, and they are here in the land of Goshen." He presented to pharaoh five of his brothers selected from their full number. Pharaoh said to these brothers, "What is your work?"

They said to pharaoh, "Your servants are sheepherders, both we and our ancestors. We have come to stay in this land, for there is no pasturage for your servants' flocks in the land of Canaan, for the famine has been severe. So let your servants settle in the land of Goshen."

Pharaoh said to Joseph, "They may settle in the land of Goshen. And if you know among them any really strong men, appoint them as livestock chiefs over the flocks and herds belonging to me."

When the famine occurred, it extended as far as Palestine and brought Israel's family within its grip. Soon people from Palestine, particularly the bedouin who were able to traverse the Sinai and had periodic connections with Egypt, began to join Egyptians at Joseph's urban source of life. To acquire food where it was to be gotten, Israel sent his sons to the Egyptian court. Benjamin, Rachel's remaining son, he kept with him.

When the brothers arrived at court, Joseph received them but they did not recognize him, so transformed was his appearance by his new identity as an urban elite. He questioned them regarding the welfare of their father and induced them to disclose to him the existence of Benjamin. Joseph accused his brothers of being spies, interested in taking advantage of the "nakedness of the land" in a possible takeover. Joseph's motivation was probably to force them to bring Benjamin to him. It is not at all clear that Joseph at this point was interested in reconciliation with the rest of his brothers or that he really cared much about his family other than his father and full brother. The emphasis is on his concern for Benjamin. But instead of taking vengeance in the tradition of Cain, as heir of the blessed line he followed the example of Abram and Lot, Jacob and Esau. Showing some concern for his brothers' welfare, he gave them food and sent them on their way, taking no security. Before they left, Joseph forbade them to reappear without Benjamin.

In secret, under orders from Joseph, Joseph's steward was able to place the silver they had paid for the food back in their baggage. It was not until they were well on their way back home that they discovered this silver. Regretting what they could only understand as an oversight, they nevertheless decided not to return.

There is a correspondence between the silver gotten by the brothers for their sale of Joseph and the silver in their bags. Judah was responsible for the brothers' gaining twenty pieces of silver for the enslavement of Joseph. In due course the brothers would return a second time to the Egyptian court, bringing with them twice ten units of silver—or twenty units. On this second visit, Judah would end up offering himself as Joseph's slave in return for this silver (half of it in the steward's hands) and one silver goblet.

The famine remained severe and Israel was forced to send them to Egypt a second time for more food. This time they were compelled to bring with them Benjamin, because Joseph, whom they had not recognized, had required it of them if they were ever to appear in his presence again. The Hebrew expression used, "to see the face," is the expression we have already encountered meaning to be reconciled. But since it is uncertain whether or how Joseph and his brothers were to be reconciled, this implication is only latent in the expression at this stage. The brothers had been able to talk Israel into releasing Benjamin into their care for this second journey when Judah had offered to go surety for him and be responsible for his person. The jeopardy the brothers were in, having never returned the silver they found in their packs, was made symbolically clear when their father sent them on their way with gifts of balm, honey, gum, myrrh, pistachios, and almonds.[1] The brothers on their way to Egypt must have looked exactly like the Ishmaelite caravan that took Joseph as a slave to Egypt, a caravan described as bearing gum, balm, and myrrh. The picture the historian paints is a cautionary one for northern Israel (the territory of the tribes of Joseph in the reign of David), suggesting that when all is said and done the only reason one would go to Egypt would be to become a slave.

When the brothers arrived in Egypt, Joseph saw them coming and instructed his steward to make ready a meal for them in the house. When they had been escorted into the house, prior to greeting Joseph the brothers were afraid on account of the silver they had found in their packs. They thought for sure that the official in charge of food supplies—again they did not recognize Joseph—intended to make slaves of them (in exchange for the silver given back to them on their first journey). They approached Joseph's steward at the palace entrance, to whom they told the story of the silver truthfully. "We have brought down with us other silver for buying food. We do not know who placed our first silver in our packs." The steward replied, "Okay, don't worry. Your god has given you a little treasure in your packs and your silver comes to me." Having bribed the steward, the brothers had reason to believe they had bought their way out of trouble or, in other words, bought their freedom from slavery.

The meal was ready. Joseph, his brothers, and his Egyptian attendants all ate separately. To their amazement, the brothers were seated according to

---

1. It is a curious feature of this story that Israel's family has wealth, including luxury items, with which to purchase food, but little food itself. They are not poor, just hungry, and, as is typical for bedouin, in a better position than the peasantry to engage in commercial transaction to acquire food.

age. Portions were brought from Joseph's table to Benjamin five times as large as the portions of the other brothers. Seeing Benjamin, Joseph had difficulty containing his emotions and once had to leave the room to compose himself. Joseph had feeling for Benjamin more than for the other brothers. He immediately formulated a strategy for sending the brothers on their way, while keeping Benjamin with him.

Joseph commanded his steward to fill his brothers' sacks and once again to return their silver. Then he instructed him to insert the silver goblet that was for his private use into the sack of the youngest, Benjamin. The brothers departed the following morning and had not gone far from the city when Joseph sent his steward after them. When he overtook them, he immediately accused them. "Why have you returned evil for good? Is this not that with which my lord drinks and which he uses for divination? You have done evil." The brothers were confused. "What are you talking about? How could we ever do such a thing? We told you before, we found silver in our packs on the way back to Canaan last time, and far from stealing it we returned it. If you find anything with one of us, let him be put to death and let the rest of us become your lord's slaves." The steward agreed but changed the terms slightly in line with Joseph's desire to retain Benjamin alone: "Have it your way, but let the one with whom it is found become a slave and the rest of you go free." The brothers pulled down their packs. The steward searched them—from the oldest's to the youngest's. Of course when he searched Benjamin's bag, there was the goblet. The youngest was left holding the bag.

By telling us that Judah had gone surety for Benjamin, J has already furnished us with the background to Judah's plea when the brothers were overtaken and it was discovered that the Egyptian lord's silver goblet was in Benjamin's sack: "In what way can we justify [the verb is from *tsedeq*] ourselves?" The goblet with which Joseph trapped Benjamin was a false token of his guilt patterned after the true token of Judah's guilt in his relation to Tamar. In the scene with Tamar, Judah was forced to face the injustice of the trick of recognition played against his father Israel in the incident of Joseph's blood-stained coat by having a similar one played on him. He was also forced to face the justice of the right of the younger—first Shelah, then Perets—and his wrongdoing compared with Joseph's refusal of relations with his master's wife.

Judah and his brothers tore their garments in distress, reloaded their asses, and returned to the palace of Joseph to find him still there. When Joseph accused Benjamin, together the ten brothers offered themselves in Benjamin's place. But Joseph was insistent that the guilty one be punished. At this point Judah took Joseph aside and pleaded in private. If Joseph were willing, he, Judah, would give himself as a slave in Benjamin's place: "Let your servant stay in place of the lad as a slave to my lord." At precisely the moment he hears these words of Judah, after so many years in which he might consider revenge, after several meetings during which he continued uncertain whether he ever wanted to be reconciled with his other brothers again, Joseph was unable to contain himself. Joseph broke down in tears and revealed his identity to his astounded and grateful brothers.

Joseph had been influenced by the Egyptians, behaving in the line of the city builders. In constructing the grain-storage cities and buying the land for pharaoh, he was preparing the way for the corvée that would later be inflicted upon the bedouin. Judah's offer to sacrifice himself for Benjamin's sake in fulfillment of his oath of surety to his father, which J would have us understand grew directly out of his judgment by Tamar, was the act that induced and clinched Joseph's reconciliation with his brothers. Once more the historian has treated his theme which he first presented in the history of Cain and Abel. But this time around, with the harmony of the national brothers at stake, it was the deference, generosity, and loyalty of Judah that was most instrumental in establishing harmony. It was Judah who redeemed Joseph, reconciling him with the brothers. The contrast with northern Israel's tendency to move into the Egyptian sphere of influence is obvious; so too the implication that the north's salvation lay in its allegiance to the Judahite court.

Ebed ("slave") is a Hebrew word formed from a root that has been a key word from the beginning of J's history, and it becomes even more so in the history of Joseph and its sequel. The underlying assumption of the history to this point is that Israel was destined to *abad* ("to work") Yahweh's grant of land to Abram. After the reconciliation of the brothers based on the threat of their becoming *ebadim* ("slaves") and Judah an *ebed* ("slave"), which threat reaches back to the brothers' making Joseph an *ebed*, then Joseph made the Egyptians *ebadim*. Finally, pharaoh made the bedouin into *ebadim*—workers on his land. Since the bedouin were destined to work Yahweh's land grant, Yahweh rescued them, in effect to make them his own *ebadim*.

When J speaks of famine or grain in the history of Joseph, the subject is the same as the basic J theme of the production and distribution of food which was essential to the monarchy's self-justification throughout J's history. At times the historian seems to be aware that famine was essentially a socioeconomic and sociopolitical rather than a natural phenomenon. Starvation was far more likely to be caused by the nature of food distribution than by the vicissitudes of the weather.[2] The famine was

---

2. Western views of famine tend to be based overwhelmingly on the assumption of a decline in the overall availability of food. It is widely recognized among historians that famines are rooted more deeply in a region's political economy and the failure of entitlement to existing food. See Amartya Sen, *Poverty and Famines: An Essay on Entitlement and Deprivation* (New York: Oxford University Press, 1981); Rony Brauman, "Famine Aid: Were We Duped?" *Reader's Digest* (October 1986): 65–72.

centered in Egypt, where grain production depended little on rainfall, depending instead almost entirely on the annual rise of the Nile, which, though it varied somewhat with the rainfall in East Africa, was practically speaking constant.[3] The shortage of grain under these circumstances, which J does not explicitly explain, must have been due to something like the inequitable arrangements which he pictures Joseph himself devising. The land of Canaan, on the other hand, was dependent for its agriculture upon rainfall which began with the great downpour in the eighth generation.

Up to this time, however, in J's conception of history, grain agriculture was only sporadic in Canaan. The Canaanites and other Hamites in the land were mostly city dwellers whose production was largely limited to perennials. The extensive cultivation of the land of Canaan in grains awaited the formation of the Israelite kingdom. Thus the land of Canaan was known at this time as a land oozing milk and honey. The meaning of this phrase can be seen clearly in Isa. 7:10–25. It refers to a land in which nothing is raised but a few sheep and goats, a more or less wild and uncultivated land populated by wild bees. Hence even the wealth of Israel's family consisted mainly in agricultural products from either trade or urban perennial cultivation, as can be seen from the stuffs brought by the brothers to Egypt. (The exception is described in Gen. 26:12.) Israel came to Egypt as Abram had during a famine, and just as Abram's presence in Egypt became the occasion for Yahweh to inflict plagues on pharaoh, so Israel's presence there became the occasion for the same. Joseph acquired wealth and substance in Egypt just as Abram had, although in Abram's case his substance followed on the plagues, while Joseph's preceded them.

The famine had five years left to go. Joseph invited his family to travel to Egypt and settle in the land of Goshen close by him. This invitation extended, as he put it, to "you and your children and your children's children." These are the eighteenth, nineteenth, and twentieth generations, and their specification is the best indication in J of the sequence of generations between Joseph and Moses, who represented the twenty-first generation.[4]

Joseph advised his brothers to accept his invitation "lest you and your children be dispossessed of all that is yours." Joseph's warning hints at what was in store for the Egyptian peasantry even while Israel and his family

3. Hermann Kees, *Ancient Egypt: A Cultural Topography* (Chicago: University of Chicago Press, 1977), 47–74.

4. The clearer enumeration of these generations comes from the P genealogy of Moses in Exod. 6:16–20. The sole use of P's genealogy to reconstruct J's genealogy at this point would be dubious if it did not fit with J's overall scheme and were not confirmed by Joseph's statement.

temporarily escaped this fate for some three generations. Joseph concluded his interview with his brothers in a passionate embrace with Benjamin. The special relationship between the two sons of Rachel comes to the fore at this point in the history.

Pharaoh offered the sons of Israel the good of the earth for their taking. The ones whom pharaoh favored during a famine would not suffer in it. He offered them carts for transporting their families in grand style from Canaan. He also gave Benjamin three hundred pieces of silver and five new garments.

Israel and his sons and their families migrated to Egypt as clients of Joseph, enjoying, but entirely dependent upon, his position in service at the pinnacle of the Egyptian regime. Israel sent Judah ahead of him to show where Goshen was. Israel now regarded Judah more favorably than ever, not only because of the bad behavior of his older brothers Reuben, Simeon, and Levi but also because of his rescue of Benjamin. Joseph mounted his chariot and rode out to meet his father. "I can die," Israel said to him, "now that I have seen your face."

Joseph arranged personally for the provisioning of his family. He hinted at the trouble that was to come and the recurrence of the struggle between Cain and Abel on the supranational or international level. Herders of sheep, he cautioned them, were an abomination in Egypt. The correspondence implied in the narrative is between Cain and Egypt, the workers of the land, and between Abel and the bedouin descendants of Israel, the shepherds of the flocks. Pharaoh designated Goshen as their pasturage in a grant of land tenure for the pasturing of their own flocks and herds and instructed Joseph to appoint strongmen as "chiefs of the cattle (*miqneh*)" over his own royal flocks and herds. This would be the consummate reversal—Abel as "chief of the cattle" over Cain—were it not for the disjunction between pharaoh's land grant to Israel and Yahweh's pending land grant to Abram. If Israel settled in Egypt, when would they take possession of the land that Yahweh granted to Abram?

Joseph sustained his father and brothers and his father's whole household with food, each according to the number of their children. Since there was no food out in the whole land, as the famine was extremely severe, the land of Egypt and the land of Canaan languished because of the famine. Joseph collected all the silver to be found in the land of Egypt and the land of Canaan in payment for the grain they were buying, and Joseph had the silver brought to pharaoh's palace. When the silver was gone from the land of Egypt and the land of Canaan, all the Egyptians came to Joseph and said, "Give us food. Why should we die right here in front of you? But our silver is gone."

Joseph said, "Give me your livestock, and I will sell you food for your livestock, since your silver is gone."

So they brought their livestock to Joseph, and he sold them food in return for their horses, their sheep livestock and cattle livestock, and their asses. Thus he guided them through that year with food for all their livestock.

When that year was over, they came to him the next and said to him, "We cannot conceal from my lord that, since our silver is gone and our livestock made over to my lord, there is nothing left to put before my lord except our bodies and our farm land. Why should we die before your eyes, both we and our land? Buy us and our land for food, so that we and our land may be slaves for pharaoh, and give us seed so that we may live and not die, and our land not go to waste."

So Joseph bought all the farm land of Egypt for pharaoh, since in the grip of famine every Egyptian sold his field rights. Thus the land became pharaoh's. As for the populace, without their lands he removed them to the cities, from one end of Egypt to the other. The lands of the priests were the only ones he did not buy. Since the priests had a statutory grant from pharaoh and ate the produce of their statutory grant that pharaoh granted them, they did not sell their lands.

Joseph said to the populace, "Now that I have bought you and your lands on behalf of pharaoh, here is seed for you for sowing the land. Of the harvest you must pay one-fifth to pharaoh. The other four-fifths will be yours for field seed and for food for yourselves and for everyone in your households, including food for your children."

They said, "You have saved our lives. May my lord continue to be gracious and allow us to be pharaoh's slaves."

Thus Joseph established the statute over the lands of Egypt to this day that pharaoh receives a fifth. Only the lands of the priests alone did not become pharaoh's.

Having provided for his family, Joseph then turned to the provisioning of the rest of Egypt. Now the category of fraternal conflict takes on a new dimension. Joseph despoiled the Egyptians on pharaoh's behalf. This means not only that henceforth Israel was to be pitted against opposing nations but even more that historical Israel (the northern hill country) was to be cautioned about the kind of king the north might produce. Such a king might be like Joseph, portrayed here as the originator of what everyone knew was the basic system of royal oppression.[5]

Once we realize that Joseph enslaved the Egyptian peasantry, it seems strange that he should do what appears to us as such an evil deed. But J's history understands Joseph's act in different terms. What Joseph did was to fulfill the curse pronounced upon Ham in the ninth generation by Noah. In the text of J as we now have it, Noah cursed Canaan, not Ham. But as we saw, the narrative implies that the object of Noah's curse was Ham, which would encompass both Canaan and Egypt. If this understanding of J's history of Noah is correct, then the curse inherited from Ham by Canaan

5. As events turned out, the Judahites should have been the ones to worry, at least until Omri seized rule in the north.

points to the rule of David in the land of Canaan, while the curse inherited by Ham's other descendants points forward to Joseph's enslavement of the Egyptian peasantry as a preview of David's rule or even (considering the socioeconomic linkage between J's Canaanites and Egyptians) as the basis of that rule. It is true that Joseph performed his deed on pharaoh's behalf, but the narrative, as a description of administration, focuses exclusively on Joseph. Thus one should understand it to be portraying a son of Shem and the sons of Ham in contrast to each other, with the peasantry compliant with Noah's pro-Davidic curse. Once again it is necessary to suppress initial moral assumptions in order to grasp the categories that J is using.

At one level J's portrayal of people in Palestine sharing a common food supply with Egypt reflects the occasional practice of Negev bedouin traveling to Egypt for either a short or a long period to seek their fortunes there or to establish some connection to enhance their economic or social advantage. There are many instances of such practice throughout Palestinian history. At another level, of significance to someone whose primary concern was political and administrative, Egypt and Canaan are treated as a single administrative unit. Whether J's portrayal at this level is a result of the famine itself or not, Canaan is presented in its relation to Egypt because it did not have Egypt's brilliant antifamine system. From J's point of view on the Canaan–Egypt connection, the release of the bedouin corvée laborers and the implied fulfillment of Yahweh's grant of land to Israel represent Canaan breaking with the Egyptian sphere of influence under David's regime and forming its own independent administrative unit, the Davidic state. In the Davidic conception, contrary to what is seen in other parts of the Old Testament (particularly the Deuteronomistic History) there is no discernible period of time, other than the period of the wasteland trek, between the disruption of pharaoh's administration by Yahweh and the division of the single administrative unit into the separate units of Egypt and Israel. The Davidic historian is intent upon stressing the administrative autonomy of the Davidic monarchy in a region that for many hundreds of years, and with only a brief gap, had been under Egyptian suzerainty.

Joseph's method of feeding pharaoh's people *and* bringing the land of Egypt under pharaoh's ownership was and is the patent means of elite urban control in agrarian societies. In the third year, the silver with which the peasantry had purchased back their grain ran out. The historian informs us, "Joseph brought the silver in Egypt and Canaan to the house of pharaoh." From a realist's point of view, it is impossible that this could refer to all the silver. J's history is not a realist's history in this sense but a schematic, symbolic, and multifaceted conception of reality as he knew it. For J, therefore, Joseph impounded all the silver. For the peasantry of Egypt or Palestine the reality would have been little different.

With no silver left and four years to go, how were the peasants to buy grain? They still had their traction animals, their means of plowing the land. These they brought to Joseph in the fourth year, and Joseph magnanimously accepted them in return for the food they required. In the fifth year, having sold their silver and their animals, they had nothing left but "our bodies and our land." Joseph graciously bought (*qanah*) their bodies and their land, turning the peasants at that point into *ebadim*, pharaoh's workers. The peasants had been forced, in one of the many typical forms of debt slavery, to sell themselves for food because the famine was severe. "And the land became pharaoh's" as Joseph sold back to the peasants what he had taken from them in the first place. J condones pharaoh's imposition of debt slavery on Egypt but rejects his imposition of corvée slavery on Israel.

In most translations of Gen. 47:21, one reads, "He made slaves of them from one end of Egypt to the other." This translation is based on the Septuagint, the early Greek translation from the Hebrew, and on the text of the Samaritan sect. As the textual note in the RSV (and most other modern translations) explains, the traditional Hebrew text says, "He removed them to [or caused them to pass into] the cities from one end of Egypt to the other." The difference in the Hebrew text that would produce these two variant translations is minor, leaving open the question as to which is original. The textual evidence is ambiguous. If we ask whether historical or sociological comparison leads us to favor one translation or the other, we have to say that such comparisons are ambiguous as well. Being made workers or slaves and being caused to move into the city are essentially the same thing, both in J's conception and the reality of his time and ours. The family without animals or land may not occupy land without the express leave of the owner of the land, and there is no motivation for families to live on the land if the food which they must eat is to be found, under urban control, in the cities. And in any case, they can always be drawn out of the cities for hired day labor. The system put in place during the crisis of the famine remains permanently in place thereafter to the continuing advantage of the rulers.

Joseph did not buy the priests' lands, because they had an allotment of food and did not need to sell their lands to acquire food. The exclusion of the priesthood from this system reflects their great importance—at great expense—for the projection of the ideological or transcendent basis that validated the system. This was the case during the New Kingdom period, and J knew it. He takes particular notice of it in order once again to draw out the contrast between the Egyptian administration, albeit headed by

Joseph, and David's administration.[6] The reason for composing his history is to narrate the history of the world of which David's monarchy was the goal and center in such a way as to reveal why a temple and a priestly establishment like that of Egypt were for David not only dispensable but also evil. Recall that we first encountered this reasoning in the contrast between the city-tower of the fourteenth generation (modeled in part on a kind of tower from just before J's time in Shechem, in the land of Joseph) and the simple earthen and stone altar of Abram at Shechem in the fifteenth generation.

Joseph's final arrangement for the peasantry was actually generous by agrarian standards. He sent the peasants back to what were now pharaoh's lands with seed from the royal stores for planting, requiring in return a mere 20 percent per annum tax on their produce. The peasantry were overwhelmed with a profound sense of joy at their enslavement. "You have brought us back to life. May it please you for us to be pharaoh's slaves." Joseph took them to mean permanently and so made it the norm "to this day," as J puts it. J thus portrays the peasantry in the bind of all oppressed peoples: they are induced to thank their oppressors for the sustenance that makes their lives possible.

After Israel had been settled in the land of Egypt, in the land of Goshen, the time for Israel to die drew near. He summoned his son Joseph and said to him, "Please, place your hand under my thigh, and I shall be kind and faithful to you. Do not allow me to be buried in Egypt. I want to lie with my ancestors. Carry me out of Egypt and bury me at their burial site."

He said, "I will do as you request."

Israel said, "Swear to me."

So Joseph swore to him. Israel bowed at the head of the bed. Then Israel pulled himself together and sat up in bed and noticed Joseph's sons, and said, "Who are these?"

Joseph said to his father, "They are my sons."

He said, "Bring them to me so I can bless them."

Israel's eyes were sluggish with age and he was unable to see well. When Joseph brought them close to him and he kissed them and embraced them, Israel said to Joseph, "I did not think to see your face." Then Joseph took Ephraim in his right hand, to Israel's left, and Manasseh in his left hand, to Israel's right, and brought them up to him. Israel, however, put out his right hand and placed it on Ephraim's head, even though he was the younger, and his left hand on Manasseh's head—he

---

6. Donald B. Redford, in *A Study of the Biblical Story of Joseph (Genesis 37—50)* (Leiden: E. J. Brill, 1970), 238–39. He argues that the evidence suggests that temple lands were taxed in the New Kingdom period and the late tenth century B.C.E. but probably not during some later periods. Redford ignores the strand analysis of the Pentateuch. Whether J was basing his description of Egypt on direct evidence is often dubious.

had got his hands crossed, because Manasseh was the firstborn. When Joseph saw that his father had put his right hand on Ephraim's head, it seemed wrong to him. He grasped his father's hand to switch it from Ephraim's head to Manasseh's head. Joseph said to his father, "Not that way, father. This one is the firstborn. Place your right hand on his head."

But his father refused. "I know, my son. I know. He too will become a people, and he too will be great. But his younger brother shall be greater than he, and his offspring shall become a plethora of nations." Thus when he blessed them on that day, he put Ephraim ahead of Manasseh.

Then Israel said to Joseph, "As I am about to die, I hereby grant you Shechem, as a man equal to your brothers." [Then Israel said,][7]

> "Gather and hear, sons of Jacob,
>   listen to Israel your father.
> *Reuben,* you are my firstborn,
>   my strength, the first fruit of my manhood,
>   outstanding in rank, outstanding in power.
> Unruly as water, you shall not be outstanding,
>   for you climbed into your father's bed,
>   then defiled the couch you got into.
> *Simeon* and *Levi* are brothers;
>   weapons of violence are their stock in trade.
> Let my spirit not join their council,
>   my self not unite with their company,
>   for in their anger they killed men,
>   and with wantonness they hamstrung oxen.
> Cursed be their anger, for it is fierce,
>   and their wrath, for it is cruel.
> I will scatter them in Jacob,
>   disperse them in Israel.
> *Judah,* your brothers shall praise you;
>   your hand shall be on the neck of your enemies,
>   your father's sons shall bow before you.
> A lion's whelp is Judah;
>   from the prey, my son, you have arisen;
>   he stoops, he crouches like a lion,
>   like the king of beasts—who would dare entice him?
> The scepter shall not depart from Judah,
>   nor the mace from between his legs;
> Unto him shall tribute be brought,
>   to him the homage of the peoples.
> He tethers his donkey to the vine,
>   his ass's colt to the choice vine.
> He dyes his garment with wine,
>   his robe in the blood of grapes.

7. The Hebrew text of the following archaic blessings is not always clear and thus is the subject of significant debate among historians. The translation here is schematic and not intended as a contribution to the ongoing debate.

His eyes are darker than wine,
   and his teeth are whiter than milk.
Zebulun shall dwell by the seashore;
   he shall be a shore for ships,
   and his flank shall reach to Sidon.
Isaachar is a bony ass,
   crouching among the rubbish piles.
He saw a resting place that was good,
   and a land that was pleasant,
   and bent his shoulder to the corvée basket,
   and became a corvée slave.
Dan shall achieve justice for his people,
   as one of the tribes of Israel.
Let Dan be a snake on the road,
   a viper on the path,
   who snaps at the heel of a horse
   so that its rider falls backward.
Gad is a band that raids,
   who raids from the rear.
Asher produces food that is rich,
   and he furnishes royal dainties.
Naphtali is a hind let loose,
   that bears lovely fawns.
Joseph is a [. . .]
The archers harried and attacked,
   and showed their hostility toward him.
But his bow let loose a steady stream,
   and his arms and hands were supple.
From the hands of the Champion of Jacob,
   from the Shepherd of the sons of Israel,
   from the God of your father, who aids you,
   the mountain God, who blesses you,
Blessings of the sky above,
   blessings of the deep beneath,
   blessings of breasts and womb,
   blessings of father and mother, man and child,
   blessings of the mountains of old,
   blessings of the eternal hills—
May they be on the head of Joseph,
   on the brow of the leader of his brothers.
Benjamin is a ravenous wolf;
   in the morning he devours prey,
   at evening he distributes the spoils.

Joseph fell all over his father's face and wept over him and kissed him. Then he ordered the physicians in his service to embalm his father. So the physicians embalmed Israel. It took them forty days, since that's how long embalming takes. They wept over Israel for seventy days in Egypt. When they had gotten through the days of weeping, Joseph said to the court of pharaoh, "Please convey this request to pharaoh: 'My father made me swear when he said, "I am about to die. Bury me in the grave I had dug out for myself in the land of Canaan." So let me go up and bury my father and then return.' "

Pharaoh said, "Go on up and bury your father, as he had you swear you would."

Joseph went up to bury his father, and all the servants of pharaoh, the senior members of his court, all the elders of the land of Egypt, and the whole household of Joseph, his brothers, and the household of his father went with him. The only thing they left behind in the land of Goshen was their children, flocks, and herds. Even chariots and charioteers went up with him. It was a splendid company.

When they arrived at Goren-ha-atad, beyond the Jordan, they observed there a great and highly solemn lamentation. Joseph mourned his father seven days. When the urban landowners of the land, the Canaanites, saw the mourning at Goren-ha-atad, they said, "This is Egypt's solemn mourning." Thus they named it Abel-mitsrayim, just beyond the Jordan.

After he had buried his father, Joseph returned to Egypt with his brothers and all those who had gone up with him to bury his father.

Then a new king arose over Egypt who did not know Joseph, that is, did not recognize the land tenure claims of Joseph and his kin.

The historian now resumes the narrative of the brothers for the last time. The climax of the history of Judah is to come with Jacob's final blessing. Hence we are told that Israel approached death. With a view toward his end, he required Joseph to swear that he would transport him to the land of Canaan for burial. Assured of proper burial and confined now to his deathbed, Israel undertook the blessing of all his sons, and his grandsons through Joseph. He began with Joseph's sons, Manasseh and Ephraim. Israel's eyes failed and he was having trouble seeing. Thus he approached the blessing of his grandsons in precisely the same condition as Isaac had approached the blessing of his sons. The result was predictably the same: the younger was given preference over the older. Joseph brought his sons up to Israel, his older son Manasseh at his left hand in front of Israel's right and his younger son Ephraim at his right hand in front of Israel's left. In this formation, Israel's greater blessing should have fallen on the older son. But to Joseph's consternation, the feeble Israel crossed his arms and reversed the blessings. "Manasseh will become great, but Ephraim will be greater." The historian refuses to bypass this opportunity to present yet one more variation on the theme of the prevailing of the younger son—in an ironic and dramatic way—and in the process probably withdraws priority from Shechem.

At last Israel blessed his own twelve sons, in the order of their birth. His blessings of Reuben, Simeon, and Levi were sharply qualified. His full-bodied enthusiasm came to the fore first with Judah, the ancestor of J's king. The blessings of the remaining first ten sons were little more than perfunctory. Israel saved his remaining breath for Joseph, whom he blessed in an effusive finale—giving the priority of blessing and prosperity to his favorite. His coda described Benjamin as a wolf at the spoil. A Benjaminite might have found the figure favorable but at the same time would have wondered at its curtness in comparison to the blessing of Joseph. J had little interest in conceding more to the tribe of David's archenemy Saul.

Israel died. Joseph had him embalmed, mourned him seventy days in Egypt, and took him to Canaan with a splendid Egyptian guard and in the company of numerous Egyptian elders. He had him buried in Canaan and mourned him seven days there. The Canaanites took notice. As this narrative draws to its close, J piles up repetitions of the words "go up." "Let me go up . . . he went up . . . he went up." These tie in with the new pharaoh's remark in the subsequent episode that the hostile bedouin might "go up" from Egypt. For the audience of this history, it is a verbal sign of things to come. Well might the Canaanites be made anxious by this anticipation of the fulfillment of the curse of Canaan. Thus it was that the sons of Israel were reconciled one with another at the death of Israel, as Esau and Israel were reconciled at the death of Isaac.

Leaving the brothers, our historian turns back to the narrative of Joseph's administration. He will not depart from this narrative line until the end of his history. The scene shifts as he now skips from the eighteenth and nineteenth generations to the twenty-first. But all that unfolds is a direct consequence of and continuation of the history of Joseph's provisioning, the history of the production and distribution of food we have been following through the history of Judah and Joseph.

Sometime during the twentieth or twenty-first generation, a new king rose over Egypt. This king "did not know" Joseph. We are already aware that the verb "know" is significant in J's history. It has to do with being in a relationship with another, either reproductively or productively. This occurrence is no different. In many previous instances, that someone "did not know" meant that they were figuratively exonerated from the wrongness attached to sex and reproduction as characterized in the first fourteen generations and the cursed lines. In this episode, which has more to do with production than reproduction, not knowing has the more specialized meaning we have so far encountered in the episode of Abram's negotiation with Yahweh concerning the number of righteous in Sodom, at which time Yahweh said, "I have known Abram." This is a relevant instance, because it refers to Yahweh's contractual relationship with his oath of blessing to Abram, and to Yahweh's grant of land to him at Bethel.

In many places in the Bible, "know" has the special meaning "to recognize the authority of, to recognize the claims of, to be in official or contractual relationship with."[8] Scholars have found a similar meaning of the cognate of Hebrew "know" in ancient Ugaritic and Akkadian texts. What J means is that this pharaoh did not acknowledge the contractual relationship between Joseph and previous kings of Egypt. That relationship was based on Joseph's service to the Egyptian court, and its main contractual term was the land tenure rights of Joseph's family, including his descendants, in Goshen. In other words, this new king reneged on his predecessor's favor and patronage of the sons of Israel.[9]

In any king-vassal or king-servant relationship in the ancient Near East, the main term of the contract was likely to be the ownership or use of land. While the king theoretically owned all the land of his kingdom, he would make grants of this land to his aides, supporters, and servants in return for their loyalty and service. In the documents drawn up to establish these relationships, the land was frequently granted "in perpetuity." It was characteristic of agrarian monarchs, however, to shift the ownership of granted parcels of land from one person to another at will, depending on the political requirements of the moment. Thus in at least one case, at Ugarit, the king granted a particular parcel to one party "in perpetuity," and before long, with no indication of hesitation, removed the parcel from the first party and granted it to a second party—"in perpetuity." This is exactly what happened to the Israelite beneficiaries of pharaoh's patronage of Joseph.

Joseph and his wider family lost their land. This loss had two important meanings. First, land tenure was the basis of any household's economic security. Israel had lost theirs and now suffered the same jeopardy as the Egyptian peasants. This launches the climactic narrative of J in which he treats fully the essential significance of the national god Yahweh for Israel's international position and role. This is the narrative usually labeled "the exodus." Second, the latent tension between Yahweh's grant and pharaoh's grant reached a crisis. Yahweh's grant had been promised but not realized. Pharaoh's grant had been realized but taken away. The protection of newly jeopardized Israel lay in the actualization of Yahweh's land grant.

8. Herbert B. Huffmon, "The Treaty Background of Hebrew *yada'*," *Bulletin of the American Schools of Oriental Research* 181 (February 1966): 31–38. See 2 Sam. 7:20; Hos. 8:2; 8:4; 13:5; Amos 3:2; Jer. 1:5; and perhaps Gen. 47:6.

9. Hebrew *meyudde'im* in 2 Kings 10:11 probably means "whose tenure rights are recognized." On the Ugaritic *md/mudu sharri,* see M. Heltzer, "Problems of the Social History of Syria in the Late Bronze Age," in *La Siria nel Tardo Bronzo,* ed. M. Liverani (Rome: Centro per la Antichita e la Storia dell'Arte del Vicino Oriente, 1969), 41–42; J. J. Finkelstein, "Recent Studies in Cuneiform Law," *Journal of the American Oriental Society* 90 (1970): 253–54; P. Vargyas, "Le *mudu* à Ugarit. Ami du roi?" *Ugarit-Forschungen* 13 (1981): 165–79. The evidence of Mari *wedum, mare wedutim,* and similar expressions requires a separate study.

21

The Bedouin Enslaved

(Exodus 1:9–12; 2:11–22; 3:1–8; 3:16—4:23, parts)

The king of Egypt said to his court,[1] "Since the bedouin people who are the descendants of Israel are more numerous and stronger than we are, come, let us show ourselves prudent in their regard, lest they increase further and, when war occurs, be added to the forces of our enemies, do battle against us, and go up from the land."

So they put over them corvée masters, in order to oppress them with their corvée labor. They had them build for pharaoh cities with grain-storage facilities, Pithom and Ramses. The more they oppressed them, the more they multiplied and burst forth, and the Egyptian elite conceived a loathing for the Israelites. So Egypt forced the Israelites to work under harsh conditions. They made their lives bitter with cruel work, in mortar and bricks and all kinds of field work, with all the work they were forced to do for them under harsh conditions.

In those times a man named Moses, who had succeeded in making this system of oppression work to his personal advantage, went out to view his kin in their corvée work. He saw, however, an Egyptian man beating a foreign slave who was one of his kin. Looking around to make sure no one was watching, Moses beat the Egyptian to death and hid his corpse in the sand.

The next day he went out. There were two foreign slaves in an angry tussle with each other. Moses said to the one in the wrong, "Why are you beating up your companion?"

He said, "Who appointed you master and judge over us? Do you intend to murder me the way you murdered the Egyptian?"

Moses became afraid and thought, "The incident must surely be known."

Pharaoh did hear about this incident and attempted to have Moses murdered. Moses fled from pharaoh. He settled in the land of Midian, beside a well.

Now the priest of Midian had seven daughters. Once when they came, drew water, and filled the troughs to water their father's flock, other shepherds came and drove them away. Moses wasted no time in saving them, and then watered their flock. When they had come back to Reuel their father, he said, "Why have you come back so soon today?"

---

1. In several places where J uses the Hebrew word *am* and English translations use "people," the correct translation is instead "the people directly in the service of pharaoh, his court or military followers." For purposes of shorthand, we use "court."

They said, "An Egyptian man rescued us from the hand of the shepherds, then proceeded to draw water for us and water the flock."

He said to his daughters, "Where is he? Why did you leave the man there? Invite him to have a meal with us."

Moses agreed to live with the man. He gave Moses his daughter Zipporah. She bore a son. He named him Gershom, because, as he said, "I am a refugee in an alien land."

Some time later, after the king of Egypt had died, Moses was out pasturing the flock of Midian's priest. He had led the flock some ways into the desert when the genie of Yahweh appeared to him in a fiery flame out of a bush. When Moses saw that the bush was burning but that the bush did not burn up, he said, "I must go over and see this remarkable sight. Why isn't the bush burning?"

When Yahweh saw he was coming over to see, he said, "Do not come near here. Remove your sandals from your feet, for the place at which you are standing is sanctified ground. I am the god of your ancestor," he went on, "the god of Abram, the god of Isaac, and the god of Jacob. I have thoroughly seen the oppression of my people in Egypt. I have heard their outcry in the face of their slave drivers, for I know their pain. I have come down to rescue them from the hand of Egypt and to bring them up from that land to a good and broad land, a land oozing milk and honey, the place of the Canaanites, the Hittites, the Amorites, the Perizzites, the Hivites, and the Jebusites. Go and gather the sheikhs of Israel, and say to them, 'Yahweh, the god of your ancestors, the god of Abram, Isaac, and Jacob, has appeared to me with these words, "I have given close attention to you and what has been done to you in Egypt, and have determined to bring you up from the oppression of Egypt, to the land of the Canaanites, the Hittites, the Amorites, the Perizzites, the Hivites, and the Jebusites, to a land oozing milk and honey." '

"They will listen to you. Then you and the sheikhs of Israel go to the king of Egypt and say to him, 'Yahweh the god of the foreign slaves has met us. We would like to make a three-day journey into the desert to sacrifice with Yahweh our god.' I know that the king of Egypt will not let you go, not even when confronted with the force of your hand. I will stretch out my hand, therefore, and beat Egypt with all my marvels which I will do in its midst. After that he will let you go. I will even make the Egyptians so well disposed toward this people that when you leave you will not leave empty-handed. Every woman will 'borrow' from her neighbor and from her who stays in her house objects of silver and gold as well as clothing. You will put these on your sons and daughters and so relieve Egypt of these things."

Moses answered, "They won't believe me. They won't listen to me. They'll say, 'Yahweh hasn't appeared to you.' "

Yahweh said to him, "What's this in your hand?"

"A staff."

"Throw it to the ground."

He threw it to the ground and it became a snake. Moses jumped away from it.

Yahweh said to Moses, "Put out your hand and seize it by the tail."

He put out his hand and grabbed hold of it, and it turned into a staff in his hand.

"This will make them believe that Yahweh the god of their ancestors, the god of Abram, the god of Isaac, and the god of Jacob, has appeared to you. Now put your hand," Yahweh went on, "inside your shirt."

He put his hand in his shirt. When he brought it out his hand had become leprous, as white as snow.

"Put your hand back in your shirt," Yahweh said.

Moses put it back, and when he withdrew it, it was again like the rest of his body.

"If they don't believe you and they don't heed the first sign, then they'll believe the second sign. And if they don't believe either of these signs and they don't heed you, take some of the water of the Nile and pour it on the land. The water you take from the Nile will become blood on the dry land."

Moses said to Yahweh, "Look, my lord, I am not a man of words—neither yesterday nor any time in the past, and for sure not from the time you started speaking to your servant. I have a sluggish mouth and a sluggish tongue."

Yahweh said to him, "Who gives a mouth to a person, or who makes a person mute or deaf, or seeing or blind? Me, Yahweh, that's who. So go, and I'll be your mouth and I'll let you know what to say."

"Look, my lord, you send anyone you want. . . ."

Yahweh got angry with Moses and said, "Is there Aaron your brother, the Levite? I know he knows how to speak, and here he is, on his way to meet you. He'll be glad to see you. Speak to him and put the words in his mouth, and I will be with both your mouth and his mouth, and will let you both know what you are to do. He will speak for you to the people. He will become for you a mouth, and you will become for him a god."

So while Moses was in Midian, Yahweh said to Moses, "Go back to Egypt. All the men seeking your life are dead." So Moses took his wife and his sons and put them on asses and returned to the land of Egypt.

Yahweh said to Moses, "When you get back to Egypt, see that you perform in the presence of pharaoh all the wonders I have put in your hand. Also, say to pharaoh, 'Thus Yahweh has said, "With regard to my firstborn son Israel, I hereby say to you, 'Let my son go, that he may work for me.' If you refuse to let him go, I will kill your firstborn son."' "

The "exodus story" is a separate story that appears to stand by itself, even for those who are minimally familiar with the Bible. Even among biblical historians the assumption prevails: this part of the great history of early Israel contained in the Pentateuch can be interpreted as a unit on its own terms. In our Bibles it begins at a major break created by the division of the text into the books of Genesis and Exodus. This break belongs, however, to a comparatively late stage in the history of the text, long after the original J had been supplemented several times, and as much as six or seven hundred years after it had been written.

The narrative of the twenty-first generation's deliverance from corvée labor in Egypt is presented as the story behind the Israelite rite of Passover. It is not known for certain whether J himself presented a clear enough conception of the rite of Passover for this connection to be a part of his history, but it is likely that it was. There is no reason to doubt that the villagers of highland Palestine in the twelfth and eleventh centuries B.C.E.

celebrated the spring barley harvest with a special festival or rite and that a feature of this rite was a feast on the male lambs born earlier that year. Because of the connection between the rite and the narrative in the text of Exodus, and the way in which the narrative is treated as a discrete unit, it is widely assumed that the narrative of deliverance was in fact the narrative basis of the barley harvest feast as celebrated prior to the time of David. This would make sense of J's incorporation of this tradition and his emphasis on it. His purpose would be to incorporate into what was intended to be the national history a well-established narrative, one that enjoyed great popularity among the people.

Our method of understanding J as a coherent whole runs against this preconception on literary and historical grounds. In literary terms, what is popularly known as "the exodus" is wholly of a piece with the rest of J. The historical reason for this is easy to see. The traditional source for this section of J is the same as for the great bulk of J that deals with the ancestors of Israel as bedouin in terms of traditions that would be typical and prevalent among bedouin, particularly those of southern Palestine. The bedouin of southern Palestine were vulnerable to just the kind of jeopardy into which Joseph's family fell. Lore celebrating escape from such captivity would form an important basis for a bedouin group's sense of political independence and autonomy. Such a tradition need not have been originally attached to the other bedouin-like traditions adapted by J. The continuity that marks J's history from Abram on derives not from the continuity of his traditional sources but from the linkages made possible by their common social and ethnic background.

While we do not know whether this story was linked to the barley festival for the first time by David and his historian, what we recognize are the many connections of the story with the rest of J. As previously noticed, the rest of J does not reflect the traditions that were prevalent and popular among the Palestinian peasantry of the Davidic nation. Instead, it draws on bedouin traditions. As this is also the case with the exodus, there is no reason to imagine that such an exodus was a significant component of the traditions of the pre-Davidic peasantry of Palestine who were being required to identify with the portrayal of Israel sketched by J, or who were simply included in it without their awareness.

If the popular understanding of the barley harvest festival as a celebration of the deliverance from Egypt did not exist prior to David, then there is no way of knowing what popular understanding stood in its place. It may also be surprising to think that a king and his scribe could simply create such an important connection. We tend to think of such religious rites and their traditions as stretching back endlessly in time or as originating in some specific historical event precisely like the exodus. A closer study of such rites and their traditions would show, however, that they often derive from political purposes, such as the formation of national identity as defined by rulers.

It is now known that the highland communities attested to archaeologically and identified as the "Israel" of the Bible did not come into being as the result of an exodus from Egypt, as the conquest model of Israel's origin would have it. Many historians have been inclined to suggest, however, that while the exodus could not be the tradition of all of the early Israelites, it could have been the tradition of a few Israelites who did experience such an event. According to this view, these few Israelites then shared it with others in the Palestinian highland, where it became the basic tradition of Israelite identity.

This view was formulated in an intellectual climate that underrated the bedouin character of nearly all of J's traditions as well as the marked distinctiveness of bedouin identity in its historical context. It does not take into account the great difficulty of assuming that a community of peasants would adopt as their tradition of basic identity a story dealing with bedouin in a region where it is unlikely they would ever go. If Palestinian peasants did regard themselves as the beneficiaries of deliverance from Egyptian corvée, they could have easily done so in terms of a story of corvée in Palestine itself, or a story in which a Canaanite ruler impressed them into slavery and shipped them to Egypt. It makes more sense instead to suppose that the village peasants of pre-Davidic highland Palestine never did identify themselves in this way but that such an identification was forged for them by the court of David.

The barley harvest festival celebrated a dual product, the barley and the flock. For the pre-Davidic villager of highland Palestine, the meaning of such a celebration would be tied up with the importance of diversification in the management of the risks that attended village agriculture in Palestine.[2] It was a foregone conclusion that the barley harvest would fail on an average of one year out of every three or four. One of the primary functions of devoting productive energy to the raising of sheep and goats, which were less desirable for day-to-day sustenance and were not raised for that purpose by either peasants or bedouin, was to provide a safety net during times of hardship or famine. From this perspective, the peasants' interest in this festival rested equally on both components. In addition, there is reason to believe that, if the barley harvest festival played a more important role in the pre-Davidic highland than the wheat and fruit harvests of late spring and late summer, then the reason for this importance

---

2. David C. Hopkins, *The Highlands of Canaan: Agricultural Life in the Early Iron Age* (Sheffield, Eng.: Almond Press, 1985), 213–51.

would be the usefulness of barley—it grows in harsher conditions than wheat—in opening up new lands to cultivation. From this perspective, the barley aspect of the festival was indispensable. Yet this is precisely the aspect that is missing in J's conception of the Passover. J focuses entirely on the lamb in a style that would be quite unexpected for the peasants' celebration.

In what sense was the lamb associated with the deliverance of the bedouin from Egypt of particular significance for them? The simplest way to answer this question is to characterize the essential features of the two main types of distinctive social identity among the producer peoples of Palestine. On what basis did the peasants and the bedouin regard themselves as distinct from one another? This is a complex question, but it is possible to give a partial answer that helps us to understand the emphasis in J on the lamb.

Village peasants were more or less tied to their locality and regarded their welfare as based primarily on their tenure by family of agricultural lands controlled by the village. A peasant's wealth and status were measured in terms of land. Bedouin also might live in villages, and of course they raised barley, but the distinctiveness of their social identity derived from the typical behavior of dwelling in tents and being able to move about within a given territory. Bedouin regarded their welfare as based primarily on the size and quality of their flocks and herds. Of these, the sheep was the most important component. The emphasis in J on the lamb, therefore, when considered in the light of the general bedouin character of nearly the whole of J, can be seen to reflect the essential item of bedouin identity. (Later in history, the camel would serve this role, but not in the time of David.)

The killing and eating of lambs at about the time of the barley harvest makes considerable ecological sense. For the peasants who are the object of J's portrayal, the period just prior to the grain harvest finds the household grain bins at their lowest level. Male lambs provide a way of filling out the diet at this time when other food is scarce. The same applies to bedouin, among whom other considerations weigh as well. The flocks are about to be moved from winter pasture in the dryland to the lowland fields about to be harvested, where stubble will be available for grazing. For both shepherds and bedouin, it would be important to cull unneeded males from the flock before moving into summer pasturage in the more densely populated and intensively farmed areas of the region, where the direct "cost" of pasturage was liable to rise. Also, the journey is back toward territory under state control, where the state typically taxes the flock: the smaller the flock, the less the taxes. The male lambs are eaten at the start of the trek so they do not have to be tended on the journey and paid for on arrival.

This then is the background for the association of the escape of the bedouin corvée workers and the lamb-slaughtering feast in early spring. The tradition is one of undertaking a lengthy trek not unlike the spring transhumance (although the escape itself is a migration), when the flock must be reduced where possible. This is what the historian has in mind as the history of the great escape begins.

Tribes of Palestinian bedouin operated regularly in the Nile delta and valley regions. From what we know about such activities, the relationships between the bedouin and the Egyptian government were usually peaceful. This is what one would expect when the government was more powerful than the bedouin and sufficiently secure to permit them entrance through the defended and controlled eastern border. Although this was normally the case, because such tribes functioned typically as paramilitary bands, they posed a potential threat to the rulers of Egypt. They periodically came to rival the Egyptian administration when it was less powerful and not in a position to control the eastern border or, in some periods, the Egyptian heartland itself. The best example of this phenomenon from the period prior to the emergence of Israel in Palestine is the rule of the Hyksos toward the end of the Middle Bronze Age (ca. 1650–1550). The Hyksos, in the view of many historians, were Palestinian bedouin who took advantage of the weakness of indigenous rule in Egypt to capture sovereignty in Egypt for about a hundred years. The New Kingdom Eighteenth Dynasty came to power in opposition to this Palestinian control of Egypt and made it the cardinal article of their legitimacy that they threw out the foreign tyrants. In some circles the Hyksos have been identified as the Israelites themselves. That this is not the case is clear from what we have said regarding the emergence of Israel. There is, however, some insight embedded in the suggestion. It makes perfectly good sense to compare the Hyksos as a type of people with the bedouin type that J takes to represent early Israel. Hence the threat that Israel posed to pharaoh in J's history was a real one, at least at any time the Egyptian rule was weak. Historically speaking, neither the period of the emergence of the highland villages of Iron I Palestine nor for that matter the period of the rise of David was such a time.

In order to prevent the descendants of Israel, whom we may now call the Israelites, from taking advantage of their increasing greatness—the result of their blessing—by opposing the current ruling house of Egypt as Palestinians had done in the past,[3] the king of Egypt impressed them into forced

3. The usual translations of Exod. 1:9 are like the RSV ("He said to his people"), taking "his people" to be all the people of Egypt, as in the New American Bible's "his subjects." This understanding has pharaoh noting that the descendants of Israel, the Palestinian migrants, have come to outnumber the Egyptians. This is absurd and misses the point. Hebrew *am* here means the military subjects of pharaoh's immediate court, whom the Israelite bedouin as a coherent military band might well outnumber.

labor, or corvée, to build cities of storage within the rich grain-growing delta region of northern Egypt. More than a variation on the theme of Cain's building the first city or of the tower-city of the fourteenth genera- tion, the impressment of Israel's labor into the building of centralized grain- storage facilities represents the climactic and fundamental recapitulation of the archetypal evil of the history's first and second generations. In the brief compass of Exod. 1:8–12, J concentrates the basic issues of his categoriza- tion of reality: land, labor in terms of both production and reproduction, urban rule, and nationalist opposition to Egypt.

The tendency in popular treatments of the "exodus" is to understand slavery as a social and economic issue. J's issue isn't primarily so- cioeconomic but political. His interest in slavery per se is secondary to his interest in the nationalism of the Davidic state. Having told without hesita- tion story after story involving the slaves of Abram, Sarai, Isaac, Rebekkah, Jacob, Leah, Rachel, and Jacob's sons, J clearly does not want to call into question all exploitation of labor but to project a particular state's definition of its subjects' national identity in terms of that form of exploitation most directly identifiable with the state.[4] Throughout his history, J chooses corvée, rather than just any form of the exploitation of labor, as his prime issue. Why? Because, as the most obvious form of the exploitation of labor by the state, corvée lends itself more readily than other forms of slavery to treatment from a nationalist stance as a nationalist issue. Contrast J's use of the motif of exploitation with that of the prophets of eighth-century Israel and Judah, who treated the exploitation of labor against the backdrop of the collapse of the state of Israel and the threatened collapse of Judah. In their view, Yahweh's solicitude for the worker superseded his solicitude for the state. Hence they focused not on state slavery but on debt slavery, a form of exploitation that directs attention to a wider class of oppressors, the urban landowners as a group, rather than the king alone, and thus to the social more than the national issue.[5]

The cities of storage were a regular feature of agrarian urban rule. They existed in Israel, as we know from the reference in 1 Kings 9:15–19 and 2 Chron. 32:27–29. Grain-storage facilities are known archaeologically from the excavation at Beersheba, where such structures were discovered from the Israelite monarchic period. It is not known whether David himself expended a great amount of energy and resources for the construction of

4. It would be inaccurate, however, to think that this nationalism of J which so over- shadows his social critique has simply transformed "slavery," or the exploitation of labor in general, as an adaptable ethical problem from a social issue into a nationalist issue.

5. At the secession of northern Israel under Jeroboam, localizing forces again came to the fore. While opposing Solomon's state corvée, Jeroboam promulgated a set of laws, related to Exod. 21:1–11, that condoned debt slavery to a limit of seven years. Cf. p. 36 n. 14.

such facilities. The reconstruction of the great administrative cities of the
Israelite kingdom which included the provision for grain storage is known
archaeologically to have occurred early in the Iron II, or monarchic, period,
but archaeologists are rarely able to distinguish between Davidic and
Solomonic construction. What is clear? For the people of Palestine identified by the court of David as Israelite, such a system for the disposal of grain
was probably a considerable departure from normal practice. The corvée
they were conscripted into denied their rights as creatures of Yahweh who,
like the first human and all succeeding humans in J's view, were not
created to be corvée slaves.

J has described the awful condition of enslaved Israel, a condition
opposed by the entire thrust of J's history. The condition demands nothing
less than complete reversal. At this critical moment, then, when all the
threads of J's history have been joined in a single focus in which everything
is all wrong, J introduces the person who will play the lead role in the
resolution required, the protagonist of the twenty-first generation, Moses.[6]
Moses differs from the protagonists presented previously in J, because J
does not define his precise genealogical connection to the great progenitor
Abram.

At this point in the Bible there occurs the story of the midwives saving
the male children of Israel, the birth of Moses, and his discovery by
pharaoh's daughter in the bulrushes. These stories are from E, who emphasizes as usual the jeopardy of sons—both stories have this as their main
theme—and who creates a Moses who, having been raised in the Egyptian
court, has an identity problem. This imparts to the following stories from J
a meaning they did not previously have, that Moses must struggle through
his ambivalence by willfully seizing upon his identity with the Hebrews. E's
Moses, a familiar of pharaoh's court destined to be the leader of the
movement of bedouin against the tyranny of corvée labor, is probably a
retrojection of Jeroboam I. He reflects a northern scribe's reshaping of the
traditions of Moses in accordance with the scribe's actual experience of the
ruler of his own kingdom. This was quite unknown to J, just as J had no
foreknowledge of the secession of Israel from the house of David a full
generation and a half after his time.

The one Egyptian characteristic that J includes in his portrayal of Moses
is his name. The names Israel and Moses must be put in another category
from those of the bedouin heroes we have encountered so far in the history.

6. Recall that in terms of J's chronological structure, the scheme of three sets of seven
generations, Moses does not fit the pattern of Adam, Noah, and Abram. Moses comes at the
end of a set of seven. The nation to settle the land, the twenty-second generation, the people
coming under David's rule, represents the critical new beginning.

J does not have an etiology[7] of the name Moses, while his etiology of the name Israel relates only slightly to the story. Moses is an Egyptian name. Moses is the element of many Egyptian names that means "born of," or "son of"—as in Ramses, in which the element -*mses* is the same as Moses. It is tempting to speculate whether J was aware that the name Moses, Yahweh's ultimate hero, means "born," in line with J's interest in reproduction, and that the Egyptian word *msi* from which it is derived means both "bear, give birth" and "form, fashion," making it the Egyptian counterpart of both Hebrew *yalad* and *yatsar,* the terms for bearing and forming, as in the garden where the first human was formed.

The great hero of J's history of Israel at its turning point—when the survival of the Israelite nation is at stake, on the brink of the generation of David himself—was an Israelite bedouin descendant with an Egyptian name. Now why would such a figure have an Egyptian rather than a Hebrew language name? What's in the name?

Many historians have noticed that a number of Israelites from the early period have Egyptian names, particularly men in Moses' own tribe of Levi. These names probably include Aaron, Phinehas, and Hophni, and possibly Miriam. When noticed, the names are usually taken to prove that there were Israelites who actually lived in Egypt and participated in an exodus out of Egypt. This interpretation has little if anything to do with the several far more important factors now known to bear directly on the emergence of Israelite society during the Iron I period.

So strange is it for J's main protagonist to have an Egyptian name that it is possible J incorporated into his history the popular notion that such a sheikh played a definitive role in the pre-Davidic history of highland Palestine. If so, then all that is preserved of such a person in J's account is his name. There is no reason to believe that J's portrayal of Moses is based on a tradition including accurate knowledge of such an erstwhile individual's activities in Egypt, the Sinai, and the Transjordan. Like the rest of J's history from the fifteenth generation on, the character of Moses is based on the typicalities of bedouin political and social life, involving relationships with Egypt or the dominant power there and the problem of leadership over a hierarchy of tribes in a critical period when the usual tribal consensus prerequisite to leadership was threatened with fracture. To the extent that J portrays actual realities, the best guess is that they occurred in or pertained to J's own day. Alternatively, it might indicate the importance of a pro-Egyptian faction in pre-Davidic Palestinian history.

Under what circumstances would such a figure have existed? Were there

7. Etiology is the study of origins. J simply adopts the name Moses without furnishing us with its significance, in contrast to the many names whose meanings are important to his history. E, on the other hand, does give a Hebrew etymology (Exod. 2:10).

such people in Palestine? Yes. We have already discussed how the bedouin leaders of Palestine, particularly the more powerful and wealthy, had close connections with the urban ruling class. When that ruling class was partly Egyptian, it would not have been out of the ordinary for a Palestinian bedouin sheikh, like any other Palestinian lord, to spend time in the Egyptian court and to adopt a supplemental Egyptian identity. Palestinian rulers have perennially taken the opportunity to adopt names from the culture of the suzerain power in control in Palestine in any given period. Many Palestinians in Egypt would also have done so. At the same time, the evidence for the Hyksos in Egypt includes many Palestinian names, including the name Jacob itself. Thus not all Palestinians automatically adopted this practice. If there was a Palestinian sheikh named Moses in the pre-Davidic period, then we must suppose he and his forces were allied with the New Kingdom administration of Palestine. We can suppose that he served, in the age-old pattern of the bedouin of this general region, as a head of military contingents maintained by the Egyptian empire as a buffer between themselves and the Hittite empire.

J says nothing about Moses' origin and upbringing. This must be stressed, given the rather common knowledge of the E stories of his youth. As we explained (chapter 2), J's history of Moses begins with the words, "In those days" (Exod. 2:11). In the present form of the text, that phrase refers to the preceding incident involving pharaoh's daughter and the raising of Moses in the court. English translations are forced to render the phrase with this meaning. Thus the RSV translates, "One day." In J itself, this phrase followed directly on Exod. 1:8–12 and referred to that charged time of the enslavement of the bedouin.

In J, Moses has no background. In view of the clear description of the origin and status of J's previous protagonists, with the partial exception of Abram, this lack of background is odd and striking, raising the question of where Moses came from and who he was. It is as though J intends this question to be raised in the audience's mind. Ancestry is the issue, and David was fatherless in terms of his royal legitimacy. The heroes in the stories of the ancestors are the younger sons. Isaac, Jacob, and Joseph are younger sons. Usurpers of royalty like David were consumed with the question of their right to the throne. When David took the throne from Saul, we see this ever-present concern throughout 1 Samuel and early parts of 2 Samuel; we see it also in J's household cult history.

For J, it is significant that Moses' importance does not stem from his background, genealogy, family connections, or from any specific links with the family of Israel as it has been traced so far. This lack is intended to point up a different basis for his importance. This different basis has to do with who he was as demonstrated by certain actions that caused Yahweh to

notice him. Something other than his background and connections established Yahweh's interest in Moses.

J goes on to say, "Moses was great." This could mean one of two things,
and both possible meanings of "was great" have already occurred in J, so
we know they are genuine possibilities. Either it means Moses grew up or it
means Moses had become a great man in some sense. This ambiguity
served the purposes of E perfectly, who supplemented the narrative at this
point as he supplemented the story of Jacob at Bethel. When the stories of
Moses' birth and upbringing were inserted just before this ambiguous
phrase, it took on the meaning, "When Moses had grown up." This is the
way it is always translated. It is likely that J intended the second meaning.
There is no reason to think that, having said nothing about Moses' youth,
he would now say he had grown up. More important, the primary issue in
the history of Moses as it develops is the nature of Moses' authority over his
people and how he came to have that authority. This is the main subject of
the episodes through which J introduces him, and it is in relation to Moses'
authority in these episodes that J announces that this Israelite, possessing
an Egyptian name, was an important man, probably in the view of both the
Egyptians and the Israelites, in a context in which most Israelites were
anything but important or great. The Egyptian administration would have
had need of go-betweens who were bedouin but, because they were
beholden to Egyptian favor for their rise in status, inclined to loyalty to
their own oppressor. A more appropriate translation should read something like: "In those days—that is, in the days of the taskmasters' severe
oppression of the Israelite corvée workers—one of the Israelites, having
adopted an Egyptian name, was noticeably upwardly mobile within the
system of the oppression of his own people."

J's point, then, is that when in a moment of distraction this man, with
such privileges as he had, impulsively identified with and took extraordinary action on behalf of the downtrodden of his own people, this extreme
reversal in his expected behavior attracted the notice of Yahweh. J's purpose in this and the next two episodes introducing this man is to explain
why Yahweh chose him rather than any other to do what he wanted done:
to lead the ancestors of Israel to the land of Abram's and Israel's land grant.

At the beginning of J's characterization of Moses, he portrays a man who
combined the salient characteristics of the heroes of the blessed generations. Like Abram, Moses would be blessed by Yahweh without the advantages of his reproductive background. Like Isaac, he is portrayed as compliant with and entirely dependent upon Yahweh, while like Jacob he was
a man who acted on his own initiative. But like Joseph, he had been
affected by the Egyptian context in which he lived.

If it is true that Moses as a great man summarized the salient characteristics of the other great men of J's history of the blessing, then at the very least it reinforces the character of J as a history of great men—the cursed "men of name" as well as those blessed by Yahweh. Elite history tends to be in terms of great men. J's history itself could be epitomized by calling it "The History of Adam, Cain, Noah, Abram, Isaac, Israel, Judah, Joseph, and Moses." The same is true of the Davidic court documents in 1 Samuel 16—2 Samuel 5 and 2 Samuel 13—20. Because we are so used to the stories of the beginning of the Bible and the habit of portraying history in terms of the actions of great men, we don't take notice of the peculiarity of this character of J's history, like most of biblical and agrarian history.[8]

For the Davidic court, the figure of Moses meant something. It could be said that the main theme of J's history of Moses is the legitimacy of the particular form and style of leadership exercised by Moses. This feature of the history of Moses comes into sharp focus in the narrative of the trek through the Sinai desert when Moses exercised the desert leadership for which he was particularly suited. Moses as a champion of the history was more than a coincidence of the bedouin genre of the history of his generation. Among the many ways he could be described, his role as a tribal military leader guiding and compelling his band across the Sinai would have been of particular interest to a royal court of southern Palestine. During most of the agrarian era, it was difficult to cross the hostile environment of the Sinai. The worst problems were lack of water and the interdiction of hostile groups. During the New Kingdom period, Egypt had positioned garrisons and stations for provisions all along the main coastal route between the Nile delta and Gaza in Palestine. But not everyone, obviously, could cross the Sinai in the care of the Egyptian military and officialdom. And by the time of David, the Twenty-first Dynasty in Egypt had long since been too weak to maintain such a system. For royalty on both sides of the Sinai, the best or perhaps only way to cross the Sinai was under the guidance and in the care of bedouin groups who knew where water was and who could defend against bandits. Even if David did not desire to cross the Sinai to Egypt, it was important for him to be allied with those chiefs who could provide such escort in order to prevent his opponents on either side from making use of their services. It is in this sense that the Davidic court's patronage of chiefs like Moses was essential and that J's making Moses so important was politically significant.

If J's concern for the nature of Moses' leadership only comes into sharp focus later on, it is nonetheless an important part of the story from the beginning. The first three incidents involving Moses are presented by J to

8. Compare the preliminary comments regarding "political biographies" of paradigmatic heroes by Jack M. Sasson, "Literary Criticism, Folklore Scholarship, and Ugaritic Literature," in *Ugarit in Retrospect,* ed. G. D. Young (Winona Lake, Ind.: Eisenbrauns, 1981), 96—98.

explain what it was in Moses' character that led Yahweh to select precisely this man to guide the bedouin away from Egypt. The man who was selected demonstrated a compassion and a sense of justice equivalent to Yahweh's as Yahweh viewed with distress the oppression of the people he had blessed.

In the first incident, Moses was moving among his people in a position to observe their harsh treatment directly.[9] (Again, it is not precisely clear whether he was privileged not to suffer similar treatment himself; although, as has been said, it is the concern of E, not J, to make an issue of Moses' Israelite identity, it is true that J also portrays a Moses who at first was not "all" bedouin. In a short while, a Midianite girl in the Sinai would describe him to her father as an Egyptian.) While watching, he saw an Egyptian beating one of his kinsmen.[10] He was impelled to come to the defense of the victim. First, however, he looked to the left and the right to make sure no one was watching: Moses' sense of right was his own, not a function of political maneuvering or the anticipation of political advancement. He killed the Egyptian and hid his corpse in the sand.

Moses' killing of this Egyptian was an all-important act. When Moses appeared, we knew nothing about him, and at this point we know only that he has killed an Egyptian slave driver. Shortly Yahweh would select

9. Moses at first regarded himself over against his own kin. The expression used for "going out to look at" is the same as when Dinah went out to look at the daughters of the area around Shechem.

10. The kinsman is called an *ibri,* usually translated "Hebrew." The meaning of this term is a vexed difficulty of Old Testament history. Its meaning in English depends a good deal on context. J appears to use it to refer to foreign, or Palestinian, slaves in Egypt. This usage begins with Joseph in Egypt, and thus fits precisely with the usage in contemporaneous Davidic apologetic documents. P. Kyle McCarter, Jr., in his recent commentary *I Samuel,* Anchor Bible (Garden City, N.Y.: Doubleday & Co., 1980), 240–41, characterizes *ibri* as the way Israelites are referred to in foreign speech. In J, the definition of Israel as a nation depends on its opposition to Egypt.

Moses will be instructed to refer to Yahweh with pharaoh as the god of the *ibriyim,* or the god of the foreign slaves. This expression virtually defines the character of Yahweh for the history of Moses and hence—because of the importance of J's critique of royal corvée from the very beginning—for the entire history. Pharaoh does not know this god, as he will repeat—it is not surprising that the king of Egypt finds it difficult to condescend to know the god of his nonnative slaves—and Yahweh's purpose through much of the history in Egypt is to make himself known to pharaoh. The content of what pharaoh is to know is precisely this characterization: Yahweh is the god of the foreign slaves, or, in other words, the bedouin whose identity becomes, in J's history, that of the Israelite nation.

It remains uncertain whether *ibri* is the same as the term *apiru* that occurs in many documents from Egypt and southwest Asia during the second millennium B.C.E. During the New Kingdom period, many of the captives—even thousands of them—from Palestine taken to Egypt and employed in royal service were called *apiru.* Although there probably is a link between this usage and J's usage, it remains problematic, and it is not essential to understanding what J means by *ibri.* See most recently Nadav Na'aman, "Habiru and Hebrews: The Transfer of a Social Term to the Literary Sphere," *Journal of Near Eastern Studies* 45 (1986): 271–88.

him to help release the bedouin on the basis of this act and two like it. Yahweh approved the killing—it was right in his eyes. There is only one way it could be defined as right, and that is if it were in return for an injustice of equal magnitude. The implication is that the Egyptians were perpetrating such an injustice. We already know from our historian what the injustice was. As part of the system represented by the city, the Egyptians' oppression of the bedouin was directly linked with Cain's murder of Abel. The rightness of Moses' killing the Egyptian defined Egypt's oppression of the bedouin as tantamount to killing them. For J, the extortion of the Palestinians' labor was murder. In modern terms, as Jean-Paul Sartre said, "To fire workers because a factory is closing is a sovereign act that tacitly assumes the fundamental right to kill."

People are often shocked by Moses' violent behavior. In personalizing their evaluation of Moses, they tend to reverse the meaning of this episode. "If God could choose Moses," who killed somebody and therefore was a great sinner, the explanation goes, "then I guess God can put up with me, and maybe even use me." This approach to the text has God bending over backward, against God's principles, to pick out Moses. The opposite is the case. God reacted to Moses not with shock but approval. Moses acted not against God's principles and passion but wholly in line with them.

The next day, Moses went out again. He observed another fight. This time two Palestinian slaves were fighting each other. Moses addressed the slave in the wrong: "Why are you beating up your companion?" J does not explain to us what gave Moses the capacity to make this judgment of right and wrong. He simply presents a character who could and did make such a determination. The man who was addressed resisted. "Who made you," he countered, "master and judge over us?" The phrase "master and judge" combines two words to produce a single meaning (hendiadys). "Master" alludes to the Hebrew term for taskmaster, and "judge" refers to Moses' presuming to judge in this incident, not to any official role as a judge. The slave complained: Moses interfered in the dispute; he was no better than an Egyptian boss. This is the first of several incidents in which the oppressed would mislocate the cause of their oppression, blaming Moses for their troubles. It is the flip side of the Egyptian peasants' gratitude to pharaoh for their oppression: "Thank you, pharaoh, for enslaving us and saving our lives."

The slave in the wrong added, "Do you intend to murder me the way you murdered the Egyptian?" It is not possible to tell the difference between "murder" and "kill" simply from the Hebrew word that is used. Since the slave would obviously regard his own death as murder, it is clear that he regarded Moses' killing the Egyptian in the same terms. Murder placed the burden on Moses. It made Moses' act wrong. The person Moses would have to deliver could not himself make the correct moral judgment that would in due course form the basis of his own liberation. Moses realized that others knew he had killed an Egyptian. Pharaoh had heard of it and now sought to have Moses killed. So he escaped toward the desert in the east. With a few deft strokes of his pen J has brilliantly epitomized the principle of divide and rule against which all liberation movements struggle.

What we observe in these terse incidents are historical dynamics generic to the history of liberation in practically every time and place in which it occurs. They have been widely recognized as part of the history of Moses. But it is perhaps not so widely realized that these dynamics, appropriated for the purposes of the Davidic court, are subordinated to the particular political purposes of that court which many people even then might have regarded as nonliberating. J's purpose is not so much to explore the precise dynamics of liberation as to claim a particular bedouin history of liberation in support of the political assertions of David's court. Recall that J, speaking for the house of David on behalf of Israelite peasantry, is representing their political identity as a liberated identity in a form they could identify with little, the flight of a band of bedouin from Egypt. It is not surprising, according to the archival documents contained in 2 Kings and 2 Chronicles, that the Passover festival in this sense might not have been observed by the peasantry of monarchic Israel and Judah prior to the seventh century B.C.E.[11]

The third incident begins with a variation on the theme of the Palestinian arriving in a foreign land and finding a wife. Moses recapitulates Abram's servant and Jacob. He sat down by a well, out in the Sinai desert. The seven daughters of a priest of Midian frequented this well. When some shepherds came and drove them away, Moses saved them and watered their flocks for them. When they returned to Reuel their father, he asked, "Why have you come home so early today?" They replied, "An Egyptian saved us from the power of the shepherds. He even drew water for us and watered our flocks." Moses, in other words, went further than Jacob and so demonstrated for the third time that he was inclined to protect, make a judgment for, and deliver the oppressed.

Reuel asked immediately, "Where is he? Why did you leave the man there? Invite him to have something to eat." We are reminded of Laban, who had a difficult enough problem with only two daughters to marry off. This priest of Midian had an even greater problem. By this time J has little interest in the themes associated with reproduction in comparison with his

11. Uncertainty remains as to whether 2 Chronicles 30 and 2 Kings 23:22 refer to the failure to keep the festival at all or the failure to keep it as the Deuteronomist intended, as a grand national festival at a single central sanctuary.

history of production, justice, and liberation, yet he does not refrain from giving Moses a validity in terms of the theme of reproduction. Moses consented to live with Reuel, and he gave his daughter Zipporah to Moses in marriage. Since J doesn't say otherwise, it is to be assumed that since the father selected Moses' wife, Zipporah was the eldest and Moses made no choice. Moses then is more like Isaac, who waited on the choice of Yahweh.

Zipporah bore a child, their firstborn son. Moses named him Gershom. This name combines the Hebrew word for sojourner *(ger)* and a word that comes close to meaning "there" *(shom),* and took the name to mean "I am a sojourner over there, in a foreign land." The meaning of Moses' and Zipporah's firstborn—Gershom—takes us directly back to the blessing of Abram with a firstborn son entirely apart from Abram's homeland and kinship and reproductive network. At the same time, "Gershom" virtually names the fundamental tension not only of this section of the history but of the entire history itself. Moses was not the only one who was a sojourner in a foreign land. The bedouin too were sojourners, having lost their earlier land grant from pharaoh and not yet having taken possession of their land grant from Yahweh in Palestine. Something must give. It is probable that J here mentions that the pharaoh who was trying to have Moses killed died.

Moses worked as a herdsman for Reuel, just as Jacob had worked for Laban. On one occasion Moses led his flocks deep into the desert. Suddenly the genie of Yahweh appeared to him in a fiery flame out of a bush. The bush was called *seneh,* which sounds much like Sinai. In this way J makes clear that Sinai is the place where in a short while Yahweh will appear to all the bedouin to instruct them as to the proper way for them to worship him at an earthen altar. This typical J wordplay ties a significant episode in J to the stay at Sinai on the trek away from Egypt to Sinai.[12]

Yahweh appeared as a fire at this sanctuary-to-be because he adopted here the character of the warrior who burns cities and destroys all that they stand for in J's history. This fire may excite the modern reader as some vague mystical entity. But its political and military significance in J is made clear by some biblical parallels (e.g., Deut. 9:1–3, shortened): "You are about to cross the Jordan to dispossess great cities, fortified to the sky; know that Yahweh passes in the vanguard, a consuming fire, who will destroy them."[13]

Moses waited for the bush to burn up, and when it didn't, he walked

12. This tie, together with other evidence, makes less likely the view expressed by von Rad and other historians of the Bible that the main episode of Sinai, especially the deliverance of law there, was originally unconnected to the rest of the narrative.

13. Fire is the city-consuming agent also in Josh. 6:24; 8:8, 19; Judg. 1:8; 9:52; 18:27; 20:48; 2 Kings 8:12; Amos 1:4, 7, 10; Isa. 1:7; Jer. 17:27; and elsewhere.

toward it to take a closer look. The genie instantly repulsed him: "Don't come near. Remove your sandals from your feet, for the place you are standing on is sacred ground." The perpetual fire at the sacred place alludes to the anticipated prescription for the notably modest altar cult of Israel and to the future construction of a pilgrimage shrine at the "sacred ground" of Sinai.

It is still not certain, and may never be, exactly where the mountain of Sinai is. The traditional site is Jebel Musa, the "Mount of Moses," located in the south of the Sinai peninsula. Many alternatives have been proposed over the ages and more recently by historians, but none of them has appealed to more than a handful of people as more likely than the traditional site.[14] During the monarchic period, there were Israelite pilgrimage way stations in the Sinai region (as indicated by Num. 33:1–49, which many think is a list of such stations, and more recently by archaeological excavations). The evidence from some periods of the Israelite monarchy after David's time indicates there was a pilgrimage sanctuary in the Sinai area (now known as Jebel Musa), the goal of a rather lengthy pilgrimage trek from Palestine backward along the traditional route of the trek away from Egypt.[15] It can be supposed, given the role of Sinai in J, that this pilgrimage existed also during the reign of David. It may even have originated at that time. There are at least three ways to view the significance of this pilgrimage and the central role J gives it in his history.

First, the pilgrimage itself was important for the political purpose of maintaining Davidic national presence in the Sinai in the direction of Egypt. Pilgrimage in the ancient Near East usually had such political or economic significance. In this case, the Sinai pilgrimage indirectly reflected in J marked the extent of the territory under Davidic sovereignty in the direction of the main enemy, the ruling house of Egypt. In terms of this purpose, the pilgrimage to Sinai in David's reign paralleled the pilgrimages to Dan and Bethel in the reign of Jeroboam I, who ruled Israel after the death of Solomon. Jeroboam's pilgrimage cults likewise marked the extent of his territory in the directions of his main opponents Aram and Judah. It makes sense to call this political feature of Palestinian sovereignty the border pilgrimage, even though this important feature of the founding of

14. The most recent unlikely alternative relocates Sinai within the boundaries of the modern state of Israel: Emmanuel Anati, *The Mountain of God: Har Karkom* (New York: Rizzoli, 1987).

15. See Zeev Meshel and Carol Meyers, "The Name of God in the Wilderness of Zin," *Biblical Archaeologist* 39 (1976): 6–10. The site referred to is Kuntillet Ajrud, a little less than halfway between Jebel Musa and Gaza.

such cults did not always persist after the territory under the rule of a particular state grew or shrank and thus changed borders.[16]

In the second place, in David's case the border pilgrimage had another significance. Until the era of mechanization, traversing the Sinai always required the assistance and services of bedouin who were resident there and on its edges. David's control of the Sinai in the direction of Palestine (for which the Sinai pilgrimage was an emblem) was based on the same kind of bedouin links and alliances that made possible his continued influence and control in the Negev. This was one more facet of the typical pattern of states using bedouin tribes as paramilitary buffer zone allies in the more arid or marginal terrain along their borders. The decision to portray Israel as bedouin included the need to incorporate such alliances, essential to the integrity of David's rule on the boundary with Egypt, his main opponent, in the portrayal of national identity.

Third, and finally, that J should depict the national law of David being revealed at just this border pilgrimage site results directly from his epitomizing Israel's national identity in terms of a massive bedouin anti-Egyptian labor movement.

Yahweh identified himself as the god of Abram, Isaac, and Jacob, that is, the god who granted those ancestors the land of Palestine. "I have seen the affliction of my people who are in Egypt, and I have heard their outcry because of their slave drivers. I know their pain." The last statement is a remarkably concise and weighty J statement. J's history has already made clear that this divinity Yahweh feels pain, pain no less than the pain of labor whether in childbirth or field work. Now J has come to the great pain of history, the culminating pain behind the national identity of David's people, and here combines his assertion of Yahweh's empathic pain with the term "know." Yahweh "knew" the pain of the Israelite laborers.[17]

So he came down to deliver them from the power of Egypt and to bring them from Egypt to Palestine, the land he granted to Abram. He describes that land as "a good and wide land, a land oozing milk and honey, the land of the Canaanites, the Hittites, the Amorites, the Perizzites, the Hivites, and the Jebusites." As we have already seen, this was an untilled land inhabited only by city dwellers. The phrase "oozing milk and honey" does not mean

---

16. The particular attachment of the name Sinai to the national house of David is manifest in the change of the mountain's name in northern Israel to Horeb, even though the mountain itself was probably the same. Which of the two names was more original, or whether both were, is uncertain.

17. See Terence E. Fretheim, *The Suffering of God: An Old Testament Perspective* (Philadelphia: Fortress Press, 1984).

that the land was currently marvelously productive but that it was sparsely populated and was the haunt of sheep, goats, and wild bees.[18]

Yahweh instructed Moses to go to Egypt and gather the bedouin elders to tell them he had appeared to Moses and that, knowing their oppression, he was to lead them from Egypt to Palestine. "They will listen to you," he assured Moses.[19]

It is easy to miss perhaps the most important point of this pivotal moment in J's history. The Israelites were in their predicament because a pharaoh reneged on his land grant. He did not "know," and can be said to have forgotten, the right of the descendants of Israel to their land in Egypt. Yahweh remembered. This marks the great difference between Yahweh and pharaoh. Yahweh's provision of land, the basic element of production and economic independence, was reliable, pharaoh's was not. Yahweh is shown to be what pharaoh was not, for production. This is *the* basic claim of the whole J history: the Davidic state reliably supplies the means for its people to prosper. Under David the people need not fear the loss of the integrity of their productive systems and relations. In the context of the selective upward mobility within David's realm, J was apparently able to get away with this assertion.

Yahweh instructed Moses to take sheikhs of Israel with him to the king of Egypt and say, "Yahweh the god of the foreign slaves has met us. We would like to make a three-day journey into the desert to sacrifice with Yahweh our god." The purpose of the Israelites' pilgrimage would have been to "serve" Yahweh, although that is not the term used in this instance. The

18. Compare Isa. 7:18–25. Two later occurrences of the expression "oozing milk and honey," in Num. 13:27 and 16:14, are sometimes thought to suggest that the expression implies that the land is to be generally fertile. It is not likely that the expression itself refers there directly to the produce of the land that the spies see and bring back samples of. Expressions for fertile agricultural land would be of the type found in Deut. 8:8: "a land of wheat, barley, vine, fig, and pomegranate; a land of olive oil and honey." The positive meaning of the expression in Numbers is good pasturage.

As is now known, adults in most human populations are deficient in the enzyme required for digesting lactose, a complex sugar in milk. During the Neolithic period a few human populations developed in relation to domestic mammals under such conditions that milk became an important part of the adult diet, and in these populations the capacity to digest milk is generally found. But this capacity can be said to be uncommon for humans in general. In the Middle East, historically the bedouin groups have a greater tolerance for milk because of its greater importance in the bedouin diet. For other groups, villagers and especially townspeople, the idea of a land flowing with milk would have considerably less appeal. The picture of Abram serving a form of yogurt to Yahweh in the fifteenth generation is one more mark of Abram's bedouin character. See Marvin Harris, *Good to Eat: Riddles of Food and Culture* (New York: Simon Schuster, 1985), 130–53 (chap. 7: "Lactophiles and Lactophobes").

19. Exod. 3:9–15 belongs to E. The E strand elaborates here on the meaning of the name Yahweh, including the intriguing phrase translated "I am who I am." Some might be surprised to realize that Yahweh is the name of Israel's god in E just as in J. Because a minority of historians erroneously regard this as an inconsistency for E, they assign the references to Yahweh in this section to J, which itself does not have an etymology of Yahweh.

sacrifice was the feast shared in Yahweh's presence over the altar and was not different from the "service" or work at the altar going back as far as Abram and even Noah.

In this pivotal context, the contrast is the same as it was between the fourteenth and the fifteenth generation, between the city-tower of Babylon and the altars of Abram at Shechem and Bethel. It is the contrast between working for what J epitomizes as the city or state, on the one hand, and working for Yahweh, on the other hand. Human beings were created to work for Yahweh, as the first human was set to work in Yahweh's pleasure orchard. As explained in connection with Abram's altars, possibly the only instruction given by Yahweh to Moses and the bedouin when they returned to this very place in Sinai after their escape from Egypt defines the precise nature of the altar preferred by Yahweh for those who did his work and service, and the altar's service. All this was alluded to in these instructions given to Moses.

"I know," said Yahweh, "that the king of Egypt will not let you go, not even when confronted with force." But he reassured Moses: "I will stretch out my hand therefore and beat Egypt with all my marvels which I will do in its midst. After that he will let you go. I will even make the Egyptians so well disposed toward this people that when you leave you will not leave empty-handed. Every woman will 'borrow' from her neighbor and from her who sojourns in her house objects of silver and gold as well as clothing. You will put them on your sons and daughters and so relieve Egypt of these things." Moses was not reassured. "They won't believe me."

Moses' response initiates the theme of the rest of his dialogue with Yahweh. Yahweh pressed this commission upon Moses, who was reluctant to assume it. Later revisers and interpreters would take this exchange as an example of the reluctance of prophets during the monarchic period to accept the commission of Yahweh to denounce the elite of their people, since they would have to bear the hostile and harsh response of these elite. This was not Moses' problem, and it would be misleading to think that J had such a "prophetic" theme in mind in composing this scene. Moses' problem was simply expressed by "They won't believe me." The problem lay with his people, the people he was charged to guide, rather than with the elite Egyptian ruler he was charged to oppose. It was true, as Yahweh had just said, that pharaoh would not heed. This became the reason for the lengthy elaboration of Yahweh's marvels in opposition to pharaoh. But this was not the issue that concerned Moses. It was not pharaoh who was to question Moses' authority—as would be the case had Moses been a "prophet"—but his own people. The significance of this for the people governed by David is obvious: he had become leader of Israel by deposing the existing leadership, and his only right to the throne was his claim that Yahweh had anointed him.

The exchange between Yahweh and Moses is worth viewing in its entirety. (Note especially the emphasis on Moses' hand. The hand of Moses, representing the hand of Yahweh, will prove more potent than the hand of pharaoh.) Moses argued, "They won't heed me. They will say, 'Yahweh hasn't appeared to you.' "

Yahweh said to him, "What's this in your hand?"

He said, "A staff."

"Throw it to the ground."

He threw it to the ground and it became a snake. Moses jumped away from it.

Yahweh said to Moses, "Put out your hand and seize it by the tail."

Moses himself was different from his people. With the genie in front of him, he had little reason to doubt him. He put out his hand and grabbed hold of the snake, and it became a staff in his hand.

"This will make them believe that Yahweh the god of their fathers has appeared to you. Now put your hand inside your shirt."

Moses put his hand in his shirt and when he brought it out it had become diseased, as white as snow.

"Now put your hand back in your shirt."

He put it back, and when he withdrew it, it was again like the rest of his body.

"If they don't believe you and they don't heed the first sign, then they'll believe the second sign. And if they don't believe either of these signs and they don't heed you, take some of the water of the Nile and pour it on the land. The water you take from the Nile will become blood on the land."

Again Yahweh was experimenting, as in the history of the creation of the second human in the garden and of the great downpour of the eighth generation. Yahweh believed the second sign would be convincing, but he had a third sign up his sleeve just in case. He probably thought that the mention of blood would put an immediate end to all doubt. The rightness, in the view of Yahweh, of Moses' killing the Egyptian defined the oppression of the Israelites as tantamount to murder. Blood was thus the issue. Yahweh could anticipate as much when pharaoh did not relent. Yahweh would be forced to confront pharaoh with the bloodiness of his system and then to shed the blood of his eldest son, of the eldest sons of all his kingdom, and ultimately the blood of pharaoh himself. Yahweh could perhaps further anticipate that he would set the bedouin slaves apart by lamb's blood. Blood epitomized the evil of Egypt. At this stage of the history, nothing else would better reveal Yahweh's determination to return blood for blood upon the line of Cain. Thereby Yahweh would exact the ultimate retribution for the blood of Abel that soaked the ground and cried out for justice.

Moses did not take the hint to end the conversation, since (as J knew) the punch line had not yet been delivered. "Look, my lord, I am not a man of words—neither yesterday nor any time in the past, and for sure not from the time you started speaking to your servant. I have a sluggish tongue." Moses was literally "heavy of mouth" and "heavy of tongue." There has been much speculation as to what exactly this means. There is little reason to think that it refers to a particular pathology.[20] The more important point is again the rhetorical one. Pharaoh's most important characteristic, as the plagues came at him one after the other, was clear: he was "heavy of heart." This means that his mind worked slowly. Moses' complaint was that his tongue worked slowly. Yahweh must grant the point and so was faced with the problem of getting a sluggish tongue to work on a sluggish brain. The history of oppression does indeed have a sluggish, resisting quality to it.

Yahweh retorted, "Who gives a mouth to a person, or who makes a person mute or deaf, or seeing or blind?[21] Yahweh, that's who. So go, and I'll be your mouth and I'll let you know what to say."[22]

"Look, my lord, you send anyone you want . . . ."

At this point Yahweh became angry with Moses and said, "Is there Aaron your brother, the Levite? I know he knows how to speak, and here he is, on his way to meet you. He'll be glad to see you. Speak to him and put the words in his mouth, and I will be with both your mouth and his mouth, and will let you both know what you are to do. He will speak for you to the people. He will become for you a mouth, and you will become for him a god."

The last line is the punch line. Moses was not the prophet, as spokesman, but Aaron was. Yahweh has made an astounding statement about Moses. From the inception of the Bible's first history, the distinction between the divine and the human has been maintained at great cost. Now Yahweh has reached the stage where a mere creature is virtually redefined as a god! Moses was to supply, like a god, speeches for Aaron his spokesman. But far more important, he was to appear before pharaoh to

20. See Jeffrey H. Tigay, "'Heavy of Mouth' and 'Heavy of Tongue': On Moses' Speech Difficulty," *Bulletin of the American Schools of Oriental Research* 231 (1978): 57–67.

21. Yahweh must have already been thinking of pharaoh. Pharaoh's problem, as it turned out, was that his sluggish mind prevented him from hearing and seeing properly, as we shall see.

22. Moses was "an agent of God whose success owed nothing to his natural endowments, but only to the persuasion worked by the words and deeds he uttered and performed under divine direction" (Tigay). The comparison with Balaam, the speaker who brings J to a resounding close, is evident.

speak as Yahweh himself. He was also to confront pharaoh with nothing less than the will of the divine creator in opposition to this enslaving regime whose presumption denied the creator. In this sense Moses was to be god in the presence of pharaoh in order to show that pharaoh, like Cain, was not a god.

Moses' resistance crumbled. Yahweh then instructed him: when he reached pharaoh he should issue a "Thus says Yahweh."[23] "With regard to my firstborn son Israel, I have said to you, 'Let my son go, that he may work for [and serve and worship] me.' If you refuse to let him go, I will kill your firstborn son." This heavily loaded threat makes perfect sense in the light of our history. The evil that began with the presumptuous acts of Cain (the firstborn in the first seven generations) and Ham (the firstborn in the second seven generations) will be resolved through a consciousness epitomized by the birth of Isaac (the firstborn of the blessed line in this third seven generations).

---

23. The expression "thus says" indicates simply that what follows is a verbatim message from a message sender.

22

A Thick Head

(Exodus 4:24—5:23)

At a place where Moses spent the night on the way, Yahweh came upon Moses and tried to kill him. Zipporah took a flint and cut off her son's foreskin. This she brought in contact with Moses' genitals and said, "You are my 'blood-groom.'" When he slacked off from him/it, she said, "A blood-groom of circumcision."[1]

Moses and Aaron went and gathered all the Israelite bedouin sheikhs.[2] Aaron spoke to them all the words Yahweh had spoken to Moses. Moses performed the signs for the people to see. The people trusted them when they heard that Yahweh had attended to the sons of Israel and had seen their oppression. They bowed down and did obeisance.

Afterward, Moses and Aaron went to pharaoh. They said to him, "Thus Yahweh the god of Israel has said: 'Let my people loose so they can make a pilgrimage feast for me in the desert.'"

Pharaoh said, "Who is Yahweh? Why should I listen to him and let Israel loose? I don't know Yahweh, and I won't let Israel loose."

They said, "The god of us foreign slaves has met us. We want to make a three-day journey into the desert to sacrifice with Yahweh our god, before he gets us with disease or sword."

The king of Egypt said to them, "Moses and Aaron, why are you giving the people an excuse to get out of their work? Get back to your corvée work. Just look

---

1. Even though Exod. 4:24–26 apparently belongs to J, we are not able to include it in our interpretation, because it is so difficult to interpret and has always been so. Clearly there are motifs already encountered, such as Yahweh's attempt to kill Moses as he killed Er and Onan, and Jacob's tussle with Yahweh. Such behavior probably strikes many modern readers as odd, but it is quite in line with the way J's Yahweh behaves. The gist of this episode remains genuinely obscure in the view of historians who have tried to make sense of it, and its relation to the main themes of J is unclear. Except for this passage and the story of the rape of Dinah, J makes nothing of the practice of circumcision, the circumcision of Isaac being part of the P strand. See Ernst Axel Knauf, "Supplementa Ismaelitica, 11," *Biblische Notize*, 40 (1987): 16–19.

2. There is no particular term for bedouin in the text. Hereafter "bedouin" will often be used in place of "Israelites" in the translation, to reinforce a point that was more obvious to the readers and hearers in David's court than to readers today.

how numerous these 'peasants' are, and you want to give them a chance to stop their corvée work?"

That day pharaoh told the slave drivers and foremen, "Don't give the people straw anymore, the way you have been, for making bricks. Let them go and gather their own straw. But continue to assign to them the same quota of bricks they have been used to making. Don't reduce it. They are lazy. That's why they are crying out, 'Let us go and sacrifice with our god.' Make the work for the men heavier. Keep them busy, and they won't have time to pay any attention to these lies."

The slave drivers and foremen went out and said to the people, "Thus pharaoh has said: 'There isn't anybody to give you straw anymore. Go and get your own straw, wherever you can find it. And your work quota is not going to be reduced one bit.'"

The people scattered throughout the whole land of Egypt to gather stubble for straw. The slave drivers pressed them: "Finish each day's work quota just as if you had plenty of straw." Pharaoh's slave drivers beat the bedouin foremen they had placed over the workers and shouted, "Why haven't you fulfilled your brick quota yesterday and today the way you used to?"

So the bedouin foremen went and cried out to pharaoh. "Why do you treat your slaves like this? They don't give us straw and yet they tell us to make bricks. We get beaten, but it's your men who are in the wrong."

Pharaoh said, "You're lazy. Lazy! That's why you say, 'Let us go and sacrifice with Yahweh.' Get back to work. Straw will not be given to you, but you must still give us your quota of bricks."

The bedouin foremen saw they were in an evil spot when they heard pharaoh repeat, "Don't reduce the daily requirement of bricks." When they bumped into Moses and Aaron waiting to meet them as they left pharaoh, they said to them, "May Yahweh look you over and judge. It is you who have made us stink in the eyes of pharaoh and in the eyes of his servants, and have put a sword in their hand to kill us."

Moses went back to Yahweh. He said, "My lord, why have you done such evil to these people? Why did you send me anyway? From the moment I went to pharaoh to speak in your name, he has done evil to these people, and you have done nothing to rescue them."

Moses returned to Egypt. When Moses and Aaron had gathered the notable and influential sheikhs of the bedouin, Aaron did all the public speaking, and Moses performed the tricks. The people believed Moses, J says, when they heard that Yahweh had noticed them in their oppression. Since the trust of Moses' people is so much at issue from this point on, it seems clear that J says they believed in order to point up shortly the brevity of their belief. "They bowed down and did obeisance." Did they bow to Yahweh or to Moses? J doesn't say. It is left ambiguous because the history of Moses is the history of his authority. It is hard to tell whether his acting in the place of Yahweh is an act of presumption or obedience on his part.

With Yahweh and the people behind them, Moses and Aaron were confident of success and went to pharaoh. J is uninterested in how this pair of slave-related individuals gained access to the king of Egypt. It was a stunning achievement. The lack of any attention to it points up the far greater importance of what exactly was said between the parties. They had a message for pharaoh from Yahweh. They introduced it in excellent messenger form, suggesting they posed as nothing more than messengers. "Thus said Yahweh, the god of Israel: 'Let my people loose that they may make a pilgrimage feast to me in the desert.' "

Pharaoh responded, "Who is Yahweh?" Who is Yahweh? Many times in the dialogues between Moses, Aaron, and pharaoh, pharaoh was to hear the words "that you may know that I am Yahweh." These two elements epitomize the entire episode of the plagues and subsequent escape of the bedouin corvée workers. The episode has a purpose: to disclose who Yahweh is, not only to pharaoh but also to the people J is addressing in David's realm. For J to ask and then answer the question of who Yahweh is does not mean simply that pharaoh knew other gods but not Yahweh and only needed to be introduced to Yahweh to add him to his repertoire of divine acquaintances. The point is not that it was well known to everyone just what Yahweh was like, so that in order to get to know him all one had to do was to be introduced. Rather, the whole of J's history defines this god precisely according to the history which he creates and to which he responds. Indeed, the history defines what it means to use the word "god," at least in the sense of the one who did nothing less than create the whole world and play the primary role in interacting with his creatures in the unfolding of this history. Hence we can rephrase pharaoh's question and Yahweh's response. The question is not just who is Yahweh. The question is who now at this stage in history is the god who created this world and interacted with the humans who in the history engaged in reproduction, production, murder, city-building, and everything else J has told us leading up to this moment. The answer, then, is not simply the being that we all generally believe in and know but exactly the one who in an act on a par with the creation of the world itself would rescue this band of enthralled Palestinian bedouin. This is the god of David's state.

J uses two expressions, "the sons of Israel" and "Israel." The first we have referred to as the bedouin. J uses this expression—a tribal designation for those who are the descendants of the bedouin sheikh Jacob or Israel— consistent with his characterization of Israel as bedouin. The second expression refers to the people ruled by David in terms of a national identity, as a nation. The term "nation" refers to a political consensus. The political consensus implied by J in his use of the expression "Israel" was not necessarily the political identity that all the people of David's kingdom would claim for themselves but one that was being projected upon them for the purposes of the court. The political identity of the diverse people included in David's realm could hardly have been represented as a consensus, except as they could be made to identify with a bedouin band like Moses', an undifferentiated unity for which supposedly the simple term Israel could suffice. Not only was J aware that such a projection of national identity functioned as a piece of Davidic propaganda. He also addresses head-on the very issue of a lack of consensus. He does so by making the chief theme of the history of Moses the issue of the people's acquiescence to a single authority and hence to a corporate identity.

Moses is David. Note that—what with all of the identifications made between J's characters and various historical or political entities up to this point, including several allusions to David—this is the first time we have made an identification with the one political figure who played the primary role in the creation of J in the first place. We must be precise, since the identification is not meant to be complete. In J's history, Moses preceded the generation contemporary with J by at least one. He was a bedouin sheikh, while David manifestly was not. In what sense, then, are they to be identified?

First, in order to answer this question we must reflect on another not so obvious question: in whose name did David promulgate the law of his kingdom? Law is like national identity. It is a conception of what the nation under monarchic rule holds in common as its norms of social interaction. Law and nation can be said to define each other. The usual practice in the ancient Near East was for the king to promulgate the law of his rule in his own name as the agent of the law-giving god of the realm, just as he promulgated, whether or not in his own name, the national identity. The striking thing about law in monarchic Israel as attested in the Old Testament is that none of it was presented as royal law. All Old Testament law in its present form is the law of Moses. Why should an Israelite king—beginning probably with David—have forgone the opportunity to claim himself as the mediating presenter of the divine law?

While some historians might wonder whether the assignment of all law to Moses is not the result of later editing of the documents contained in the Old Testament, most believe that the kings of Israel and Judah did in fact publish the law of their realms in the name of Moses. For historians who have read the early history of Israel directly out of the Old Testament, this has meant that an actual Moses played such a significant role in the creation of the law of premonarchic Israel that the kings of Israel had no choice but to continue to attach his name to any law they themselves wished to enforce. Such a view does not account for what sort of person Moses was as portrayed in the traditions, beginning with J, nor for the peculiar character of traditions like those in J or E as royal propaganda.

Everything that can be said to be meaningful in J's portrayal of Moses is meaningful precisely in terms of the part it plays in the presentation of J's entire history as Davidic propaganda. That Moses should play the primary role in David's projection of national identity and possibly as the giver of the law of David's realm (contrary to the ancient practice of the king himself giving the law) stems from the linkage already noted between nation and law, both as nationalist categories. Moses led the unified people and gave them their law, starting with the cult, just as the creation of a political consensus required the creation of a juridical consensus. David displaced the projection of the origin of law from himself to Moses for the same reasons that he displaced the projection of the origin of most of his people from the peasant villages of their homeland to the tents of Negev bedouin far off in Egypt. Principal among these reasons was that David gained political leverage with both peasants and bedouin by focusing the identity of Israel on a few wealthy sheikhs. This focus provided the optimum vehicle for conceptualizing the common opposition to Egypt which united his subjects in what David wanted to foster as a common cause. In addition, it appears from the way Moses figures in E, the narratives regarding Elijah and Elisha in 1 and 2 Kings, and other biblical traditions, that Moses was an important traditional juridical figure in the northern heartland of early Israel. By making Moses the lawgiver, J may also have been enhancing David's appeal to northern loyalties.

We broke into pharaoh's response in order to comment on its significance. "Who is Yahweh," he went on, "whose voice I should heed by letting Israel loose? I do not know Yahweh, and I won't let Israel loose."

Knowing Yahweh was in direct contrast to the "knowing" of the man and the woman that led to Cain's history. Knowing Yahweh was to acknowledge the authority of and to be in agreement with the god who responded to the first fourteen generations of history by blessing Abram and Sarai in order that in knowing him they might counteract the history of Cain. Knowing Yahweh was to work for Yahweh and to serve and worship Yahweh. Work, serve, and worship are not mentioned here just to make a religious point.[3] The point was mainly political. The contrast was with the king of Egypt, who did not "know."

Moses and Aaron made their request. "The god of us foreign slaves has met us." This was their first designation of Yahweh. Once again, we have translated "Hebrew" as foreign slaves in order to reinforce the generic meaning of this god. It is necessary first to grasp this generic meaning before leaping to David's nationalist meaning, which is dependent upon it. Without careful attention to the generic meaning, it is not possible to keep

---

3. Comparison with the semantic development of the term "liturgy" is often made.

in mind the basic question raised by the whole history: who exactly is this god? This is the question lying behind the question J is asking on behalf of David: who is Israel's god? This insistence on the generic meaning of J's god continues the concern expressed from the beginning of J's history in reference to "Yahweh, a god."

When Yahweh's envoys said, "Let us make a three-day journey into the desert to make sacrifice to Yahweh our god—otherwise he may plague us with pestilence or with the sword," pharaoh was unimpressed. He responded, "Moses and Aaron, why are you giving the people an excuse for getting out of work? Get back to your work gangs. Look how numerous the people are. And do you want to give them a chance to stop their work?" Anxious to squelch any resistance, pharaoh dispatched his slave drivers and the bedouin foremen to increase the work load of the people. Henceforth they were to receive no straw for their bricks, yet were forced to produce the same quota of bricks. "Do not reduce their quota," said pharaoh. "They are lazy." The king of Egypt was no different in his view of the oppressed from all who say that oppressed peoples feel oppressed because they are lazy. "Keep them busy, and they won't have time for these lies," he added.

The word "lies" poses the question: whose version of reality is true, the king of Egypt's or Yahweh's? The two were different, and only one could be true. The truth of Yahweh that proved the Egyptian king's view of reality a lie emerged in Yahweh's struggle against him. The truth was sealed when Yahweh killed the firstborn and eventually the king himself, and in place of the king of Egypt gave the people land. Of course, Yahweh's truth was also a royal truth, namely, David's.

Pharaoh's charge begins an episode whose main subject is the bedouin foremen. J portrays them as being on the side of the slave drivers. This is realistic in terms of the history of labor's resistance, and by paying attention momentarily to the foremen, J is able to sharpen the profile of Moses. The foremen and Moses had a common intermediate status; both were greater than mere slaves but less than their masters. The foremen identified with upward mobility, whereas Moses identified with downward mobility.

When the bedouin corvée slaves were unable to fulfill their quota, the slave drivers of the king of Egypt beat the bedouin foremen whom they had placed over the workers and demanded of them, "Why have you not completed your prescribed amount of bricks yesterday and today as before?" The foremen stomped into court and complained to pharaoh, "Why do you treat your slaves like this? They don't give us straw and yet require us to make bricks. We are beaten, but it is your thugs who are in the wrong." The foremen seemed to recognize the source of their oppression, but unlike the slaves and Moses, they failed to recognize the source of their deliverance. The slaves cried to Yahweh; the foremen cried to pharaoh.

Pharaoh had no more use for them than the slaves. "You are lazy. Lazy! Get back to work." The foremen went back to work and gave their own people as hard a time as they were receiving. "Fulfill your quota." On their way back, they met Moses and Aaron, for whom they had unkind words. "May Yahweh take close notice of you and judge. It is you who have made us stink in the eyes of pharaoh, and in the eyes of his servants, and have put a sword in their hands to kill us." The punch line of the foremen episode reveals they did not recognize the source of their oppression after all.

As always, the system of oppression was maintained by those who were able to keep themselves above the lowest while blaming the truth-tellers, those who identified with the lowest, for all the trouble. When the pressure increased, the foremen, as those in the middle, put pressure on the ones below rather than the ones above. They had bought into pharaoh's view that the oppressed were the cause of their own trouble. Far better to adopt the position of J's Egyptian peasantry: thanks be to pharaoh for saving our lives.

The story here rings true, and its perennial appeal and wonder come in part from the profound sense of recognition that has accompanied the reading and hearing of it over the ages. This would be particularly so for those for whom the taxation or extortion of their labor was a live issue. In every age the history of Moses has been politically appealing in the same way that liberation theologies are politically appealing. All of us can recognize liberation or freedom as something we want. It is important for us to acknowledge the appeal of this sense of recognition not just because it informs our own knowledge of the truth but also because it was precisely this appeal that made this narrative so useful as a vehicle for increasing the popularity of the rule of David.[4]

Moses went back to Yahweh, put off by his assignment and the results achieved so far. "Why have you treated this people so badly?" he asked Yahweh. "Why did you ever send me anyway? From the moment I went in to pharaoh to speak in your name, he has made things worse for this people, and you have done nothing to rescue them." This was a critical

4. See J. Severino Croatto, *Exodus: A Hermeneutics of Freedom* (Maryknoll, N.Y.: Orbis Books, 1981); Michael Walzer, *Exodus and Revolution* (New York: Basic Books, 1985); Nahum M. Sarna, *Exploring Exodus: The Heritage of Biblical Israel* (New York: Schocken Books, 1986); and George V. Pixley, *On Exodus: A Liberation Perspective* (Maryknoll, N.Y.: Orbis Books, 1987). For a critical analysis, however, of the implications of Walzer's book for the history of modern Palestine, see the review by Edward W. Said in Edward W. Said and Christopher Hitchens, eds., *Blaming the Victims: Spurious Scholarship and the Palestine Question* (New York: Verso, 1988), 161–78.

moment. Moses had not simply lost his temper, become discouraged, or reached the end of his rope. Rather, he had adopted the view of the foremen who had just rebuked him. In this view, the problem was not pharaoh but someone else. For Moses, this someone was Yahweh. Both Yahweh and pharaoh had, as the Hebrew says literally, "done evil" to the people. By using this language in reference to both Yahweh and pharaoh, it appeared that Moses could no longer distinguish between them.

We may imagine that when Yahweh heard Moses' complaint, he realized he was in a potential blind alley just as he had been at the close of the fourteenth generation. At that time everyone was affected by the evil and hence cursed condition of human society. There was no exception. To move history forward in his own conception—to change history—Yahweh had to introduce a new concept into history. In the fifteenth generation it was the blessing. Now, in the generation of Moses, it was manifest to Yahweh again that everyone was affected by the distortion of perception that caused the oppressed—everyone under the power of pharaoh—to blame their oppression on someone other than pharaoh or on some other source of immediate evil than the Cain-inspired system. Yahweh had lost the man he had found. The man he had found was the Moses who killed the Egyptian slave driver and who thus demonstrated that he could properly identify a source of committed evil. When he questioned why Yahweh had done evil to his people, that man no longer existed. It was time to give this man a new assignment that would deliver him, his people, pharaoh, and all the rest of the world from their misperception.

23

The Great Escape

(Exodus 6:1—15:21, parts)

Yahweh said to Moses, "Now you will see what I will do to pharaoh. Forced by my hand, he will let the people loose. Forced by my hand, he will drive them out from his land." Then Yahweh said to Moses, "Pharaoh's head is thick. Since he refuses to let the people loose, go to pharaoh in the morning, when he is going out to the water, and stand there to meet him on the bank of the river. And take in your hand the staff that turned into a snake. Say to him, 'Yahweh, the god of the foreign slaves, has sent me to you to say, "Let my people loose so they can work for me in the desert." But so far you haven't listened. So now Yahweh says, "By this you shall know that I am Yahweh: with the staff in my hand I shall beat upon the water in the river, and it shall turn into blood; when the fish in the river die, the river will stink, and the Egyptians will loathe to drink water from the river."'"

He raised his staff and beat the water in the river with pharaoh and his servants watching. All the water in the river turned to blood. The fish in the river died, and the river stank so that the Egyptians loathed to drink water from the river. Pharaoh turned and went back into his palace, and gave no further thought to what he had just witnessed. All the Egyptians dug in the vicinity of the river for water to drink, since they were not able to drink the river water.

Seven days after Yahweh beat on the river, Yahweh said to Moses, "Go to pharaoh and say to him, 'Thus Yahweh said, "Let my people loose so they can work for me. If you refuse to let them loose, I will plague your whole country with frogs. The river will swarm with frogs, and they will come out and get into your house, your bedchamber, and on your bed, in your servants' quarters, onto your courtiers, in your ovens and your kneading bowls. The frogs will get all over you and your court and your servants."'"

Pharaoh summoned Moses and Aaron and said, "Intercede with Yahweh, so he will take the frogs away from me and my court. I will let the people loose so they can sacrifice with Yahweh."

Moses said to pharaoh, "Assume then all honor over me, and say but when I should intercede for you, your servants, and your court, to take away the frogs from you and your palace and leave them only in the river."

He said, "Tomorrow."

Moses said, "As you wish, that you may know that there is none like Yahweh our

239

god. The frogs will leave you, your palace, and your courtiers. They will be left just
in the river."

Moses and Aaron left pharaoh. Moses cried out to Yahweh over the frogs he had
appointed for pharaoh. Yahweh did as Moses requested. The frogs died off in the
palace houses, courtyards, and fields. They piled them up in heaps everywhere, and
the land stank. When pharaoh saw at last that there was a breathing space, his mind
went blank and he paid no attention to Moses and Aaron.

Yahweh said to Moses, "In the morning, stand in pharaoh's way when he goes
out to the water, and say to him, 'Thus said Yahweh: "Let my people loose so they
can work for me. If you don't let my people loose, I will let loose on you and your
servants and your court and your palace swarms of flies. The houses of Egypt and
the ground they stand on shall be saturated with flies. At that time, however, I will
set apart the land of Goshen where my people stay, so there won't be flies there,
that you may know that I am Yahweh in the midst of the land, and that I make a
distinction between my people and your people. This sign will occur tomorrow."'"

Yahweh did exactly that. Severe swarms of flies came into pharaoh's palace, his
servants' quarters, and the whole land of Egypt.

Pharaoh shouted at Moses, "Go, sacrifice with your god somewhere in the land."

Moses said, "No that's not the way it is. The Egyptians would abominate our
sacrificing with Yahweh our god. If we were to do what the Egyptians abominate by
sacrificing before their very eyes, would they not stone us to death? Three days'
journey into the desert is where we must go, to sacrifice with Yahweh our god the
way he told us to."

Pharaoh said, "Okay, I will let you loose to sacrifice with Yahweh your god in the
desert. Only you must never go far. And intercede on my behalf."

Moses said, "The minute I leave you I will intercede with Yahweh to take the flies
away tomorrow from pharaoh, his servants, and his court. Only pharaoh must not
persist in mockery by not letting the people loose to sacrifice with Yahweh."

Moses left pharaoh. When he interceded with Yahweh, Yahweh did as Moses
requested. He took the flies away from pharaoh, his servants, and his court. Not one
was left. But pharaoh let his mind go blank this time as well, and did not let the
people loose.

Yahweh said to Moses, "Go to pharaoh and say to him, 'Thus said Yahweh, the
god of the foreign slaves, "Let my people loose so they can work for me. But if you
refuse to let them loose and continue to hold on to them, then the hand of Yahweh
will fall on your livestock in the field, on horses, asses, camels, herds, and flocks, in
the form of an extremely severe pestilence. But Yahweh will set a division between
the livestock of Israel and the livestock of Egypt, so that nothing belonging to the
sons of Israel shall die."'" And Yahweh set a definite time and said, "Yahweh will
perform this word in the land tomorrow."

On the morrow Yahweh did it. All Egypt's livestock died, while of the livestock of
the Israelite bedouin not one animal died. Pharaoh sent out for news and found out
that not one of Israel's livestock had died. Yet he let his mind go blank, and did not
let the people loose.

Yahweh said to Moses, "First thing in the morning, stand in pharaoh's way and
say to him, 'Thus said Yahweh, the god of the foreign slaves, "Let my people loose
so they can work for me. This time I'm going to deliver all my blows to your mind,

and against your servants and your court, so that you will know that there is none like me in the whole world. By now I could have put forth my hand and beaten you and your court with pestilence such that you would have been effaced from the earth. But for this reason I have left you in place, to make you see my power, so that my name can be told about in the whole world. Since you insist on impeding my people by not letting them loose, this time tomorrow I am going to rain on you an extremely heavy hailstorm, the likes of which has not occurred in Egypt from the day it was founded until now. So send orders to have your livestock and everything else that is yours out in the field sheltered. When the hail comes down on them, any person or animal still out in the field and not brought into house will die.' ' "

Those servants of pharaoh who by this time feared the word of Yahweh hurried their slaves and livestock into house. Those who paid no attention to the word of Yahweh left their slaves and livestock out in the field.

Yahweh said to Moses, "Stretch your hand toward the sky, so there will be hail on the whole land of Egypt, upon the people, the livestock, and all the field crops in the land of Egypt." Moses stretched his staff toward the sky. Yahweh caused peals of thunder, with hail. Lightning bolts crackled to the earth. Yahweh made it rain hail on the land of Egypt. While it hailed, lightning flashed in the midst of the hail. The storm was so fierce that there had been nothing like it in the whole land of Egypt from the time it had become a nation. The hail beat down on everything in the fields in the whole land of Egypt, from people to animals. The hail beat down all the field crops and splintered every tree in the fields. The only place it did not hail was in the land of Goshen, where the Israelite bedouin were.

Pharaoh sent word to Moses and Aaron. "I have sinned; this time I admit it. Yahweh is in the right, and I and my court are the ones in the wrong. Entreat Yahweh. We've had enough thunder and hail. I will let you loose. You won't have to stay any longer."

Moses said to him, "The moment I leave the city, I will spread my hands toward Yahweh. The thunder will cease, and there won't be any more hail, so that you may know that Yahweh owns the earth."

Now the flax and the barley were beaten down, since the barley was in ear and the flax in bud. But the wheat and the spelt were not beat down, since they come up later. When Moses left pharaoh's presence and the city and spread his hands toward Yahweh, the thunder ceased and hail and rain stopped pouring toward the earth. When pharaoh saw that the rain, hail, and thunder had ceased, he sinned again and let his mind go blank—he and his servants.

Moses and Aaron went to pharaoh and said to him, "Thus said Yahweh, the god of the foreign slaves, 'How long do you plan to refuse to submit to me? Let my people loose so they can work for me. If you refuse to let my people loose, tomorrow I will bring locusts within your borders. They will cover every square inch of the land so you will not be able to see the land. They will eat up everything that was left over that you saved from the hail, and they will eat up every tree that has since begun to grow in the field. They will fill your palace, the houses of all your servants, and the houses in all of Egypt. Neither your fathers nor grandfathers have seen anything like it, from the day they arrived on this land to this day.' " Then Moses spun around and left pharaoh.

Pharaoh's servants said to him, "How much longer are you going to let him bait us? Let the men loose to do some work for Yahweh their god. Will it be by the time you know that Egypt is being destroyed?"

Pharaoh had Moses and Aaron brought back and said to them, "Go ahead and work for Yahweh your god. Who all will be going with you?"

Moses said, "We will be going with our youth and elderly, with our sons and daughters, with our flocks and herds, since this is a pilgrimage feast with Yahweh for us."

"Yahweh help you," pharaoh said, "if I let you loose with your children. Clearly you have some evil in mind. No way. Just you men go and work for Yahweh. That's what you've been wanting." With that, pharaoh had them driven from his presence.

Yahweh said to Moses, "Stretch your hand over the land of Egypt, for locusts, so that they will come up over the land of Egypt and eat all the grain of the land left by the hail."

Moses stretched his staff over the land of Egypt. Yahweh started an east wind blowing over the land, and kept it going that whole day and all through the night. The next morning the east wind was bearing the locusts. The locusts came up all over Egypt and settled throughout the entire territory of Egypt. They were an extremely heavy swarm. There hadn't been locusts like these ever before, and there won't be ever again. They covered every square inch of the land. The land darkened. They ate all the grain of the land and all the tree fruit left by the hail. Not one green shoot on tree or grain stalk was left in the whole land of Egypt.

Pharaoh quickly summoned Moses and Aaron. He said to them, "I have sinned against Yahweh your god and against you. Forgive my sin once more. Entreat Yahweh your god only to remove from me this death."

He left pharaoh and entreated Yahweh. Yahweh changed the wind to a gale from the west that carried off the locusts and blew them into the Sup Sea. There was not one locust left in the entire territory of Egypt. Yet Yahweh thickened pharaoh's head, and he did not let the Israelite bedouin loose.

Moses had a new assignment. He was to announce to pharaoh the series of "plagues" about to descend on him and his land. "Now you will see what I will do to pharaoh. Forced by my hand, he will let the people loose. Forced by my hand, he will drive them out from his land. Pharaoh's head is thick."

This last phrase, along with "his mind went blank," is our translation of Hebrew "his heart is heavy." Heart in Hebrew means what we mean by mind, thought, will, and intent. It is the organ of thought rather than feeling, though from our perspective there might be a close connection between the intent that is connoted by "heart" in Hebrew and the feeling that is connoted by "heart" in English. We have seen that "heavy," when applied to the heart in Hebrew, means thick, dense, or sluggish. In other words, pharaoh's mind and hence both his thought and his will were sluggish. He found it difficult to "know." Yahweh's purpose was to make pharaoh know him. Given pharaoh's sluggish mind, this turned out to be impossible. It is as though pharaoh were in a perpetual stupor. What the god of the oppressed was trying to say to pharaoh was absolutely unintelligible: as prophets later put it, as though the hearer had no ears.

This of course is a characterization of all elite oppressors. The theological problem that occurs to a lot of people, as to whether God was the cause of pharaoh's heart being thick, as the historian in fact says once or twice, is not a question that the historian deals with; it has no significance for the overall history. Sometimes Yahweh made pharaoh's heart thick. Or pharaoh himself hardened his heart. To focus attention on such a problem is to come close to falling into the mind-set of Yahweh's responsibility for the evil in the world that the narrative undertakes to dispel. The irony that "Yahweh caused pharaoh's mind to be sluggish" is not different from Yahweh's instructions to Isaiah when he commissioned him to address the elite of Judah: "Go and say to this people, 'Hear but do not understand, see but do not perceive.' Make the heart of this people fat [that is, make their minds sluggish], their ears heavy, their eyes shut, lest they see and hear and understand." It is not that God wants the people not to hear. The instruction is given rather with a view to the anticipated outcome, shown by subsequent history to be inevitable, or is simply narrated in retrospect. The people addressed are so incorrigibly dense that you might as well ensure they don't understand—the result will be the same in any case. This ironic point of view is also taken by the historian when, for the sake of his narrative indictment of pharaoh, he portrays Yahweh as knowing that no matter what is done, pharaoh will not awaken from his moral stupor. Many affluent readers of the Bible find it difficult to understand what this stupor is like, because we may suffer from it. The oppressed often instantly recognize what J means.

Pharaoh's dense mind is one of the main motifs of the episode of the plagues. After each plague, even when pharaoh seemed to be changing his mind, his "heart became heavy," and Yahweh, not yet known to him, proceeded to the next plague. The full episode of the plagues could be characterized as the interplay between Yahweh's drive to be known as the unique god of the whole earth who does not tolerate the enslavement of his people and the density of pharaoh's senses.[1]

The episode of the plagues is the longest single dramatic episode in J. In one sense, the episode contains much of interest, as is proved by its popularity over the ages. In another sense, however, compared with much that has gone before in J, the episode is somewhat monotonous, with the

1. In P, pharaoh's heart is not heavy but "stiff." For P, the issue is not that pharaoh's mind cannot work but that his will is stubborn. Throughout his narrative, P pays particular attention to Yahweh's commandments and people's obedience to them. To P, pharaoh is not so much senseless as disobedient.

same small repertoire of elements repeated several times. There is some development through the stories but not enough to explain, in view of the more complex character of J, why J devotes so much attention to this episode. The reason has to do with one of the chief themes of J: the liberation from unjust extortion of labor.

The history of Moses and pharaoh can best be characterized as the history of a rising labor movement. The problem of the organization of workers for resistance is by no means limited to the industrial era, and this part of J can be illuminated by our looking at it from the perspective of modern labor movements. The episode of the plagues is essentially an extended negotiation between a labor leader, Moses, and the boss, the king of Egypt. Viewed in this way, it is not at all surprising that this history, one of whose purposes is to project a national consensus in terms of the resistance of labor, should devote so much attention to the primary relationship at issue in a labor movement.

"The ego of the organizer is stronger and more monumental than the ego of the leader. The leader is driven by the desire for power, while the organizer is driven by the desire to create. The organizer is in a true sense reaching for the highest level for which man can reach—to create, to be a 'great creator,' to play God."[2] Moses in J's portrayal is such a creator. The leader in J's history is pharaoh. As for David, J intends to contrast him with pharaoh and represent him in Moses. Hence in J's portrayal David himself, as the figurehead of the national identity he desires to foster, comes across more as the labor organizer than the leader.

The history of labor organization and of the labor organizer Moses (hence David) in the twenty-first generation captures the essence of J. The theme of labor that was established at the outset, through J's history of the creation of human beings for a purpose other than to be corvée workers, is brought to fulfillment as the main theme of the entire history. David's nationalism as expressed in J can be characterized as a massive anti-Egyptian labor movement in fulfillment of the nature of human beings as laborers created by Yahweh, the god of David's nation. Israel's god and worship were then seen to sanction this identity of the laborer rather than the identity imposed upon the working populace by the usual temple monarch. David's strength was still mainly political rather than monumental. It did not require a large standing military or monuments like a palace, temple, city walls, and garrison fortresses. The essence of the people's backing of David is viewed in J, and portrayed and projected there, as based on liberation from the labor tax that such monuments require. In

2. Saul David Alinsky, *Rules for Radicals* (New York: Random House, 1971), 61.

J, the essence of the projected national political consensus is freedom from an unjust tax in labor.

This comparison allows us to make better sense of the variation and development in the episode of the plagues. The main point of the repetition is to represent the gradual escalation of the threat that labor's resistance represents and the king of Egypt's response to that threat. Workers are typically at such a disadvantage that they rebel and walk out only in the extreme situation when all alternatives have been exhausted, when negotiation has been carried on at great length and finally broken down for good. The plagues initiate an extended negotiation. The extension of the negotiation points to the magnitude of the density or senselessness of the boss. For the workers it provides an increasing sense of frustration and finally impels them to take the otherwise extremely risky decision to walk out.

The other main development in the episode is the nature of the plagues themselves. The plagues came in this order: bloody river water, frogs, flies, pestilence affecting livestock, hail, locusts, and, as we shall see, darkness, followed by the culminating act of the killing of the firstborn sons. The order is one of increasing severity, including darkness, which had its own particular role. The plagues began as inconveniences. The pestilence on the livestock was more serious. Here, the Egyptians' insurance against possible crop failure was affected and, more important, their traction animals, their means of plowing and transporting, were disabled. The hail and the locusts destroyed the produce of the land directly and completely. The death of the firstborn symbolically disrupted the total system of property and inheritance—everything that the line of Cain had built—presided over by the king.

The sequence of inconvenience, stock, land, and persons can be placed next to a similar sequence in the process of the enslavement of the Egyptian peasantry: silver, stock, land, and persons. This represents what the peasants gave up to the king of Egypt in order to survive. Hence the plagues brought upon pharaoh evils that corresponded to the evils brought upon the peasantry by their enslavement. The consequence of the plagues could be described as the enslavement of pharaoh. He never came to "know" the progressive encroachment upon his power. Nothing was left for Yahweh to do but to kill pharaoh—the final outcome of being enslaved. Enslavement is tantamount to death. The point remains the same as when Moses killed the slave driver.

The sequence of plagues also represents the gradual ruining of pharaoh's realm. This sometimes causes people to wonder why Yahweh made all the Egyptians suffer when only the king and his court were responsible. We have already seen that in J's view all the Egyptians were considered part of the cursed line of Cain, Ham, and Canaan.

The sequence also represents the gradual distinguishing of Israel from Egypt, in which Israel is treated as a national entity and thus Egypt is too. For David, the national distinction takes precedence over the social distinction. The history concentrates ever more intensely on the culpable insensitivity of the individual king. At the same time, it augments ever more intensely the nationalist categories that were essential to the Davidic court's projection of anti-Egyptian Israelite national identity. Once again we see that while J's history, especially in the section about Moses, is a history of liberation, it is not based primarily on the notion that the agrarian oppressed as a class are the ultimate measure of justice. The village population of David's realm are scarcely in the picture. J is nationalist state propaganda. For J, the ultimate standard of justice is the god of the Davidic state who represents the self-proclaimed character of state rule. David enjoyed the opportunity to claim that his rule liberated his nation from the unjust extortion of their labor. We are nowhere told what the villagers, who made up the bulk of his nation and who may have served him in corvée, thought, beyond the intrinsic appeal of the walkout of Moses and his people, about this claim and David's Yahweh, nor can we probably ever find out.

The first plague was the turning of the Nile to blood. No doubt J intends to make a point by making the first and the last plague have to do with blood. The blood killed the fish in the river, and the river stank atrociously. Yahweh wasted no time in answering the complaint of the bedouin foremen, who had said to Moses, "You have made us stink in the eyes of pharaoh." If they thought Moses was the one who made them stink rather than the king of Egypt, then their perception was to be changed through a process that began by Yahweh making pharaoh's river stink.

The second plague reinforced the point: frogs came up from the river and invaded the land, getting into everything, including the bed in which pharaoh had fathered his dynastic house. When the frogs died, they were gathered into heaps, "and the land stank." When pharaoh saw that there was a "breathing space"—it was again possible to breathe because the stench had subsided—he "made his mind thick" and would not heed Moses.

Yahweh said to Moses, "Stretch your hand toward the sky so there may be darkness over the land of Egypt such that a person can feel the darkness."

Moses stretched his hand toward the sky, and there was a close darkness in the whole land of Egypt for three days. People could not see the people next to them, and they couldn't move from where they were for three days. All the Israelite bedouin, however, had light in their settlements.

Pharaoh called for Moses and said, "Go, work for Yahweh. But your flocks and herds must stay put. Your children may also go with you."

Moses said, "You also have to let us take meal offerings and burnt offerings for us to serve to Yahweh our god. Also our livestock must go with us. Not a hoof must be left behind. We have to take them to work with Yahweh our god, since we don't know what we will need for work with Yahweh until we get there."

Yahweh thickened pharaoh's head so that he was not willing to let them loose. Pharaoh said to them, "Get out of here. And watch out you don't ever see my face again. The day you see my face, you will die."

Moses said, "Have it your way. I will never see your face again."

While Moses stood there, Yahweh said to him, "I have one more plague to bring upon pharaoh and upon Egypt. After that, he will let you loose from here. In fact, he will absolutely drive you out of here. Discreetly tell the people to 'borrow,' each man from his neighbor and each woman from hers, objects of silver and gold."

Yahweh had made the Egyptians well disposed toward the people. The man Moses, moreover, was held in very high regard by both pharaoh's servants and the court.

Moses said to pharaoh, "Thus said Yahweh, 'About midnight I will go out into Egypt, and every firstborn in the land of Egypt shall die, from the firstborn of pharaoh seated on his throne to the firstborn of the slave seated at the handmill, and every firstborn of the animals. There will be a great outcry in all the land of Egypt, such as has never been, nor will ever be again. But against all the Israelite bedouin not even a dog will growl, against either person or animal, so that you may know that Yahweh makes a distinction between Egypt and Israel.' Then all these your servants will come down to me and bow down to me and say, 'Leave, you and all the people at your feet.' After that, I will leave." Then Moses left pharaoh's presence in deep anger.

He summoned all the sheikhs of Israel and said to them, "Select out by families sheep for yourselves and slaughter the 'pass' sheep. Then take a bunch of hyssop, dip it in the blood in the slaughter basin, and with it slap blood from the basin onto the lintel and both doorposts of your houses. Let not one person go out through the door until morning. Yahweh will pass by, on his way to wreak slaughter in all Egypt, will see the blood on the lintel and doorposts and pass that doorway and not let the destroyer get into your houses to do any slaughter there."

The people bowed low.

At midnight, Yahweh killed every firstborn in the land of Egypt, from the firstborn of pharaoh seated on his throne to the firstborn of the prisoner who is in prison, and every firstborn of the animals. Pharaoh got up that night. So did all his servants, and all Egypt. There was a great outcry in Egypt, for there was not a house where someone did not die.

He called for Moses and Aaron during the night and had them told, "Get out of here, away from my court, right now, both of you, and the Israelite bedouin. Go work for Yahweh, the way you said. Take your flocks and herds, the way you said. Bless me by getting out of here."

The Egyptians were firm in urging the people out of the land quickly, thinking that otherwise they would all die. The people, therefore, took their dough before it was leavened, and their kneading bowls wrapped in their coats on their shoulders. And the bedouin followed Moses' instructions: they "borrowed" from the Egyptians objects of silver and gold as well as clothing. Thus Yahweh made the Egyptians well disposed toward the people. They "borrowed," and so relieved Egypt.

The Israelite bedouin set out, about six hundred companies of men on foot, apart from the children. A great swarm of animals went up with them, flocks and herds, a great horde of livestock. They baked the dough they had brought out of Egypt into unleavened loaves, as it had not leavened, since they were driven out of Egypt and were not able to linger even so long as to pack some provisions for themselves.

Yahweh went in front of them during the day in a cloud pillar, to show them the road, and during the night in a fire pillar, to give them light, so they could travel day and night. Neither the cloud pillar during the day nor the fire pillar during the night ever left its place in front of the people.

It was reported to the king of Egypt that the people had fled. The minds of pharaoh and his servants were changed regarding the people. They said, "What have we done by letting Israel loose from working for us?" Pharaoh had six hundred choice chariots and all the rest of Egypt's chariots harnessed, took his court military with him, put a firing officer on each chariot, and chased after the bedouin, who had left with a raised hand. Chasing after the bedouin, Egypt caught up with them camped by the sea.

Pharaoh had gotten close by the time the bedouin looked back and realized Egypt had taken off after them. In great fear they said to Moses, "Were there no graves in Egypt that you had to take us to the desert to die? What have you done for us by forcing us out of Egypt? Is this not just what we were telling you in Egypt when we said, 'Leave us alone so we can work for Egypt'? It was better for us to work for Egypt than die in the desert."

Moses said to the people, "Don't be afraid. Just stand there and see the liberation of Yahweh which he will perform for you today. You may see the Egyptians today, but you'll never see them again, ever. Yahweh will fight for you. You just watch quietly."

The cloud pillar moved from their front to their rear and positioned itself between the camp of Egypt and the camp of Israel. The cloud turned into darkness. The [fire pillar] lit up the night. Neither camp approached the other to do battle the entire night.

While it was night, Yahweh made the sea move forward with a strong east wind. By having the waters divide, he turned the sea into dry land. At the watch just before dawn, Yahweh gazed toward the Egyptian camp from the fire and cloud pillar and threw the Egyptian camp into confusion. When pharaoh tried to turn the wheels of his chariot, he could only get them to turn sluggishly, for all the mud caused by the sea water. So Egypt said, "I've got to get away from Israel. Yahweh is fighting for them against Egypt."

As morning arrived, the sea returned to its normal depth. As the Egyptians fled toward it, where they had thought to find dry terrain, Yahweh shook the Egyptians into the sea. Not one of them was left.

Thus Yahweh liberated Israel on that day from the hand of Egypt. Israel saw Egypt dead on the shore of the sea. Having seen the "great hand" that Yahweh had done against Egypt, Israel trusted Yahweh and Moses his servant.

The oracle Miriam took a tambourine to hand, and while all the women followed out after her with tambourines and dance, Miriam sang for them the whole of the song that begins, "Sing to Yahweh, for he is gloriously triumphant. Horse and chariot he has cast into the sea."[3]

3. It is probable that the whole song in Exod. 15:1–18 celebrating Yahweh's victory, there ascribed to Moses, followed here in J as Miriam's song.

The seventh plague was darkness.[4] Like blood, darkness is closely tied to the main themes of J, although not perhaps at first glance. Observe the punch line. Pharaoh said, "Get out of here. Watch out that you don't see my face again. If you see my face again, you will die." Moses said, "Whatever you say. I will not again see your face." The punch line of the penultimate plague leads us directly back to the field where Cain and Abel stood in each other's presence and could not see each other's face because "the face of Cain was fallen." This mark of Cain's irreconcilability was then reversed several times when the various sets of brothers in the history of the blessed line saw each other "face to face" and were reconciled. Moses and the king of Egypt were not to be reconciled. This is the meaning of darkness. Estranged as they were, these two could not have seen each other's faces if they had tried.

The darkness foreshadowed not only the night of deliverance in which Yahweh would skip the dwellings marked by lamb's blood but also the night Yahweh would kill the king of Egypt. This connection is made explicit by the connection between the concluding lines of the plague of darkness regarding seeing the face of pharaoh no more and the lines that introduce the event of pharaoh's death during that night: "Station yourselves and see the victory of Yahweh. . . . While you see Egypt now, you won't see them again, forever." Here is the ultimate though not the last reversal of the "seeing" that had begun with Adam and Eve in Yahweh's pleasure orchard.

Yahweh at last revealed to Moses the culminating event, the killing of the firstborn of Egypt. The killing of the firstborn represents justice done to Cain, the requital of the killing of Abel. Abel's death was not avenged against Cain at first, and we noted J's reasons for this in terms of the institution of blood revenge as viewed and revised by the court of David. We can now see that it has a further meaning in specific reference to this critical juncture in the overall history. Cain did not suffer revenge at that time, because his revenge was being saved until the murder of Abel could be shown eventually in its fullest meaning. It was not simply a family matter that could be settled by the convention of blood revenge. Its significance was ramified throughout the basic social system of J's world, includ-

---

4. Counting darkness and the killing of the firstborn, there were eight plagues. It is likely that J thought of his sequence as seven plagues plus one culminating deathblow. Some historians have thought that the plague of darkness did not belong to the original J sequence. Psalm 78 refers to all the plagues in J, with the exception of darkness. It is probable that this psalm comes from the Davidic court and hence possible that its writer knew J in an original form that did not include the plague of darkness. This explanation is in line with the expectation that J would list seven plagues. We include it in our text of J because of the J-like character strongly indicated by the motif of "seeing the face." The priestly edition of J turned J's seven plagues plus one culminating deathblow into ten by the addition of the plagues of gnats and boils. This is just what P had done by turning J's eight generations to Noah into ten and his fifteen generations to Abram into twenty by the addition of names to J's genealogy.

ing the nationalist categories essential to the rule of David. Everything that
has been derived by J from the birth of Cain as the firstborn of the creatures
of Yahweh, including the entire system of urban culture epitomized by
Canaan and Egypt, and treated by J as intrinsically unjust, is here included
within the persons of the firstborn sons of everyone in Egypt except the
bedouin corvée slaves. This negative meaning of the firstborn sons of Egypt
is further defined by the full panoply of the positive meanings of Isaac and
the consequences of his birth for his generation and succeeding generations
of his offspring.

Many later prophets whose words are preserved in the Old Testament
treat their social world in terms that include a class analysis. If J also does
this, he discontinues use of that analysis here to focus attention fully on the
nationalist distinction between Egypt and Israel. This is the great emphasis
of Yahweh's speech, repeated to pharaoh apparently during the last interview: "Every firstborn son in Egypt will die, from the firstborn of pharaoh
who sits on the throne to the firstborn of the maiden slave who sits behind
the lowly millstones—even the firstborn of their beasts." When this happened shortly afterward, J repeated these lines but varied the language
slightly: "From the firstborn of pharaoh to the firstborn of the prisoner who
is in prison." Clearly the whole social spectrum of Egypt is included in J's
condemnation.

Lest the point be missed, the most important phrase during the entire
episode of the plagues—"that you may know that I am Yahweh"—now
took on a new meaning. "A great cry will arise in the land of Egypt the likes
of which has never been heard nor ever will be." The Egyptians would cry
out just as the bedouin did, but they would not be saved. Their cry would
not be against the sons of Israel. "Against the sons of Israel not even a dog
will bark—that you may know that Yahweh makes a distinction between
Egypt and Israel." The phrase "that you may know," as it is used with the
plagues, points to the nature of Yahweh in contrast to the whole social
system of urban culture. But it is now shown to have a specific meaning
that can override the social meaning: Yahweh is the god of Israel the
nation.

As he had promised at Sinai, Yahweh gave the bedouin favor in the eyes
of the Egyptians, and "also the man Moses was exceedingly great in the
land of Egypt in the eyes of the servants of pharaoh and in the eyes of the
court." Moses was introduced in J's history as a great man, presumably
becoming greater, who relinquished his increasing greatness when he
killed the Egyptian slave driver. Now J tells us that as the history of Moses
approached its critical moment, the moment of the deliverance of his
people, Moses was once again great. Indeed, he was very great, far greater

than he was before—and in the eyes of the very people who had, in the nationalist conception of J, the greatest reason to look down on him.

The history of Cain's murder of Abel was the history of the firstborn and the blood he shed. In order to distinguish now between his own firstborn, the bedouin Israel, and the firstborn of Egypt, Yahweh instructed Moses to have his people mark themselves by means of blood. They were to slaughter lambs, take a hyssop branch, dip it in the blood, and slap blood on the lintel and side posts of the entrances to their huts or tents. The word "slap" carries far more weight than the usual translations suggest (e.g., RSV "touch"). It comes from the same root as the word "plague," which could just as well be translated "stroke" or "blow." The plagues began with and culminated in blood. Their final meaning is the distinction between Israel and Egypt. This distinction is marked, verbally, by Yahweh's having Israel "slapped" with blood to deliver them from the last slap against Egypt.

It is not certain whether J described the institution of the Passover rite in full. The description of the rite that might come from J, focusing on the redemption of the firstborn of the flocks and of the sons of the Israelites themselves, would certainly fit the main themes related to the history of the deliverance of the bedouin, but the literary analysis is uncertain.[5]

While several references are made to Yahweh killing the firstborn of Egypt, J once refers to what the RSV calls "the destroyer." This destroyer, who carried away the lives of the firstborn of Egypt as they lay sleeping at night, was, like every other such being whom the ancients dreaded, a demon. J mentions demons only twice. The first time, Yahweh warned Cain that sin was a "crouching demon" at the doorway, referring to Cain's act of murder. That demon did get Cain. Now its successor, the destroyer, was to repeat its success. It was to enter the dwellings of the descendants of Cain and get them.

In the middle of the night, Yahweh slaughtered all the firstborn sons of Egypt. Pharaoh and his people got out of bed and let loose an enormous cry. Moses and Aaron were summoned. "Get away from here, you and all your sons of Israel. Go work for Yahweh. Take your flocks and herds with you. Go! And bless me also." Except for pharaoh's death itself, this is perhaps the critical moment of J's history. The king of Egypt released his bedouin corvée workers, the sons of blessed Abram and Sarai, from their work for him and sent them to work for Yahweh, requesting in return their blessing. His request was right: the release of the workers was tantamount to his blessing them, and he could thus rightly expect their blessing in

5. See John van Seters, "The Place of the Yahwist in the History of Passover and Massot," *Zeitschrift für die alttestamentliche Wissenschaft* 95 (1983): 167–82.

return. The king of Egypt was now on the brink of acknowledging that the mission on which Yahweh sent Moses, to make pharaoh know Yahweh even as Abram knew Yahweh, had been a success. The killing of the firstborn of pharaoh would have served the same purpose for pharaoh as the birth of the firstborn Isaac served for Abram's family. Through that birth, Abram's family came to know the new meaning of Yahweh in reference to the meaning of human procreation for the preceding fourteen generations. For the sons of Israel to bless him now would bring the history of Yahweh and his creatures to a resolution of ultimate reconciliation, the reconciliation of the worst of the sons of Cain through Ham with the sons of Israel. This, however, was not to be.

The bedouin fled in haste. They are said to have numbered six hundred *'eleph*s. The *'eleph* here does not mean a thousand but a much smaller unit (although there is no question that J considers the entire band to represent the whole nation).[6] The troop is described as including what is often interpreted, and as the RSV translates, as a "mixed multitude" of beasts and people. This has been taken by many historians to be a social description of early Israel, suggesting that early Israelite society was socially mixed, including elements from a variety of classes and groups. The term simply means a great swarm. It refers to the huge migrating bedouin horde, with an emphasis on its Abram-like wealth in flocks and herds, and says nothing about a social mixture, much less anything about early Israel.

In his earlier speech to Moses which unveiled what the culminating blow to Egypt would be, Yahweh had referred back to his declaration at the burning bush that the bedouin would "borrow" goods from their Egyptian neighbors and thus despoil them. As the bedouin took flight, they were loaded down with this wealth. They looked just like Abram with his "weighty wealth" when he left Egypt. This wealth taken from the Egyptians was tantamount to compensation for the uncompensated labor performed by the bedouin. The general shift in interest in J from reproductive to productive themes is illustrated by this connection. While Abram had been compensated for the misuse of his wife, his bedouin descendants were compensated for the misuse of their labor.

The bedouin set out at night. Guiding and protecting them was a miraculous column that looked like fire at night and smoke during the day. With this column in their vanguard, they could trek night and day. No doubt they expected to be in Palestine within six or seven days at most.

Yahweh as the god who warred against the king of Egypt appeared as fire in the column as he had in the bush at Sinai. As already indicated, fire was

6. George E. Mendenhall, "The Census Lists of Numbers 1 and 26," *Journal of Biblical Literature* 77 (1968): 52–66.

a commonplace in the conception of the warrior deities of the world of J. Fire was the most effective and thorough weapon against the cities, citadels, and fortresses of the urban elite. Although a city's foundations were of stone, most of its construction was of wood, dried brush, and mud. Once started, a conflagration would normally destroy the entire city. Fire was by far the commonest cause of the complete destruction of urban sites in the archaeological record. This significance of fire can be seen in a number of biblical passages. For example, in the several speeches against kings and cities that begin the Book of Amos, Yahweh announced repeatedly, "I shall send fire against the walls of the city." Since this god had revealed himself as the god of such fire first to Moses at Sinai, there is every expectation that he would lead his people to the same mountain and then, in the person of David, against the cities of Canaan.

The king of Egypt was told that the bedouin had fled. "The mind [heart] of pharaoh and his servants was turned," J says. "What have we done by releasing them from working for us?" The possibility of a blessing for the king of Egypt, and in this way a grand positive finale to J's history, was thus removed. From this point to the killing of pharaoh—the only possible response now from Yahweh—was a short step.

The king of Egypt harnessed six hundred choice chariots, one for each unit of escaping bedouin, along with other chariots, all fully manned—an inordinately overwhelming force—and went after the fugitives. The bedouin fled "with a raised hand." In line with the many similarities between the history of Moses and labor revolts, including peasant revolts, the phrase "with a raised hand" refers to the active rebellion of a group of workers. The imagery of a raised hand is that of a fist raised in aggressive revolt. It belongs to individuals with a fresh sense of resistance and pride on their faces. It marks the development of the workers' rebellion from negotiation to the use of force. From the moment he raises his hand, the rebel laborer is his own man. In Moses' day and ours, the same holds for women.

But J intends more than this image. A "hand" cannot be a simple image for J. Its fuller meaning comes clear later, following the defeat of pharaoh: J draws together the motifs of "seeing" that defeat and the "hand" of Yahweh in support of the bedouin. "Yahweh saved Israel on that day from the hand of Egypt, and Israel saw Egypt dead on the shore of the sea, and Israel saw the 'great hand' which Yahweh did against Egypt, and the people feared Yahweh." The upshot of the entire climactic incident was that Israel "saw the hand of Yahweh."

This idiom has two meanings. The first is clear from the previous paragraph: they saw Yahweh's support on behalf of their revolt. The "hand of Yahweh" borrows a phrase popular with the pharaohs of the New Kingdom and turns it directly against their tenth-century successor. The pharaohs styled themselves variously as "Great of Arm," "Strong of Arm," "Possessor of a Strong Arm," and "Powerful of Arm Who Subdues the Nine Bows." (In this first meaning, hand and arm are synonymous, can be used in parallelism, and refer in an identical way metaphorically to military power.) The word "arm" was widely used in the throne names of Nineteenth and Twentieth Dynasty royalty. Ramses III, who ruled less than two hundred years before David, calls himself "Lord of a Powerful Arm Who Smites Asiatics."[7] "From the reign of Ramses IX [just over a century prior to David] comes a report from the High Priest . . . that the king, in what must have been a minor skirmish near the Red Sea, defeated some bedouin. The report says, 'the strong arm of Pharaoh my lord has entirely cast down the Shasu [bedouin] of the Red Sea region.'"[8] It is the reversal of precisely such an event—probably not atypical of Egyptian royal activity or of the manner in which such an event was celebrated in official Egyptian terminology— that J makes into the pivotal moment of his history. The ironic taunt behind the "hand of Yahweh" would not have been lost on J's court and bedouin hearers.

The second meaning derives from J's use of the expression "to see the nakedness of" (or his allusion in other terms to the meaning conveyed by this expression). The first of these (every other instance was derived in some way from the result of this first instance) was when the first man and woman saw each other naked and the sight of the human genitalia signified for the one seeing the power of godlike creation and killing. This is the comprehensive foil to "seeing the hand of Yahweh." The Hebrew word *yad* means not just hand or arm but also phallus. To see the hand of Yahweh was the ultimate outcome of the fathering of Isaac: Israel now saw the phallus of Yahweh, as it were. The full significance of this can be grasped only in the light of the now fully developed themes of reproduction and production, sexual potency and economic power. J saves such an important moment, in a sense the culmination of the strand of his history that began with Adam and Eve seeing each other's genitalia and producing Cain, and that included Yahweh's fathering Isaac, until this climactic moment when he could at last make clear the full meaning of this strand in terms of its sociopolitical significance for the rising house of David.

J's reference to the bedouin's raised "hand" includes the suggestion that the bedouin, with their power regained and the firstborn of Egypt dead, were on their way out with an erect penis. This meaning of "raised" is fully

---

7. "Asiatics" refers to Palestinian lords like David, and bedouin like Moses.

8. James K. Hoffmeier, "The Arm of God Versus the Arm of Pharaoh," *Biblica* 67 (1986): 378–87. The quote is from p. 383.

in line with the meaning of the Hebrew word involved (*ram*). This is the term that also occurs in the name Abram. Abram means, as explained previously, "the father is high." One of several potential meanings of the name is that the father has a good erection—an ironic meaning in view of J's history of Yahweh's displacing of Abram in the fathering of Isaac.[9]

The Egyptians chased after the bedouin. They caught up with them as they were encamped momentarily by a large body of water—the "sea."[10] As the king of Egypt drew closer with his mighty force, the bedouin, facing the sea on one side and Egypt on the other, panicked. They turned on Moses, as they would during the entire trek: "Were there no graves in Egypt that you had to bring us out to the desert to die? We told you to leave us alone and let us work for Egypt. It was better for us to work for Egypt than to die in the desert." The bedouin felt trapped by the sea, as though the sea itself were in the service of the king to assist in their destruction.

The complaint of the bedouin that they might die in the wilderness, whereas in Egypt they could work, provides the perfect foil for J's view of what the deliverance from Egypt meant for the bedouin. That Egypt's firstborn sons had to die, and now the king of Egypt himself must die, means that Egypt's enslavement of the bedouin was the same as murder, requiring the killing of pharaoh and his forces in return. For J, slavery in Egypt wasn't better than death, it was death.

There has been much discussion of what kind of sea this was and where it was. It is not at all important to know the answers to these questions to understand what J wants to get across by means of this motif. We saw earlier that the form of J's history owes a great deal to the genre of which it is a modified example, the monarchic cult and world history usually labeled simply the myth of Baal. His use of sea derives from the all-important role of the cosmic sea in the mythology of the temple state in Syro-Palestinian and other ancient Near Eastern societies. The subduing of the chaotic waters of creation present in the Baal myth, as well as in P's history of the world in Genesis 1, has been displaced to the climactic moment in J's history. Baal, the deity who stood for royalty, was able to have his temple built after he defeated and destroyed Sea. Then he was able to rule the world—the kingdom—from his temple and give it life. In the mythology of J's age, the defeat of Sea was the essential basis of the establishment of a stable, temple-centered, king-controlled state. J, writing for a king who distanced himself from this mythology, nevertheless

9. The connotations of "hand of Yahweh" together follow on J's use of the idiom "send forth the hand" in Gen. 3:22 and Exod. 4:4 with related actions.

10. The meaning of Yam-Sup, usually translated Sea of Reeds, is uncertain. The traditional identification with the Red Sea is widely rejected. See the excellent discussion of Bernard F. Batto, "The Reed Sea: *Requiescat in Pace*," *Journal of Biblical Literature* 102 (1983): 27–35.

adopted its essential moment, the defeat of Sea. But he reversed it. Instead of having the king of Egypt defeat the sea, he had the sea, under the power of Yahweh, defeat the king of Egypt. He did not need to have Yahweh himself defeat the sea, because he was not interested in portraying Yahweh as a god requiring a temple.

J combines his adaptation of the defeat of Sea and Death in the single event of the death of the king of Egypt in the sea, even though the motif of the king's failure to control death goes all the way back to the beginning in the Bible's first history.

In J's version, Yahweh was completely in control of both the sea and pharaoh. "Yahweh will fight for you," said Moses. "You just watch quietly." The pillar containing the battle fire of the nationalist Yahweh moved from in front of the bedouin column and positioned itself at its rear, between the bedouin on one side and the Egyptians on the other. The fire lit up the night, and neither camp attacked the other. The whole night long, Yahweh blew up a strong east wind. This caused a dry way through the sea to appear, as the waters divided on both sides of the dry way. This amounted to "splitting" the sea, as is said of Baal and other royal deities in their myths. It is not at all clear that in J the bedouin themselves crossed through the sea on this dry path. The sea blown aside washed over in the direction of the Egyptians, turning the ground into mud.

As dawn approached, Yahweh looked down from his pillar and put Egypt to rout. The drivers turned their chariots into the mud, thick like pharaoh's mind (the Hebrew word for mud and thick is the same), and their wheels turned sluggishly. Just as night turned into day, Yahweh allowed the sea to return to its usual place. Yahweh shook the Egyptians off their chariots into the sea. (The picture of shaking is borrowed from the full song of Miriam that comes under Moses' name in the present Old Testament text and was probably included in J's history.) Thus Yahweh's hand had won deliverance for the bedouin sons of Israel. When they "saw" the hand and power of Yahweh in this light, they believed in Yahweh and in Moses his servant, as they did not always believe. Miriam took musical instruments, gathered some women around her, danced, and sang the victory song ascribed to her.

24

Who's in Charge Here?

(Exodus 15:22–25a; 16—17, parts; 18:1–11, parts;
19:1–15, parts; 20:22–26; 24:1–2, 9–11, parts;
34, parts; Numbers 10:29—12:15)

Moses had Israel depart from Sup Sea and proceed toward the desert of Shur. They trekked for three days in the desert without finding water. They got as far as Marah, but could not drink the water at Marah because it was too bitter. That's why its name is Bitter. The people complained to Moses, "What are we going to drink?" Moses cried out to Yahweh, and Yahweh showed him a tree. This he threw into the water, and the water became sweet.

Yahweh then said to Moses, "I am about to rain down for you bread from the sky, a daily supply of which the people should go out and collect each day." When morning came, there was a layer of dew around the camp. When this layer of dew evaporated, there was left on the surface of the desert a thin, flaky substance, a thin substance like frost, all over the area. The bedouin looked at it and said to each other, "What's that?" They didn't know what it was. So they named the stuff *man*. It was like coriander seed, but white, and tasted like honey wafers. This *man* they ate until they got to the edge of the land of Canaan.

When Yahweh had brought Israel out of Egypt, Moses' father-in-law took Zipporah, Moses' wife, whom Moses had sent back to him, and his two sons—the first's name was Gershom, from the statement "I was a refugee in a foreign country," and the second's name was Eliezer, from the statement "My father's god was my help and rescued me from the sword of pharaoh"—Moses' father-in-law came with his sons and wife to Moses in the desert where he was camping. He sent word to Moses, "I your father-in-law [Reuel] am coming to you with your wife, and her two sons with her."

Moses went out to meet his father-in-law. He bowed and kissed him, and they said hello to each other and went into the tent. Moses told his father-in-law everything Yahweh did to pharaoh and Egypt on Israel's account, all the hardships they had suffered on the way, and how Yahweh had rescued them. [Reuel] rejoiced at all the good Yahweh had done for Israel by rescuing them from the hand of pharaoh.

[Reuel] said, "Blessed is Yahweh who rescued from the hand of Egypt and from the hand of pharaoh, who rescued the people from beneath the hand of Egypt. Now I know that Yahweh is the greatest of the gods, particularly in the case of Egypt's arrogance toward the bedouin."

The bedouin trek[1] to Sinai resumed at a less compulsive pace. Before reaching Sinai, the horde faced two hardships: lack of water and lack of food.[2] They went without water for three days. When they finally came to a water hole, at Marah, the water was "bitter" (*marim* represents a wordplay on Miriam's name in the preceding episode). When his people complained, as they inevitably did, Moses cried out to Yahweh. Yahweh showed him a stick. He threw the stick into the water, and the water turned drinkable. With this first major incident in the desert, our historian emphasizes that Moses was the prime leader with exclusive prerogatives upon whom all the others were dependent.

Marah was in the desert of Shur. The last time J mentioned Shur was when Ishmael's mother, Hagar, fled from Sarai toward Shur. Just as Yahweh disclosed the well of water to the thirsting mother and child on the way to Shur, so here at Shur the thirsting people found water. For J, Shur seems to designate the main route between Palestine and Egypt, the route traversed periodically by the tribe of Ishmael and hence the route by which Joseph, later Israel, and then all his family came to Egypt. The incident at Shur indicates that the bedouin were to return by the way they came.

Then the bedouin ran out of food. So Yahweh provided them with manna. As it stands in the Bible, the point of the story of how they were fed with manna is supplied by P. The people must gather only enough food to cover the needs of each day. No food was to be provided on the seventh day, so on the sixth day they had to gather food for two days. P's concern with the provision on the sabbath is of no interest to J. There is little doubt that J did contain the basis for the story about manna that P greatly expanded, but it is difficult to know just what J's original version was. In our interpretation, we will treat only those parts of the story most likely derived from J.

Yahweh told Moses that he would rain on the bedouin food from the sky and that the people could collect food daily. (It was the Hebrew way of expressing this last point—"food for each day on its day"—that P devel-

---

1. On the bedouin character of this trek and of the issues it covers, see Zev Meshel, "An Explanation of the Journeys of the Israelites in the Wilderness," *Biblical Archaeologist* 45 (1982): 19–20.

2. Some have suggested that J's history went directly from Egypt to Sinai without intervening incident. Most of what is contained in Exodus 16—17 consists of doublets of the stories of interdiction that J placed in the desert trek following the bedouin's departure from Sinai. These doublets were composed and revised by E, D, and P or related writers. It is likely that what J did narrate during this stage of the trek was the two incidents concerning water and food. One indication that they come from J is that when the Israelites complained a second time regarding meat, in what is now Numbers 11, they referred to manna as though they had been eating it for some time. The presence of characteristic J themes, and the fact that the incidents fit well J's history as a whole, are further reasons for ascribing these incidents to J.

oped into his main point.) The next morning, there was a layer of dew all around the camp. When this dew evaporated, on the ground there was a thin layer of what looked like frost. The bedouin "saw" and then said to each other in Hebrew, *"man hu,"* "What's that?" (using the archaic word *man* for "what"). They asked because, as J puts it, they did not "know" what it was. Hence they called this frostlike food *man* (Eng.: "manna"). It was like flaky honey wafers, and hence a foretaste of the wild produce of the land toward which they were headed. J's reason for making the story pivot on the term *man*—on seeing without knowing—is to stress the failure of the Israelites to draw the implication from Yahweh's feeding of them that loyalty to their leader Moses was essential.

Following the feeding of the people, Moses' father-in-law[3] brought Moses' wife Zipporah and Moses' two sons to Moses in the desert. J again explains the meaning of the name of Moses' first son and explains for the first time the meaning of his second son's name, previously unmentioned. Gershom meant "I was a sojourner in a foreign land," and Eliezer means "Yahweh rescued me from the sword of pharaoh." The two names form a sequence: first caught in a foreign land, then rescued. Having paused to explain these names, J then restates in a slightly different but perhaps significant order that there came to Moses his father-in-law, his sons, and his wife. Reuel approached and said to Moses, "I am your father-in-law, and I have come to you with your wife and your two sons." The stress falls on Moses' wife and two sons, now mentioned three times. Once again J integrates the themes of reproduction and production. When Moses married and fathered his first son, his role in J's reproductive scheme was tied directly to the injustice of the king of Egypt. Moses came to his wife while fleeing the king and named his son in reference to the injustice of the king. Now, precisely when that king, the heir of the line of Cain, had been killed by Yahweh, along with the son of the king, there appeared the wife of Moses—the successor of Sarai and the other wives of the blessed generations—and the sons of Moses. Their names again make explicit reference to the history of injustice and its resolution in this generation, reminding us once more of how the history of injustice was initiated through the theme of royal reproduction.

Following greetings and formalities, they went into Moses' tent. There Moses explained to his father-in-law all that Yahweh had done to pharaoh and Egypt on account of the descendants of Israel (he tells him a nationalist story like J's), as well as the hardships—lack of water and food—they had encountered on the way and from which Yahweh had delivered them.

---

3. Exactly as in Exod. 3:1, E or a writer copying E's diction has inserted the name Jethro. To judge from the story of how Moses married, J calls Moses' father-in-law Reuel.

Moses' father-in-law rejoiced over the good that Yahweh had done for Israel. Then the most remarkable piling up of terms ensues: in the midst of his *blessing* Yahweh, J has the father-in-law repeat the word *yad* ("hand, phallus, power") four times and follow it immediately with *yada'ti* ("I know"). This is the way it goes: he rejoiced at the good, "how Yahweh had delivered them from the 'hand' of Egypt. And he said, 'Blessed is Yahweh who delivered you from the "hand" of Egypt and from the "hand" of pharaoh, who delivered the people from beneath the "hand" of Egypt. Now I know that Yahweh is greater than all the gods.' " There are few places in J where so many important themes come together in one place.

J's description of the bedouin's stop at Sinai is framed by two conversations between Moses and his Midianite father-in-law or brother-in-law. In the first conversation, Moses' father-in-law as the representative of Midian blessed Yahweh and by implication Yahweh's creature Israel. This blessing, according to the rule of the blessing of Abram, would produce for Midian a blessing in return. The Midianite bedouin and the Israelite bedouin were in alliance. The Midianites in J stood for the bedouin allies of David who exercised effective control in the Sinai. They were David's bedouin clients, necessary for guaranteeing the track from Palestine into Sinai, as far as the sanctuary at the mountain of Sinai, and the rest of the boundary between Israel and Egypt. This function of the Midianites is made explicit in J's description of the conversation that occurred as Israel prepared to depart from Sinai. Moses said to his father-in-law, "Don't abandon us, for your purpose is to guide us in the desert and to be our eyes there." With the role of the Midianites fresh in mind, we are not surprised to discover that the track Israel was following led directly to Sinai.

Israel came then to the desert of Sinai and camped in that desert, in front of the mountain. Yahweh said to Moses, "I am about to come to you in the smoky cloud so the people can hear me speak with you, so they will trust you from now on." (Moses had reported the people's words to Yahweh.) Yahweh said further to Moses, "Go to the people and sanctify them today and tomorrow. Have them wash their garments and get ready on the day after tomorrow, for on the third day Yahweh will come down, in view of all the people, onto the mountain at Sinai. Bound off this mountain on all sides from the people with these words, 'Watch out you don't go up the mountain or touch its edge. If you do, you'll die. Whoever touches it, person or beast, will be stoned or shot and will not recover.' When the horn sounds, then let them come up to the mountain."

Moses went down from the mountain to the people. He sanctified the people, had them wash their garments, and said to them, "Be ready on the day after tomorrow. Don't go near a woman."

On the day after the morrow, as morning came, there was thunder and lightning, and a heavy cloud over the mountain. The sound of the horn got louder and louder, and all the people in the camp trembled. The whole of the mountain at Sinai began to smoke as Yahweh came down on it as fire. The smoke went up like smoke from a furnace. While the whole mountain shook severely and the sound of the horn got louder still, Yahweh came down above the mountain at Sinai, onto the top of the mountain.

Yahweh summoned Moses to the top of the mountain, and Moses went up. Yahweh said to Moses, "Go down and warn the people not to break through to Yahweh and see him, or many of them will fall. Let even the priests approaching Yahweh be sanctified, lest Yahweh explode against them."

Moses said to Yahweh, "The people aren't able to come up the mountain at Sinai, because you yourself warned us, 'Set bounds around the mountain and keep it holy.' "

So Yahweh said to him, "Then you go down."

Moses went down to the people. Then Yahweh said to Moses, "Thus you shall say to the Israelites, 'Having seen that I have spoken with you all from the sky, you shall not make like me gods of silver or gods of gold. Instead, make an altar of earth for me and thereon sacrifice your whole burnt offerings and community meal offerings, your flocks and herds. In every sanctuary where I make my name proclaimed, I will come to you and bless you. If you insist on making an altar out of stones, never make it out of hewn stones; if you strike any part of it with an iron tool, you will profane it. And you shall not go up on my altar by steps, so that your nakedness will not be uncovered on it.' "

Moses was told, "Come up to Yahweh, you, Aaron, Nadab, Abihu, and seventy of the sheikhs of Israel, and bow down at a distance. Then Moses alone shall approach Yahweh. The others shall not approach; the people shall not go with him." So Moses went up with Aaron, Nadab, Abihu, and seventy of the sheikhs of Israel. They saw the god of Israel. Beneath his feet was a sapphire tilework, as clear as the sky itself. When Yahweh did not strike out at these Israelite bedouin chiefs, they stayed to eat and drink.

Then Yahweh said to Moses, "Come up to me on the mountain and stay there, so I can give you the stone slabs with the customary law that I have inscribed for their legal instruction."

[. . .][4]

Yahweh said to Moses, "Go up from here, you and the people I brought up from the land of Egypt, to the land I swore to Abram, Isaac, and Jacob, 'I will grant it to your descendants.' I will send before you a messenger. I will drive away the Canaanites, the Amorites, the Hittites, the Perizzites, the Hivites, and the Jebusites in the land oozing milk and honey. But I will not go up myself in your midst, because you are a stubborn people, and I don't want to be tempted to exterminate you." When the people heard this evil word, they went into mourning, and did not deck themselves with their usual ornaments.

Moses used to take the tent—called the meeting tent—and pitch it outside the camp at some distance. Anyone who wanted to consult Yahweh would come out to the meeting tent outside the camp. Whenever Moses went out to the tent, all the people would come out and stand at the entrances to their tents and watch until Moses disappeared into the tent. Whenever Moses went into the tent, the cloud pillar would come down and stand at the entrance to the tent, where it would

---

4. It is possible Exod. 32:9–14 was an original part of J.

speak with Moses. Whenever all the people saw the cloud pillar standing at the entrance of the tent, they would all proceed to bow down, each at the entrance to their own tents. Yahweh would then speak to Moses face to face the way a person would speak to a companion. Then he would return to the camp.

Moses said to Yahweh, "Look, you keep telling me to take these people up, but you haven't let me know whom you're going to send with me. You've said, 'I know you by name,' and 'I find favor with you.' So if you are favorably disposed toward me, let me know what you're going to do, so I can know you, and so continue to find favor with you, because look, this nation is *your* people."

Yahweh said, "I will go along in person, and give you rest."

Moses said to him, "If you're not going along in person, then don't take us up from here. And just how is it to be known that I have found favor with you—I and your people? Only if you go with us, and we, I and your people, are distinguished from all the people on the surface of the earth."

[. . .]

"You shall not make for yourselves metal figures of gods.

"You shall keep the pilgrimage feast of unleavened bread ('pass' feast), during which you shall eat unleavened bread, as I ordered you to, for seven days at the prescribed time in the month of Abib, since you left Egypt in the month of Abib. Every firstborn of cattle, sheep, and asses you shall redeem with a lamb. If you don't redeem it, you shall break its neck. Every firstborn son you shall redeem. You shall not see my face with nothing to offer.

"You shall keep the pilgrimage feast of sevens, at the first of the wheat harvest, and the pilgrimage feast of the fruit harvest at the end of the year in autumn. Three times a year every one of your males shall see the face of the lord Yahweh, the god of Israel. Since I will drive away the nations from you and widen your territory, no one will covet your land when you come up to see the face of Yahweh your god three times a year.

"You shall not offer me the blood of sacrifice with leavened bread. You shall not let the meat for the 'pass' feast in Abib remain overnight until morning.

"The very first of the crops of your ground you shall bring to the cult of Yahweh your god.

"You shall not boil a kid in its mother's milk."

When Moses came down from the mountain of Sinai, Moses said to Hobab his brother-in-law or to Reuel his father-in-law, the Midianite, "We are about to pull out on our way to the place about which Yahweh said, 'I shall give it to you.' Go with us, and we'll make it good for you, as Yahweh has pronounced good for Israel."

He said, "I can't go. I want to go back to my land, birthplace, and kinship network."

Moses said, "Don't leave us. You know where we can camp in the desert, and you can be our eyes. If you go with us, whatever good Yahweh brings about for us he will bring about for you, too."

And so the bedouin arrived at Sinai. This was the sacred place where Yahweh had first appeared to Moses as the perpetual sacrificial-military fire rather than as a genie or man. The presence of Israel at Sinai concentrates on the sanctification of the mountain where Yahweh reappeared as fire. Here the national history singles out Moses as the sole great authoritative representative of Yahweh on earth. Rebellion against Moses is futile. So, too, is rebellion against the ruling house of David.

Yahweh said to Moses, "I am about to come to you in the smoky cloud so the people can hear me speak with you, so they will trust you." Moses told this to the people. Then Yahweh instructed Moses, "Go to the people and sanctify them"—that is, prepare them for the sacred encounter they were about to experience—"on the first and second day. Have them wash their garments and get ready on the third day, for on the third day Yahweh will descend, in view of all the people, onto the mountain at Sinai."[5]

"Bound off this mountain from the people," Yahweh continued, "with these words: 'Watch out you don't go up the mountain or touch its edge. If you do, you'll die. Whoever touches it, human or beast, will be stoned or shot.' When the horn sounds, then let them come up to the mountain."

Moses came down from the mountain and set about doing as he was instructed. His reiteration of Yahweh's instructions contains the pointed addition, "Do not approach a woman," which connotes military-like preparation with implications stemming from J's reproductive theme.

On the morning of the third day, the thunder and lightning started, the cloud descended onto the mountain, the sound of the horn grew louder and louder, and the people trembled with fear. The mountain was enshrouded in smoke because Yahweh descended upon it in the fire. As the sound of the horn grew still louder, Yahweh reached the top of the mountain and thunderously summoned Moses to the summit. Moses ascended. When he reached the top, Yahweh said to him, "Go down and warn the people lest they break through to Yahweh and see him, and many of them fall." For the duration of the trek, people were not to "see" Yahweh directly. Instead, they were to see him in Moses and especially in the nation Israel. "Let even the priests approaching Yahweh be sanctified lest Yahweh explode against them." This reference to the priests of Yahweh's cult is the first clear indication of what was soon to come, the prime commandment delivered at Sinai which describes the form of the altar for the service of Yahweh wherever it might be performed. This commandment dealt with David's national cult not only at the pilgrimage sanctuary of Sinai but also at Jerusalem and probably elsewhere.

Moses said to Yahweh, "The people aren't able to come up the mountain of Sinai, as you earlier indicated they should, because you yourself warned

---

5. J's portrayal of Yahweh's appearance at Sinai is possibly influenced by the cultic traditions of highland sanctuaries like Bethel. Those sanctuaries were not necessarily located on high mountains, although this feature of J's portrayal, reflecting the terrain of the lower Sinai peninsula, is implicit in the symbolism of the cult wherever it was practiced.

us, 'Set bounds around the mountain and sanctify it.' " Yahweh answered, "Then you go down." So Moses descended.

He arrived with this message, describing the altar worship of Yahweh: "Having seen that I have spoken with you all from the sky, you shall not make like me gods of silver or gods of gold. Instead, make an altar of earth for me and thereon sacrifice your whole burnt offerings and community meal offerings. In every sanctuary where I make my name proclaimed, I will come to you and bless you. If you insist on making an altar out of stones, never make it out of hewn stones; if you strike any part of it with an iron tool, you will profane it. And you shall not go up on my altar by steps, so that your nakedness will not be uncovered on it."

This is an all-important paragraph in J, usually not even attributed to J. In it J defines the essence of the cult of Yahweh in such a way that the essential features of Israel's national history as beneficiaries of the blessing of Yahweh could be called to remembrance in the course of a modest and probably multi-sited national worship. The cult rejected gods portrayed in precious metals, the metals of kings. The altar was of soil, from which the workers of the world, royalty included, were formed. If the altar were of stone, it should not be of hewn stone, since the transporting of and construction with hewn stone almost invariably were carried out by corvée labor. Solomon and his builders attempted to circumvent this law promulgated by David: "When the temple was built, it was with stone prepared at the quarry, so that neither hammer nor ax nor any tool of iron was heard in the temple, while it was being built" (1 Kings 6:7). Many altars at the center of state cults were large and did indeed require steps. Royalty and the priesthood periodically exposed themselves on their way up to the altar so as to demonstrate their power before the people, just as David did while conducting the ark to his cult shrine in Jerusalem (2 Sam. 6:16, 20). J concludes his description of the cult with a clear reference to the moment when humans in the pleasure orchard first saw their nakedness, thereby initiating J's history of good and evil.

The cult of sacrifice on such a modest altar must itself have been modest. The heart of that cult was the provision of meat for the official state priesthood. Meat in the quantities the priests enjoyed through the cult was a privilege of the elite, as in most agrarian societies. In the case of David's priests, however, this privilege was characteristically circumscribed. The modesty of the cult of Sinai must also have been due to the sparse grazing in that part of the desert. In settled areas of Palestine, David's priestly establishment no doubt grew apace.

The law of the altar[6] makes reference to what can be described as the

---

6. For a discussion of the extent of law in J, see J. Alberto Soggin, "Ancient Israelite Poetry and Ancient 'Codes' of Law, and the Sources 'J' and 'E' of the Pentateuch," *Supplements to Vetus Testamentum* 28 (1975): 185–95.

primary interest of J's history at the point of transition between the fourteenth and the fifteenth generation, between the time of the curse and the introduction of the blessing. Recall that at that time all humanity were dispersed from the building of a great city-tower which threatened the divine prerogative of Yahweh and seemed (to the readers and hearers of J) to refer to citadel temples in the Palestinian highlands. The reversal of this in the first generation of the blessing was Abram's earthen altar at Shechem. J is concerned throughout with the cult of David. J emphasizes the character of the altar of David's cult of sacrifice—a cult not significantly different from other such cults as far as we know—because of the importance of the relationship between cult and the court's own understanding of the national political economy. This, after all, is what a history such as J's was typically all about.

Throughout the biblical period in Palestine, priests, cult, and sacrifice provided the prime sanction for jurisdiction, the right to interpret and apply law, with which cult was inextricably integrated. All forms of law—standards, norms, regulations, examples, customs, penalties, taboos, and historical sanctions—emanated from cults. David's national law regulating his political economy, though not laid out in J, was no different. Hence the history of the cult addresses in turn the essential features of the model cult of David: the altar, the validation of seventy elders (standing for the magistracy under David's authority), the peculiar authority of Moses (and thus David), and the rules for the periodic keeping of the pilgrimage to the shrines of David's jurisdiction. The Deuteronomistic construal of *man* (manna), which figures in episodes occurring immediately before and after the bedouin stop at Sinai, points to the jurisdictional significance of the cult defined at Sinai: "I fed you *man* to make you know that people don't live by bread only, but by every law and admonition that comes forth from the mouth of Yahweh" (Deut. 8:3).

In the history of the composition of the Pentateuch, the various writers and editors over the centuries paid close attention to what happened at Sinai and greatly expanded the original version of J. In J's conception, Yahweh addressed Moses with the basic cultic stipulation pertaining to the state, coupled with the requirement to keep the requisite pilgrimage feasts. This then became the literary locus of every government's presentation of its receipt of state law through Moses. The clearest instance of this concentration on Sinai for literary historians is the material from P found in what is now Exodus 25 up through Num. 10:10. Except for Exodus 32—34, within this entire section there is little from J, E, or D. E and D were, however, also especially interested in this location in the history. They added much material to J, and the combination of J, E, and D, along with P, in Exodus 19—24 is extremely complex. Older literary criticism assumed a good deal of J within these chapters. So far in our treatment of Exodus 19—20 we have discussed the arrival of Moses' Midianite family, the meeting of Yahweh and the bedouin at Sinai, and the delivering of the law of the altar. After that, it is not clear there is much J at all.

When Exodus 32—34 is scrutinized, it becomes clear that the J portions have been revised in the style of J to take account of the secession of Israel from the house of David, the establishment of a new royal cult at Bethel under the direction of a priesthood putatively descended from the family of Aaron, and the struggle of Rehoboam in the south to delegitimate that cult. As part of the establishment of his rule, Jeroboam promulgated an alternative history of Israel, probably a revision of J, that included and even emphasized Moses delivering a state law for Israel at Sinai, redesignated Horeb. It is likely that E's placing of its state law at this point in the history (Exod. 21:1—22:19, approximately), along with Rehoboam's attempt to counter the implications of this, has led to the introduction of further J-like laws in this section of the history that were not there originally. In Exodus 19—24, the sequence of events and their literary connections is extremely muddy. For example, it remains a point of considerable debate as to what literary strand the Ten Commandments are to be ascribed. (They seem to play a definitive role beginning with D.) A first reading of this section of the Pentateuch will leave a reader bewildered as to how many times and exactly why Moses went up and down the mountain.

In the J parts of Exodus 24, Moses went back up the mountain with three leaders—Aaron, Nadab, and Abihu—and seventy sheikhs. They all bowed down at a distance. Then Moses approached Yahweh alone. The others stayed where they were, and together they saw Yahweh, the god of Israel. Beneath his feet they saw a very fancy and luxurious pavement. In the presence of this all-powerful creator, they were doubtless overwhelmed with awe. Yahweh, however, did not harm them, and so they ate and drank in his company.

Coming immediately after the law of the altar, the contrast is obvious: while on earth, Israel, epitomizing Yahweh's creatures made of earth, were to sacrifice at an earthen altar—that is to say, eat and drink in the presence of Yahweh at the earthen altar. Here on the mountain high in the sky, they dined with Yahweh in surroundings that expressed the great distance between creator and creature, the difference between sapphire and dirt. Who is privileged to dine in the creator's own home? The three and the seventy stand for the national elite of David's realm. They reflect the reality that only a few people in David's kingdom possessed the privilege of worshiping within the precinct of David's royal cult at the capital. The seventy were what in the medieval period would be called the magistracy. They were the major landowners who exercised the military and judicial leadership of the realm. They are referred to in an episode after the bedouin's departure from Sinai as the seventy or so leaders of Israel who possessed the spirit of Moses and so could adjudicate cases at law. J's failure to define the law beyond the royal cult is an indication that David was in little position to curb the autonomy of his magistracy.

One of the better known incidents at Sinai is the one involving the golden calf. Again, the literary analysis of Exodus 32—34 is extremely complex. There seem to be pieces of text that do in fact come from the original J history of the time of David. These, however, have been recast in reaction to the establishment of Jeroboam's national cult at Bethel. Much of the text in these chapters might be characterized as supplements from the time of Rehoboam in the style of the Davidic court historian J of two generations before. There are also additions in the style of the Deuteronomist from even later, along with parts whose literary affiliation is harder to define.

We can identify a few more incidents at Sinai as J's. Yahweh told Moses to lead the people from Sinai to Palestine, where he would drive out the Canaanites. Yahweh was not to lead them himself, but by means of a "messenger," who was apparently Moses or a genie. Yahweh was angry with the bedouin. In fact, he regarded them as so stubbornly malcontent he was prepared to destroy them. The discontent of the bedouin had already been exposed in their grousing about water and food prior to arriving at Sinai and would occur again in their complaints about food, and directly against Moses' authority, after leaving Sinai. J talks about this stubbornness in terms of their lack of faith, which was referred to at the very beginning of the history of Moses. The stubbornness of the bedouin is the primary foil against which J presses the authority of Moses.

J proceeds to explain how Moses was to be singled out in his relation to Yahweh as the primary leader of this people. Moses took his tent and pitched it outside the camp, separate from the rest, and named it the "tent of meeting." Here Moses would meet with Yahweh. When he went there, all the other people would stand outside the entrances to their own tents and watch as Moses entered the tent of meeting. Then the column of cloud would descend and stand at the entrance to the tent, and Yahweh would speak with Moses. The people would see the column at the entrance and bow down at their own tents. Moses would speak with Yahweh face to face. Moses himself did not want to lead without Yahweh's backing and presence. He insisted, as a leader representing the values of J's history might, that the distinctiveness of Israel as a creation of Yahweh could be manifest to the world only if Yahweh himself were with them on their trek. Many people in J's history have so far talked with Yahweh face to face.

Henceforth this privilege was reserved for Moses.[7] The expression "face to face" is of course a loaded one in J, signifying the reconciliation of fraternal conflict that was so important to the Davidic state. It is as though J were suggesting that this national reconciliation was now available to all in Israel through their acquiescence to a leadership like Moses', namely, David's.

Like E, D, and P later, J narrates the pronouncement of laws in addition to the law of the altar. These are the laws in Exod. 34:17–26 dealing with the three pilgrimage feasts, appropriately the chief events to occur at the national altars, and the provision of any priests who might serve there. Whether these or other laws were recorded on tablets of stone—the practice at the time of David—is not known.[8]

As the bedouin prepared to move camp, Moses' father-in-law or brother-in-law[9] declined to depart with them. He wanted to return to his own settlement area in the heart of the Sinai. Now at this stage Moses pressed on him the Midianites' importance to the bedouin as their guides and fellow guardians in the desert.

They left the mountain of Yahweh. By the time they had been traveling for three days, the people were complaining badly in Yahweh's hearing. Yahweh heard them and got angry. Yahweh's fire flared up against them and ate up the edge of the encampment. The people cried out to Moses, and when he prayed to Yahweh the fire subsided. They named that place Taberah, because the fire of Yahweh flared up against them.

When the camp followers among them were gripped with a craving for meat, the Israelite bedouin started weeping again, too. "Who's going to feed us some meat? We remember the fish we had to eat in Egypt—for free—and cucumbers, melons, leeks, onions, and garlic we had there. But now we are famished, and there's nothing to look at but *man*." *Man* was like coriander seed, and looked like bdellium. The people would go about and gather it up, then grind it in a mill or pound it in a mortar, cook it in a pot, and make it into loaves. It tasted like cakes baked with olive oil. Whenever at night dew fell on the camp, *man* fell with it.

Moses heard the people weeping, each family at the entrance of its own tent, and that Yahweh was angry. It looked evil to Moses. He said to Yahweh, "Why have you brought this evil on your servant? Why have you not been well disposed toward me, by placing upon me the burden of all these people? Was it I who was pregnant with all these people? Did I give them birth, so that you should tell me to carry them at my bosom as a nurse might carry a sucking child, all the way to the ground you swore to their ancestors? Where am I going to get meat to give all these people who are wailing at me, 'Give us meat to eat!'? There is no way I can support all these people by myself. They are too heavy for me. If this is what you are going to

7. In the unlikely event that Joshua plays any role in J at all, he is first introduced as a servant of Moses who stayed at the tent of meeting when Moses returned to camp.

8. See F. E. Wilms, *Das jahwistische Bundesbuch in Exodus 34* (Munich, 1973).

9. The present text, "Hobab the son of Reuel . . . the father-in-law of Moses," may be composite.

do to me, just kill me now, if you don't mind, so I won't have to see any more evil for me."

Yahweh said to Moses, "Gather together for me seventy of the sheikhs of Israel, men you know as the people's sheikhs and foremen, and take them to the tent of meeting and have them stand there with you. I will come down and talk with you there and take some of the spirit which is in you and give it to them so that they might bear with you the burden of the people, so that you don't have to bear it alone. Then say to the people, 'Sanctify yourselves for tomorrow. You are going to eat meat. Since you cried so Yahweh could hear you, "Who's going to feed us some meat? We had it better in Egypt," Yahweh will give you meat, and you're going to eat it. You're not going to eat it for one day, or two, or five, or ten, or twenty, but for a whole month, until it's coming out of your noses and it disgusts you, because you spurned Yahweh, who was with you in your midst, and cried before him, "Why did we ever come out of Egypt?" ' "

Moses said, "The people around me include six hundred units on foot, and you're saying you can feed them meat for a month? Are we supposed to slaughter the flocks and herds for them so they can get some? Are we supposed to gather in all the fish of the sea?"

Yahweh said to Moses, "Is the hand of Yahweh short? Now you will see whether what I said will happen or not."

Moses went out and told the people what Yahweh had said. He gathered together seventy of the sheikhs of the people and had them stand around the tent. Yahweh came down in the cloud and spoke to him. He took some of the spirit which was in him and gave it to the seventy sheikhs. When the spirit came to rest in them, they started making utterances, and kept on doing it.

The spirit came to rest in two more men left in the camp, one named Eldad and the other Medad. Although they were on the list of sheikhs, they failed to go out to the tent, yet made utterances in the camp anyway. A boy ran and told Moses, "Eldad and Medad are making utterances in the camp." Moses said to him, "Are you jealous for me? I wish all the people of Yahweh were makers of utterances, that Yahweh would give his spirit to all of them."

Moses and the bedouin sheikhs were brought back into the camp. A further wind departed from Yahweh and swept in quail from seaward and deposited them over the camp area two yards deep and a day's journey out on all sides. All that day, that night, and the next day, the people went and collected quail. The people who got the least collected about fifty baskets of them. They spread them out for themselves all around the camp. The meat, however, no sooner came between their teeth, without their even biting, when Yahweh became angry with the people. Yahweh killed a great many of them. So they named that place Qibrot-hatta'awah, "The Graves of Craving," because there they buried the people who had the craving.

Miriam and Aaron spoke against Moses on account of the Cushite wife he had taken (he had taken a Cushite wife). "Does Yahweh speak only with Moses? Does he not also speak with us?"

Yahweh heard it. Now Moses was the most humble human on the face of this earth. Suddenly Yahweh said to Moses, Aaron, and Miriam, "The three of you go out to the tent of meeting." So the three of them went out. Yahweh came down in the cloud pillar and stood at the entrance of the tent. He called Aaron and Miriam and those two went over to him. He said, "Listen to me. If you have a maker of utterances for Yahweh, I make myself known to him in visions, or I talk with him in dreams. But that's not the way it is with my servant Moses. In all my cult, he is the sure one. I speak with him mouth to mouth, and not in riddles. He sees the form of Yahweh. Why aren't you afraid to speak against my servant Moses?"

Yahweh became very angry with them and left. When the cloud had departed from over the tent, Miriam was left leprous, white as snow. Aaron said to Moses, "I beg of you, my lord, do not lay on us the sin we have so foolishly committed. Let her not be like a stillborn infant, just out of its mother's womb with half its flesh consumed."

Moses cried out to Yahweh, "O El, heal her!"

Yahweh said to Moses, "If her father had spit in her face, would she not conceal herself for shame for seven days? Let her be confined outside the camp for seven days, and then be brought back."

Miriam was confined outside the camp for seven days. The people did not start out until Miriam had been brought back.

J's history of the bedouin's trek in the desert is structured according to a number of places whose names are explained in terms of the two themes that characterize this part of the history: the people's complaints about food and questioning of Moses' authority. The first place mentioned is Taberah, which means "burning." There, when the people complained, the fire of Yahweh flared up and consumed the edge of the encampment. The people appealed to Moses, who in turn appealed to Yahweh, and the fire subsided. It was already hot in the desert during this time of the year, between the spring of their escape and the late summer when they first scouted the Palestinian highland, and Yahweh's fire made it hotter. It was clear that Yahweh as a god of war, symbolized by the fire, would continue to tolerate no resistance to his purpose of creating a society directly opposed, in the conception of David, to the system and pretension of the king of Egypt. It may even be that J wished to publicize David's willingness to suppress resistance to his power by similar means.

The next place they came to was to be called, once the events that gave it its name had occurred, Qibrot-hatta'awah ("the graves of desire"). Here were found the graves of bedouin who upon following Moses out of Egypt desired something besides *man* to eat. "We wish someone would give us some meat. We remember the fish we ate in Egypt, for nothing. We remember the cucumbers, melons, leeks, onions, and garlic we had there. But now our throats are dry. We have nothing to look at but *man*." They wanted something crunchy and juicy, something flavorful, for this hot and dry desert trek, instead of the flaky, seedlike crust of *man*. *Man* appealed to them about as much as turkey appeals to us after it has been prepared ten different ways all week long after Thanksgiving. Moses heard the wailing of the people at their tent entrances. He didn't like it, and Yahweh was angry too.

Moses said to Yahweh, "Why have you brought this evil on me? Why have I not found favor with you? Why have you placed on me the burden of this whole people?" The word "burden" is an important clue to the rest of the episode. The story develops along parallel tracks, connected with two meanings of burden. One track deals with the burden of feeding the disgruntled multitude, the other with the authority of Moses and the burden of adjudicating the people's complaints. This episode is J's version of what will be repeated by E in Exodus 18 and by D in Deuteronomy 1: the appointment of the chief judicial officers of the realm. The parallel tracks interconnect. It is best to discuss this episode in the sequence in which it occurs rather than to disentangle each issue in a separate analysis.

Moses complained that he didn't want to be his people's mother. "Was it I who was pregnant with all these people? Did I bear them, so that you should tell me to carry them at my bosom as a nurse might carry a sucking child, all the way to the ground you have sworn to their ancestors? Where am I going to get meat for all these people who are wailing so? There is no way I can support all these people by myself. They are too heavy. If this is what you want, kill me if you favor me and don't let me see this trouble."

Yahweh told Moses to gather seventy of the elders and bring them to the tent of meeting. "I will come down and speak with you there and take some of the spirit which is in you and give it to them so that they might with you carry the burden of the people so that you don't have to carry it alone." The moment the jurisdictional function is broached, however, Yahweh switched to the other theme. "Gather tomorrow and you will eat meat. You won't eat it for one day, nor for two, nor five, nor ten, nor twenty, but for a whole month, until it's coming out of your noses and it disgusts you, because you spurned Yahweh and complained, 'Why have we come out of Egypt?' "

Moses had no idea where he was going to find meat for six hundred units of bedouin. "Are we going to slaughter all our sheep and cattle at once? Are we going to gather in all the fish of the sea?" Yahweh had a pointed response. "Is the hand of Yahweh short?" The hand of Yahweh, which has been rich with meaning so far in J, is now deployed to provide food for his people directly: potency and produce are two sides of the same coin.

Moses gathered the sheikhs as instructed. When they had received the spirit of Moses, they "prophesied," falling into ecstatic and incoherent utterance for a time. In addition to the seventy outside the camp at the tent of meeting, there were two within the camp, Eldad and Medad, who likewise began shouting ecstatically. A boy ran to Moses to tell him. With less power than Moses, he was more anxious. Moses said to him, "I wish all the people would prophesy, that Yahweh would give all of them this spirit." Eldad and Medad were left alone and all returned to the camp.

The spirit of Moses here is the spirit of Moses' leadership, which has been described by J in full since he first introduced Moses. It is the spirit of initiative for the deliverance of these corvée slaves in the name of Yahweh, the spirit behind the history that sanctioned David's law. This spirit was to be shared among the people as long as it retained the precise meaning that it had in connection with Moses himself. The seventy or so possessors of the spirit were the same as the seventy diners with Yahweh. They may be the elite, but their spirit and consciousness of the defeat of the king of Egypt and the worship of the Yahweh of J at altars of earth were the very basis of a just administration and the provision of food to the realm. These were guaranteed together, as J recognizes that judicial right and the right to food are inseparable. The pilgrimage services of jurisdiction were at the same time services of the three major food harvests.

In Hebrew, the same word is used for spirit and wind *(ruach)*. The spirit, or wind, blew up and swept in countless quail from seaward, depositing them about the camp and covering the ground two yards deep the distance of a day's journey on all sides. The people collected this meat in great quantity. When they went to eat it, however, the moment it touched their mouths Yahweh's anger flared up and he killed a large number of them. Hence the name of the place, "graves of desire."

The next episode in which the authority of Moses was questioned involved Aaron and Miriam. Recently it has been suggested that this episode, along with some others like it in Exodus and Numbers, reflects the tensions between two opposing priestly groups in early Israel, those tracing themselves back to Moses and those tracing themselves back to Aaron.[10] Given that David's administration included two main priests and that Jeroboam I established a priesthood tracing to Aaron at Bethel and one tracing to Moses at Dan, this view may be correct. It is not likely, however, that this is why J included the story. It is the role of Miriam that is of interest in this episode. Her role was not that of bedouin leader. She complained that Moses presumed to be the only one through whom Yahweh spoke. Her role therefore was probably that of an oracle, a mantic or divinitory figure.[11] She objected that her special skill, knowledge, and

10. Frank Moore Cross, *Canaanite Myth and Hebrew Epic* (Cambridge: Harvard University Press, 1973), 198–206; Richard Elliot Friedman, *Who Wrote the Bible?* (New York: Summit Books, 1987).

11. Not too much is to be made of Miriam in J. She appears in the history only twice, briefly—when she led the bedouin women in a victory song and dance at the death of the

status within the community were being diminished by the exclusive authority of Moses.

She began her complaint by speaking against Moses' right to have a black African wife.[12] This complaint is not explained. That Moses took an African wife, perhaps in a marriage alliance with the Cushite elite as a part of an anti-Egyptian pincer movement, is a mark of Moses' special authority. This time Moses had taken as his wife whom he would, a characteristically J way of confirming his authority. Whatever the reason, Yahweh was incensed at the complaint of Miriam and Aaron. He drew all three aside to the tent of meeting and there asserted that Moses did indeed have unique authority. He did not speak with Moses in a vision or dream but "mouth to mouth." Nevertheless, he was, J avers, "the most humble man of all humanity who were on the face of the earth." Yahweh himself said of him, "He sees the form of Yahweh. Why do you not fear to speak against my servant Moses?"[13]

As the cloud pillar of Yahweh retreated from the tent, Miriam was left leprous "like snow." Since the sign that set Moses apart from Miriam was the whiteness of her leprosy, the blackness of Moses' chosen wife served as a foil for this sign. That is how J combines the main issue of Moses' authority with the question of his black African wife. Moses himself was made similarly leprous at the moment when Yahweh commissioned him and set him apart with unique authority at the burning bush. At that time, Yahweh removed Moses' leprosy immediately. Miriam's leprosy was not removed until Moses interceded with Yahweh on her behalf at the request of Aaron.

---

king of Egypt, and here. In J, Miriam can be understood in terms of the normal behavior of a bedouin woman. Her behavior does not compare with that of extraordinary women leaders in folk tradition, like Deborah, Jael, or Judith. Miriam's exact relationship to Aaron and Moses is not made clear by J.

12. This wife of Moses is described as Cushite. This time Cush refers to the black African peoples of the upper Nile, southern Sudan and Ethiopia.

13. There may be a clue to the meaning of this incident in the poetic form in which defiance typically is expressed in the context of deference in bedouin society. See Lila Abu-Lughod, *Veiled Sentiments: Honor and Poetry in a Bedouin Society* (Berkeley: University of California Press, 1986).

25

Getting There

(Numbers 13:17—21:18, parts)

Moses said to scouts, "Go up through the Negev and up into the hill country, and see what kind of land it is. See whether the people resident in the land are strong or weak, few or many, whether the land they are resident in is good or bad, whether the cities they are resident in are open camps or fortified, and whether the land is fruitful or barren, with trees or not. Be bold enough to seize some of the fruit of the land, since it is the beginning of the grape harvest."

The men went up through the Negev and came to Hebron. Ahiman, Sheshai, and Talmai, descendants of Anak, were there. (Hebron was built seven years before Zoan in Egypt.) When they got to Wadi Eshkol, they cut down a grape branch and a single bunch of grapes. They carried it off with a pole slung over the shoulders of two of them. They also carried off some pomegranates and figs. That place is named Wadi Eshkol, Grape Bunch Stream Bed, on account of the bunch of grapes the Israelite bedouin cut down from there.

When they got back to Moses, they related their story to him. "We came to the land you sent us to. It was indeed a land oozing milk and honey, and this is an example of its fruit. Only the people resident in the land are strong, and the cities are great fortified ones, and we even saw some descendants of Anak there. The Amalekites occupy the land of the Negev, and the Hittites, the Jebusites, and the Amorites hold the hill country, and the Canaanites are resident in the seacoast and Jordanian lowlands."

Caleb hushed the people's talk like that in front of Moses. "We're going to go up and take it," he said. "We can do it!"

When, however, the men who had gone up with him insisted, "We aren't able to go up against those people. They're too strong for us," the people wept that night. "Why is Yahweh leading us into this land, only to have us fall by the sword? Our wives and children will be taken as spoil. Wouldn't it be better for us to go back to Egypt?"

So they said to each other, "Let's appoint ourselves a leader and return to Egypt."

Yahweh said to Moses, "How much longer are these people going to spurn me? How much longer are they not going to trust me, and all the signs I have done in their midst? Let me kill them with pestilence and disenfranchise them, and I'll make you into a nation greater and stronger than they."

"You would do that," Moses said to Yahweh, "even though the Egyptians have heard you brought up these people right out of their midst with your power? They told the lords of this land they had heard you are Yahweh in the midst of these people; you are Yahweh, who appears eyeball to eyeball, and your cloud hovers over them, and in a cloud pillar you travel in front of them during the day and in a fire pillar during the night. But you killed these people, the whole lot, the nations are going to say when they hear about your doing this, because of Yahweh's inability to bring these people to the land he swore to them—that's the reason he slaughtered them in the desert.

"So now, let the power of my lord be great, as you have said—'Yahweh is long-suffering, abundantly kind, forgiving wrong and transgression, yet not letting a person off free, but bringing the wrongs of the fathers down upon the sons of the third and fourth generations'—forgive these people their wrong, in accord with your great kindness, as you have forgiven and carried them from Egypt to here."

Yahweh said, "I hereby forgive them, as you wish. But as I live, and as the majesty of Yahweh fills the earth, all these men who have seen my majesty and my signs which I did in Egypt and the desert will by no means see the land I swore to their ancestors, and any who spurned me will not see it. But my servant Caleb, because a different spirit is in him, and he follows me without question, him I will bring to the land he is going to, and his offspring shall inherit it. Now, since the Amalekites and the Canaanites are resident in the lower elevations, turn around tomorrow and set out back through the desert on the way to Sup Sea."

The people grieved deeply. First thing in the morning, they went up to the crest of the nearby hills and said, "This time we're going to go up to the place Yahweh said, because earlier we sinned."

Moses, however, said, "Why now do you want to transgress the order of Yahweh? It won't work. Don't go up, because Yahweh is not in your midst. Don't. You will be beaten back before your enemies. The Amalekites and the Canaanites face you up there, and you will fall by the sword, because you turned back from following Yahweh, and Yahweh will not be with you."

But they heedlessly went up into the hills, and the Amalekites and the Canaanites resident in those hills came down and attacked them and pushed them back as far as Hormah.

Now Dathan and Abiram, the sons of Eliab, and On the son of Peleg, sons of Reuben, were men of name. Moses sent a summons to Dathan and Abiram, the sons of Eliab, but they said, "We will not come up. Is it not enough that you have brought us up from a land oozing milk and honey to have us die in the desert, that you should also persist in acting out the role of commander-in-chief over us? You have not brought us to a land oozing milk and honey and given us land grants of fields and vineyards. Are you going to gouge those men's eyes out? We will not come up."

Moses got very angry and said to Yahweh, "Do not turn with favor toward their offering. Not one ass have I carried off from them, and not one of them have I done any evil to."

Moses proceeded to go to Dathan and Abiram, and behind him went the sheikhs of Israel. Dathan and Abiram had come out and stood by the entrances of their tents with women, sons, and small children.

Moses said, "By this you shall know that Yahweh has sent me to do these deeds I have done, and that it wasn't my idea. If these people die the way all people do, and if they meet their maker the way anyone else does, then Yahweh didn't send me. But if Yahweh is creative, and the ground opens its mouth and swallows them and everything they own, and they go down alive to the nether world, then you all shall know that these men have spurned Yahweh, not me."

At the moment Moses finished speaking these words, the ground beneath them was split, and the earth opened its mouth and swallowed them and their households. They and everything they owned went down alive to the nether world, and the earth covered them over. Thus they were liquidated from the community. All the Israelites around them fled at their shrieks, fearing that "the earth might swallow us, too!"

From Qadesh, Moses sent envoys to the king of Edom with the message, "Thus says your brother Israel: you know all the hardship that has befallen us. Our ancestors went down to Egypt and resided in Egypt for many years. The Egyptians treated us and our ancestors with evil. We cried out to Yahweh. He heard our cry and sent a genie, who brought us out of Egypt. Now here we are in Qadesh, a city on the edge of your territory, and we would like to pass through your land. We're not going to get into your fields or vineyards. We're not going to drink the water in your wells. We want to travel on the Royal Road, and won't bend right or left until we have passed through your territory."

Edom said, "You may not pass through me. If you try it, I will come out to meet you with the sword."

The Israelite bedouin said, "We just want to go up by means of the highway. If I or my livestock should drink any of your water, I will reimburse you. There's no harm in our passing through on foot."

He said, "You shall not pass through."

Edom came out to meet them with a heavily armed force and a strong hand. Edom reiterated their refusal to allow Israel to pass through their territory, so Israel veered away from them. They set out from the highland of Hor on the Sup Sea road to detour around the land of Edom. On the way the people's patience began to wear thin, and the people spoke against Moses. "Why have you brought us up from Egypt to die in the desert? There's no food and there's no water, and we're fed up with this inane food."

Against the people Yahweh sent burning snakes. They crawled around biting the people, and a large number of bedouin Israel died.

The people came to Moses and said, "We have sinned, for we have spoken against Yahweh as well as against you. Pray to Yahweh to remove the snakes from us."

Moses prayed on behalf of the people, and Yahweh said to Moses, "Make a model of a burning snake and attach it to a pole. Anyone bitten who sees it will recover."

Moses made a bronze snake and attached it to a pole. Thereafter if a snake bit people, if they looked at the bronze snake they recovered.

The trekking bedouin now approached Palestine. They had departed the Nile delta in the spring, and reached their destination in late summer when the grapes of the southern Palestinian highlands had fully ripened. They had survived the desert's dry season, the most difficult time in it.

Moses sent scouts from the Negev into the highlands around Hebron to find out what kinds of people lived there, their defenses and their product. In the vicinity of Hebron they collected ripe grapes, for which this area has always been famous, and pomegranates and figs. These are perennial fruits, urban fruit produce in line with J's conception of the Canaanites as exclusively urbanite.

When they returned to the encampment the scouts reported to Moses, "We went into the land you sent us to, and it was indeed oozing milk and honey, and this is its produce." While much of Palestine was uncultivated, pastoral land with goats and wild bees, here in the desert in the summer the bedouin had seen so little productive potential in mile after mile of desert land that they were overwhelmed with the productivity of the small stretches of urban property in the Judahite highlands that produced their samples. The productive system they viewed was just what J has previously described for the land of Canaan. They reported that they saw a strong people ensconced on urban estates in the land.[1] They lived in fortified cities and towns. This description applies not to the Late Bronze cities and towns contemporary with the actual emergence of villages all over the highland of Palestine usually identified with early Israel but to urban centers in David's time. Archaeological investigation has shown that during the time of the emergence of the Iron Age villages of Palestine, most urban sites were unwalled.

The scouts then characterized the inhabitants they saw. They were all "offspring of Anak." All we know about Anaq is that he was large and strong, an exemplar of the well-nourished and well-trained urban "men of name"—a giant in the eyes of peasants. The scouts located them in the three distinctive geographical regions of southern Palestine. In the Negev were the Amalekites. These were the great Negev opponents of David, the antagonists of the account of David's rise to power from his own court (1 Samuel 15—2 Samuel 1). In the highland resided the Hittites, the Jebusites, and the Amorites. These were urban-based Canaanites in J's conception. The Canaanites by name dwelt along the coast and in the Jordan valley. So according to the scouts, the population of Canaan was an urban population just as it was earlier in J's history.

1. The RSV translation "the people who dwell in the land" is too general. The singular *yosheb* ("inhabitant") does not match the singular *am* ("people"). The phrase *yosheb ba'arets* in many uses connotes the established and elite holders of the land, who had been granted their tenure directly from the royal family and other high families of the territory. See Norman K. Gottwald, *The Tribes of Yahweh: A Sociology of the Religion of Liberated Israel, 1250–1050 b.c.* (Maryknoll, N.Y.: Orbis Books, 1979), 512–34.

The most obvious omission from the scouts' report was the Philistines. Surely the scouts must have seen the Philistines on the coast as well. But J is not describing all the inhabitants of this region, only those inhabitants who represented in a schematic way the urban royal culture epitomized by Canaan and Egypt, traced back to Cain, and largely opposed to David. Those who were allied with David in his rise to power and his royal dominion were not so conceived. The Philistines were in league with David, as J made clear in his history of Isaac. For the scouts, the Amalekites loomed large and the Philistines were nonexistent. In actuality, for David the Amalekites proved relatively insignificant, while the Philistines were essential to his rule.

The bedouin had now entered the region that played a crucial role in the rise of David and his early exercise and consolidation of power. David ruled first in Hebron, the main city of the Judahite highlands. J has already featured a figure who represented the bedouin of southern Judah and the Negev, who were allied with David and clustered about Hebron as one of their centers. This was Abram. Now J addresses another significant component of the urban elite of Hebron. While all the other scouts were fearful of the large Canaanites they had seen and attempted to dissuade the bedouin from attacking, Caleb alone urged the force to invade. Caleb is introduced for the first time in J with this approach to Hebron. He was known at the time of David as the ancestor of what was probably the dominant family of Hebron. He is viewed in a positive light by J's treatment. In fact, he is made unique among all the twenty-first generation who had left Egypt. He alone (assuming Joshua does not appear in J), excluding even Moses, would join the twenty-second generation in taking the land of David's Israel. J is clearly catering to a family who doubtless played an important role in supporting David's rise to power in and over Hebron and the rest of Judah.

It is likely that Nabal in 1 Samuel 25 was a Calebite sheikh near the center of power in that influential clan of Hebron. By marrying Nabal's wife Abigail, David became a part of the clan and thereby laid the ground for his assumption of rule in Hebron. Calebite support did not fall readily to David, who sought it continually. If Abigail was David's sister, as seems probable, then David began by sanctioning her marriage to the Calebite chief, to David's potential benefit. Then when the chief failed to support him, he had him killed and took his place in the clan. The chief Hebron clan still resisted: the center of Absalom's revolt against David was in Hebron, and Absalom's chief officer in that revolt was Amasa, a son of Nabal. Following Absalom's death, David was quick to appoint him commander of his army. Chronicles preserves genealogies that transfer David to the Calebite line. It is clear that David greatly desired this political tie, and it is therefore not surprising that his cult history (J) should give Caleb such a unique role near its conclusion.[2]

Discouraged by the scouts, the bedouin longed to return to Egypt, to reverse the course of Yahweh's deliverance. This desire they expressed immediately as a threat to Moses' authority. "Let us appoint a head [instead of Moses], that we might return to Egypt," they said. Yahweh went to Moses and said, "How long will this people spurn me? How long will they not trust me?" The question of trust directs attention back to one of the main issues in the commissioning of Moses, the necessity of leading the bedouin in Egypt to trust in his and Yahweh's headship for the creation of a nation over against Egypt. "Let me kill them with a plague, so that I can make you into a nation greater and stronger than they," Yahweh responded. The only way Yahweh could have done this was to make Moses the husband of hundreds of wives. J seems almost to be playing with his portrayal of Moses as the most humble man in the world, a man whose authority was not his own but wholly from Yahweh. Only such a man could have a hundred wives and thousands of children without threatening the reproductive prerogative of the creator of human beings.

Moses wasn't humble as we would use the term. He was the head sheikh of an extremely large encampment of potentially powerful bedouin. He had killed at least one man. J does not portray Moses so much as humble. Rather, J portrays him as in complete agreement with and subordinate to the conception of power represented by Yahweh and the political values safeguarded by that power.

Moses made this subordination clear by the response to Yahweh's proposal to make him the father of thousands: "If you do that, the Egyptians and the Canaanites will hear about it and will say that it was because you were not powerful enough to bring this people to the land you had granted them that you slaughtered them in the desert." In a typical Hebrew complaint on behalf of his people, Moses appealed to Yahweh's self-respect. He specified that self-respect in the main terms of power in which J is interested: that the overturning of Egypt and Canaan represented the establishment of a new consciousness and a new socioeconomic order in history— the epitome of David's most grandiose nationalist claim.

Moses went on, "Let your power be great, and manifest in mercy rather than by killing this people." Moses, faithful to the purposes of this Yahweh as always, was trying to refocus Yahweh's attention on his main purpose: the saving of these offspring of Abram for the land grant to Abram. Moses

2. Jon D. Levenson, "I Samuel 25 as Literature and as History," *Catholic Biblical Quarterly* 40 (1978): 11–28; and Jon D. Levenson and Baruch Halpern, "The Political Import of David's Marriages," *Journal of Biblical Literature* 99 (1980): 507–18.

was reminding him that if he killed this people to make Moses the father of thousands, he was running the risk of ruining his reputation. This would be disastrous from Yahweh's point of view. It was essential to Yahweh's purpose that all humanity, especially the kings of the world, not just the king of Egypt, should "know" him. It would not do for them to know him as the killer of the people delivered by the overthrow of the king of Egypt.

Hence Yahweh concluded with a great emphasis on the visibility of his "glory." "I swear, as I live and my glory fills the whole world, that all the men who saw my glory and my signs which I did in Egypt and the desert will not see the land I granted to their ancestors, and all those who spurned me will not see it. Only Caleb, who has a different spirit"—the spirit of Moses, presumably—"will I bring to the land and have him take possession of it." The seeing of Yahweh's power and purpose provided the occasion for setting apart the generation that saw the fall of Egypt from the generation that took the land, the twenty-first from the twenty-second, with Caleb, the head of the dominant family of Hebron, binding the two. It was to be the sons and daughters, not the fathers, who would receive the land grant. If Moses was not to be the father of a new generation, neither would the fathers of the generation that would have been replaced participate in the fulfillment of the history. The twenty-second generation is the last one in J's history and comes closest to representing J's present, the time of David.

Yahweh then instructed the bedouin that, "since the Amalekites and the Canaanites are ensconced in the land," they were to turn about and head back to the Sup Sea where the king of Egypt had been killed. Our historian's continued attention on the Amalekites comes not from Yahweh's or the bedouin's inability to defeat them, but from the historian's particular interest in preserving them for David to deal with in his own age.

J focuses on two particular peoples toward the end of the desert trek: the Amalekites and the Edomites, those who represented the greatest threat and challenge to David on the southwest and southeast of his center of power and whose conquest was essential to his rise in power. J's awareness of this importance of the Amalekites and the Edomites is reflected in the curses that conclude his whole history, curses against Edom, the Amalekites, and the offspring of Cain.

The bedouin were so shocked by Yahweh's intent to let their generation die in the desert that they determined to invade the land after all. This was in disobedience to Yahweh's most recent instruction to turn back to the desert. Moses reminded them that such contravention would not succeed: "Don't go up in the highland. Yahweh will not be in your midst. The Amalekites and the Canaanites are there in front of you, and you will fall."

They insisted. The Amalekites and the Canaanites descended on them and killed many. David would have much mopping up left to do in the Negev.

As J's history rapidly approaches its conclusion, allusions back to the beginning of the history accumulate. There are also numerous internal allusions toward the end of the history; several terms in the episodes that immediately precede the end of the history flash forward to the last episode of Balaam.

This method of tying his history together with allusions is one key to understanding the rebellion of certain sons of Reuben. These sons were "men of name." They were offspring of Reuben, the firstborn son of Israel. Presumably this made them feel superior with the normal (rejected by J) sense of superiority belonging to the firstborn. Their names indicate the interest of "men of name" in procreation. One was Eliab, "my god is a father." Another was Abiram (a name nearly identical to Abram), meaning "my father is high." A third was On, whose name was virtually the same as Onan's, the son of Judah who refused to maintain his brother's name through offspring. While these names are in themselves ambiguous and could suggest that their holders deferred to Yahweh (as they have previously), in this context they mean the opposite: as sons of the firstborn Reuben and as potential fathers themselves, they venerated the god of virility and procreation. (The significance of the name Dathan is not certain.)

Moses summoned these men, and they refused to come. "We will not come up," they said at the beginning and the end of their short response. In Hebrew their refusal carried the double meaning of "we will not go up" to Moses or the land. This double meaning itself had two meanings. What they meant was that they would refuse to "go up" to Palestine. What they did not mean was what happened to them for refusing: indeed they did not go up but down.

The rest of their response was also filled with irony. "Is it not enough that you have brought us up from a land oozing milk and honey to kill us in the desert, that you should also persist in acting out the role of commander-in-chief over us? You have not brought us to a land oozing milk and honey, and we won't go up." According to J, Egypt was not a land oozing milk and honey. In addition, these men accused Moses of killing them. This too runs directly against the fundamental thesis of J's history, that pharaoh's impressment of the bedouin into corvée labor was tantamount to murder, from which Moses then delivered them. The charge that Moses persisted in acting as a commander-in-chief refers directly back to the moment when Moses, having killed the Egyptian taskmaster and thus shown that pharaoh's slavery was murder, returned the next day to adjudicate a dispute between his kin and was confronted with the question, "Who made you master and judge over us?" The word "master" used then was the basis of the verb "act as commander-in-chief" now. Just as the bedouin disputants at that time first rejected Moses' authority, so now the sons of Reuben did. This would be the last time that the bedouin would do so in J's history. The consequence was too dreadful to risk repeating.

Moses became angry and said to Yahweh, "Don't turn to their offering. They have no just complaint against me." Moses' request put his opponents—offspring of the firstborn Reuben—in the position of Cain—the prototype of all firstborn—whose offering Yahweh did not notice.[3]

Rebuffed by these men, Moses went to them, taking many of his seventy magistrates with him. J focuses on Dathan and Abiram. As Moses approached, they came out of their tent with their wives and children to meet him. Moses minced no words. "By this you will *know*"—Moses was addressing the bystanders—"that Yahweh sent me to do these things, and that I didn't think them up myself. If these people die a natural death, then Yahweh did not send me; but if Yahweh creates a new thing[4] and the ground opens its mouth and swallows them, and they go down to the underworld alive, then you will know that these men have spurned Yahweh [and not just me]." "People" is *adam* in Hebrew, and "ground" is *adama.* J's diction is the same as at the beginning of his history, when the first human *(adam)* was formed from the ground *(adama).* That Dathan, Abiram, and their families are swallowed up by the ground springs directly from the beginning: what was taken from the ground and given life could be returned to the ground if it refused to recognize the significance of Yahweh as the creator of live human beings and the deliverer of humans condemned to a living death by the extortion of their labor. It is fitting that the last of the bedouin resisters should be treated to a fate that directs attention back to the beginning of the history.

The motif of "swallowing" also makes a person think of food. As J's history progresses to its conclusion, especially in the twenty-first generation, more and more is made of the bearing of the history on food production, distribution, and acquisition. Most of the episodes in the desert have revolved around food. If the beneficiaries of Yahweh's deliverance may be regarded as so many "swallowers," then those who reject that deliverance might justly be swallowed. The human being was created as a living *nephesh.* The RSV translates *nephesh* with the unfortunate word "soul." A

3. The mention of offering became the basis of an elaborate expansion of J's narrative by later priestly writers, which makes Numbers 16 much longer than the part treated here.

4. The Hebrew expression twice uses the root *bara'.* This root is usually regarded as characteristic of P, as it is the word translated "created" in Genesis 1. It probably appears, however, in J in Gen. 6:7.

nephesh, however, is not so much a soul as an appetite. J's history could be characterized as the history of how this *nephesh* and all the others like it came to be fed—from the first pleasure orchard to the land of milk and honey.

The Hebrew verb *bala'* ("swallow") also flashes forward to Balaam, whose name looks at first as though it was formed on the same root: *bil'am*. This is an example of how J begins to employ and concentrate wordplays at the end of his work.

Now the Bible's first history proceeds to deal with the last of the kingly resisters, the final royal interdictions that recapitulate the resistance of pharaoh: the king of Edom and the king of Moab. The king of Edom came first, not only because he was the first bedouin encountered as Israel continued their trek but also because his name furthers the wordplay of the preceding episode between *adam* and *adama*. The king of Mo*ab*, the nation whose name J thinks contains the word "father" *(ab)*, is saved until last.

Repulsed from the northern Negev, the bedouin moved east toward Edomite territory and halted at the border of Edom. Moses sent envoys to the king of Edom. That Edom had a king in J is a reflection of the time of David. When the Iron Age villages first appeared in highland Palestine, the territory of Edom was also experiencing the expansion of settlement. Like western Palestine, it did not come under royal dominion (that is, the standing right to tax the agricultural product of fixed villages and to establish an urban capital on that basis) until the eleventh century B.C.E. Moses' envoys requested leave to transit Edomite territory by means of the Royal Highway, in Hebrew "the Way of the King." Their request was stated in generous terms: along the way they would consume no food or water belonging to the king of Edom. Their offer was no doubt genuine, although there may have been an element of hyperbole which the king of Edom, sharing their culture, would have recognized: perhaps they would take just a bit of food or water. The king of Edom refused transit on the King's Highway. The envoys offered to pay for water, but still the king refused.[5]

Following their rejection by the king of Edom, the bedouin embarked on a wide swing to the east, around the territory of Edom. This way lay out in the eastern desert, a region as arid and hostile to the traveler as the Sinai desert. The people became short-tempered. Yahweh, having run out of

---

5. The next brief episode probably does not come from J, even though like much of this part of J it concerns a section of the Negev of great importance to David and contains words and motifs reminiscent of J. The king of Arad, a city in the Negev, attacked the bedouin and took prisoners. The bedouin took an oath: if Yahweh would put Arad in their hands, they would completely destroy all its supporting villages. Yahweh heeded their plea and delivered up the king of Arad to them. They desolated the area and named it Hormah, desolation. The difficulty with including this section in J is that it sends the bedouin back in the wrong direction, breaking the logic of the journey around Edom that comes next.

patience long ago, sent burning snakes—with inflaming and deadly bites—to afflict the bedouin. When they acknowledged their wrong and that Moses stood for Yahweh, Moses interceded for his people and at the instruction of Yahweh fabricated a bronze snake as a prophylactic talisman. If persons bitten and dying looked at the snake, they recovered.

The snakes are an allusion to the snake in the pleasure orchard. The same word *(nahash)* is used in both places, though there are many Hebrew words for snake. The original J snake launched the history of good and bad. These snakes in the desert help bring the J history to its conclusion. Just as the snake at the beginning of the history was a talking animal, so the ass of Balaam, soon to appear, would be a talking animal. Just as the voice of the snake led to the first curse, so these snakes lead into the "divination" of Balaam (J uses the root *qasam*, which is parallel to the word *nahash*, meaning both "snake" and "divination") that produces the last of the blessings and curses. That such a word "snake" would flash backward and forward in the history parallels the technique seen with the word "swallow." J expects his audience to pay attention to the word *nahash* (snake, divination), since the word for bronze *(nehoshet)* also sounds as though it was formed from the same root.

As the bedouin proceeded north on the edge of the desert, they approached the territory of Moab, also under the rule of a king. In this final episode, J returns to the pivotal issue of his history, the relationship between curse and blessing in the history of royalty. Yahweh's oath to Abram stated: "Those who bless you I will bless, and those who curse you I will curse." This plan made possible the beginning of the amelioration of the curses of the first fourteen generations. An important early incident in the implementation of this plan showed a Canaanite king, the king of Sodom, who did not bless Abram, and a king of (Jeru)Salem who did. All along, we have been particularly attentive to the royal successors of one or the other, especially the Egyptian king of Joseph's generation and the Egyptian king of Moses' generation. Now we have come to the last generation and the last king presented in the history. This king wanted one thing: to curse the blessed offspring of Israel, to reverse the blessing of Abram.

26

The Triumph of the Blessing

(Numbers 22:1—24:22a)

Moab became quite worried about the people, because of their numbers, and conceived a loathing for the bedouin Israelites. Moab said to the sheikhs of Midian, "Soon this community is going to lick up everything around us the way an ox licks up grass in the field."

At that time Moab's king was Balak, the son of Zippor. He sent envoys to Balaam, the son of Beor, at Petor, by the river in the land of the sons of his people, to summon him. "Some people have gotten out of Egypt, and now they are covering the surface of the earth and have taken up residence just opposite us. So come curse these people for me, for they are mightier than we. It may be that then we can attack them and drive them away from the land. For I know that whoever you bless is blessed, and whoever you curse is cursed."

With divination fee in hand, the Moabite and Midianite sheikhs traveled off, came to Balaam, and repeated to him Balak's words. He said to them, "Spend the night here, and I will give you an answer, according to what Yahweh says to me." So the Moabite chiefs stayed there with Balaam.

God came to Balaam and said, "Who are these men with you?"

Balaam said to God, "Balak, the son of Zippor, the king of Moab, has sent them to me with the message, 'The people who got out of Egypt now cover the surface of the earth. Come curse them for me so that I can go out in battle against them and drive them away.' "

God said to Balaam, "You may not go with them. You may not curse the people, because they are blessed."

Balaam got up in the morning and said to Balak's chiefs, "Go back to your country. Yahweh has refused to allow me to go with you."

The Moabite chiefs came back to Balak and said, "Balaam refused to go with us."

Balak again sent chiefs, this time more numerous and weighty than the previous ones. They came to Balaam and said to him, "Thus said Balak, son of Zippor, 'Do not decline coming to me. I can make you highly wealthy and honored. Whatever you say to me, I will do. Just come and curse these people for me.' "

Balaam answered Balak's servants, "Even if Balak gave me the whole of his household, silver and gold, I would not be able to defy the order of Yahweh my god, in a little thing or great. Stay here tonight, you as well, that I may know what Yahweh will say to me this time."

That night God came to Balaam and said to him, "If these men have come to summon you, go ahead and go with them. Yet you must do what I tell you."

In the morning, Balaam got up, saddled his ass, and went with the Moabite chiefs. God became angry that he was going, so the genie of Yahweh planted himself in the road as an opponent to him. While he was riding on his ass, with his two boys with him, his ass saw the genie of Yahweh planted in the road, with a drawn sword in his hand. The ass veered out of the road and walked into the field. Balaam beat the ass to swerve it back to the road.

The genie of Yahweh stood in a narrow lane in the vineyards, with a stone wall on each side. When the ass saw the genie of Yahweh, it squeezed against the wall, and in the process squeezed Balaam's foot against the wall. He beat it again.

The genie of Yahweh passed them again and stood in a tight spot where there was no room to lean to either side. When the ass saw the genie of Yahweh, it just crouched down beneath Balaam. Balaam became incensed and beat the ass with his stick.

Then Yahweh opened the mouth of the ass and it said to Balaam, "What have I done to you to make you beat me these three times?"

Balaam said to the ass, "Because you have been playing games with me. If only there was a sword in my hand I would kill you."

The ass said to Balaam, "Am I not your ass, on whom you have ridden all along until today? Have I been in the habit of treating you this way?"

He said, "No."

Then Yahweh uncovered Balaam's eyes, and he saw the genie of Yahweh planted in the road with his drawn sword in his hand, and Balaam bowed low and did obeisance.

The genie of Yahweh said to him, "For what reason did you beat your ass these three times? I came out as your opponent because the way was [. . .] before me. The ass saw me and veered out of my way these three times. If it had not veered out of my way, I would have killed you and let it live."

Balaam said to the genie of Yahweh, "I have sinned, for I did not know you were planted in front of me in the road. Now, if you regard my going as evil, I will go back."

The genie of Yahweh said to Balaam, "Go with the men. Just be sure you say only what I tell you to." So Balaam went with Balak's chiefs.

When Balak heard that Balaam was coming, he went out to meet him at the Moabite city on the Arnon border, at the edge of the territory. Balak said to Balaam, "Did I not urgently send to summon you? Why didn't you come to me? Do you doubt I can give you wealth and honor?"

Balaam said to Balak, "Now that I've come to you, do you think I will be able to say just anything? I can speak only the word that Yahweh places in my mouth."

Balaam went with Balak, and they came to Qiryat-hutsot, the City of Streets. There Balak sacrificed cattle and sheep and handed out portions to Balaam and the chiefs who were with him. When morning came, Balak took Balaam and led him up to Bamot-Baal. From there he saw the edge of the people.

Balaam said to Balak, "Build me seven altars here, and prepare for me seven bulls and seven rams."

Balak did as Balaam said. Then Balak and Balaam sacrificed a bull and a ram on each altar.

Balaam said to Balak, "Station yourself by your burnt offering while I go off. Perhaps Yahweh will meet me, in which case I will report to you the word Yahweh has me see."

He went to a bare height. God did meet Balaam, who said to him, "I have arranged the seven altars and sacrificed a bull and a ram on each altar."

Yahweh placed a word in the mouth of Balaam and said, "Go back to Balak and speak thus."

He returned to him and found him standing next to his burnt offering with all the Moabite chiefs. He then pronounced this oracle:[1]

Balak has brought me from the East and told me to curse Jacob and malign Israel. How can I curse whom God has not cursed, and how can I malign whom Yahweh has not maligned? From the top of the cliffs I see him, and from the hills I behold him, a people distinct among the nations. Who can count even a fraction of the offspring of Israel? May my posterity be like his!

Balak said to Balaam, "What are you doing to me? I brought you here to curse my enemies, and here you are blessing them."

He answered, "Do I not have to watch out to speak only what Yahweh puts in my mouth?"

Balak said to him, "Come with me to another spot from which to see. You've only seen the edge of them. You haven't seen all of them. You can curse them for me from there."

So he brought him to the lookout ground on the top of Pisgah. He built seven altars and sacrificed a bull and a ram on each altar.

He said to Balak, "Station yourself here by your burnt offering while I wait for something to happen over there."

Balaam did encounter God. He placed a word in his mouth and said, "Go back to Balak and say thus . . . ."

He returned to him and found him standing next to his burnt offering with the Moabite chiefs. Balak said to him, "What did Yahweh say?"

In response, Balaam pronounced this oracle:

Now hear this, Balak. God is not a man: he does not say one thing and do another. He told me to bless. He has blessed, and I cannot change it. He sees nothing wrong with Israel. Yahweh is with them. Their battle shout is as good as any king's. God has got them out of Egypt, and there is no divination against them. They are like a lion stalking its prey. It will not relax until it eats it up and drinks the blood of slain, so watch out.

1. The texts of Balaam's archaic blessings and curses are of a different kind from the text of J's narrative. J probably adopted them, perhaps from another source as he had the blessings of Israel and the Song of Miriam, and adapted them for his purpose. In their present form, their meaning is not always clear and thus is the subject of significant debate. Because of these difficulties, we have chosen to paraphrase their main points rather than attempt to translate them verbatim. The translation is intended as schematic and not as a contribution to the ongoing debate.

Balak said to Balaam, "If you can't manage to curse them, at least don't go ahead and bless them."

Balaam answered Balak, "Didn't I tell you I would have to do everything Yahweh told me to?"

Balak said to him, "Come on, let me take you to still another spot. Perhaps it will seem proper to God to have you curse them for me from there."

Balak took Balaam to the top of Peor, overlooking the desert. Balaam said to Balak, "Build me here seven altars, and prepare for me here seven bulls and seven rams." Balak did as Balaam said, and made an offering of a bull and a ram on each altar.

Balaam saw that it seemed good to Yahweh to bless Israel, so he did not walk off as he had the previous two times but instead gazed out intently toward the desert. Balaam raised his eyes and saw Israel encamped by tribes. The spirit of God descended on him and he pronounced this oracle:

> The oracle of Balaam, the man whose eye is opened. The oracle who sees what God sees, with his face to the ground but eyes uncovered. How good are your tents, Jacob, and your encampments, Israel. Like extended fertile wadies, like pleasure orchards beside the river, like aloes planted by Yahweh, like cedars beside the waters. Water shall flow from him, and his offspring shall be like many waters. His king shall be higher than Agag, and his kingdom more exalted. God has brought them out of Egypt. They shall devour their national adversaries. Blessed be everyone who blesses you, and cursed be everyone who curses you.

Balak slapped his hands together in a fit of anger and said to Balaam, "I summoned you to curse my enemies, and here you have done nothing but bless them these three times. Get out of here. I said I would weigh you down with wealth and honor, but Yahweh has held you back from these weighty awards."

Balaam said to Balak, "Did I not already tell the envoys you sent to me, 'Even if Balak gave me the whole of his household, silver and gold, I would not be able to defy the order of Yahweh my god, to perform good or evil on my own'? What Yahweh said, I said. Okay, I'll go back to my people. But first, let me advise you what these people are going to do to your people in time." He then pronounced this oracle:

> The oracle of Balaam, the man whose eye is opened. The oracle who sees what God sees, with his face to the ground but eyes uncovered. I see, but not now. I behold, but not the present. Israel shall crush Moab.

Then this:

> Edom shall become someone else's possession, his enemies' possession, while Israel shall gain wealth and might.

Then he saw the Amalekites, and pronounced this oracle:

> The head of the nations is the Amalekites, but its rear will be the booty of the destroyer.

Then he saw the Kenites, and pronounced this oracle:

> Your dwellings last and you have nested among the crags, yet you are for burning, Cain.

Then Balaam left and returned to his locale, and Balak went his way.

For the final episode of the Bible's first history, J presents a grand expansion of the last clause of the blessing of Abram on which his history pivots. This finale features a king, a son of Shem this time, who was forced to bless Israel despite himself. If this determined king could not accomplish his purpose to curse, and the king of Egypt was dead, then what king could accomplish his curse? If no king could effect a curse, then the second clause of Yahweh's blessing of Abram was hardly any longer applicable. The implication of the final episode of the history is that to the extent no one may curse, all may be blessed.[2] The blessing that was initiated through Abram may now, through David, imbue the world and history. David's self-understanding was grand indeed.[3]

Historians are nearly unanimous in regarding the Balaam episode of Numbers 22—24 as a composite of J and E. The main reason for their conclusion is that both Yahweh and Elohim are used frequently. This is not by itself sufficient reason, since both strands use both terms. If we look at a typical example of one of the supposed E passages, we will see the difficulty of this literary assignment. One such passage is Num. 22:7–14. The sheikhs of Moab and Midian came from Balak to hire Balaam. Balaam told them to remain with him for the night, so he could hear what Yahweh had to tell him. That night Elohim came to Balaam and conversed with him. Proponents of the view that this passage comes from E point out that in addition to the use of Elohim, God appeared to Balaam at night, and it is assumed that this was in a dream. But no mention is made of a dream. In J, Yahweh has appeared to people at night. One can cite Yahweh's tussle with Jacob at the Jabbok during the night as well as the nightlong deliverance of the bedouin from Egypt, the climactic moment of the whole J history. The conversation between Balaam and God is much more in line with the familiarity between people and Yahweh in J than with the distance between people and Elohim in E.

What other explanation for the use of Yahweh and Elohim in the history of Balaam might be possible? If we examine the episode closely (leaving

2. From the beginning of history, Yahweh has striven to catch up with human events, to become full author, not responder. With this final episode, Yahweh catches up.

3. Many scholars have been dissatisfied with the idea that J originally concluded with Balaam, because such a conclusion does not seem to say anything about the great themes we have come to think of when we think of the Pentateuch, such as covenant and conquest. As we have seen, these are not the main themes of J. In fact, they are not present at all. An ending with Balaam fits the emphases of J. The history concludes at just the point when the bedouin would cross the Jordan to march up to Jerusalem. For a work that concentrates so heavily on the Negev, this approach to Jerusalem might seem strange. But it makes perfect sense in a work that is set to catapult its audience into a future whose glory is centered in Jerusalem.

aside the poetic oracles, which parallel Yahweh and Elohim as a matter of course), we find that with only a few exceptions Elohim is used in narrative and Yahweh in speech.[4] There is one other place in J's history where both Yahweh and Elohim are used. That is in the very first episode, in the pleasure orchard (chapter 7). There Yahweh is used in narrative (along with the qualifier *elohim,* a god) and Elohim in speech, as a byproduct of J's characterization of the first set of seven generations as a period when humans did not know the name Yahweh. In order to round out his history, J has borrowed this feature of the first episode and reproduced it in mirror image in the last episode.

There are only two talking animals in the Bible, the snake at the beginning of J and the ass at the end of J. In the scene with the snake, all the occasions in which only Elohim is used are in speech. In the scene with the ass, all the occasions in which only Yahweh is used are likewise in speech. The mirror image expresses the basic reversal of the history with which its final episode is preoccupied, the reversal of the general curse into a general blessing. Just as the speech of the snake led directly to the three curses, with four to follow (on Cain, the men of name, Ham and Canaan, and the tower builders), so the speech of the ass leads directly to the three blessings, with four quickly following.

The exceptions are the following. The name Elohim is used in speech in Num. 22:38 and 23:27. The first represents Balaam's first address to Balak, when Balak didn't yet know who Yahweh was, and occurs with the expression "place a word in my mouth." The second represents the only time Balak had occasion to mention God, and occurs with the expression "in the eyes of." Balak did not call God Yahweh because, like pharaoh, he did not ever "know" Yahweh. These two exceptions highlight the concern of this episode for "the word which Yahweh will cause me to see," the concern to relate word and view, what is seen to what is said in curse and blessing. The name Yahweh is used in narrative throughout the scene involving the ass. That reverses the usage in the scene with the snake at the beginning of the history. Otherwise, Yahweh is used in narrative in Num. 23:5 and 24:1. These balance the two exceptions in the use of Elohim. The first balances the use in 22:38, with the same expression "place a word in my mouth." The second balances the use in 23:27, with the same expression "in the eyes of." That leaves one genuine anomaly, the use of Yahweh in narrative in 23:16. This anomaly is removed by comparing the

4. The difference between narrative and speech is of course not the difference between J and E. It would be quite a coincidence indeed if in three whole chapters J just happened to be all speech and E all narrative. Even a brief reading of the episode shows that this is not the case.

Greek translation, which uses God. The Greek here is consistent with the overall scheme and therefore appears to represent the original Hebrew of J.

Like pharaoh, the king of Moab was afraid of the bedouin offspring of Israel because of their multitude. He turned to some sheikhs of Midian, bedouin chiefs in alliance with Moab. Part of Midian was still allied with Balak, as most were apparently allied with David. Balak complained that the assemblage of the offspring of Israel would eat up his entire realm as an ox eats up the grass of a field. He sent envoys to Balaam[5] at a place called Petor. Petor was located "by the river in the land of the sons of his people," a statement that does not seem to make complete sense. One would expect the location to be more specific, especially since Balaam's first oracle locates him in Aram, or Syria. Many historians emend "his people" (Heb.: *ammo*) to "Ammon": "by the river in the land of the Ammonites." This is possible. We might ask, however, what sense the Hebrew as it stands makes in relation to the rest of J. Examine the name Balaam in Hebrew—*Bilam*. J could construe Balaam as composed of *bil* ("not") and *am* ("a people"): "not a people." Balaam thus means not a particular people. This meaning of his name is confirmed by Balaam's origin, by the river in the land of the offspring of his people, which are not any particular people. If Balaam belongs to no particular people, he can be thought of as representing all people, as he does in pronouncing the unintended blessing on behalf of the last hostile king in J's history.

Balak instructed his envoys to deliver this message: "Come curse this people for me. They are stronger than I. Perhaps I will be able to beat them and drive them out of the land." Note how similar this language is to what the pharaoh who "did not know Joseph" said to his advisers. Balak continued, "I know that whom you bless will be blessed and whom you curse will be cursed." Nowhere in J do we get a better sense of the weighty effect of words spoken in a solemn ceremony for the sake of their magical power. Words spoken in such a context make reality. This was the significance of Yahweh's oath to Abram, with its grant of land and its introduction

---

5. It is possible J did not make up the name Balaam. About a decade ago, archaeologists discovered a rather lengthy but fragmentary text in the Jordan valley, written about 700 B.C.E., some three hundred years or so after J, that refers to a prophet named Balaam. Unfortunately nothing can be extracted from this text regarding the nature of this Balaam other than his name. For most historians, this chance discovery has been taken to indicate that Balaam was the name of a traditional mantic figure in this area and that J made use of this traditional name and figure in composing the Balaam episode. It is less likely, though possible, that the name became traditional as a result of J's coinage. See Baruch A. Levine, "The Balaam Inscription from Deir 'Alla: Historical Aspects," in *Biblical Archaeology Today: Proceedings of the International Congress on Biblical Archaeology, Jerusalem, April 1984* (Jerusalem: Israel Exploration Society, 1985), 326–39; and Jo Ann Hackett, "Some Observations on the Balaam Tradition at Deir 'Alla," *Biblical Archaeologist* 49 (1986): 216–22.

of nothing less than the blessing. This is the significance of the solemn word upon which Balak now wished to draw.

The envoys from Moab took payment for Balaam's divinatory services in hand and went to Balaam. When they had repeated their message, he responded, "Stay here for the night. I'll answer you in the morning the way Yahweh tells me to."

Balaam arose in the morning and summoned the envoys. "Go home," he told them. "Yahweh has refused to allow me to go with you."

The envoys returned to Balak and conveyed Balaam's response. Balak was not to be dissuaded. This time he sent to Balaam "many and weighty chiefs." J's emphasis is on "weighty," which in Hebrew involves the same root as the wealth and honor that Balak the king presumed to be able to offer Balaam. His presumption contrasts with Yahweh's ability to make people "weighty," as when Yahweh, having blessed Abram, made him "weighty" with wealth and honor in Egypt. The envoys came to Balaam and said, "Thus says Balak: 'Don't refuse to come to me. I will make you extremely wealthy and give you very high honor [both these meanings are based on the root meaning weighty]. Whatever you say, I will do. Just come and curse this people for me.' "

Balaam responded, "Even if Balak were to give me the whole contents of his kingdom, silver and gold, I would not be able to defy the instruction of Yahweh my god, in a little thing or great. Stay here again tonight, so that I may know what Yahweh will say to me this time."

This time God said, "If the men have come to call you, go with them. But do only what I tell you to do."

Starting in the pleasure orchard, what humans see has been of utmost importance to J. Now the historian's interest in "seeing" comes to its grand climax.[6] The issue is what a person sees when seeing Israel, this horde of delivered corvée workers. Balak had summoned Balaam to "see" the Israelite bedouin as a cursed people and so to define them as such. Balaam was forced by Yahweh to "see" them instead as blessed by Yahweh. Before Balaam arrived to do not Balak's but Yahweh's bidding, our historian reinforces the rule that Balaam saw only what Yahweh made him see. This he does in the incident involving Balaam's ass and the genie of Yahweh.

In the morning, Balaam saddled his ass and went with the envoys. As the group journeyed, the genie of Yahweh positioned himself in front of Balaam's ass with a sword in his hand. The ass trotted out of the path and into the field. Balaam struck the ass to get it back on the path. Eventually the group came to a narrow path with vineyard walls on each side. Again

---

6. Robert Alter, *The Art of Biblical Narrative* (New York: Basic Books, 1981), 104–7. Alter's treatment of God as the exclusive source of vision in the Balaam episode is to the point, even though he does not relate it to the rest of J.

the genie stood before the ass, which attempted to squeeze by the genie on one side and so scraped Balaam's foot against the wall. Balaam hit it again. Finally the genie sprang ahead and took up position in a passage so narrow that there was no room at all to squeeze by. When the ass approached, it simply stopped and squatted down. Balaam took his stick and struck it harder than ever. He was incensed: "If I had a sword in my hand, I would kill you."

During all of this, the genie was invisible to Balaam. The ass was mystified. It complained, "Am I not the ass you have ridden all your life? Did I ever do these things to you for nothing?" Balaam admitted it had not.

Then Yahweh opened the eyes of Balaam and he saw the genie there with his sword. He fell down on his face in obeisance. The genie spoke. "Why have you struck the ass these three times? I have set myself to oppose you intentionally. The ass saw me and rightly turned aside. If it had not, I would have killed you and let it live." We are reminded of the eyes of the first humans being opened in the pleasure orchard. On that occasion, the opening of their eyes led to the humans exercising their own godlike procreative powers, causing Yahweh to curse them. In the concluding episode of the history, everything is reversed. It is the human Balaam, who tries to curse those Yahweh has blessed, who has his eyes opened to see Yahweh and his own impotence to curse. As the tree of life in the original pleasure garden was protected by a flashing sword following the institution of the curse, so in the era of the blessing Balaam is prevented from cursing by the appearance of Yahweh's genie with a sword in his hand. And whereas it was the talking snake that lured the first humans into being cursed with death by Yahweh, now it is another talking creature that seeks to prevent Balaam from being killed by the genie with the sword in his hand.

Balaam confessed, "I have sinned. I did not know that you were stationed before me in the way. If you don't want me to go to Balak, I will go back." The genie then repeated what Yahweh had said to Balaam in the night, to go but speak only what Yahweh told him to speak.[7]

Balaam arrived, and Balak went out to meet him on the northern boundary of Moab. Balak questioned Balaam: "Why didn't you come right away? Am I not able to give you great wealth and honor?" Balaam was quick to respond: "I'm here now but I can only say what God puts in my mouth." Then Balak and Balaam went together to a "city of streets," where Balak had a great sacrifice performed to solemnize the pronouncement of

---

7. "It seems fairly clear that the ass in this episode plays the role of Balaam—beholding divine visions with eyes unveiled—to Balaam's Balak" (Alter, *The Art of Biblical Narrative*, 106).

Balaam. The next morning he took Balaam up on a height from which he could get a good view of the passing bedouin.

The first thing Balak did was to perform seven sacrifices at the instruction of Balaam. J is a history of the world, with Israel's cult at its center. In his concluding scene, he makes certain that the disclosure of unjust and just royalty defined by Balaam's blessings and curses is accompanied by cultic sacrifice to reflect the cultural assumption that political economy and religious cult embodied the same reality. In true J style, Balak's morning sacrifice involved seven bulls and seven rams on seven altars. Out by the desert and requiring ad hoc altars, they would be forced to construct them out of dirt or unhewn rocks, as Yahweh had prescribed at the desert shrine of Sinai. The seven sacrifices corresponded to the seven blessings and curses by which Balaam would define Israel and its royalty.

Then Balaam told Balak to stand by the altars while he went to find out what Yahweh wanted him to say. J calls that "the word which Yahweh will cause me to see." This is J's way of saying that what Yahweh forced on Balaam was both words and the point of view they represented. When Balaam came to him, Yahweh put a word in his mouth and sent him back to Balak, who was still standing by the sacrifices on the seven altars. Against this backdrop, Balaam pronounced his first oracle:

Balak has brought me from the East and told me to curse Jacob and malign Israel. How can I curse whom God has not cursed, and how can I malign whom Yahweh has not maligned? From the top of the cliffs I see him, and from the hills I behold him, a people distinct among the nations. Who can count even a fraction of the offspring of Israel? May my posterity be like his!

Many of the main J themes appear even in this brief oracle. Balaam avoided the curse, saw Israel from Yahweh's vantage, noted their uniqueness, and was amazed by and envious of their reproductive success.

Balak was shocked and incensed. "What are you doing?" he demanded. "I brought you here to curse my enemies, and here you are blessing them." Balaam answered, "Do I not have to watch out to speak only what Yahweh puts in my mouth?"

Balak, convinced that Balaam was not getting the right picture, said, "Come with me to a different place from which you can see [Israel as Balak saw them]. You've only seen the edges of the horde and not the whole. You can curse them for me from there."

Off they went to the second location, where they built another seven altars and sacrificed another seven bulls and seven rams. Again Balaam left Balak by the altars to go to Yahweh. Yahweh put the words in his mouth and sent him back to Balak. There Balaam uttered his second oracle:

Now hear this, Balak. God is not a man: he does not say one thing and do another. He told me to bless. He has blessed, and I can't change it. He sees nothing wrong with Israel. Yahweh is with them. Their battle shout is as good as any king's. God has got them out of Egypt, and there is no divination against them. They are like a lion stalking its prey, so watch out.

The reiteration of J themes continues. The history began on the note that Yahweh and his creatures were of two different kinds, gods and humans. Here J states it in so many words. The blessing could not be reversed. The people of Israel were mighty militarily despite their lack of palace, temple, and grain-storage facilities. They could even conquer other kingdoms.

Balak was furious. "If you can't curse them, don't say anything at all!" All Balaam could say was that he had told Balak only what Yahweh told him to speak. Balak decided to have one more go at it. Perhaps at some third place the angle would be right and Balaam could get on with his assigned task. So he led him to a mountaintop overlooking a desert wasteland. His strategy was clear: perhaps against this desolate backdrop, the truly desolate character of Israel would be manifest. By this time, Balaam had gotten Yahweh's point and did not need to go off to hear from Yahweh. After the seven altars, seven bulls, and seven rams, Balaam launched into his third oracle:

The oracle of Balaam, the man whose eye is opened. The oracle who sees what God sees, with his face to the ground but eyes uncovered. How good are your tents, Jacob, and your encampments, Israel. Like extended fertile wadies, like pleasure orchards beside the river, like aloes planted by Yahweh, like cedars beside the waters. Water shall flow from him, and his offspring shall be like many waters. His king shall be higher than Agag, and his kingdom more exalted. God has brought them out of Egypt. They shall devour their national adversaries. Blessed be everyone who blesses you, and cursed be everyone who curses you.

Balaam, now able to see with Yahweh's eyes, though with his face to the ground (we recall all that has been said about the face throughout the history), had looked out toward the desolate desert to view this people. They had trekked in the desert all the way from Egypt during the hottest time of the year and had now been forced out into the eastern wastelands of Moab. He might well have seen, as Balak wanted him to, a desolate and God-forsaken people. But what he saw was just the opposite. Instead of a desert, he saw lush gardens, and water everywhere. He saw a people who embodied the closest thing to the pleasure garden of God's original creation since Yahweh desolated the lush region chosen by Lot in the first blessed generation by the destruction of the city and Canaanite subjects of the evil king of Sodom. What Balaam saw as Israel was a national equivalent of the garden of Eden. This final blessing of Israel concluded with the simple restatement of the blessing of Abram.

The mention of Agag ties the blessing directly to the time of David. Agag, according to the history of Saul and of David's rise, was the Amalekite chief killed by Samuel. The direct consequence of Samuel's having to kill him was the anointing of David as king over Israel.[8]

By this time, Balak was livid. "I summoned you to curse my enemies, and you have blessed them three times. Get out of here. I promised you wealth and honor, but Yahweh has deprived you of it."

Balaam responded, "I told you from the beginning that even if you were to give me the whole contents of your kingdom, silver and gold, I would not be able to defy the instruction of Yahweh my god, to perform either good or bad [another theme originating in the pleasure garden] on my own.[9] I'll go, but first let me advise you as to what these people will do to you."

Balaam had pronounced three blessings. Now he would pronounce four curses in staccato progression, the residue of curse in David's blessed world, seven speeches in all. The first fell on Moab, the next on Edom, the next on the Amalekites, and the last on the sons of Cain.[10]

The oracle of Balaam, the man whose eye is opened. The oracle who sees what God sees, with his face to the ground but eyes uncovered. I see, but not now. I behold, but not the present. Israel shall crush Moab.

So much for Moab.

Edom will become someone else's possession, his enemies' possession, while Israel will gain wealth and might.

So much for Edom, whose baleful "blessing" from Isaac is thus reiterated. Next he "saw" the Amalekites:

The head of the nations is the Amalekites, but its rear [posterity and future] will be the booty of the destroyer.

8. As already explained, the emphasis on the killing of the Amalekites in 1 Samuel 15 comes from a post-David source. This source, however, makes use of the references to David's fight against the Amalekites in 1 Samuel 27—2 Samuel 1, from a source contemporary with David.

9. "On my own" is Hebrew "from my heart." The heart is the mind. Balaam had the mind of Yahweh. Hence he contrasts with the divine-human "men of name" in the first set of seven generations, whose minds devised evil, and especially with the king of Egypt, whose mind, in the virtual presence of Yahweh, was sluggish.

10. The cursing of Assyria (Num. 24:22–24) is a later addition.

So much for the Amalekites, the arch opponent of the rising David. Finally Balaam "saw" the "Cainite" (Kenite[11]), the personified son of Cain:

Your dwellings last and you have nested among the crags, yet you are for burning, Cain.

Cain, the untamed metal craftsman who works with fire, is for burning by the fire seen at Sinai. David can get his weapons from elsewhere, including through his bedouin friends. The blessing under David now controls history. So ends the Bible's first history.

---

11. Recall that the "Cainites" (Kenites) were a nomadic group in Palestine who operated as metalworkers in David's time. His control of them was an essential ingredient of his rule. On the relation of these last curses to Judahite tradition, see Hans-Jürgen Zobel, "Beiträge zur Geschichte Gross-Judas im früh- und vordavidischer Zeit," *Supplements to Vetus Testamentum* 28 (1975; Edinburgh Congress Volume, 1974), 268–71.

27

What's Different?

Once J's story—the Bible's first history—has been told this way, it seems a reasonable approach, though it is evident that many aspects of interpretation require further research. The story is clear and compelling enough, however, to raise the question why, with all the scholarly study that has been devoted to J in the past and on which this study depends, J's story line has not previously been presented in this way. It also raises the question of what implications such a story has for the way we think about the Bible. The first question we address in this chapter, the second in the concluding chapter.

What concerned past historians when they studied J? A glance at past agendas of interpretation should furnish some idea of how the present study is indebted to previous studies and how it departs from them.[1] What past historians did with J can best be seen in terms of the questions they undertook to answer. The first question, starting a little under three hundred years ago, was whether there is such a thing as J. Can Genesis and Exodus be separated into components that are then to be regarded as sources or strands combined into the present text? Although this matter was essentially settled a century or more ago, there are still historians for whom this remains the main question and who answer it in the negative, usually by insulating literary analysis from other significant historical issues. Many students still leave classes on the Bible with the impression that what scholars want to prove is whether J exists or not, and with no idea as to what difference it might make one way or the other for how they read the Bible or understand the world.

The next question was what parts of the Bible belong to J. What in

---

1. Many useful recent reviews of the study of J in Pentateuchal literary criticism are available. Brief but excellent is Douglas A. Knight's survey in *The Hebrew Bible and Its Modern Interpreters*, ed. D. A. Knight and G. M. Tucker (Philadelphia: Fortress Press, 1985), 277–82.

Genesis, Exodus, and Numbers comes from J and what doesn't? Like the first question, this one also continues to be asked, but more understandably so. Which literary strand is being dealt with is more evident with some passages than with others. The approach taken in this book has differed from most treatments of this issue. Rather than giving a uniform list of J passages, as is the custom, thus conveying the impression that all J passages are equally easy to identify, some indication has been given as to the relative degree of certainty with which an identification can be made. The weight of interpretation has then fallen on those passages which are more clearly derived from J in the light of the overall interpretation.

The question of what belongs to J leads naturally to another question: where does J end? For a long time it was thought that passages from J were to be found in Joshua, Judges, and 1 and 2 Samuel. At that time it seemed obvious that a historian who made the land grant to Abram so important would conclude with the conquest of that land, in either Joshua or Samuel, or even with the construction of the temple in Kings. In the 1930s and 1940s, however, the studies of the historian Martin Noth showed that these later biblical books all belonged to a single document we now call the Deuteronomistic History, or D. If the strands like J and E were sources for this history, then they were no longer at all visible as such in the present text. Now and then a scholar claims to have found J and E in Joshua or one of the later books, but most others disagree and Noth's view has held the day. Why we end J where we do in our treatment of his document should now be obvious to anyone who has followed the development of the narrative from beginning to end.[2]

Yet another question used to be asked often: is J itself a literary composite? Was there a J-1 and a J-2, and perhaps other Js, which were combined into what we call J? One historian proposed a source L, a "lay" source, behind much of what is now called J, while another proposed an N, or "nomadic," source. L and N and others like them have found little support. Nevertheless, cumulatively all the passages usually listed as J do most likely form a composite document. There is too little evidence, however, to say much about its composition in more than one stage. In the view presented here, the great bulk of J belongs to a single source, to which later additions were made in Jerusalem some two generations after its initial composition. A small number of these additions, like those in Exodus 32, are more or less identifiable. This view is in line with what most scholars who have dealt with J in detail have found.

With the turn of the century, form criticism came to the fore in biblical

2. Hans Walter Wolff is the primary spokesperson for those who think J concludes in Numbers.

studies. As applied to J, form criticism posed the question of what traditional type of work J is, and what types of traditions are present in its
constituent parts. Form criticism brought a new focus to the question of the
date and context of J. Rather than being regarded simply as the earliest of
the strands, dating from sometime prior to the seventh century B.C.E., J was
located more exactly in the court of Solomon, during the second half of the
tenth century B.C.E. At first this theory went against the majority view, but
it gradually came to prevail. It was assumed that J was a compiler of
traditions, ones connected with the cults of premonarchic Israel, and that J
reformulated them in the secular and urban context of Jerusalem, a new
and different political center for Israel. Thus J desacralized the traditions.
Also, J composed some narratives on his own rather than from Israel's
rural traditions, narratives whose mythic character was foreign to the ethos
of his people. J appended these to the front of his melded traditional
history. This preface now appears as the J portions of Genesis 2—11 and is
thus often called "the Primeval History." This is a misleading phrase, since it
suggests that even for J this material is of a different type from the rest of J.
The value of this insight, however, was the recognition that J was not
simply a repository of supposedly naive rural traditions and that J laid out
many of his chief ideas in this first distinctive part of his history. This form
critical investigation was led by the continental scholar Gerhard von Rad.[3]
He conceived of biblical study as the study of the history of traditions, their
origins, transformations, and recording in the documents contained in the
Bible. His method, an important extension of form criticism, is called
tradition history. His work was and remains the most influential treatment
of J in this century. Even the latest introductory treatments of J are deeply
indebted to it.

The weaknesses in von Rad's tradition history of J are numerous, however, as even those who follow it are inclined to recognize. Von Rad
proposed that the original short core of the oral traditions which were
eventually transformed into the lengthy J document was the brief summary of events recorded in Deut. 26:5—9. Few historians today would
agree with his assumption that an earlier form of a tradition should be a
shorter form. Von Rad believed that the summary in Deuteronomy 26 was
early, while most historians now believe it comes from late in the history of
the monarchy, perhaps several hundred years after Solomon. Von Rad
hypothesized that J came together primarily out of two blocks of tradition,
each related separately to a festival of early Israel: a body of law from the
spring wheat harvest festival and a narrative from the fall fruits harvest
festival. It is now widely doubted that law and narrative were kept so

3. Gerhard von Rad, "The Form-Critical Problem of the Hexateuch," in *The Problem of the Hexateuch and Other Essays* (New York: McGraw-Hill, 1966; London: SCM Press, 1938), 1—78.

separate in early Israel's traditions. Von Rad furthermore overstated the "secular" character of J. By uncoupling the early traditions from their cultic festival settings reflective of a supposed early Israelite piety and by merging them artificially in a secularized urban context new in the history of Israel, he thought that J was modifying the underlying character of the traditions from sacred to secular. In this way von Rad was probably attempting to address the distinction between little and great traditions. For many scholars in the 1930s and 1940s, it was an attractive idea that the tension felt between the sacred and the secular had been resolved in such an imaginative way within an early constituent part of the Bible itself. What gives von Rad's essay its perennial appeal is its idealism. Von Rad interpreted the work of his Yahwist as the spiritualizing and the secularizing of cultic traditions that had a material significance in their original settings. Once transferred away from Israel's rural cults, however, the traditions' ostensibly material topics like famine, inheritance, and land tenure ceased, in von Rad's view, to have material significance to the writer and hearers of the traditions. It is now realized that within the urban context compositions such as J (i.e., compositions of J's type, the category essential to precisely von Rad's form critical question) were directly related to the cult of the city and that the issue was not secularization but the particular, and material, form and meaning of the sacred which such compositions expressed.[4] This is what we have attempted to explain in this book.

Nearly all studies of J after von Rad were indebted to his treatment of the place and meaning of J. That J was composed in the court of Solomon is something of a received opinion of biblical scholarship, even though one of the primary reasons for this dating is von Rad's view of the supposed secularization of the traditions.[5] As previously explained, our view that J was written in the court of David, not Solomon, is based in large measure on the realization that J is indeed a sacred document, a history attached to and reflecting a cult. And, since the temple built under Solomon is emphatically not a part of the cult reflected in J, it must have been written before Solomon. The most widely used of the studies following von Rad and building on his work was the study of Hans Walter Wolff in Germany,[6] and

4. For a recent critique of this part of von Rad's work, see J. Barton, "Gerhard von Rad on the World-View of Early Israel," *Journal of Theological Studies* 35 (1984): 301–23.

5. Most of the other reasons explain why J is not *later* than Solomon. That J might be earlier than Solomon has scarcely been considered. A smaller number of scholars perform the valuable service of continuing to test the cogency of the early dating of J by arguing for various later datings, from the ninth to the sixth century B.C.E.

6. Hans Walter Wolff, "The Kerygma of the Yahwist," in *The Vitality of Old Testament Traditions*, Walter Brueggemann and Hans Walter Wolff, 2d ed. (Atlanta: John Knox Press, 1982), 41–66. Wolff interprets J as proposing something akin to the Marshall Plan for Solomon to apply to parts of his empire. For an excellent critique of Wolff's interpretation, see Ludwig Schmidt, "Israel ein Segen für die Völker? (Das Ziel des jahwistischen Werkes—eine Auseinandersetzung mit H. W. Wolff)," *Theologia viatorum* 12 (1975): 135–51.

in this country the works of Peter Ellis[7] and, from a more critical perspective, Walter Brueggemann.[8] Another stream of interpretation found its source in the work of Martin Noth, who conceived of J as a merging of discrete traditional themes that had largely developed before J adopted them. This continues to be an influential approach to J and E in combination, especially from the perspective of the history of oral traditions.[9] Together von Rad and Noth have set the agenda for the study of J for the last two generations.[10]

Still, few historians or students ever read J in its entirety as a coherent history, to see what precisely its version of history was and how a better understanding of that history could assist in answering the important questions that dominated earlier study.

The insights of von Rad, Noth, and their followers involved oversights that could not be generally recognized until the recovery of a social perspective on biblical history. Perhaps the most serious fault in von Rad's work is his assumption, shared with most of his contemporaries in biblical studies and still widely held, that despite Israel's social diversity, which von Rad was keenly sensitive to, Israel was a social unity, a variegated but seamless fabric that could be named and analyzed in the singular. On this assumption, it was possible to talk about the "traditions of Israel" as a social unity even while conceiving of them as diverse in their particularity but not in their social character. Since Israel was one, the "traditions of Israel" included by von Rad in his J expressed the identity of all Israel in a basic sense. It was also assumed that since such traditions belonged to all Israel, they must have had something to do with what happened because over time the community as a whole served as the guardian of the traditions' accuracy.[11]

7. Peter Ellis, *The Yahwist: The Bible's First Theologian* (Collegeville, Minn.: Liturgical Press, 1968). This is the best book on the subject in English because until now it has been the only one. Fortunately it has remained in print.

8. Walter Brueggemann, "David and His Theologian," *Catholic Biblical Quarterly* 30 (1968): 156–81; and idem, "Yahwist," *The Interpreter's Dictionary of the Bible*, Supplementary Volume (Nashville: Abingdon Press, 1976), 971–75. See also the studies by Brueggemann cited in chapter 5; and Donald E. Gowan, *When Man Becomes God: Humanism and Hubris in the Old Testament* (Pittsburgh: Pickwick Press, 1975).

9. Martin Noth, *A History of Pentateuchal Traditions* (1948; reprint, Englewood Cliffs, N.J.: Prentice-Hall, 1972). The deleterious sectioning of the Pentateuch into the themes of "Promise to the Patriarchs," "Guidance out of Egypt," "Revelation at Sinai," "Guidance in the Wilderness," and "Guidance Into the Arable Land" (a vestige of the nomadic infiltration model) maintains a heavy influence on biblical studies.

10. For perceptive critical comments on the influence of von Rad and Noth, see Rolf Rendtorff, "Der 'Jahwist' als Theologe? Zum Dilemma der Pentateuchkritik," *Supplements to Vetus Testamentum* 28 (1975): 158–66. Rendtorff takes Noth's sectioning to an extreme in his provocative work *Das überlieferungsgeschichtliche Problem des Pentateuch* (Berlin: Walter de Gruyter, 1977). See also Knight in *The Hebrew Bible and Its Modern Interpreters*, 265–76.

11. For recent developments and the current state of the discussion of J, the following may

Quite a different view has been presented here. Some implications of these departures from previous approaches are the subject of the final chapter.

---

be consulted: A. Graeme Auld, "Keeping Up with Recent Studies: The Pentateuch," *Expository Times* 91 (1980): 297–302; Walter Brueggemann, "Recent Developments," in *The Vitality of Old Testament Traditions*, 127–41; Otto Kaiser, *Introduction to the Old Testament: A Presentation of Its Results and Problems* (Minneapolis: Augsburg Publishing House, 1975), 67–91; Hannelis Schulte, *Die Entstehung der Geschichtsschreibung im Alten Israel* (Berlin: Walter de Gruyter, 1972), 8–77; Conrad E. L'Heureux, *In and Out of Paradise: The Book of Genesis from Adam and Eve to the Tower of Babel* (New York: Paulist Press, 1983); Isaac M. Kikawada and Arthur Quinn, *Before Abraham Was: The Unity of Genesis 1–11* (Nashville: Abingdon Press, 1985); John Van Seters, "Recent Studies on the Pentateuch: A Crisis in Method," *Journal of the American Oriental Society* 99 (1979): 663–73; Ludwig Schmidt, "Überlegungen zum Jahwisten," *Evangelische Theologie* 37 (1977): 230–47; Werner H. Schmidt, "A Theologian of the Solomonic Era? A Plea for the Yahwist," in *Studies in the Period of David and Solomon and Other Essays*, ed. T. Ishida (Winona Lake, Ind.: Eisenbrauns, 1982), 55–73 (Schmidt's essay is a particularly outstanding treatment. The view that J serves to legitimate the Davidic-Solomonic kingdom is convincingly argued in several recent works in German. Schmidt opposes this view in favor of the alternative view that J is mainly a quasi-prophetic critique of the excesses of the Israelite monarchy itself, especially Solomon. In the light of our own treatment, this latter view is probably erroneous); John Van Seters, "Patriarchs," *The Interpreter's Dictionary of the Bible*, Supplementary Volume 645–48; idem, "The Yahwist as Historian," *1986 SBL Seminar Papers* (Atlanta: Scholars Press, 1986), 37–55; Simon J. De Vries, "A Review of Recent Research in the Tradition History of the Pentateuch," *1987 SBL Seminar Papers* (Atlanta: Scholars Press, 1987), 459–502, especially the concluding remarks on 500–502. Recent questions raised concerning the cogency of talking about a coherent J narrative, especially by Rendtorff, have been sympathetically discussed by Niels P. Lemche, *Early Israel: Anthropological and Historical Studies on the Israelite Society Before the Monarchy* (Leiden: E. J. Brill, 1985), 357–77. It is our view that the coherence of J has been prematurely discounted.

28

Implications

The final or canonical form of the text of the Old Testament can claim a unique authority only on the basis of an antibiblical authority, because it cannot claim to comprehend the constituent traditions of the Bible, written during eight hundred years of the recorded history of God. It cannot claim to comprehend them, because it does not in fact preserve them but instead blurs or distorts them for its own purposes of consolidation. While much is preserved, often what is most distinctive in a constituent tradition can get lost in the canonization process. We now proceed to explicate these conclusions.

The contention is widespread that the final form of the canonical text lends itself most readily to appropriation for teaching and preaching in our modern context. That is to be expected of a library of texts patronized by a scribal class adjunct to the landowning priesthood of Persian and Hellenistic period Jerusalem, at the top of the pyramid of power and privilege in Palestinian society at that time. The canon is the product of a particular historical process involving the consolidation of authority in the hands of a class of capital scribes. In the case of the Old Testament, the scribes who had the final say in determining the basic meanings of the canon were supporters and beneficiaries of the power and authority of the Persian empire in Palestine. In view of the lack of any anti-Persian word whatsoever anywhere in the canon, as well as other indications, the Old Testament canon could fairly be characterized as the "Persian canon."

Whereas the canonization process thus favors hierarchical authority deriving from imperial power centered outside Palestine and potentially inimical, like the Palestinian state itself, to the interests of Palestinian people, the canon itself is made up of earlier constituent traditions, oral and written, that engage in questioning such power and authority. The J document questions such imperial power and authority in the name of

304

independent Negev bedouin and on behalf of a Davidic state that could justly claim as far as we can tell to benefit many Palestinian bedouin and peasants temporarily. In other words, canonical authority cannot authenticate itself successfully precisely because it results from a process that the text itself calls into question. Canon as norm emerges from near the seat of pharaoh, the epitome of hierarchical rule—in terms of the biblical story— and so canon itself does not permit the hierarchical normalizing of canon. What is canonical is the history of Israel's God revealed in the historical, processive dimensions of the biblical canon.

This contradiction comes into focus by the kind of reading the J document itself requires, which is to locate the determinative part and interpret the document as a whole in the light of that part. We have seen that the determinative part of J—the one story that controls all the other stories in it—is the story of the rebellion and escape of a band of disenfranchised corvée slave laborers. This rebellion is against the agency in society from which written and functional canon springs. The resolution of this contradiction for middle-class readers comes only through the process of a critical reading of the canon, a reading which is itself responsible to the historical processes of human liberation as these are presented in the constituent texts of the canon.

We have said from the outset that J deals with issues of sex, violence, injustice, and justice. Clearly, J looks at these issues the way many do today, as interrelated rather than unrelated. Some of the correspondences between J's concerns and claims and what a similar writer might say today are quite straightforward. Much has been written over the ages about the importance of human liberation. The God of our tradition is the God of freedom. For readers and hearers of the Bible over the ages, the history of Moses and the Israelites has been the basic way of conceiving and talking about God in this sense. It is as essential today as it has ever been.

Any attention given to the history of Moses and the bedouin Israelites may be taken to affirm the central role that this history plays in the Bible. For Jews, this history has remained central over the ages. Among Christians, the tendency has been to neglect Moses' history. In one sense this neglect is surprising. The history of Moses and the escape from Egypt is, after all, the determinative event in the history that became the basis of the Pentateuch, which itself forms the basis of both the rest of the Old Testament and the New Testament. In another sense, this neglect is perhaps not so surprising, given the Christian emphasis on Jesus Christ. What has frequently been lost, however, is the realization that the history of Moses and the Israelites is as fundamental to the understanding of Jesus Christ in the Gospels of the New Testament as it is to Passover. Mark, which lies behind Matthew and Luke, interprets Jesus primarily in terms of a new understanding of the history of Moses and the Israelites and the way that that history was interpreted in later prophets, especially Elijah, Elisha, Isaiah, and Jeremiah. It is no coincidence that the climax of the life of Jesus as pictured in Mark's Gospel occurs with his execution on the first day of Passover, the feast that celebrates the escape from Egypt. This Gospel intends to say that as always that event is fundamental, and that even the meaning of Jesus Christ is based on it. In the Gospel of John also, Jesus is portrayed as Moses and as the Passover lamb.

The salvation made possible to humanity by Jesus Christ in the New Testament portion of the Christian canon differs in part from the salvation represented by Moses in J. J is interested in the salvation of humanity by means of David's nation. The Gospels, written in view of the fall of the state in Palestine, are interested in the salvation of humanity by means of a single person who represents all persons unjustly put to death or whose lives have been foreshortened by the lack of justice in the world. In the Gospels, the political descendant of David's nation, the nation of the Palestinian heirs of Judahite identity defined by the temple in Jerusalem, was treated as a barrier to rather than the means of salvation. Hence the Gospel of Mark tells the history of Moses and the Passover essentially backward from J, beginning with the crossing of the Jordan or Sup Sea, trekking through the desert, coming to the time of Passover in Jerusalem rather than Egypt, and suffering on Passover day an agonizing defeat filled with ostensible shame in contrast to the victory over pharaoh. Without undermining the significance of this reversal, the Gospel nevertheless makes the escape of Moses and the Israelites from Egypt the basis and paradigm for understanding Jesus Christ not simply because that escape was the heart of the Scriptures but also because the salvation was essentially the same. In both cases it is a salvation from oppression, a salvation that leads to freedom.[1]

What is meant by freedom depends on whose freedom is involved. What group is claiming the history of Moses and the Israelites as the basis of their identity? What are the parallel groups today? These questions make it possible for us to take advantage of the specific results of our analysis of J's understanding of history. The group whose freedom J made central was the Davidic nation in their role as laborers. In J's view, the subsequent blessing of all humanity, or their release from subjugation to patterns of systemic socioeconomic exploitation, hinges on the blessing of Abram which leads to the blessing of the Israelites under David's rule. In its own context, in comparison with the great kingdoms of its age, the Davidic nation was a

---

1. For an insightful treatment of a number of motifs from J in their Christian gospel meaning, see Dale Aukerman, *Darkening Valley: A Biblical Perspective on Nuclear War* (New York: Seabury Press, 1981).

small power whose integrity and even existence were in constant jeopardy of being lost to rulers greater than David. The immediate parallel to J's Israel, whose freedom in J's view is essential to the freedom of all humanity, cannot therefore be one of the great powers of our age.

This point is not at all obvious to most Americans who read the Bible. But think about it just for a moment. Is it not of the essence of J, the history of the miraculous escape of Israel from the power of the king of Egypt, that Egypt is great and Israel is not? That difference in power and influence is not incidental to J's history, which has Israel forced to resort to Egypt for food. Any history about sex, violence, and injustice is about power. The relations of power in such a history are fundamental. Though Yahweh created a world in which socioeconomic oppression epitomized as murder emerged as the apparent norm, Yahweh proceeded to create a history in which an oppressed nation was delivered from its oppression and in which the recognition and acknowledgment of that deliverance became the new and essential norm of human behavior and society.

If in reading J we do not define for our own time the nature of international socioeconomic oppression, we will be unable to understand what J is saying to us, or we will misunderstand it, or we will unconsciously adopt the meanings of the pro-imperial canon. Many of us might be in the habit of defining the character of socioeconomic oppression in our time in terms of the evil behavior of the opponents of the United States, especially its great power opponents, and in terms of the duty of the United States to defend freedom and all good, here and elsewhere, against those opponents. For this purpose, we say, it is necessary for the United States to be the most powerful nation in the world.

If we say that the relations of power among nations are essential to the understanding of J, that in J God delivers a weaker nation from the most powerful, and that the United States is the most powerful nation, then it is impossible to believe that the United States plays the role of J's Israel today, or that today's Israel does in the context of the Middle East. One hardly need add that in J's conception the role of the United States would be that of J's Egypt.

For many people these are understandably repugnant thoughts. How can that be? We are bombarded with reasons for believing ours is a benign nation, even a Judeo-Christian nation. We understandably strive to convince ourselves that ours is the best nation in the world by focusing our attention primarily on the genuinely valuable and laudable features of our history and society. If we want to know how it is possible to think of the United States (or if we were Soviet citizens, the Soviet Union) as the equivalent of J's Egypt, then we will have to listen to the equivalent in our time of J. J might be those theologians, historians, and publicists of small nations like Nicaragua or Poland, Peru or Czechoslovakia, the Philippines or Angola, who decry the influence and dominance of the great powers in the economics and politics of their nations, and assert that only by the complete liberation of their nations from that dominance will their nations be blessed and the world find hope and freedom.

From the prevailing American and Soviet points of view, such people do not know what they are talking about. Do these nations not know how necessary the United States or the Soviet Union is to their survival and prosperity? J's Israel stands for those nations which are led by God to spurn such gratitude, as Israel was led to spurn dependency and forced labor in Egypt in favor of land from God—for them their own foundation of blessing. Such nations refuse to say to us what the Egyptian peasants said to pharaoh: "Thank you for selling back to us what you took from us and saving our lives."